Education of an E-Designer

Edited by Steven Heller

ALLWORTH PRESS
NEW YORK

School of
VISUAL ARTS

05   04   03   02   01   00   5   4   3   2   1

Published by Allworth Press
An imprint of Allworth Communications
10 East 23rd Street, New York, NY 10010

Copublished with the School of Visual Arts

Cover design by James Victore, Inc.
Interior design by Jennifer Moore

Page composition/typography by Sharp Des!gns, Lansing, MI

ISBN: 1-58115-193-4

LIBRARY OF CONGRESS CATALOGING-IN-PUBLICATION DATA
Education of an e-designer / edited by Steven Heller.
p. cm.
ISBN 1-58115-193-4
1. Web sites—Design—Study and teaching. 2. Multimedia systems—Study
and teaching. 3. Graphic arts—Study and teaching. I. Heller, Steven.
TK5105.888 .E38 2001
005.2'76—dc21
2001003497

Printed in Canada

Contents

ACKNOWLEDGMENTS

E-design is changing at such a fast pace that some of the articles destined for this book became obsolete during the proofreading stage. It takes a certain amount of prescience to keep up with the flow. So I would like to thank the authors and educators who contributed to this volume, and who have kept up, better than I have, with progress. It goes without saying that this book would have been impossible without their enthusiastic and generous contributions to the field.

Thanks also to the support team at Allworth Press, Nicole Potter, editor, Jamie Kijowski and Liz Vanhoose, associate editors, Bob Porter, associate publisher, and Tad Crawford, publisher. Tad has been an unyielding supporter of this series of *Education of . . .* books and of critical writing about graphic design.

— SH

Introduction: Give Me an E. . .

STEVEN HELLER

You can be a graphic designer without ever touching a pixel in virtual space. But you cannot be an e-designer without knowing the language of graphic design. In the final analysis, the fundamental tools used to convey messages in both print and digital media are type and image. The result is often different, but, so far, the ends, if not the means, are the same. Or are they?

The e-designer is fast becoming a distinct and separate part of the larger visual communications industry. To refer to e-design simply as a subsidiary of graphic design is akin to asserting that graphic design is still a subset of printing, or advertising Graphic design evolved in the late nineteenth century from the primordial ooze of the commercial-job printing shop, but by the early twentieth century it had become an integral activity, indeed a profession unto itself. Similarly, e-design, which is identified by a variety of names at this stage, has quickly developed its own identity, rules, and standards. What began as a sideline within a graphic design studio has emerged as its own reason for being.

Not too long ago, graphic designers tentatively designed Web sites to supplement print endeavors. Currently, entire design firms are devoted to Web development—sometimes with a print component on the side. Some designers today have never even composed print pages. This isn't meant to imply that the supercilious mantra of the mid-nineties, "the end of print," has finally come to pass, but it does suggest the bifurcation every design-school graduate must work in the print medium, it is possible, given the state of the field, that once out of school, they will never do it again.

It would be foolish to assert that a viable e-design education must use old practices to bolster new methods. After the widespread adoption of cold type in the early sixties it became unnecessary for graphic designers to revisit hot type. Sure, it is useful to understand past processes—and what better way than to learn how to set metal type—but a designer's innate ability does not hinge on learning antiquated procedures. It is important for a magazine or book designer to understand page flow, but this skill does not automatically translate onto the Web. The principles of navigating page versus screen are decidedly different. Some say that the Web is more akin to film, which is true enough. Others argue it is more mathematical and logical. However, in the present commercial Web environment the front page of a newspaper is an apt metaphor for the screen, because it has become crucial to pack a lot of information on a home page. Whatever the case, the tenets of sophisticated graphic design are not necessarily transferable.

A good graphic designer, or any designer who can negotiate spatial relationships, can easily design a basic Web site using the conventional page as a model. The terminology might be different, but the issues are the same. You need a title page, a table of contents, feature pages, etc. Many very handsome Web pages are constructed on this simple foundation. But handsome alone is proving insufficient to grab viewers, stimulate consumers, and otherwise capture a significant audience. What an audience will accept in the print environment is not compelling in an interactive or experiential one. Viewers have become accustomed to frequent changes in content, innumerable effects, and links, not all of which are novelties. As the practice is currently evolving, designers who see their roles as making appealing packages, striking posters, and aesthetically pleasing whatever, are not the best candidates for becoming e-designers.

E-designers must know the language of type, yet need not always be exquisite typographers. The limits of technology and the demands of the medium are not geared to the subtleties and nuances endemic to fine typography. But the type expert may have little understanding—and perhaps even less patience—for the complexities of Web navigation. A solid e-designer must possess a strong grasp of how to move a viewer around in both predetermined patterns and random ways. Skills and taste—with music, sound, motion, and other sensory tools—are necessary to stimulate interest. For some graphic designers, this is a wonderful opportunity to expand the boundaries of conventional graphic design; for others it is more unwanted baggage.

With the recent boom and bust of early dot-coms, e-designers are in a state of professional flux. Despite these failures, however, the Web is here to stay and a new kind of designer is needed to orchestrate and construct the future—perhaps one who is as much content-provider, or author, as aesthetician and technician—therefore, it is crucial to develop practical educational programs for the e-designer. The question, of course, is whether to separate this activity from traditional graphic design education or integrate it throughout undergraduate and graduate institutions. Should fundamental graphic design practices be taught with a kind of "premed" approach before embarking on more specialized design? Should classes focusing on specialties kick-in after the basics are totally absorbed?

In some schools, graphic design and computer arts are totally separate, with no crossover. In others, visual communications is an umbrella for all disciplines. E-design, however, demands even more inclusion. Basic graphic design and computer courses must today be augmented by animation, film, sound, even script writing. For those who truly want to be e-designers, graphic design, though important, is definitely not an adequate course of study. It is not enough to go into the world knowing how to make type move on a screen. Taken as a whole, the positions taken in the essays and curricula in *The Education of an e-Designer* suggest a very intensive course of study that involves formerly unconventional classes for designers, including business, psychology, editing, entrepreneurship, games, and interactive science.

One of the underlying questions addressed in this book is not how should e-design be taught, but how important is graphic design in this overarching, constantly developing field? Surely this book's contributors are not always in agreement, because the field is very young and the theories are still mutable. But as this book reveals, despite the e-designer's need to understand graphic design principles, the education of an e-designer has transcended typical graphic design pedagogy. We are now at the point where all e-designers must be imbued with graphic design, although not all graphic designers will become e-designers. This is not simply a matter of a designer's preference; ultimately, the demands made on an e-designer require a unique educational experience.

Education of an *E*-Designer

What Was Graphic Design Education?

Recent Directions in Graphic Design Education

KATHERINE MCCOY

STEVE HELLER ASKS, "Where is theory now? Has it taken a back seat in graphic design education?"

No, reports of its death are premature. In fact, the field requires more theoretical grounding than ever. And there are a great deal more theoretical resources available, thanks to the new design Ph.D. programs and the continuing development of design publishing.

But we certainly hear less about post-Structuralism and deconstruction. In the past year, in conversation with both Rudy Vanderlans of *Émigré*, and CalArts' Louise Sandhaus, each noticed a decreasing enthusiasm for post-structural theory among graduate students. This could be the natural result of the past fifteen years' in-depth exploration of critical language theories for new design ideas. Only so much can be squeezed out of one theoretical field.

Of note is a decidedly non-verbal quality in much of the interesting new work coming out of graduate design schools. Laurie Haycock Makela noted recently that Cranbrook crits are less verbal and talkative. And the work is far less about cerebral word play than during the post-structuralist years. Instead, I would characterize much of their work, and work from other graduate programs as well, as sensory, preverbal, or subverbal. Sensuality, character, and emotion seem to be a focus, especially in motion-graphics experiments. This is a shift from the verbal to the sensory, from the brain to the body—to the experiential.

Which leads us to what is new. If critical language theories prompted an outpouring of experimental design in the past fifteen years, certainly the new world of interactive electronic communications design is driving even more experiment now. Technology is the force behind design change today. In fact, I can't imagine a more exciting time for communications design— we are in a technological revolution that is hungry for exploration, invention, and eventually codification. We are on a wide-open playing field where the rules are suspended and pedigrees do not yet exist. The best methods from traditional design provide a foundation, but so much more awaits discovery. And it is hard not to notice how lucrative this field can be, as a number of our colleagues become Internet millionaires.

This does not mean that post-Structuralism, deconstruction and literary criticism are no longer relevant to graphic design. In fact, these theories provide particularly useful strategies for interactive communications design, where each reader negotiates a nonlinear personal experience. The post-structuralist understanding of meaning as constructed by the audience, not the sender, is very useful. Ideas about open meaning and multiple readings can create interactive environments full of dialog, discourse, and debate.

In addition, many other theories are necessary to guide successful interactive electronic communications design. This is a far more demanding design realm. Simply rendering a clever idea in inventive or refined graphic form is no longer enough—and neither are slick HTML skills. This new immaterial medium is highly conceptual, challenging designers to create resonant and knowable conceptual spaces. With the new focus on the user's needs and experiences, methods from the social sciences, anthropology, and ethnography help designers better understand audiences. Nonlinear interaction requires complex navigation and orientation solutions, grounded in cognitive and perceptual psychology and information design. The organizational relationship between nonlinear temporal structure and content is far more complex than in tangible print media. And whole new grammars are waiting to be invented to replace the conventions of the page and page-turning in this new digital space animated by interactivity, motion, and sound. Schools need to keep pace with proprietary design methods like the ones developed by E.lab (now part of Sapient) and TSDesign (now part of Razorfish).

Yet, this new domain demands more than analytical theory and method. Interactive media is largely about experience—the user's experience in conceptual spaces. In fact, many contend that this new field should be characterized as experience design. How does one animate character and quality in fleeting dematerialized spaces? To synthesize rich and memorable experience in a highly competitive communications environment, we need bold explorations of new formal expressions full of culture, emotion, and sensuality.

Certainly graphic design education is reaching and running to catch this wave, just as the profession is. The Advance Design group, under Meredith Davis's leadership, is just now drafting first attempts at a curriculum. Faculty positions in interactive media are open at many schools since most of our senior faculty are largely lost in this field. I find that my most rewarding challenge since Cranbrook is inventing a personal vision of how to teach interactive communications design at IIT's Institute of Design.

Things are pretty chaotic at the moment, and we hear the usual laments that design is losing out to unpedigreed usurpers of our rightful territory. However skilled the code writers and the software whizzes might be, this challenging new media offers design an unprecedented opportunity. Its breadth assures that many different schools of design thought will be welcome and necessary. For comprehensible and compelling interactive communications, the design education community is exploring the forms of experience and the methods to structure it.

 **The New Design Basics**

LORETTA STAPLES

EDUCATORS AND STUDENTS aren't in agreement about what still matters in design. Teachers struggle to synthesize "principles" and "tools," while the tools continue morphing into something else, deconstructing the principles along the way. Students struggle to stay current, motivated by market opportunities ("how can I get a job?"), and are seduced by the powerful allure of the tools themselves. The digital has exploded our expectations, blurred our boundaries, and rendered obsolete what we thought we cared dearly about. What are now "the basics" in teaching and learning design?

Technology (and technique) has moved to the forefront of design education in the past ten years. Before then, "the principles" were upheld by stripping as much technology as possible out of the picture. As a matter of course, foundation classes in graphic design delved into the basics of form and structure through black and white, manipulated through the direct techniques of the hand. Even "color" impinged upon this simplicity by introducing more complexity than your average freshman was thought able to bear.

The widespread adoption of digital technology in the early 1990s didn't just streamline the processes of production, though a number of schools chose to treat it that way initially. By relegating digital tools to the "layout and pre-press" arena, many educators were able to stave off the "basics" issue, at least for a while. But rapid developments in software and hardware, along with pressure from (paying) students for digital empowerment, demanded that the technical issues of design be addressed earlier and earlier in the education process. To some extent, this worked (and still does). All those black-and-white basics—line and shape, form and composition—seem almost tailor-made for computational manipulation. Copying, pasting, and duplicating—all the standard editing operations—make it easy to cover the basics of form and pattern quickly, collapsing multiple iterations into abbreviated time frames. The computer even enables additional learning to be leveraged in the design education process through simple scripting, programming, and markup languages like HyperTalk, DBN, and HTML.

All this is good and exciting. The mesmerizing power and sophistication of software tools invites the kind of exploration that students relish. But there's a downside, too. Increasingly, teachers are relegated to the status of software "trainers," walking semesters' worth of students through the latest version of soon-to-be-upgraded software. On the faculty front, curricular debates devolve into arguments over which software package would provide the best instructional platform for teaching X, while students—who can only appreciate the brand names they see in the job ads—balk at not having the latest, greatest, and most expensive options at their fingertips. The infrastructure demands of computer instruction are immense: costly, unsustainable, and very difficult to scale and support. But, of course, this is never a student's problem (nor should it be).

And that's not the only problem. The sheer time it takes to learn the software cuts into the time that would have been spent on the "other stuff." In days of yore, there were reasons why the details of offset printing weren't covered in Graphic Design II. It simply wasn't the priority. It wasn't what the class was about. But these are different times. Design and production are one and the same in the digital realm. It's good in that it re-couples concept and form, revitalizing a sense of craft in the practice of designing. It's bad in that it demands an awful lot (of time) from both teacher and student—more than can fit conveniently into semester and trimester time slots.

With so much time given over to the technical side of things, less and less time is available for focusing on the "other stuff" that surrounds and permeates design: history, audience, social context, cultural critique. Some programs bring these neglected topics to the forefront in belabored theoretical programs that students scarcely understand, but are somehow able to mimic ("is it syntactic, semantic or indexical?" ugh.) The best efforts strike a balance between the technical, the cultural, and the critical. (The computer is a cultural appliance after all.)

It's more crucial than ever for designers to critique through design. Design seems to have emerged as the new lingua franca, flowing through commoditized daily life as never before. Conspicuous design is everywhere: on every kitchen shelf, atop every desktop, enveloping every body. Design increasingly reaches into the intimacy of nature, through bioengineering and cosmetic surgery alike. Yet the vastness of design's influence scarcely creeps into your average design curriculum; How can it, when we have so much software to keep up with?

So where does that leave us?

In comparing the past and the present, it's easy to feel sentimental about the good old days of design basics, yet those times (and the pedagogies that went with them) were fraught with their own glaring omissions. Formal beauty accompanied a supposedly neutral visual rhetoric ("information design") in design pedagogy, which tended to ignore the larger cultural and symbolic contexts of design and the corporate imperatives underlying them. The "communications" component of graphic design education tended to consist of some mix of marketing messages and "information," with an occasional semiotics lesson thrown in. That part of things hasn't gotten any better in general, though deconstruction has replaced semiotics as the philosophical underpinning of the moment, and vague references to "interactivity" abound.

So, given the current mix of opportunism and technological enabling, what still serves us in the long haul? I offer a partial list of study topics:

Structure Structure is the organization of form in space. It is the means through which design lends order to the built environment. Because structure is at work in nature and in culture, it serves as common ground, linking human intention to order in the natural world. Structure is a fundamental organizing principle.   **Context** The objects we design are situated in the world. They are nestled within the boundaries of social and formal order. Their location therein—be it historical or cultural—attaches particular value to the act of designing and the objects of design. Our awareness of design's location empowers us. Through that knowledge we can literally reshape underlying "value propositions" by proposing new things and places where design happens. Design is a potentially disruptive opportunity that lets us interrogate culture (if we choose to use it that way).   **Spatial Systems** Extending the ideas of location and situation, the objects of design live in space, and our understandings of space are systematized and culturally informed. Cartesian space, and the XYZ coordinate system, "coincides" with an understanding of perspective. This particular system continues to mold our spatial understanding as an embedded default of today's computer modeling programs. In recognizing spatial conventions, we can identify new opportunities for situating the objects of design in space, resystematizing order in radical ways.   **Stillness/Motion** If the objects of design are indeed situated in space, their relative stillness or motion becomes an attribute for the designer to exploit or not.   **History/Future** Design happens in time as well as space. Knowing what happened in the past helps us project into the future. Envisioning particular futures, by necessity engages our knowledge of the past.   **The History of Design** Many histories exist, not just one. By studying any given history of design and observing what was left out, we can expand the cultural space of that history to be more inclusive and whole. In doing this, we simultaneously critique the history of design and the design of history.

Technologies Technologies augment the designer's hand (and intentions) through new tools and materials. They afford new design opportunities by expanding the scope of what it is possible to make. For example, the "virtuality" of digital space has afforded radical new inventions (like Web sites!) that have transformed the world of commerce by affording new distribution channels for goods and services.   **Materials** We design things made out of other things. The material quality of design is sensuous and symbolic. Tools interface with materials in the act of designing.   **Process** Design happens in a certain order. The sequence of steps taken to give form to material constitutes design process. Design processes are wide ranging, allied with particular professional practices, cognitive predispositions, and resource considerations.   **"The Hand"** "The digital" raises serious questions about where the hand begins and ends. The intersection of hand and material describes the craft of design. Critical examination of the extension, replacement, and augmentation of the hand lets us consider the intersection of design and nature within the context of our own bodies. The hand is a compelling metaphor for the humanity of design.   **Communication** Design conveys meaning to particular audiences familiar with its codes. Mass production supports the widespread distribution of specific messages and underlying values. Design influences.   **Notation** "Notation" describes the linguistic dimensions of design the mark-making, coding, and sign-making that designers conventionally engage to craft design's messages. If design communicates, it must be because it is indeed "read." In this linguistic sense, designers are "writers." The objects of design convey a wide range of meanings—status and utility among them. The encoding of these meanings through sign systems constitutes notation.

Discourse   Design occupies a cultural space that embodies the values of particular audiences and practitioners. In this sense, design is a cultural practice, a means by which designers and audiences engage in critical "conversations" about value in the society at large. **Continuum**   Design "marks" space and time through styles that map to specific moments. Those markings and the space between them describe a trajectory uniting space, time, and culture.   **Style** Style expresses a particular confluence of social forces that gives rise to a set of attributes, collectively named. Styles mark the trajectory of space and time, and form a basis for the examination of economic forces, encompassing production and distribution. Style and fashion intersect.   **(Dis)appearance** Much design conspicuously engages the visual—the way things look. The optical channel is the focus of design education. But a lot of design happens behind the scenes too. The complexity of problems designers engage in this digital age requires a broader understanding of scope and possibility, beyond that which is seen.   **Audience** We don't design just for ourselves. Audiences engage our work. And audiences are implicit in what we choose to design.   **Collaboration** The complexity and magnitude of many design problems require specialized expertise residing in many individuals. The task of designing an e-business, for example, engages skills in business strategy, visual communications, finance, branding, culture, and software engineering. In complex collaborations, design is a robust social activity that demands new kinds of relationships and organizational structures.   **Commerce** The business of design is the infrastructure that moves the objects of design through the world, deploying it to various audiences through sales and distribution channels. We need to understand this infrastructure pragmatically to circulate our work. Knowledge about the ways of business can also critically inform how we choose to act as designers.   **Responsibility** Designers act on behalf of many: themselves, clients, audiences, and end users. We're advocates and champions. We do our best to make life more useful, beautiful, and purposeful, by design.

The Wrong Horse?

GEOFFRY FRIED

AS RECENTLY AS seven years ago, computer facilities at our school consisted of just ten Mac SE computers, and we were furiously trying to find resources for the purchase of new equipment. Happily, we have dramatically better technology today (better, but never enough). Now the big question is whether or not we are teaching the right things, or in the right way, to prepare our students for the twenty-first century. We are furiously trying to decide what to keep in the design curriculum, what to jettison, and how to make room for an ever-expanding wave of media skills that our students seem to want and need.

Planning an education program always involves placing a bet on the future. In a time of flux—both in the use of technology and in the structure of design practice—this future is harder to predict. When knowledge increases in any field, there are several possible responses: increasing use of reference materials and systems, increasing specialization, and increasing need for collaboration among those specialists. While we see evidence of these trends in graphic design, it is not at all clear what the future of design practice or design education will be.

How much will undergraduates need to know in order to become successful designers in an electronic environment, as opposed to print, environmental design, or any other graphic specialty? Can we provide that knowledge in the context of a general graphic design education, or should we provide specialized educational tracks for different kinds of design? I have maintained a strong commitment to the idea of a general undergraduate education, but I often find myself wondering if I am backing the wrong horse, or if I should be hedging my bets.

Ours is a small program, with approximately 100 graphic design majors. If we restrict our program to a single specialty, or try to divide students into separate tracks, I'm not sure we would find enough students for any one course of study. When students enter the program, they are usually not aware of the wide range of possibilities available in design practice, and therefore specialization at an early age seems premature. They have a variety of aptitudes and interests. It takes time to sort out who will enjoy or excel at different design activities—making images, developing verbal and visual concepts, organizing information, planning strategies, or visualizing spaces—that eventually sort themselves into professional specializations.

If we did want to develop some specialized tracks, what would they be? One natural division seems to be between design for print and design for the Web or interactive media. But this particular "media divide" ignores several other important areas: broadcast and environmental design. It is also at odds with the need for multiple media skills in many areas of professional practice, such as corporate design, advertising, or publishing. On the other hand, a division into professional specialties creates an impossibly long list: advertising, book design, publishing, Web design, packaging, environmental design, film and television, corporate design, information design, etc. It also begs the question of which design skills and principles need be taught in which specialty. Principles of typography, identity, visual communication, and the organization of information are useful in every area of the profession.

Still, the world of print and the world of the Web may just be different enough to require some form of specialization. Students currently make this distinction themselves by gravitating toward electives in the areas where they feel most comfortable. There is so much new material for them to learn—new concepts in interactivity, navigation, and time-based media, along with an endless array of new or updated software—that it seems difficult to fit it all into a four-year undergraduate curriculum. Since they learn best through constant practice, with specific projects in specific media, it seems to make sense for them to develop an initial "expertise" or facility in one area of practice.

Nevertheless, I persist in placing my money on the more general approach. The solution is not to add to the curriculum, but to restructure it entirely, to embrace the environments and media in which tomorrow's designers will be functioning. New principles of interaction, information architecture, and collaboration must be folded in, while traditional principles of perception, conceptual thinking, and design processes are adapted to tomorrow's tools. We have been working at this slowly and incrementally; now is the time to take what we have learned and risk everything on a bigger bet.

Up until this point, access to technology has been a critical issue. We know that students need as much time as possible to develop facility in any media. We now encourage use of computers, and learning new software as early as possible. We offer minicourses that allow students to pick up basic skills whenever they need them. This also makes it easy to add new skills, such as Flash or HTML, when those become necessary, or eliminate software that goes out of favor. None of this has interfered with teaching design, as was originally feared. In fact, it has made it easier for design faculty to focus on their core issues and develop new ways of teaching. They still have to help students use software correctly, but they don't have to start at the most basic level.

It has also been important to hire new faculty who are conversant in new media and who are currently working professionally in the Web environment, or in advanced areas of interaction design, or in broadcast and film. No matter how much training I provide for my faculty or myself, some of us will never cross the "generational divide" that defines current professional practice. Instead, we can encourage younger faculty who share common goals. For design courses, such as "Type in Motion" or "Designing for Interactive Media," we are careful to work with people who share our design values, not just those who have new media skills. But we are also open to having our students learn from faculty in other departments. Fine artists and photographers who are exploring digital imaging and interactive media have much to offer our students in both technical and conceptual areas. As always, artists of all kind are trying new things and students cannot help but be influenced by them.

All this computer activity creates enormous pressure for new equipment and constant software upgrades. It is clear that we cannot keep up with this demand and keep tuition reasonable—at this point every design studio needs to be a computer lab. We are actively exploring ways for students to buy or lease their own equipment which, when combined with wireless technology, will complete the integration of the tool into the studio environment.

Once this occurs, we will be challenged to teach in ways that we are only just beginning to develop. Design and media will no longer be artificially separated; basic skills and concepts will be taught in new, and sometimes dramatically more efficient ways. More traditional hand and thinking skills, such as research, sketching, and drawing, will not disappear, and will need to be taught, but not in some kind of "opposition" to other media skills. For example, students often learn about sequence in basic design classes by painting a series of panels. There is no reason why this exercise could not include some basic digital animation techniques, if the tools and software were immediately at hand. In typography, we use letterform drawing to sensitize students to the shapes and nuances of letterforms; these exercises can easily extend to practice in drawing with Bézier curves.

More profoundly, the new curriculum will also reverse the order of things. New media courses were once considered "advanced electives" for those who already had good basic design training. Now, however, they will be part of that basic training. The basic exercises of any new media class—those that introduce students to concepts like navigation and feedback—need to be incorporated into design classes at every level, instead of being taught as separate concepts.

We also need to encourage collaboration and teamwork. Students are going out into a working world that values this behavior, precisely because they can no longer be experts at all things. This has been a difficult area for many instructors who are used to doing their own work and to showing students how to work independently. Perhaps design faculty can model this behavior for their students by collaborating with faculty in other curricular areas, such as the liberal arts and sciences. The value of students' work increases exponentially when they have a deeper understanding of the content of a project, and design faculty cannot possibly provide that depth in all areas.

While it has been a struggle to gain access to new technology, a struggle to learn to use it, and a struggle to find its place in the curriculum, the advantage of this effort has been to shake out what are enduring values in design, and what are merely artifacts of a particular technology or method of training. I certainly don't miss my rapidographs or plaka, my T square, or hours of doing pasteup, but I continue to think about how to get students to see and think more precisely, how to care about craft in any particular media, and how to use materials or equipment to students' best advantage in any working process.

I also continue to be fascinated by the promise of design, to enlarge and inform our choices in whatever media or specialty we choose to work in. Some level of specialization is inevitable, but I do not believe that it should be the primary focus of undergraduate design education. The qualities of mind that favor exploration and iteration, understanding of information structures, playing with words and images, and empathetic problem solving, are qualities I wish to encourage in all of my students. When they bring those to the table—be it the small table of their own studio, or the large conference table of a collaborative new media venture—they are extending the discipline of design, and sharing the values of that discipline with the world.

Interactivity is Not an Elective

MELISSA NIEDERHELMAN

DESIGN FOR INTERACTIVITY is an elective area of study for many design students today. Unfortunately, in light of changing modes of communication and the expanding diversity of the design profession, design education cannot afford to make designing for interactivity a choice any longer. Like other fundamental areas of study, such as typography or color theory, design for interactivity should be included as part of a student's core curriculum even before addressing the digital aspects of the subject. In this information age, teaching interactivity as a principle of effective visual communication, rather than just a series of technical skills, is not an elective, but a requirement.

Designing Strategies and Other Intangible Products

Questions about interactivity and how students are dealing with the subject began to concern me in relation to my own teaching. Do students really understand the principles of designing for interactive solutions, regardless of the product or outcome? Can they identify the elements of design in an interactive environment that make it unique? Is it possible to teach design for interactivity as theory first and application second? Like many other design faculty, I had been struggling with how to teach more subjects on interactivity without immediate access (or funding) to more computers or technology. The current saturation of computer access at our university, as well as limited software licenses, made it difficult to offer more digital subjects to some thirty or forty students. What to do? Not having enough access was not the students' fault, yet they needed more exposure. When I began to explore the idea further, I realized that it was not my students' deficiencies in software that was the issue, but rather their perception of interactivity as a specialty area within the design world. Many of them didn't realize how this aspect of the design discipline would affect them in the future, whether they learned the software or not. In addition, there was this naïve impression that interactivity was just like any other design problem, just with a different outcome. Their design process revolved around a print-based model—brainstorming, sketching (on paper), variation, critique, refinement, production (on computer), and final product. They needed a new model. They needed the opportunity to study the principles behind this complex communication method.

I set out to develop a new course—the Principles of Interactivity. In the course, I made clear to the students that we were not going to focus on the product so much as on the *planning*. This course was about preparing for interactive solutions, about the computer as a medium and not just a tool, about understanding information and content before ever working with rollovers or Java script. The semester was comprised of basically one project that was broken down into several phases: content and definition, information design and navigation, and interface and identity. It took some time to help students understand that what they were designing was not an object or product, but a plan. The deliverables took the form of presentations that summarized the exploration and decisions the students had made in preparing for a hypothetical interactive design solution. These presentations also doubled as mini interactive projects because they were prepared and given digitally. Regardless of the vehicle, however, the objective was to make a thorough investigation into what they were proposing as an interactive solution, whom it would benefit, how it would work, what content was included, and how design would make this information more accessible in an interactive environment. They studied users, they analyzed the Web and existing interactive design, they researched authoring tools, new technology and project plans, and they organized information and designed navigation. There seemed to be so much to cover before we could think about application.

Throughout this process I realized how neglected this aspect of design for interactivity has become in design education. Clearly, it is necessary to prepare our students technically, in addition to theoretically, but somehow the concept of interactivity as a principle within design curriculum has been undervalued. Why aren't we teaching interactivity with the same fundamental approach we give to composition or typography? Interactivity is a unique form of design in that it accommodates the element of choice within the communication process. Choice and the ability to control sequence and time create a very different relationship between the user and the information, and make the designer's task infinitely more dynamic. This element of choice makes designing for interactivity very different than designing for print or other physical products and should be presented to students this way. It is misleading to imply that the process students have learned in a traditional approach to design problem solving will seamlessly translate to interactive solutions.

Ideally, the study of interactivity would include a thorough investigation of the inherent characteristics of interactivity and how they are unique, such as choice, sequence, navigation, and time. A well-rounded study of the subject would also incorporate the exploration of user-centered issues, human factors, interdisciplinary work methods, and information theory and design. I am not the first design educator to address the principles of interactivity in an undergraduate course, but perhaps it is time we were more explicit about the principles and theories of interactivity as a fundamental element of design education and not just an elective.

Interacting with the Real World

In considering a more theoretical approach to the subject of interactivity, it may be useful to address the contexts that surround design and information today and why teaching interactivity is a timely objective for design education.

Whether surfing the Web, adding appointments to your palm pilot, or using an information kiosk at a museum, exposure to interactive design is as common today as using the telephone. As the modes and methods of communication change, people have more choices than ever before of how to access information. This, in turn, creates a new set of issues for designers responsible for finding ways to facilitate information and transfer messages. Once, the designer needed only to be concerned with communicating a message in a passive way, but designers must now address the far more dynamic relationship between user and information. In light of these shifting contexts, designers could benefit from an area of study that was more holistic in its approach to technology and our interaction with information today.

Curriculum that deals with interactivity on a more fundamental level will also benefit students once they graduate. Regardless of whether students have taken courses in new media or not, they will inevitably encounter some form of interactive design in their experience as professionals. The days of specialization in design are over, and the majority of young design professionals find themselves in work environments that are more diverse than ever before. Even if the student isn't directly involved with such projects, he or she will more than likely be working with a colleague or team of people who are. How will these new design professionals contribute and participate, even if their role is not technical? We do design students and design education a huge favor by requiring a well-rounded understanding and application of interactivity in design solutions.

For many design students, subjects like Web design are very intimidating. Unfortunately, the root of this fear is related to things like not knowing or understanding the authoring tools for creating interactive solutions. Just the mention of HTML, JPEGs or Web-safe colors is enough to send some students running from the computer lab. As a result, the student equates designing for digital solutions with complicated code and unfamiliar software. What is most unfortunate about this is that students overlook the real value they bring to the interactive design process. The ability to organize information, manage large projects, and work with users will be critical for designers in the future, not just their knowledge of the latest software. Max Bruinsma, in his essay, "Design Interactive Education," comments: "In multimedia communication, the role of the designer is shifting from visualizing to conceptualizing."[1] Students must be taught to see themselves as contributors to the design process, as essential members of a team effort, and not just as "visualizers" of the concepts generated by others.

Elective Design and Other Ironic Choices

In many cases, courses on interactivity and new media are taken as electives and only benefit those students who choose to take them. As a result, this important aspect of design education may not reach all students. In light of the overwhelming presence of interactivity in communication today, why are design curricula still offering it "*in addition*" to the core program of studies? Even before a student launches Dreamweaver, is he really prepared to tackle the unique requirements that designing for interactivity represents? Teaching the principles of interactivity to design students, not as an elective, but as a set of fundamental methods and ideas, can go a long way in helping students see designing for interactivity as a unique process.

Classes on interactivity are usually reserved for third and fourth year students in under-graduate design education. For some reason, students are apparently not "*prepared*" to take on the complicated subject earlier in their educational experience. Unfortunately, this segregation of subjects only promotes the idea that interactivity is a "*specialized*" area within the design dis-cipline. Students choose to follow this path or not. The problem with this choice is that as the design profession becomes more diverse every day, students still cling to the notion that inter-activity is something they can avoid in their careers. As ridiculous as this is, design curriculum is not doing much to present the subject as a fundamental principle in design. The principles of interactivity can be taught much earlier in a design curriculum and be presented alongside other more traditional subjects. By introducing the principles of interactivity at the freshman or sophomore level, we prepare students better for the technical aspects of the subject later. A more contemporary curriculum would find ways to balance the traditional principles of design education with issues and methods of interactivity. Perhaps an earlier introduction of digital media from a theoretical standpoint would encourage students to be less anxious about the subject and more inclined to include it in their course of study.

Ego Trips and Team Dynamics

Another timely aspect of a more concentrated study of interactivity in design is collabora-tion. Interactivity by nature is also interdisciplinary and requires designers to work with a variety of people and experts in different fields. Katherine McCoy comments on team work in design education: "The 'Big Idea' or individual intuitive approach is no longer sufficient. We are moving into the next round—solving problems by creating experiences. As a result we need to teach students to work with others."[2] Ironically, design students often take courses in interactivity and are never exposed to this collaborative element. Design students, in many cases, need to be taught how to work in team situations, especially in areas of interactive design. The result of working as an individual on so many projects in their educational careers, makes compromise, and the ability to accept another agenda, difficult for many students. There are new things to learn about consensus, time management, methodologies, language, and expectations, all of which are part of the interdisciplinary team dynamic. Large interactive solutions aren't driven by just one person toiling away alone in his or her studio; designing for interactivity is about work-ing with others. Beyond the boundaries of the official design camp, interactive projects require the expertise and participation of people like writers, business consultants, and researchers, among others. Teaching the principles of interactivity as a unique design process, would give students more exposure to interdisciplinary work methods and the opportunity to see the benefits of team contribution.

In Support of New Technologies and Traditional Theories

The results of my class on the Principles of Interactivity have so far been very positive. "I began to realize it is possible to make connections between anything. As a result, designing the interaction is essential to helping users make the right connections," said one of my students about the course. Another student commented, "I feel like I am learning new design skills that are different from the ones I have been concentrating on. Less visual and more about planning large projects and developing content." At this stage the course is still only available to seniors in graphic design, but it could easily be modified to reach underclassmen and students in areas like industrial design, interior design, or even business.

Within a design student's curriculum today, exists an interesting collection of studies that can encompass the traditional exploration of typography alongside the introduction of new media. As design programs strive to offer courses in the multiple dimensions of the design discipline, everything from Web design to experience design, a more fundamental and comprehensive approach to design for interactivity is required. Designing for interactivity is only one such area that calls out for a theoretical component to complement an otherwise technical approach. By making design for interactivity more of a subject of investigation and less of an elective on new media, we do a better job of preparing designers to help people access and interact with information in the future.

N O T E S

1. Max Bruinsma, "Design Interactive Education," *The Education of a Graphic Designer* (New York: Allworth Press, 1998).
2. Katherine McCoy, "Design for Experience," *Lecture*, Arizona State University, School of Design, February 17, 2000.

A Philosophical Approach and Educational Options for the e-Designer

BRUCE WANDS

THE EDUCATION OF an e-designer has gone through radical changes in the past few years. To adapt to the explosion of the Internet and the development of new media, designers must learn the digital technologies necessary to keep pace with their clients' needs. Early digital equipment did not have the sophistication of traditional design methods, but this has been overcome. Digital software and hardware now offer the designer more choices and options than they ever had before. In addition, media integration is allowing designers to broaden their focus from just one area, i.e., print or broadcast, to several areas, including print, Web, video, and animation. Because the demands on e-designers are becoming so great, it is important for them to gain an intimate understanding of the software and hardware they will be using, and to have a firm grounding in the traditional approaches to their craft. This essay will discuss my philosophy of education for e-designers, and will explore the educational options available to those who want to become successful e-designers.

Educational Philosophy

My educational philosophy is that students should be allowed and encouraged to develop in three essential areas: creativity, traditional art skills, and computer art skills.

1 | CREATIVITY This is the most important of the three. It includes the development of a unique and individual design style and the ability to come up with creative solutions to design problems. Creativity is always difficult to define and very difficult to teach. It is a talent that needs to be nurtured and developed. Some people seem to be "born creative," while others are able to develop their creativity through long hours of hard work. The elusive nature of creativity is part of its value. The ability to see and create designs that are new and innovative is a very important part of the education of an e-designer. Without innovation, design becomes stale and ordinary. When considering educational programs, it's important to select those with courses that focus on creative development.

2 | TRADITIONAL ART SKILLS The development of traditional art skills is critical to becoming a

successful e-designer. Although the computer is an extremely powerful tool, it should be thought of as just that: one tool in the arsenal of the e-designer. Another powerful tool is still the pencil. The invention of the computer does not invalidate traditional design methods, just as television did not signal the end of photography. When used in conjunction with each other, traditional art skills and digital art skills are an extremely powerful combination. For e-designers, a comprehensive knowledge of typography, design, layout and the concepts underlying composition, form, color, and visual communication are the foundation upon which a design career is built. It is important that classes in these disciplines be a part of your e-design education. I highly recommend keeping a sketch/idea book with you at all times. It is also important practice is to continually create and exhibit your own personal art. This personal creative work and the satisfaction and joy you receive from doing it, is the cornerstone upon which your professional career is built.

3 | COMPUTER ART SKILLS Computer art skills begin with learning software. To be an effective e-designer, one must know the software inside out, upside down, and backwards. Only by knowing what the software can do (and what it cannot), is one able to rise above the limitations of the medium and create significant work. In the early days of digital design, one of the major limitations was the huge difference between what the image looked like on the screen and what it would look like in print. The resolution of most screens is 72 dots per inch, but the resolution of print is much higher. Further, color on the monitor is based on RGB in an additive color system, while print is based on the CMYK color system and ink. The early limited typographical controls of computers have now been updated to give designers all of the control they used to have with traditional typesetting equipment, and more. The speed and precision of the digital environment is a great aid to the designer. In the digital world, more time is spent designing and less time is spent on the production process. Changes in drawings and layouts are easier to make and take less time. It is now possible to show clients more variations of a design idea, and designer and client can sit down together at the computer to refine a design. Since e-designers need a wide range of knowledge in order to understand the design concepts and underlying parameters of different media, it is valuable to take classes in many disciplines. E-design is very different from traditional design. Print is static; the Internet is not. Animation, audio, and video are now an integral part of designing for the Internet.

Educational Approaches

There are a variety of ways to get an education as an e-designer. One can learn through self-teaching, the Internet, continuing education, undergraduate programs, graduate programs, internships, or studio training programs. The three most common choices people make are continuing education, undergraduate education, and graduate education.

1 | CONTINUING EDUCATION Continuing education comes in a wide variety of forms, the most common of which is night classes at local colleges. There are also professional training centers that offer classes, and course material is increasingly becoming available on the Internet. Continuing education is a good option for those who only need specific additions to their design education. Most continuing education classes are skills-based and the content of the courses is narrow. For example, someone who has already had training and experience as a designer and who only needs to learn Web design, or software packages like Adobe GoLive, Macromedia Flash, or Director, would benefit from a continuing education class. However, someone who has been trained in the software, but needs more help with design skills, should take a traditional design or typography class.

It is very helpful to put your résumé and portfolio together, and meet with an advisor at the school of your choice for guidance on which classes to take. You can further refine your selection of classes by reading faculty biographies; it's important to study with individuals who *do* what they teach on a daily basis. Another important issue is lab access. If you have a computer and the appropriate software at home or at work, this is not a major problem. But if you do not, it is important to find a school that will allow you to work on its machines outside of class. Many schools also have lab assistants who are on duty to answer your questions and provide limited tutoring.

2 | UNDERGRADUATE EDUCATION The advantage of an undergraduate education is the comprehensive nature of the experience. Being a designer is not just about having design skills and knowing how to use the software. An education in art history and design theory, and having your work critiqued by professionals and faculty are all part of the undergraduate experience. With four years of study, you can explore a wide range of subjects and get a broad education that will make you a better designer. A firm foundation in the humanities, intellectual growth, and the development of critical thinking skills will have a significant impact on the way a designer approaches his or her work. Because design is not only a visual process, undergraduate programs also allow for the development of content-creation skills. If you should be approached by a client like the *National Geographic*, your coursework in biology, the environment, and cultural studies will come in handy.

When choosing an undergraduate institution, take a close look at the curriculum, the faculty, and the facilities, in that order. Does the curriculum include the type of design courses you are looking for? Is the curriculum dynamic and does it keep pace with the new developments in the Internet and new media? Who are the faculty, how many of them are there, what do they do professionally, and how much access would you have to them? Finally, what are the school's facilities like? Are they state of the art? Do they have the latest hardware and software? Are new machines and software added every year? How many people use the facility and what are the access policies? What is the placement record of the school and where are the graduates working? These are all important questions to be asked when choosing an undergraduate school.

3 | GRADUATE EDUCATION Graduate programs for e-designers are on the increase. Many schools are responding to the demand for programs that combine design education with new technology. Other schools have been involved with computer art and design for a long time. The MFA Computer Art program at my institution, the School for Visual Arts, was the first in the United States and has been in existence for almost fifteen years. We recently added an MFA program in Design. I have seen the MFA Computer Art program evolve over the years, both in curriculum and facilities. None of the original computer equipment has remained, and the new facilities include a T1 and DSL line, Webcasting hardware and software, and a DVD authoring system. The curriculum has changed dramatically to adapt to the creative uses of new technology. New classes are added each year to allow students to stay abreast of the latest trends in art and design. Recent additions include Web Design, Advanced Web Programming, and Advanced Digital Video.

The approach of graduate programs to new media design and computer art is different from that of undergraduate programs. Because the time spent in a graduate program is much shorter and the students are more experienced, the programs tend to be more highly specialized. Graduate programs also focus more on theory and criticism than on software instruction. If one is only looking for software skills, a graduate program is not the right choice. Continuing education classes are shorter, more skills-based and less expensive. Graduate programs are for those who want to take their careers to a new level, and to concentrate on developing art and content-creation skills, as well as an individual creative style and approach to the work. Most graduate programs have a Thesis or Final Project course—the body of creative work one generates to earn the degree. Very often, it is also a portfolio for entering a new phase of one's career.

When looking at graduate programs, many of the same criteria as undergraduate programs apply. However, the curriculum and faculty are even more important when considering a graduate program. Make sure the curriculum is flexible and matches your needs, and check all available options. Some graduate programs are small, with everyone taking the same classes, while some are large, have several disciplines, and offer opportunities for interdisciplinary study. Art schools tend to have their curriculum structured around creative work, while large universities take a more academic approach.

Clearly define your goals before choosing a graduate program. Read the faculty biographies to make sure the people you are going to be studying with are well-known in their fields and are experts in the areas you are interested in. Look at the facilities and what access you will have to them. Finally, look at the graduates of the program, what they have done, and where they are working. Visit the Web sites—most graduate schools have them. It is also highly recommended that you visit the school and meet with the advisor or chair before making your final decision.

4 | THE EVOLUTION OF AN E-DESIGNER Whatever educational option you choose, keep in mind that developing a career in e-design is an evolutionary process. We are in the middle of a technological revolution that has important cultural implications. The Internet is a global phenomenon. People from different cultures are sharing information at a rate unheard of only a few years ago. The symbols, images, and content of a designer's work now have multiple cultural implications and access to international markets. Design work now must cross several different media. We have seen this in the recent redesigning of many large corporations' logos. What used to work well in print now has to work well in video, CD-ROMs, DVDs, and the Internet. To create the work that uses these media effectively, designers must have a comprehensive knowledge of the new media. All of this, and the continual innovation in hardware and software, has created exciting and challenging career opportunities for e-designers.

Distance Learning and Teaching in the Twenty-First Century

RAYMOND PIROUZ

FOR THE VERY first time in the history of teaching, the Internet is allowing instructors and their students to gather, share ideas, engage in deep discussions, and learn from one another's discoveries and observations without having to brush teeth, wear a stitch of clothing, or commute in ungodly traffic conditions (although brushing teeth is highly recommended nevertheless).

While this phenomenon is happening on a limited scale now, in a very short time the Internet will dramatically change how colleges and universities conduct their business—if not completely, then at least partially. To ignore this trend in education is to use an Xacto knife while blindfolded.

Distance learning programs in design are not new concepts. We all know of the correspondence courses in the 1920s and 30s. While the idea of the correspondence course was truly revolutionary in that time period, people quickly dismissed it and migrated to more traditional forms of schooling, due to one of the most obvious weaknesses of the traditional correspondence course: lack of immediate feedback. On the Internet, not only can you post an assignment for all students to see immediately (without waiting for the postman to deliver it), you (and any other student enrolled in the course) may immediately view and respond to any assignment posted by any student. If you compare this way of learning with what goes on in the traditional design classroom setting, you will see that there are many similarities between the two. In fact, the Internet goes one step beyond the traditional design classroom setting by offering the opportunity for students and instructors alike to create new discussions and maintain ongoing discussions about any aspect of any lesson or assignment throughout the entire life of the course. If you can imagine a discussion beginning on the first day of class and ending on the very last day, you can begin to imagine the rich body of topics that may be discussed online. In the traditional classroom setting, when class is over, most discussions are also over and are rarely revisited, because they are not documented in any way, shape, or form. The Internet allows for a written transcript of every conversation between teachers and students to facilitate and promote offspring discussions and sideline conversations—all of which enhance the process of discovery and learning.

Of course, it should be noted that distance learning is not for everyone. There is something to be said about the real, face-to-face human conversation, bonding, and mentoring that simply cannot be replicated in a virtual environment. With all of its strengths, online learning can't provide its student body with the same level of live flesh-and-blood community that might be experienced in a traditional educational environment. This is where the online experience may turn off a great percentage of prospective students. While it would be ridiculous to assume that everyone will be attracted to the online experience in the same way, it's safe to say that there is a growing techno-savvy minority out there who feels comfortable enough with the technology to be satisfied with the virtual learning experience.

At R35 edu, we have developed a multidisciplinary curriculum to address the learning needs of the growing Internet strategy, design, development, commerce, and marketing fields. While our program has its roots in traditional design and entrepreneurial business thinking, it goes beyond these two fields to merge the two and apply them to doing business in the new Internet economy.

R35 edu works very much like a real school. Students enroll with us and are sent a registration confirmation, and are later given the usernames and passwords with which to access the school (this can be compared to the tradition of receiving one's locker combination and student ID number). Students attend school by logging into the system, where they are visually presented with their classrooms, based on the class(es) they have enrolled in. Each student's desktop is unique in that it may be modified and customized according to the student's preferences. In addition to classrooms, students are able to join an ongoing discussion (by way of posts) in a student lounge (where administrators also participate). R35 edu is very much like a community in that it is a private environment filled with people who have the same interests and are there to share their love for the craft. Students read the lessons as they are posted to classrooms by instructors, and can then leave the environment to conduct any research and/or perform the necessary tasks to fulfill the requirements of each assignment. Once complete, the students' results are posted to the classroom for all to see. This is very much like what happens in a traditional "crit-wall" situation. One benefit here is that the R35 edu crit wall for each week's lesson remains up throughout the quarter. This way, the lessons are available for a longer time and discussions relating to the findings are also possible outside of any "time limit." For the most part, R35 edu imposes no "timing" restrictions on student activity. People may log in at any time, read their lessons at any time, and post their findings at any time before the next lesson is presented. This flexibility allows students to work full-time jobs and still participate in our program.

While the technology can be fascinating to examine, it would be foolish to assume that technology alone is what drives the school. Without passionate instruction combined with a genuine willingness to absorb and learn from the real human beings involved in the process, R35 edu would not be a functioning reality. Many traditional schools have tried to go online, and most assume that you can simply can courses and deliver them in a robotic manner. This would be true if you had robots for students, but this is rarely the case. Real human beings require real human conversation, emotion, mentoring, and passion in order to function within a learning environment. While technology makes our school possible, people are what make it function.

Technologically speaking, the R35 edu distance-learning program operates completely online. In fact, our entire third quarter of the year 2000 (including classrooms, students, all conversations, and art files) was archived on a 650-megabyte CD. Setting up a virtual school is not anywhere as difficult as building a real one out of bricks. In fact, a dual processor server with an ample amount of ram and hard drive space is all it takes for a solid foundation. Of course, it's always a good idea to have redundant technology for the sake of backups and disaster control. Therefore, generally speaking, it's always a good idea to have two of everything just in case. As for software, R35 edu runs on Centrinity's FirstClass, which is a client server–based collaborative environment. FirstClass enables us to add students using a client-license model, which is perfect for scalability. We can host several hundred students simultaneously on one machine without a problem. In fact, FirstClass is one of the premiere off-the-shelf collaborative environments used by many schools throughout the United States. What's great about FirstClass is that its interface is excellent for customizing, using an icon-based desktop approach. With a little bit of technological fiddling, one can set up a very unique and customized virtual interface. Of course, an alternative to going with something off-the-shelf is to code an application from scratch, but this is rarely cost-effective or logical—especially when you haven't had time to study user behavior to determine the services and technologies to incorporate in your custom solution.

Only time will tell if Web-based distance education will replace or augment traditional learning environments, but our guess is that it will do a little of both, depending on the market being served. For instance, at R35 edu, we attract a global student body—we have students from the United Kingdom and other parts of Europe, Singapore, and Hawaii. These are students who don't live close to a geographic area where a high-caliber design program is being offered. We also attract students who live in metropolitan areas, but cannot find a program similar to ours. Because smaller, online schools can innovate and custom-tailor their programs faster than traditional brick-and-mortar schools, whose movements are constrained by red tape and bureaucracy, small online schools may be more commonplace in the near future. This trend may enable a new class of teacher/entrepreneur to emerge, offering its unique knowledge base to a growing global community of wired students.

A Matter of Degrees: The Ph.D. in Design

CAROLYN MCCARRON

TO BE OR not to be . . . a doctor of design? To many, the idea of obtaining a doctoral degree in design seems ludicrous—especially in a field where it's not necessary to earn an undergraduate degree to find gainful employment. When asked what the response was from their colleagues and friends when they decided to enroll in a doctoral program in design, a few students confirmed that most designers don't understand it. "I usually have trouble explaining myself to designers who work in a traditional design setting," one student says, "especially when they don't see the need for higher education in design."

In an age of digital information, products, and environments, designers are expected to know and do more, and they are feeling the pressure and returning to school to obtain an advanced degree. Deane Richardson, cofounder and chairman emeritus of Fitch, confirms: "Designers need better research skills and increased capabilities to be able to work on more complex design problems, and on a team basis. Designers have always been creative thinkers and doers with a unique set of skills, but designers have not always been well-utilized by upper management in other industries. Advanced education will help maximize the contributions designers can make to economies around the world, both strategically and tactically. Design education must anticipate the expanding needs of the design profession and Ph.D. programs are one of those paths."

Meanwhile, Illinois Institute of Technology's Institute of Design (ID), which launched the first Ph.D. program in design in the United States nine years ago, has been so successful in developing its doctoral program that other schools are starting to follow suit. North Carolina State University launched a Ph.D. program last fall, and Carnegie Mellon University will open the doors to its new doctoral program this year. Other schools that now offer doctoral programs in design include the University of Minnesota, Georgia Institute of Technology, Stanford University, and MIT. Ohio State University has plans to launch a Ph.D. program in the near future.

The introduction of the Ph.D. in design programs across the country raises a lot of questions. An obvious one is: In a field where practitioners take pride in self-taught visionaries and consider the bachelor's degree to be superfluous, how will doctoral education in design be justified? Design educators want to promote design from a trade to a *profession*—via doctoral education.

Can Doctoral Programs Really Advance the Profession?

The key difference between undergraduate and doctoral programs is that undergraduate and even master's studies prepare students for professional practice, while doctoral programs are driven by research. Through research, doctoral students are pushing the boundaries and defining new areas of design. They are assessing corporate design policy and strategy, design for education, design for the workplace, how people use technology, and design's impact on economic and cultural issues. In short, they are identifying unmet human needs and untapped opportunities for design to enrich and improve people's lives.

The goal behind generating this type of research is to create an original body of knowledge unique to the design profession. The point? To not only uncover new ways to use design to enhance our lives, but to advance our profession among more established and widely accepted professions—both nationally and internationally. In the past, designers have relied on other fields for research and data. The concepts and methods, which are borrowed from other professions, have become a weaker form of design research. Pioneers of doctoral programs want the design profession to establish its own body of research, so that other professions will turn to *us* for data, information, input, and research. Until we establish this body of original knowledge, many leaders in design assert that design will remain a trade, and not become an established profession.

With this argument in mind, Patrick Whitney and the ID faculty started a doctoral program in design at ID. Whitney has long believed that the principal failing of the design world is its lack of depth in theory and methods—defining elements of a profession. He states: "I think professional practice is very healthy right now because of the economy, but I believe that more rigorous methods will help designers work and do projects in less time and at higher quality. Business schools have specific methods they teach their students that help them to work, that are good and reliable. Engineering schools do the same. I believe design education needs to develop the same rigorous body of knowledge that is represented in methods and theories that allow practitioners to work faster and better. Every professional field has a growing body of knowledge that feeds into practice, and the practice is observed and feeds back into that body of knowledge. And design is being held back because there's no segment of the field that is about growing a body of knowledge. That's what Ph.D. education should be: the small, small segment of the field that should be the intellectual engine. Otherwise, it will remain a craft like plumbing."

Originally, ID dealt with this problem through their Master of Design program. The General Electric Foundation was so impressed with the original ideas and supporting research coming out of the program—in fact, they considered it to be doctoral-level work—that they offered the school a generous two-year grant to expand the curriculum into America's first doctoral program in design.

Nine years later, due to the success of both the master's and doctoral programs, ID dropped its undergraduate program altogether so that faculty members could devote their time to developing the graduate-level programs, and contribute—along with their students—research that will feed a body of original knowledge. Whitney emphasizes that not having an undergraduate program, growing their master's program to a community of 100 students, and developing a doctoral program has allowed the school to create a culture that supports both research and a higher-level education. He believes that this type of setup is analogous to business schools that have both MBA programs and Ph.D. programs. Larry Keeley, board and faculty member at ID and the president of the Doblin Group, further justifies this decision: "We feel that there is over-capacity in design schools at the undergraduate level, anyway. We believe that what really makes designers able to contribute something important to the world is to not only understand and master design well, but to be able to contribute original ideas to the profession." He continues: "An undergraduate design degree buys you nothing in the world. The bus drivers in Chicago are better paid, on average, than designers with undergraduate degrees. And so we wanted to move the field to a higher level."

Market, scientific, and other types of research are becoming increasingly important to corporate executives who need to reach many different audiences at once. According to Meredith Davis, chair of the graphic design department and faculty member in the new interdisciplinary Ph.D. program in design at North Carolina State University (NCSU), research-driven professions are therefore securing front-end positions in corporate management, while designers remain at the bottom of the food chain. She explains: "Designers frequently question the reliability of data and the validity of responses from focus groups who have difficulty discussing objects with which they have no prior experience or that do not yet exist. However, designers can offer little in rebuttal because they lack credible research and a [professional basis] in which individuals hold express responsibility for generating new knowledge."

But Is It Relevant?

Because doctoral programs are research-based, many professionals question the relevancy of such a degree to professional practice. They are concerned that the profession's participation in heady academic discourse will remove design from the real world. There is also the accusation that doctoral students are often those who stay in school to avoid the working world, thereby becoming "professional students."

Some creative directors and company executives say they do not see the need to hire Ph.D.s, since there are other qualifications besides education that they look for in applicants, such as skills, talent, and experience. Clement Mok, chief creative officer at Sapient, comments: "We have hired quite a few Ph.D. recipients here [in other fields], so we do value that kind of training. But the problem I have with Ph.D. programs is that they can be all thinking and no doing. It's really important to be able to conduct critical analysis, but also to be able to provide insight into acting upon that analysis. Sometimes I find myself saying, 'Boy, these people are smart, but what should I do with these great ideas?' Yet, I respect the model of Ph.D. programs; the rigor is needed in the design field. If we can come up with a Ph.D. program in design that strikes a balance between research and implementation, then that would be a great thing. But in terms of hiring right now, if we look strictly at Ph.D. recipients, well . . . it's just not enough."

Peter Seidler, chief creative officer at Razorfish, echoes Mok's sentiments: "Doctoral programs can develop a great deal of intellectual validation for design. But the quality of their work is more important. We look for a great portfolio."

Although Larry Keeley was active in developing the Ph.D. program at ID and is excited about its potential, he feels that it is unrealistic to expect design consultancies to *need* Ph.D.s. He clarifies: "Ph.D.s in design are essential to bringing the field to a higher level. Thus, their ideal role is in teaching, research, writing, and perhaps consulting—*in that order*. As a member of the staff at ID, I love the fact that we are running the most robust design Ph.D. program in the world and am proud of the quality of the students that result. Of course when these young people get their degrees they know something specific very, very thoroughly, which does not usually make them [great general consultants]." At the same time, Keeley points out that the reason many technology and design consultancies may not currently need Ph.D.s is because they operate in high-growth sectors, producing large volumes of design work without conducting primary research on emerging sectors of the field. This is the precise issue that doctoral programs are attempting to address. He says: "At Harvard Medical School or Sloan Kettering, they are doing many things that expand the frontiers of medicine. Where is the design equivalent? Not at consultancies, which can and should develop urgently needed Web sites as fast as possible. So it comes as no surprise that they see little or no need for Ph.D.s. What is interesting is to question how the field itself progresses, and where the breakthrough new services will come from that reinvent consulting in our profession."

Many educators are aware of the danger of separating design education from the real world. Richard Buchanan, chair of the School of Design at Carnegie Mellon University, reminded his colleagues at a conference that the opportunity lies in the potential of research and new ideas to affect both design practice and education, thereby possibly redirecting the course of design. He also warned against losing sight of the power and grace of aesthetics to excitement over new research agendas. He reminds us that aesthetics helps to enhance people's lives, and that research and aesthetics need to be effectively combined in order for research to be truly beneficial.

Are Doctoral Students Connected to Reality?

Despite their concerns, the professionals quoted above said they would be willing to sponsor Ph.D. research if doctoral students could provide original ideas that could help advance their firms' business. For example, Peter Seidler sees a need for research in "design for new platforms and digital business," while Clement Mok cited "missing cultural artifacts: What are the things that are being replaced and displaced by new technology? How is it being displaced? And is this a good thing, or a bad thing?" Mok also cited a need for research in social, cultural, and generational biases in interaction with technology. "These are all important issues," he states, "that we have not taken a good, hard, serious look at."

The idea of these three firms sponsoring projects is key: This is how faculty members of Ph.D. programs are keeping doctoral curriculums and research connected to the real world—via corporate sponsors. Companies provide not only funding but also professional input for projects, and, in the end, implement the doctoral research and prototypes into their own corporate policies and projects.

Motorola, Steelcase, and Arthur Andersen are three major corporate sponsors at ID. At the cost of up to $200,000 each, all are members of the "Tangible Knowledge Consortium," an arena that permits a multitude of corporations to exchange information and ideas with faculty, students, and colleagues, while having a say in the research agenda. According to Whitney, there are many more possible sponsors: "We have a European management consultancy thinking of joining. We also have a major role-player in the barcode industry, a database company, and a telecommunications company. So, the way we're going to fund our program is through corporations who believe they need design methods. Our main sponsors, Motorola and Steelcase, are helping us bring in other companies."

By sponsoring doctoral research, Motorola hopes to stay one step ahead of its competitors. Joe Laviana, director of User Experience Research at Motorola Labs, confirms: "Through sponsorship, Motorola expects to gain access into the discovery of new processes and tools that will broaden our ability to produce new technologies and products based on an understanding of user needs." Doctoral students at ID are helping Motorola to explore new ideas in experiences and environments, such as new products for the car, office, body, and home.

Charles Bezerra, a student from Brazil who just received his doctoral degree, has been invited to Steelcase before he returns home to see if there are ways his dissertation research can be used within the company. Other students have helped Steelcase redesign their showrooms. According to Jim Hackett, president and CEO of Steelcase, doctoral students addressed the question: What do visitors really expect when they come to a trade show? He says, "We redesigned the showroom around the user's experience. Before, it was designed around the display of the product. We completely changed that perspective using some of the doctoral students' research. The research that they've done on cognitive experiences and structured planning really helped us get a better result. It's funny," he ponders, "we started raising our expectations of certain jobs and employees because of what we see in these students." When asked why Steelcase chose to sponsor doctoral students instead of hiring a professional design consultancy, he answers: "Doctoral students look much further out with much less—let's call it accountability for the economics of it. They push the boundaries. That's very valuable to business because here in the company, we are not always allowed to take those routes. So the students ensure that we get a really deep perspective on things. We also learn a great deal by staying in touch with what they're currently teaching in the universities. It helps the business stay fresh and on top of things."

At North Carolina State University, doctoral students are currently researching new opportunities for design application and technology in education—specifically, middle-school math and science courses—via a grant from the Kenan Institute for Engineering, Technology, and Science. The American Institute of Graphic Arts (AIGA) is a partner on this project.

Corporate sponsors and projects like these are often what attract students. Jay Melican, one of the few American doctoral students, decided to attend ID's program when a faculty member, Sharon Poggenpohl, recruited him to explore the potential of interactive multimedia in education via a grant from the Joyce Foundation in Chicago. The project was concerned with technology policy at all levels, from local to national school policy, as well as with schools' access to technology in lower-income communities. The project ended in a paper and a series of multimedia prototypes.

Melanie Joh, a student from Korea, is consulting for Arthur Andersen's Experiential Design

Practice, advising on their online strategies. She has also consulted for Ernst & Young LLP, working on their online consulting service. With a background in corporate design and strategy, she is researching design's role in corporations and applying her research to her consultant work. She writes, "Design has the ability to help people understand, both users and employees within the company, and to turn this understanding into successful strategy formulation."

Deane Richardson showed an interest in hiring Ph.D.s by attending an international conference about doctoral education in design with several of his colleagues from Fitch. He says, "An increasing number of our employees have advanced degrees, including Ph.D.s, but usually in allied fields of market planning and research—not yet in design. However, Fitch has been creating strategic partnerships with institutions which give us the opportunity to be more technically specialized and better planners and researchers to more accurately anticipate user needs and economic opportunities. The Ph.D. programs in design will only enhance what is already happening in the profession."

Who Teaches Ph.D. Students?

To date, there have been only two Ph.D.s in design conferred from an American institution—neither one to an American. Thus, a fundamental question is raised: Who teaches on the doctoral level in the United States? Most faculty members, who sometimes have master's degrees, are recruited to teach on the undergraduate or master's level. Now they are expected to teach on the doctoral level and contribute research of their own. Could it become a problem for doctoral students who are pioneering a dissertation in design when their advisor does not have a Ph.D.? Both Whitney and Davis claim that it is not a problem, as long as faculty members are active in a research consortium and have experience with consultant work. "We have to start somewhere," they both said.

Some students, however, say it can definitely be a problem, and they have to turn to Ph.D. recipients in other fields for research direction, organization, and methods. For this reason, schools like ID and NCSU assign three advisors to each doctoral student—two within the design department, and one Ph.D. from another department within the university.

Another strategy in successfully growing doctoral programs is to limit enrollment. In fact, ID did not admit any new students this year since they are already up to thirteen. Whitney affirms that this helps to ensure a closer relationship between researchers and corporate sponsors, and students get more attention from the faculty. Davis believes keeping the number small also helps to ensure that doctoral programs attract the right type of students. "Even though there is an emerging research culture in design, the general understanding of what constitutes design research is still limited," she says. "The goal is not to produce a lot of students, but to generate new and useful information about design and how it works. We have no problem interesting companies and funding sources in our research agenda, but the students who can meet those demands aren't going to be found through visual portfolio reviews and the traditional admissions practices used by design schools." The answer, she asserts, is going to lie in challenging undergraduate and master's programs to diversify their curricula and make undergraduate designers more aware of futuristic research and new ideas in the field.

One way undergraduate students are being introduced to the concept of original research is that Ph.D. students are teaching on the undergraduate and master's levels while they are enrolled as doctoral students. Eventually, there will be Ph.D. recipients teaching design courses, thereby raising the bar for design academia.

Why Aren't There Any American Ph.D.s in Design?

Up until now, doctoral design education has been mostly an international phenomenon: Ph.D. programs in design have existed only in other countries, and even with the advent of doctoral programs in design in the United States, most students come from overseas to attend these new American programs. In 1998, however, Ohio State University was the host of the first international design conference on doctoral education in design, which was organized in partnership with Carnegie Mellon University. Due to the fact that there are so few American designers currently interested in pursuing a Ph.D. in design, the number of international attendees outweighed American designers and design educators; fewer than fifteen Americans joined attendees from nineteen other countries. With the explosion of new doctoral programs in the United States, however, American design educators and leaders hope this will change soon, bringing American designers up to par with their international colleagues.

One of the goals of new doctoral programs in the Unites States, obviously, is to recruit more American designers who want to assume leadership positions in an international market of design research. The reason doctoral education in design has mostly been, up until now, an international issue is because foreign governments are willing to sponsor their citizens in doctoral education overseas, whereas this kind of financial support in higher education does not yet exist in the United States. American corporations, however, are increasingly willing to cash in on doctoral programs and projects, paying for students' tuition and research expenses, and offering their doctoral researchers a stipend. Whitney agrees that the lack of interest in doctoral education among American designers could be due to finances. "The funding is very important, because it not only covers tuition, but it covers the expenses of the research. Look at Ph.D.s in other fields outside of the sciences and engineering: Students may get tuition waived by the school, but they get no support to actually pay for the research they're doing. So it takes them a long time, often they don't graduate, and they're limited by what they can look at because they're limited by money. It was easy to create a Ph.D. program in design nine years ago, but our corporate-funded research agenda has only existed for the last two years. Getting corporations interested in becoming sponsors has been a milestone for us, and for American doctoral education in design in general." Corporate funding of American designers has allowed them to pursue leadership positions in an international arena of design research. For example, American students recently presented their work at conferences in Italy and France, and are having work published in international design publications.

For some designers, however, the lack of funding has not been the issue. There is just not an interest in design research, even if it is needed. There is a preference to pass off the research aspect of a project onto another member of the team from another field, and focus strictly on the creative aspect. Davis states, "I find it very odd and somewhat troubling that some designers don't believe there is a body of knowledge about design and that it is worth adding to. Even more troubling is the notion that we should yield responsibility for finding out about some of these issues to another field. It is almost a fear that examining something too closely will spoil it. Imagine where medicine, technology, or other more established fields would be with this kind of attitude. Every mature discipline has people who do research as their primary activity. Why not design?"

Why *Not* Design?

Three curators—each representing a different design discipline—of "Design Culture Now," the National Design Triennial Exhibition at the Cooper-Hewitt National Design Museum in New York, proved that the boundaries between professions are disintegrating and design problems are becoming more complex, requiring more skills and collaboration across disciplines to solve them. Steven Skov Holt, one of the curators and vice president of Creative Culture at frogdesign, writes: "Enormous opportunities for the design profession are being driven by the possibility to meaningfully combine features, objects, materials, technologies, and ideas previously considered to be separate. There are more new unions of content and commerce than at any point in history. E-commerce is driving a whole new generation of design, and e-design is changing the world of products as we know it. . . . The designer as the singular creator of discrete objects has been supplanted by a new vision of the design professional as orchestrator of complex systems in which information, materials, sensation, and technology are in a state of flux." Advanced education is becoming increasingly important in providing the knowledge to solve such complex design problems. Despite the small number of doctoral students in design, the research they are conducting and prototypes they are building in collaboration with corporations hold tremendous power to affect the direction of the design profession.

In fact, a doctoral student from MIT, David Small, had his dissertation project featured in the exhibit. Based on digital information, Small's project proves that design students probably have the most opportunity to uncover new information that could lead to inventive ideas. Neglecting research in future areas of design could eventually exclude designers as equal partners on multi-disciplinary teams. Deane Richardson confirms, "In the past, advanced degrees have been required if designers wanted to teach or move into research, but were not important in the professional world of practice. Today, advanced degrees are more important in industry and will be more so in the future. We need to therefore encourage the Ph.D. programs that are evolving, if we designers are to be better maximized by upper management in other industries."

Unanswered Questions

Since doctoral education in design is a new venture, many more questions remain unanswered and can only be addressed with time. For example: Will Ph.D.s raise the bar for design practitioners and educators? Although design educators are out to raise design from a trade to a profession, many doctoral students stated they do not care about advancing the profession, but rather are in it for their own intellectual and professional development. Despite personal motivations for obtaining a Ph.D., it remains to be seen if Ph.D.s will inadvertently progress the profession, especially since upon graduation they will most likely work in academia, or in research and development for corporations.

In addition, all of the current doctoral programs were established in universities with other departments to act as additional resources. Could this mean that university departments will start collaborating more, reflecting the way professionals are now working? Furthermore, one wonders if art and design schools will follow suit in establishing new doctoral programs, or leave this form of higher education to universities?

Because ID is the pioneer for establishing not only the first American doctoral program in design, but also a corporate-funded research agenda that could pay for American students' tuition and expenses, their program was covered more in this article than new-sprung programs. But in the course of the next ten years, with companies such as Motorola and Steelcase leading the way as corporate sponsors at ID, it will be interesting to watch new doctoral programs—such as Carnegie Mellon, NCSU, and even Ohio State—develop their own research agendas, and see who becomes their sponsors.

In their infancy, doctoral programs are merely reflecting what is happening in the field, mirroring the growing complexity of design problems and providing advanced training to solve them. In light of unanswered questions, it is exciting to speculate on how doctoral curricula will continue to grow, who will join the arena, and what new areas of design will be forged by doctoral dissertations. In essence, how are these doctoral programs going to ultimately affect the design profession?

This article first appeared in *Communication Arts Design Annual*, November 2000.

Typographic Education in a Digital Environment

SEAN ADAMS

"PLACE YOURSELF IN the background," wrote William Strunk, Jr. and E.B. White in *The Elements of Style*. The directive to the writer was to focus on content rather than style. By extension, if we think of typography as pictures of words, then designers of text should not decorate words, but use them plainly and directly, too. In a pre-computer typographic environment, this directive was fairly easy to enforce. The typographic education of designers followed clear and methodical practices. A well-established history of teaching specific skills based on agreed-upon standards was adhered to. Typography teachers were assured, then, that graduating design students could make a clean chart, or set body copy with a correct line length, not exceeding fifty-two characters, or use display fonts only for display, or not use Hobo in any context.

The Modernist approach to typography followed educational models of the Bauhaus and incorporated the pragmatic American concept of plain speaking. Eliminating decoration or flowery language is based on the desire of eighteenth-century American colonists to distance themselves from Europe. Early Americans associated corruption in European government and business with ulterior motives behind a baroque vernacular. By speaking directly, we would shed corruption and deception. This idea develops further in typography—by teaching designers to utilize only functional or *honest* typography, they would create work that spoke clearly and authentically.

A lack of options was key to this modernist approach. In 1982, during my first year at CalArts, a metal type shop was donated to the school. My work/study job in the type shop consisted of cleaning and organizing the metal slugs and type cases. During my first week, *bad* typefaces, as judged by the faculty, were emptied into a large bucket. The fonts discarded and removed from our menu of choices were primarily odd display fonts, fashionable during the seventies. What remained were fonts considered "basics" at that time: Bodoni, Baskerville, Garamond, Franklin Gothic, Futura, and Univers. The intended result was for students to use a limited palette of agreed-upon classic fonts, and it was enforced. There was no room for font-choice error.

"Rich, ornate prose is hard to digest, generally unwholesome, and sometimes nauseating," continue William Strunk, Jr. and E. B. White. And when applied to typographic education, we perpetuate basic American pragmatism and enforce "good design." However, in the bargain we ignore the possibilities of digital technology. There is definitely a motivation, in many students' typographic work today, to embrace style and excess as opposed to intelligent reasoning and conceptual thinking related to content. We can blame the digital technologies and mixing of media, from print to interactive, for this instinct, but it is more about information and the way this information is delivered and processed that informs contemporary typographic solutions.

Victorian book typography is dense, tight, and often gray. The primary delivery vehicle of information in nineteenth-century western civilization was the newspaper. In the early twentieth century, concurrent with the advent of radio, there was a relaxing of typography—looser leading and stronger contrasts. Black-and-white television paved the way for classic "big idea" design, which gave central image predominance and predicated the typography to remain simple and unobtrusive. Our processing of information under a barrage of messages in the digital age has opened the door to multiple typographic messages, often dissimilar or schizophrenic, complexity of form, and a relaxing of standards in relationship to letterform design.

"Work from a suitable design," caution Strunk and White. To ask students in the current design curriculum to set this process of receiving and re-presenting information aside and work from a strong structure, international style Swiss grids, for example, is a valuable exercise. Yet, to forbid them to investigate new ways of seeing and making meaning is archaic. Here, then, is one of the principal dilemmas of current typographic education. In order to break rules; a student must know the rules. In order to choose odd letterforms and compositions to promote unexpected meaning, a student must know which letterforms are not odd.

Recently, when I asked a student what typeface she used on a cookbook assignment, she could not remember. "It was one of the fonts in the As on the CD," she told me. This CD-ROM, is surreptitiously passed between the design students and is said to contain two thousand boot-legged fonts. Many of the students cannot remember most of the font names, and tend toward use of fonts with names like Alpaca, Andover, Bora, and Collier. The choice of fonts on projects is inspired, not by specific criteria, historical relevance, formal associations, or oblique conceptual issues, but on which fonts are listed first on the CD—hence the predominance of fonts beginning with A, B, or C. Allowing students to have access to all two thousand typeface choices, with no sense of a grid or proportions, may achieve surprising, even appropriate, results with a very personal energy and spirit. But this is the exception, not the rule. There are just too many choices.

"Do not take shortcuts at the cost of clarity," affirm Strunk and White. The relaxing of typographic standards is common. There is little need for fine details in a 72-dpi broadcast or Web environment. Kerning is often damaged by technical restrictions in these environments, and the difference between a badly cut version of *Firmin Didot* and a beautiful cut is often undetectable. The democratization of typography has also led to the personalization of letterforms. Making a custom font is like a signature. It reflects the author's personal concerns and issues. If a sloppy curve on a capital G is considered to be part of the personal vision and reflection of the author, then we cannot fault it. Our ability to critique based on aesthetic concerns is impaired.

It is possible to forgive these offenses as personal exploration. But typography is a craft and the quality of a finished piece is often dependent upon a skilled typographic hand.

Conveying this to a student can seem at odds with the need for personal expression. The student working in several digital environments is drawn to the eccentric because it is easy to create. Typography, like all graphic design, is a tightrope walk between discipline and freedom.

In a school environment, mistakes and explorations are encouraged. Graduating a student who has never moved beyond the comfortable and expected is a disservice to the student and the profession. Students should be interested in and anticipate change. They should be able to typographically express an idea in print, online, and in motion. The results should be unexpected, yet appropriate; the typography should be well considered, whether it is minimal or complex. The decisions made, in addition to the obvious technical issues, like small serifs on the screen, should be deliberate. To reach this place, the typographic education of the student must have included the same skills taught throughout history—addressing issues of structure, form, hierarchy, meaning, and context. Today it must also place a priority on expression, experimentation, personal understanding, process, and a willingness to be subversive. Combining these often-alternative ideas is not easy. It is a challenging task.

"Writing is an act of faith, not a trick of grammar. . . . What you are, rather than what you know, will at last determine your style," conclude Strunk and White. Armed with clear guidelines for excellence based on traditional skills, and encouraged to explore and expand with a belief in his/her value, the student is ready to face the profession. Perhaps it is presumptuous to assume that the students will be missing out on something valuable. Perhaps the subtext of typographic anarchy in a digital environment is not a comment about the current state of design education, but rather about the promises we made to ourselves as students that we may have forgotten under the guise of maintaining order and tradition.

There's No *e* in Illustrator

DUGALD STERMER

TAKE AWAY THE modem and the Internet, and the illustrator's computer becomes little more than a lavish airbrush, typewriter, and filing system. But with those two, the combination has completely changed the art and business of the field, the latter far more than the former.

I'm much less interested, not to mention incompetent, to write about the use and misuse of the computer as an illustrating tool than I am to discuss the enormous effect it has had on all other areas of our lives as practitioners. From promotion to pricing, from competition to copyright violations, and from our traditional roles as visual interpreters and communicators to an increasing—and mostly disagreeable—job as marketers of our own off-the-shelf inventory, e-mail and the Internet has rendered our field nearly unrecognizable to the likes of the late Robert Weaver, much less the earlier N. C. Wyeth and Norman Rockwell.

The notion of having a portfolio of my work instantly available to anyone, anywhere, anytime, was so irresistible several years ago that I purchased a computer, scanner, CD writer, and printer. This was, as anyone who knows me can attest, a revolutionary act. That I didn't have a clue how to connect it up, plug it in, or turn it on, much less do anything useful with it, wasn't the real hurdle. I still needed to figure out what this thing was going to help me with that *would* be useful.

First, while the computer, once installed, would certainly allow me to view my own Web site, I was entirely incapable of building it. I had to hire that out, and did. But in the process I did learn how to scan my work. Now, instead of the expensive and time-consuming process of having 4" × 5" transparencies made of every piece, in order to maintain a reproducible record, the file can be built and maintained quickly, cheaply, and much more efficiently with a scanner, a computer, and some CD-ROMs or zip disks. I may have been near the last on my block to realize this, but it was nonetheless a revelation, the first of many.

Following shortly thereafter, it occurred to me that if I could build a decent scan of a picture for my own files, why bother to send the original to the client, risking damage or loss in the round trip. For a time, insecurity prompted me to send both a disk and the original to clients, offering them the choice. Unsurprisingly, they nearly always chose to shoot from the original. Many art directors and production managers still prefer to scan from original art, and feel that they are paying for the privilege; and most are. But some have come to welcome digital files. One client, a magazine for which I have been producing a regular feature for several years, has printed from my scans for the last four or five issues, and I can't discern any qualitative difference. From my perspective, perhaps the ultimate distinction is that if I make the scan, I can adjust my own illustration to more closely approximate my vision of what it should look like. The production manager is stuck with having to try to match the original.

It quickly became apparent to me, once my Web site was up, that this was sooner or later going to make the traditional illustrator's portfolio obsolete. In fact, I haven't put one together, much less packed it and shipped it, since the site has been operational. Often, during the introductory phone call from a prospective client—art director or art buyer—he or she is browsing the site as we converse, fees and deadlines are discussed, all in minutes instead of days or weeks. What this foretells for the traditional roles played by reps will be, of course, worked out by them, individually or through groups like SPAR (Society of Professional Artists' Representatives). But one thing is certain: What they now do, in general, is not worth anything like 25 percent of an illustrator's income, not in the digital age, and not to me.

Recently, that which some of my less technologically challenged colleagues have long been predicting, all-digital transactions start to finish, has nearly come to pass. I have received e-mails that said, approximately: "I saw some of your work on theispot [an online commercial Web site that rents space to illustrators. There are others, with more entering the field by the minute.], linked onto your Web site, and sent samples from it on to the editor. We would like to e-mail you a manuscript and have you illustrate it for a magazine page. . . ." With the details ironed out, again by modem, I read the piece, did the sketch, scanned it, and e-mailed it to the client. Upon acceptance, I finished the job, scanned it, and sent the file along with the invoice, again by e-mail. So far, I haven't been paid electronically, at least not by domestic clients, but that can't be far away.

It should be mentioned that one problem remains to be satisfactorily solved. Just because someone has their own Web site, like the clichéd tree falling in the forest, if no one knows how to get there, for all intents and purposes, it doesn't exist. Even theispot has not come up with much more in the way of promotion than advertisements in the trades, more or less preaching to the choir. So far, the best I've done are snail mailings, sending cards announcing my site's address to the usual suspects (who move around with the frequency of deadbeat dads). It is to be hoped that some of the more farsighted reps will figure out more inventive ways to get the word out, but I'm not counting on it. Solutions will likely come from among those who are now illustration students; mine, I hope, so I can steal their ideas.

I've nodded sympathetically when friends bemoan the lack of human interaction this electronic process implies. But privately, I'm a little shamed to find out just how much of a hermit's life I can slip into with ease. After all, if I want to chat with a client, nothing stands between me and the telephone, except my own inertia. And it's been a very long time since I've lived in the same state as most of my clients, much less the same city, so face-to-face encounters are almost always out of the question. My guess is that most art directors and designers I work with don't encourage time-consuming conversations any more than I do. One of my very best friends, a well-known editorial art director, has said flatly, "I won't work with any illustrator who doesn't have e-mail," and clearly he includes me in this fiat. My experience suggests that, rather than reducing correspondence, e-mail has increased it exponentially. I am in regular contact with vastly more people now than when we had to depend on writing letters, sending faxes, or even dialing a phone. I cannot explain this phenomenon satisfactorily even to myself; I just know it's true.

One of the most useful and wondrous abilities of the Internet, one that most of my students knew well before me, is research. Damn, such a wealth of pictorial and informational material rests in this box. Again, I feel like the last person on the planet to get it, but what a marvel, not to mention a marvelous time-saver, unless one is a browser, easily and thoroughly distracted, as I am.

So much for the good stuff.

The Web has rendered our copyright laws meaningless at worst, and unenforceable at best. It has also made possible an enormous glut of imagery instantly available worldwide at insanely low fees, making a mockery of the already misleading and demeaning term "stock art." These abuses have led to several truly dismal trends, undeniably changing the field forever and, at least so far, for the worst. And neither of these "paradigm shifts" (the first and last time I'll employ this trendy term, but it fits) would have been logistically possible without the Internet.

First, the Web invites outright theft of images. So what if the resolution is not the best. In many places throughout the world, the available paper and printing is none too good either. Further, much of the theft has to do with moving the stolen pictures to other sites on the Internet anyway, basically dot for dot. None of us has the time, will or the resources to try to track down these illegal acts, and the thieves know it. Further, unless we take the considerable time and trouble to register each of our pictures with the U.S. Copyright Office, even if we did track down an offender, all we can do at best is get a cease and desist order, which the thief may or may not choose to obey. Forget damages or fees; that's not going to happen.

Second, corporate publishers got wise to the possibilities inherent in the Internet long before we did. No surprise there. They, or their lawyers, just rewrote their contracts with illustrators and photographers to include electronic transferal (read "the Web"), as well as "all known media and that yet to be invented," or some such all-encompassing phrase, *for no additional fee.* When I have discussed such phrases in the contracts with, say, the *Washington Post*, it was explained that they use the Internet as their traditional morgue, that it has only replaced microfilm for storage and research. Fair enough, as far as that goes, but it also automatically adds an infinite number of readers to their potential circulation, and makes abuses far easier to accomplish; just click and copy. Many other publications now attempt to retain all primary and secondary rights forever, using the Web as their shop from which to sell used pictures worldwide.

So far, the undisputed leader in this greedy race to grab up all the possible rights for future income is undoubtedly Conde Nast, publisher of such image-heavy publications as the *New Yorker, Vogue, GQ, Vanity Fair, House & Garden*, and *Architectural Digest*, among many others. Their current contract, once signed, gives the company *all* rights to *all* of the signer's pictures *ever* published by *any* of their magazines, forever and in all media. Consider that for a minute: This amounts to no less than a retroactive work-for-hire contract, without any of the benefits such an agreement normally confers. Can you imagine the meeting where the corporate attorneys introduced that particular notion to the board of directors? Some v.p. must have cautioned, "They'll never go for it." And the shysters' answer was probably, "Sure they will. They'll grumble, but they have no choice. It's either that or they get no work from us, ever." Unfortunately, so far they're right about a number of us. Either through oversight, or because they need the work, many illustrators go along. The problem is, once signed, that contract means that everything the signer does for any of their magazines, or ever did, or ever will do, is theirs, not his, forever.

An equally pernicious effect the Internet has had on the whole field of image-making—photography as well as illustration—has been the proliferation of huge online stock houses, like Corbis, Getty Art and S.I.S. (Stock Image Source). Without getting into the small print of any of these corporations' contracts, they can sell any of the images in their catalog for any price to any client for any use, take as much as half to two-thirds of the fee for themselves, and remit the remainder to the artist; that is, the images they don't already own outright. The details change from company to company—some have literally no bottom on their fee schedule—but the results are pretty much the same. The maker of the image is, if anything, a minor player in the deal, and apparently an annoying one at that. Recently an executive of one of these companies said, for attribution, "We could make a lot more money if we didn't have to pay artists," and he meant it seriously. Well, duh.

Of course, it's not only a matter of money, although many of us illustrators think it unseemly to talk about the subject, lest we compromise our art with mammon. We also have a sense of ourselves as communicators, however quaint that sounds today, and not just decorators. Our best work has been done in response to specific needs, not just to fill space for lazy, or greedy, or penurious, or inefficient publications and their art directors. It is a stretch, not to mention disheartening, to think of ourselves as purveyors of interchangeable inventory.

My friend and esteemed colleague, Brad Holland, has often pointed out "that in America, we can purchase something good, or fast, or cheap; we might get two of the three, but not all three at once, that is, not until now." After all, with the purchase of limited rights to an existing piece, the buyer gets it immediately and risk free. There are no annoying sketches on which to secure client approvals, maybe including discussions about ideas and imagery, the normal back and forth of traditional art direction. The art is presumed to be of high quality, in part validated by its provenance. It seems that logic would suggest that such a simplified, speedy, and trouble-free transaction would cost the buyer more, not less. But leave it to us illustrators to accept less than half for re-use rights, compared to what we would, on the average, receive for an assignment. We swallow, seemingly without reflection, the argument that, "After all, you already did the piece," as if we were being paid by the hour, and not essentially renting our copyright. ("Why should I pay full rent for the apartment? The place is built, and besides, it has been previously lived in.") No wonder Conde Nast, Getty Art, Corbis, a number of reps, designers, art directors, and others in related fields often treat us as commercially inept. Frequently we've justified their low opinion of us as business people: "They're artists, and you know how *they* are."

On the other hand, many of us have run relatively successful small businesses, sometimes for decades, with no support staff, quite by ourselves. This is no small feat in the United States, where small businesses fail four to one in the first six months. It seems obvious to me that now, finally, we all would be well-advised to educate ourselves, organize, and address some of these Web-related issues as a group or several groups. Otherwise, we might just find ourselves working in a kind of worldwide, work-for-hire, generic image-making industry, where the idea of specific commissions to interpret ideas and emotions in an imaginative and personal way is but a fond but hazy memory. Some of us have begun to get it together, as with The Illustrators Partnership, The Graphic Artists Guild, the almost annual Illustrators' Conference in Santa Fe, and within theispot's lively chat room. Often, it all seems like trying to herd a swarm of fractious and suspicious bees. We illustrators are not noted for our ability to play well with others, but maybe it's time to learn some new skills.

Gestures in TypeSpace

BOB AUFULDISH

MAKING GOOD TYPOGRAPHY is difficult even under the best of circumstances, and so the problem teaching typography for a digital environment is a difficult one. Typography usually depends on the typographer exerting maximum control over the form of the text, but in a digital environment that level of control is not always attainable, or desirable. So how to proceed?

First, some background: At the California College of Arts and Crafts, all graphic design students take the same curriculum through the first two semesters, after which they may choose to concentrate in New Media. The New Media concentration is a series of six studio classes completed over two semesters, at the end of which the students rejoin the rest of the program for their Theses. TypeSpace is in the first semester of the concentration. In the typography sequence, Typography 1: Introduction, covers the traditional basics in 2D print-based typography with close attention paid to form/content relationships. Typography 2: Intermediate, moves into areas of systems and sequences, also from a print perspective. Simultaneously, students are learning the software needed to produce their work in a separate class. So when students enter the New Media concentration, they have a solid background in print-based typography.

When the students enter TypeSpace, the course I teach with David Karam of PostTool Design, they—and we as their instructors—need to operate on a number of levels. First, the course is the next level in the sequence of typography courses, so it needs to look at its subject more deeply; second, the class is an introduction to typography in the digital environment; and third, the class requires the use of software—After Effects, Infiniti-d, Premiere—that most of the students are unfamiliar with. As instructors, David and I need to balance all three.

This brings up a topic that is perhaps an essay in itself: the demographics of the students attracted to this kind of work. Broadly speaking, the faculty at CCAC noticed some years ago that the kind of students interested in graphic design had shifted. Many of the students had liberal arts degrees before studying graphic design. Software for print production became more sophisticated, allowing people to enter the field who might not have had the hand skills essential to previous generations of designers. Now we have students who have spent their entire lives with personal computers, and the demographics are shifting again—toward students who learn software continually and intuitively.

This leads to the fundamental tenet of our course—we don't teach software. Demo's are given at the beginning of each project and technical questions are answered (by David, since I lack the expertise), but the primary focus in class is on the project at hand. We have come to believe that the students will best learn the software on their own in the process of producing their work. We find it's better for them to ask first, "what does this need to be," rather than, "what can I (or the software) do?"

TypeSpace consists of three projects, each with a different focus, but all dealing with gesture to some degree. By "gesture," we mean the movement of the letter(s) or words in space and time in the pursuit of transferring meaning. We encourage the students to physically act out the gestures they want their letterforms to have and then try transferring those gestures to animation. (An especially beautiful example of this was a student's animation of the name Ahab from *Moby Dick*. The "Aha" moved forward smoothly, and the "*b*" trailed behind, complete with scraping sound, to express how Ahab's wooden leg—severed by Moby Dick—had permanently altered Ahab's gait.) Later in the semester, we talk about the gesture of the camera—how the motion of the camera itself can help impart meaning.

The first project deals exclusively with gesture. The students are randomly assigned an emotion and asked to animate a single letterform to express that emotion. This is similar to the form/content relationships they had investigated in previous courses, with the added complexity of motion, time, and sound.

The second project deals primarily with navigation. The students are asked to take a short text of their choice and explicate it using three-dimensional space. The project they make is an animation of how the navigation might work—a demo. We don't ask the students to program their spaces so that they work; our concern is that they investigate how the navigation could operate. Here, the gesture of the camera comes into play as a way of defining the user's point of view. The gesture of the camera can be poetic, or more straightforward and transparent.

The third project deals primarily with storytelling. The students are asked to make an animated sequence that translates a story into an abstract typographic environment. The students edit their stories down to a series of key events that are translated into key frames. The students then build the frames in Infiniti-d to work out the characters and environment. Gesture plays a key role in this assignment in that the characters need to express more complicated emotions and interactions than in the first assignment. Imagine the name "Gregor" from Kafka's *Metamorphosis*, swelling up, twitching, and scurrying off into a corner to the horror of his family, expressed by a gasping "O" from the word "mother."

Currently, we find that having a print typography background prepares students well in that they have a basic formal vocabulary. Eventually, when New Media is spun off into a separate major, we'll have to deal with digital typography from the ground up. At first, I suspect that we'll use a model similar to the traditional typography sequence. However, the work of the students will cause everything to shift again, with unpredictable, but always interesting, results.

Learning the Languages of Babel: An Approach to New Media Pedagogy and the Relevance of Graphic Design

DIANE GROMALA

Introduction

The emergence of practices variously termed New Media Design, Interaction or Interactive Design, Interface Design, and Human-Computer Interaction Design, is territory contested by many disciplines and practices. Fields as diverse as Computer Science, Engineering, Cognitive Psychology, Library and Information Science, English, Film, Communications, and Graphic and Product Design, to name a few, each claim its tradition and area of expertise as essential to new design practices.

Unarguably, electronic technologies do affect, extend, and transform these traditional disciplines. In academia and in industry, each discipline struggles to define its design practice and value, as well as the notion of what the term "design" itself means. Increasingly, diverse practices borrow from one another's knowledge bases[1], as multidisciplinary approaches, teams, and academic programs emerge.

Most recently, we have witnessed an increase in the calls for developing a new and distinct discipline of interactive design, one that comprises knowledge bases from a variety of relevant fields. Janet Murray, among others, has offered persuasive arguments for the necessity to develop what she terms interactive design as "an independent discipline, with its own goals, methods, and competencies."[2] Yet, while many universities ostensibly embrace the idea of multidisciplinary programs, numerous impediments often quash any timely realization of such efforts. Universities stand in a seemingly inimical relation to the speed of technological and social change. Impeded by structures that inhibit the ability to quickly change, universities additionally struggle to cope with the expense of buying, maintaining, and updating equipment and software that continually changes. Attracting and retaining faculty who lack a wide-ranging education in programs that do not yet exist, but who have nonetheless developed expertise, is exceedingly difficult in the face of lucrative corporate alternatives and a strong economy. These faculty members themselves face the difficulties of building labs and sustaining new research that has yet to be systematically valued in the academic realm. Finally, the traditional disciplinary boundaries and the institutional structures that maintain them seem to render the problem intractable.

Yet, universities do change and adapt. Evidence of this is clear, from the ubiquity of e-mail as a primary mode of communication, to online library and World Wide Web access, to a preponderance of computer labs, distance-learning programs, and the primacy of technological development in university mission statements. Given time, multidisciplinary programs are sure to arise, just as traditional disciplines themselves have been reconfiguring curricula to adapt to the demands of interactive design, to the increasing centrality that technology assumes in the structure of academia, and to the intense demands of students who understand technology to be essential to their futures. What then will be, could be, the role of graphic design in such multidisciplinary programs?

Where are Graphic Designers?

Graphic designers often decry their absence in contributing to and defining the direction of emerging technologies.[3] They tend to operate on the assumption that the experts who currently have the greatest say in determining the direction of technological development and design—Computer Scientists, Engineers, and HCI (Human-Computer Interaction) experts—simply do not respect them, ignore them, or are ignorant of their practices and value. This belies a certain sense of entitlement, that the inclusion of graphic design should be self-evident, when in fact other disciplines must contend and compete for such status. Few graphic designers[4], however, make sustained contributions to the rough-and-tumble process of contributing to and defining technological innovation, where claims to expertise are rigorously tested and contested, adjudicated, and legitimized by professionals and academics.

Reasons for the relative absence of graphic designers in technological development and design are multiple. First, the few designers who learn the paradigms of other disciplines are often unrewarded within their own. With some exception[5], the graphic design profession does not value or recognize technological innovation that requires, but also extends beyond, mere aesthetic form, until more widespread adoption and understanding of technology occurs among them en masse—that is, when technological innovation is no longer new in other professions. These designers then must contend with the regular conflicts that arise in the way differing knowledge bases or epistemologies value and legitimize knowledge[6], often single-handedly. Second, although technological developments are crucial to the history of graphic design, educational programs often offer only limited interest in focusing on this historical aspect, which itself would go far in creating a bridge to other disciplines. In addition, graphic design education rarely offers examinations of emerging forms of technology and their implications, since few graphic designers are involved with it to begin with. Third, graphic designers seem relatively unable to articulate their knowledge base and methods of legitimizing this knowledge, which is perhaps the most crucial component for multidisciplinary inclusion. Finally, historical and institutionalized prejudices have resulted only very recently in Ph.D. programs in graphic design. This will finally allow designers to be on equal footing with other academics through the easily understandable mark a Ph.D. confers.

At the end of the day, however, such prejudices and conflicts need to be overcome if graphic designers are to assert their relevance. This relevance becomes more obvious with the fast-expanding availability to millions of users of, say, the World Wide Web, interactive media, and "smart" appliances, and with increased and widespread commercial use. As Meredith Davis suggests, however, respect is not given—it is earned.

The role of graphic design in interactive design, however, is not an either/or proposition. To maintain relevance to the growing realm of interactive design, graphic design needs to work in at least two realms: within the discipline of graphic design itself, *and*, perhaps more importantly, in its contribution as an essential component to emerging multidisciplinary practices in industry and in academia.

A Working Instance of How Graphic Design Can Be Incorporated in a Distinct Interactive Design Program

Long an advocate of a distinct, multidisciplinary program in interactive design, I have taught components of it and have developed new curricula in traditional programs of graphic design and communications. More recently, I joined a program that exists in a department already constructed to be multidisciplinary (the School of Literature, Communication, and Culture), with strong and shared links with computer science. Among the handful of new graduate programs in interactive design is the Information Design and Technology Program (IDT) at Georgia Tech. The faculty have expertise in art, graphic design, communications, film and film studies, literature, math, television, and theatre and performance studies. Nearly every faculty member has a background in cultural studies, and is thus concerned with theory and practice, and with understanding how the new practices of interactive design relate to their diverse historical antecedents[7], knowledge bases, cultural contexts, and critical discourses. In addition, the department within which IDT resides is one that comprises the GVU (Graphics Visualization and Usability Center), along with Computer Science, Architecture, Engineering, and Psychology. Thus, both within the program and within the university, the faculty practice multidisciplinary, collaborative inquiry on a daily basis.

This program, along with others like it, is fairly new and is far from providing a magic bullet or one, uniform exemplar. Such a program still struggles to define a distinct discipline. However, it offers a working instance of how a multidisciplinary program in interactive design can and does incorporate graphic design in ways that emphasize its relevance. It also positions its students to develop effective skills in working in collaborative teams within which they will be certain to find themselves in professional and research contexts. The effectiveness of the program depends on its ability to engage a variety of disciplinary and cultural perspectives.

Four Strategies of Incorporation

The cornerstone of the program at Georgia Tech rests on an equal emphasis on the conceptual and pragmatic production of digital artifacts with the study of the cultural, historical, and critical discourses relevant to that production. Perhaps more important than the class in Graphic Design, the history and principles of graphic design are essential components in the four approaches that constitute an integration of disciplinary practices across courses.

1 | AN EXAMINATION OF DISCIPLINARY PARADIGMS First, we examine the paradigms of disciplines that contribute to new media and interface design research, from Computer Science and Cognitive Psychology to Graphic Design and the Humanities. We identify and articulate the assumptions of differing knowledge bases: what constitutes knowledge and expertise, how it is understood and legitimized, how it is practiced, and its effect on making. Since these knowledge bases differ and often are in conflict with one another, it is essential to articulate these differences and examine how, why, and where they contribute to a distinct discipline in interactive design. This approach offers students an ability to share common perspectives and terminologies in collaborative groups in academia and in industry, to position and articulate their work in terms acceptable to diverse organizations and conferences, and to articulate the value these different disciplines bring to bear on interactive design. IDT students often take electives in, for example, Video Game Programming and Design or HCI in the Computer Science department, while students in Computer Science take IDT classes in our joint HCI program. Thus, the examinations of these paradigms are immediately useful for students in other classes. IDT faculty also collaborate on research projects with Computer Science faculty and with graduate students in both departments, which provides all concerned with an opportunity to develop productive methods in the ways that paradigms can and do overlap, and work in new configurations.

Graphic Design is valued in IDT, in its own right and as it intimately relates to other visual practices in interactive design, such as Video and Interactive Narrative. Graphic Design is also valued in the Computer Science department, where IDT faculty often present, for example, lectures on the Graphic Design component of HCI courses.

2 | THEORY VERSUS PRACTICE, THEORY INFORMING PRACTICE, THEORY AND PRACTICE INEXTRICABILITY Second, by examining existing media, their uses, and the cultural forms they have brought into being, faculty provide a context for exploring the new creative possibilities of interactive design. Students learn theoretical approaches to the critical assessment of new media both within IDT classes, and by taking seminars in cultural theory, cognitive science, and historical studies of technology. By engaging theoretical concerns, students gain intellectual frameworks for understanding the field, their processes of creating interactive media, and broad, conceptual concerns in their use, value and implications in varied cultural contexts.

An example that illustrates the interplay between theory and practice is the CD-ROM *Griffith in Context*, developed by IDT faculty Ellen Strain, Greg Van Hoosier-Carey, and graduate student Patrick Ledwell. As a tool for cultural analysis, *Griffith in Context* encourages multiple modes of inquiry pertaining to a single historical artifact, from theoretical to pragmatic, and in this case, the relation between the two. Thus, students who use the CD-ROM develop series of skills applicable to the study of cultural materials beyond those presented on the CD-ROM.

The Birth of a Nation (1915) is a historical drama by D. W. Griffith, crucial to the study of film history. Even though it is one of the most technically lauded films of all time, some educators won't include it in their curricula because of the film's racist propaganda. Nonetheless, it introduced a groundbreaking set of cinematic techniques to the production lexicon. But by situating *The Birth of a Nation* within contextualizing corollary materials that make the film's cultural and cinematic impact tangible, *Griffith in Context* enables critical and technological analyses. The CD-ROM contextualizes the film through its use of an interactive, annotated "filmstrip" interface. This interface enables frame-by-frame textual analysis, juxtaposing the filmic image with voice-overs from leading historians and film scholars, and with archival materials surrounding the production and reception of the film. What makes the interface innovative, however, is the combination of this aspect of the CD-ROM with a hands-on editing engine. On formal and technological levels that are inextricable from theoretical concerns, this editing engine allows students to analyze the meaning-producing mechanisms of film editing by dissecting and re-editing clips from the film.

The design of the interface itself emphasizes the ideological aspects of the film's racist propaganda and its historical contexts, allowing students to recognize how the meanings of cultural artifacts are dependent on socio-historical context, and how articulations of national, regional, racial, and sexual identity can become "wedded" and take on the appearance of inevitability.

Similarly, the editing engine of *Griffith in Context* enables students to conduct formal clip analyses and editing exercises, strengthening their skills in "reading" film as an artistic and narrative medium, and creating an awareness of the relation of production techniques to how these techniques influence how the visual language of film produces meaning. Thus, the theoretical aspects of Cultural Studies deeply and inextricably inform the approach to pedagogy, content matter, and interface design in *Griffith in Context*.

The graphic design of this CD-ROM is crucial to its innovative aspects, from the appearance and functional characteristics of the interface, to issues of visual language (among film, graphic, and multimedia or time-based design), and to the historical posters and printed artifacts that constitute the film's contextual milieux.

3 | EXAMINING EMERGING TECHNOLOGIES AS TECHNOLOGIES OF REPRESENTATION Third, students learn principles of interactive design, how to effectively use digital tools and applications that already exist to explore new forms of expression, how to think procedurally, and how technological aspects *work* in the production of meaning. The tools themselves are conceived of as technologies of representation, and as a nascent medium in its own right. An important emphasis is in going beyond existing software by examining and experimenting with emerging forms of technology, such as Augmented Reality (AR).

One example of how students examine, work in, and reconceive new technologies is demonstrated in a research project that grew out of a class in AR, cross-listed and taught by IDT faculty Jay Bolter and Computer Science faculty Blair MacIntyre. Building on the findings of this class, a research project titled "Ghosts of Sweet Auburn: Augmented Reality as a New Media Form" evolved, supported by a research grant from GVU, and the efforts of collaborators from both departments.[8]

In AR systems, users typically use a head-worn, see-through display to augment their experience of the physical world with an overlay of computer-controlled graphics and sound. The collaborative team is building such an AR system to create what they refer to as "ghost movies": recorded video experiences in which individual figures appear to float, ghost-like, in the physical world. The collaborators believe that these ghost movies may constitute a new narrative form, and are inventing appropriate conventions and uses for this form, just as early filmmakers invented conventions for their medium. Their first application is a series of virtual recreations of the Sweet Auburn area in downtown Atlanta. The history of this African-American cultural and economic center promises to provide a compelling test of the narrative power of the so-called ghost movies, providing users with multiple points of view and historical interpretations of the significance of Sweet Auburn.

As with the interface design of *Griffith in Context*, "Ghosts of Sweet Auburn" necessarily depends on principles and practices of graphic design in innovative technological contexts. The interface in this case requires not only knowledge of interactive, time-based graphic design, but also its updating, on a continual basis, with the physical environment.

4 | THE CHANGING ROLE OF GRAPHIC DESIGN Fourth, in IDT, a distinct program in interactive design, the role and the importance of the designer is altered in at least two ways. The designer is understood to be a generator of concept and content, singularly or in a team, rather than merely the visual stylist at the end of a production cycle. In addition, the importance of the interface in interactive design, including its visual appearance and visual language, and the importance of visual metaphors and their influence on how users navigate through content, emphasizes the importance and knowledge of graphic design.

These two factors, of content-produce in the strict sense, and as content-produce at the level of the interface, are foregrounded in IDT by historical recognitions of the role that graphic designers have traditionally played in making new technologies understandable and available on a mass scale.

Conclusion

While the IDT program, like others, is fairly new, it is only one example of how graphic design is an essential constituent of a distinct program in interactive design. In this case, graphic design is offered as a class, but more importantly perhaps, reverberates through each class and through research projects. Rather than losing its identity and relevance, graphic design becomes an integral component in interactive design, tightly imbricated with other issues of visual language, such as film, interactive narrative, and visual culture, as well as the interactive and multi-mediated characteristics of new media forms. Our approach, we believe, extends familiarity of the importance and value of graphic design across disciplines. In doing so, it brings designers closer to positions from which they can contribute to technological innovation nearer its inception, and allows designers to collaborate in new and meaningful ways with disparate disciplines.

N O T E S

1. To cite only one example in software design: Terry Winograd, John Bennett, Laura De Young, Peter S. Gordon, Brad Hartfield, eds. *Bringing Design to Software*. (Reading, MA: Addison-Wesley, 1996).

2. Janet Murray. "Interactive Design: A Profession in Search of Professional Education." *The Chronicle of Higher Education* (April 23, 1999): B4.

3. Although it is important to recognize the innovation that graphic designers offer during the early adoption stages of existing applications, as well as novel experiments using existing technology, I refer here to techno-logical innovation at its very inception—at the stage of research, before applications are realized, marketed, and used on a mass basis. One example would be the contributions of graphic designers in the inception of the graphic-user interface at Apple Computer, or Hugh Dubberly, Doris Mitch, and others to the interface design for one of the earliest instantiations of multimedia, HyperCard (Apple Computer, Inc.)

4. One sustained effort is the American Center for Design's annual Living Surfaces conference.

5. Notable exceptions are Aaron Marcus, who has sustained a strong presence in Computer Science and HCI for decades; the visual designers and typographers who contributed to the first graphical user interfaces and software at Apple Computer, Inc., and Adobe Systems, Inc.; and visually trained designers at research entities such as Xerox PARC, Interval Research Corporation, and Microsoft Research. In design education, Daniel Boyarski (Carnegie Mellon University), Lorraine Justice (Georgia Tech), and Linda Wyman (Art Center) are in the forefront of interface design education within the disciplines of graphic and product design.

    A more recent example of how visually trained designers contribute knowledge to the larger practice of interface design includes Kevin Mullet and Darrell Sano. Their work, or the sustained efforts of other graphic designers, seemed to have moved Jakob Neilsen, who wrote the forward to their book, from the seeming intransigence of his former position that graphic design inhibited usability. (Kevin Mullet and Darrell Sano, *Designing Visual Interfaces: Communication Oriented Techniques*. Upper Saddle River, NJ: Prentice Hall, 1995.)

6. These conflicts are not limited, of course, to mere discussion of the differences of knowledge bases, but extend to conflicts in practice and in more general cultural orientations. The largest rift seems to regularly occur between the sciences and the arts and humanities. Although C. P. Snow wrote *The Two Cultures* in the 1950s, the book still retains relevance about those conflicts today. (C. P. Snow, *The Two Cultures*. Cambridge: Cambridge University Press, Reissue edition, 1993.)

    In a less scholarly vein, Fred Moody documents this conflict as it played out in Microsoft. (Fred Moody, *I Sing the Body Electronic: A Year With Microsoft on the Multimedia Frontier*. Collingdale, PA: Diane Publishing, 1998.)

7. An example of this concern is a book by two faculty members: Richard Grusin, Jay David Bolter, *Remediation: Understanding New Media*. Cambridge: MIT Press, 1998.

8. From IDT: Professors Jay Bolter and Kavita Philip, along with graduate students Noel Moreno, Lauren Keating, Frances Hamilton, and Yu-Cheng Hsu. From Computer Science: Professor Blair MacIntyre and research scien-tist Wendy Newstetter.

It's Brain Surgery, After All

Education of a Digital Designer

LYNDA WEINMAN

I'M NOT A big advocate of rules—almost everyone I admire has broken rules in order to attain greatness. In thinking about this topic of becoming an e-designer however, I am searching for generalities that might be helpful. These are merely my insights and suggestions—be sure to question all rules and make sure they make sense to the situation at hand. Be sure to break some rules once you've learned them—those who play it safe all the time usually don't go very far.

Design versus Technology

Design existed long before the technologies we grapple with today. There are basic design skills that aren't gained by knowing a computer program, but are acquired through studying the principles of design. Issues such as color, composition, typography, communication, message, metaphor, interaction, experience, and theater all play a strong part in any successful designer's skill set. If you're entering the e-design market by understanding technology only, you're missing a major part of the equation.

Technology

It's really important to be comfortable and knowledgeable about technology. Good design skills alone don't make an e-designer. Getting the comfort and knowledge can be anxiety producing. It's really important to feel safe and confident in the process of "not knowing." Be sure to grow your skills before you market yourself as an e-designer. Do projects for free and for experimentation until you are comfortable with the tools and challenges of the medium.

Admit When You Don't Know

Don't fake knowing what you don't know to get a job. Be honest—the honesty will be more appreciated than the pretense of knowing something that you don't. This deception will result only in failure, and a loss of trust and faith on the part of your client. It's important to be confident in your not knowing. Insecurity is very disquieting to a client, but the act of questioning and gaining clarification is very comforting.

Everyone is Important

Just because you know more than the person who works below you, doesn't mean that person won't leapfrog into an important position someday. The longer you are in business, the more likely it is that people will recycle into your business life. The person you treated poorly might be in a position to hire you later. Good communication and respectful relationships are key, no matter what the hierarchy of knowledge or talent.

What is the Message?

It's not enough to want to add animation, hyperlinks, a guest book, or a streaming video. Those are just tools with which to communicate. Figure out what the message is and the goals of the project before you settle on a path to get there.

Think about Contrast

Contrast allows some ideas to be more dominant than others. Contrast can be achieved with color, with scale, with type, with movement, with an element of surprise. Think about design as an experience that you craft in order to communicate an idea or a goal.

Don't Stop Learning

Technology changes rapidly, and there are always new things to learn. If you don't embrace those changes and consider them part of your work life, then you are choosing the wrong business. This is not like other mediums because of the changing nature of delivery mediums and software.

Be Willing to Share Your Process

Digital design is a process. Don't make something too polished before you show it to your client. Expect lots of iterations and changes, and create a comfort level in which they know you're okay with that.

Share What You Know

E-Design is an evolving medium and has an ethics system built on generosity. Unlike ceramicists who covet secret glaze recipes, or photographers who use a custom printing scheme, e-designers must share in order to survive. It's a karmic cycle—the more generous you are the more you information you'll receive. Join user groups, message boards, and subscribe to magazines. The e-designer who stays on top of what is current will be the most successful.

Your Portfolio is Paramount

It doesn't matter where you've schooled or what kind of degree you have—clients are interested in whether you can do the work or can't. Your portfolio is your biggest asset. If you want to do online design, you must have your own online portfolio presence or only a fool will hire you.

Don't Work For Yourself Right Away

Being in business for yourself is a great goal, but one that should be earned. You can learn a lot on someone else's nickel about all kinds of things that can't be taught in art school or universities. Spend a few years in the job market before you start your own company.

Your First Job is Not Your Last

Many e-designers experience angst over where to take a first job. It almost doesn't matter, because it will only be your first job. The days of working for one company an entire lifetime are long gone. Each job will be a stepping-stone to the next.

Take a Job Beneath You

If there's a certain person or firm that you want to study with (i.e., work for), be willing to do anything to get your foot in the door. Very few people walk out of college and into a dream position. If you hold to your ideals too tightly, you will miss important opportunities.

Be Selective

Once you've got your land legs as a designer, the projects you choose have everything to do with knowing what you're good at, what you enjoy, and being aware of how you want to grow. You can direct the quality of your work, the direction of your career, and the types of clients you work with as long as you are discriminating. You might not have this luxury out the hatch, but experienced and successful e-designers are always very selective.

Why Designers Need to Learn Programming

DAVID YOUNG

WITH DYNAMIC INTERACTIVE media, the role of the graphic designer has changed. In these new media, the assignments designers face are increasingly complex. In order to succeed at these projects, additional conceptual skills and tools are required. Computer programming satisfies these needs, allowing designers to conceive new categories of solutions, and providing the technical ability to realize them.

A cross-disciplinary approach is widely acknowledged as necessary, yet is only beginning to be practiced. Schools (and industry) have tended to keep their existing structures and hierarchies. Few have provided means by which students can learn both skills. Programming is not something that should simply be *tacked on* to an existing education. It needs to be embraced by all aspects of the curriculum—to be tightly woven into all courses.

What follows is a list of reasons why it is important for graphic designers, both students and professionals, to learn programming. And why that education will enable the creation of truly unique designs—possible only with a dual education—that will help redefine what it means to be a designer.

It's Easy to Learn

Programming, like design, is based on a few basic principles and rules. It is through practice and working on projects that students apply those basics and use them as foundation for expanding their skills and knowledge. To a student who has never been exposed to programming, it can at first seem like a lot to learn; but it is no different for a new student of graphic design, where the basics can also seem overwhelming. The first step is to approach it with an open mind and curiosity.

As with design, one learns programming best by doing it. Through practice, students better understand the basic aesthetics and principles of the activity. Over time, students gain improved skills, and are able to use those skills as a base from which to expand their understanding and knowledge. Gradually, a student develops an intuitive understanding of what makes a program aesthetically successful, and then begins to develop a personal style and approach to projects.

Programming and Design Are Identical

Programming and design are remarkably similar activities. This may sound strange; the common perception is that graphic design is a visual and creative activity, while programming is a technical and mechanical exercise in simply getting the computer to do something (and with some archaic tech-language).

What's forgotten is that both graphic designers and computer programmers are creative problem solvers. For either group, an assignment begins with the need for some information to be communicated, a problem to be solved, or a tool to be created. To arrive at a solution, each group uses their education, their experience, and various tools. Successful solutions are those that not only satisfy the original assignment, but do so with creativity, intelligence, and personality. In both fields, there is never a single "correct" solution; instead, successful solutions are those that express the creativity and style of the designer.

It might be argued that programming involves more strict rules, that if a program is not written correctly, it will generate errors or crash. But the same thing might be said of visual design. If a design does not effectively communicate its information, then it, too, is "buggy." Both design and programming require a certain technical competence, but it is the creativity of the solution that can elevate it to the level of "art."

Change How You Think about "Content"

Content is not arbitrary material that gets poured into a design. When content is created, it needs to be authored specifically for an intended medium. This affects the manner, format, and structure of the information—whether it's intended for a book or magazine, or for television or film. Unfortunately, it is rare for content to be authored specifically for a richly interactive project. Too often, video footage or long paragraphs of text appear on Web pages and CD-ROM screens though they were not authored specifically for interactivity. Nobody would think of scanning a poster, putting it online, and calling it interactive. So why would anyone do the equivalent with video?

For true interactivity, we must redevelop our content. When you begin a project by first considering programming, you often start by designing data structures to organize the content and by observing interconnections within the data. The results of this process can be eye-opening: Not only is content now the base upon which the entire design rests, but its structure and connectivity can be more transparently displayed, accessed, and navigated. In addition, by more loosely structuring content (i.e., by breaking the linearity inherent in other mediums) users are able to create their own narrative paths through it, in ways often unimagined by the original author.

Make Big Changes Fast

One of the problems with current design tools (such as Adobe Illustrator or After Effects) is that they are production oriented. They assist in a relatively narrow range of design activities—primarily where the designer takes a concept and finishes it. But sketching, and making big changes to an existing design, is often impractical with these tools.

Working on a design through programming allows you to work at a more conceptual level. It allows you to quickly sketch and to more easily make global changes. For example, when designing using a traditional tool, editing transitions, movements, or rollovers may require a manual change for each. A program makes it possible to make global changes through the modification of a few lines of code. This ability to easily make changes allows the designer to more freely experiment and, thus, to focus on sketching, exploration, and designing, instead of on the production details that can kill the creative process.

Think Abstractly

Less and less, designers create pieces that are fixed—frozen and unchanging on paper or video. Instead, designs evolve and grow, expanding beyond their initial scope. They change as new content is added, and as users interact with them on different platforms and devices. New technologies will continue this abstraction, with designers working at increasingly conceptual levels.

Understanding programming encourages designers to think more abstractly. By thinking of the visual representation of a design as fluid, and more easily adaptable to changes, designers will be more comfortable with the changes their designs undergo. It is the original conceptual structure and style that is most important.

Work Better with Others

Not all design students graduate into the world and begin programming their own designs. Many work as team members on projects whose scope may be beyond that of the individual designer. In these situations, it is important for the designer to be involved with all aspects of the project. The visual design must be integral to the overall structure and organization of the project. The design should not be a "look" or "style" applied to a disconnected structure.

When the designers understand programming, they are able to work much more closely with the programming team members. Knowledge of programming will allow designers to communicate more intelligently and to have much closer collaborations, resulting in projects where the design and underlying structure are tightly interconnected.

It's Fun!

Programming, like design, can be a very enjoyable and satisfying activity. You see your work come together as you code. It is highly interactive because, as you shape the code, you see the design change in all sorts of, often unexpected, visual and dynamic ways.

As the designer's programming skills develop, the programs become more advanced, achieving designs that might not have been possible to conceive of prior to starting a project. The designs begin to take on a life of their own. When integrated with programming, the design process becomes more like giving birth to something that will continue and evolve long after the designer/programmer has moved on to other projects.

Things Will Change

Students often worry about what skills they need and what tools they should learn. Yet, the field, and the world, is changing so quickly that by graduation, new tools will have been developed and old tools will have changed. And with these changes, designers will often need to rethink the design process. Likewise, the choice of a programming language can influence a design. Clearly, a specific tool-based, skill-based, and medium-specific education will not have a long lifespan. The challenge is to determine what core curriculum will be the best foundation for a successful career.

Just as there are fundamentals to design, there are fundamentals to programming. With a solid understanding of these basics, the choice of design tool, or programming language, is secondary. New tools and languages can be learned, since they exist only to serve the designer's intent. But it is these fundamentals, including programming, that allow the designer to keep up with a changing profession.

The Need for Programming Will Not Go Away

Too often, designers are at the mercy of the tools they use. The work produced is a clear product of the features and limitations of those tools. Certainly, the tools will improve over time, providing richer libraries of built-in behaviors and dynamics. Still, designs resulting from their application will have the feel of their ready-made effects. Furthermore, software application tools are not made with your content's or your design's specific requirements in mind. Programming will always allow the designers to transcend their tools, and create designs which are uniquely their own.

Introducing the Macintosh: Teaching Basic Computer

RACHEL SCHREIBER

I BEGAN TEACHING Introduction to the Macintosh in 1989, at a time when the Macintosh Operating System did not allow multiple open applications, grayscale monitors had just been introduced, and only a handful of software programs were available. The most difficult concept to teach was, as Suzanne Bloom and Ed Hill noted, "to Save or to Save As." While this concept may still be difficult for some beginners to grasp, it has been replaced by comparable issues. Many of my students need much review before they understand the difference between quitting an application versus switching to the Finder, or understanding why enlarging a 72-dpi image will result in a bad print.

Introduction to the Macintosh was easier to teach in 1989 than it is in 2000. We started by learning how to use a mouse, and we completed the course with a layout for a newsletter in Adobe PageMaker, incorporating photographs scanned into Adobe Photoshop and a logo made in FreeHand. At that time, I still believed the computer to be a tool, not a medium; and the technical issues to be covered were minimal. Electronic art has certainly since become a medium—I define a medium as a means of making work that has its own discourse. Introducing students to this medium therefore necessitates an introduction to its theory as well as its practice. Additionally, the complexity of the medium requires an entirely different pedagogical approach. It is no longer adequate to teach students an array of software programs; rather, it is necessary to teach students self-reliance in relation to the computer environment.

In the fall of 1999, I was hired by the Maryland Institute, College of Art (MICA) in Baltimore, Maryland, to teach a variety of digital courses. Chief among my responsibilities was a course then titled Basic Computer. During my first year at MICA, I contributed to the definition of a framework for the curriculum of that course, which is now titled Introduction to Electronic Media and Culture, in order to achieve some consistency across the twelve or more sections we offer each academic year. Although most of the students in the course are freshmen (the course is offered through the Foundation Department), there may be a range of students from every year and major. The course is required for students majoring in Graphic Design, Illustration, and Photography, as well as for students pursuing a concentration in Digital Media Arts or Animation. All other students may take it as a studio elective. The course is also a prerequisite for many advanced digital courses, such as Web Design, Interactive Design, and Digital Image I and II. Therefore, the various sections need to be, on the one hand, similar enough to qualify as a prerequisite for the advanced courses (so that advanced instructors will be able to count on their students having a certain skill set), while, on the other hand, allowing each instructor the freedom to design his or her own syllabus.

The faculty who teach the course come from diverse backgrounds, including graphic design, illustration, photography, video, media studies, programming, and sound. When we came together, we found that all of our syllabi overlapped a good bit. Yet, it also became clear that to try and define the common parameters of the course would be a great challenge. Since the applications of this medium are diverse, ranging from print and Web design to installation, video, sound, and more (and all combinations thereof), it is difficult to decide what counts as fundamental. The question of what belongs in an introductory-level course has become quite complex, on two levels. First, on the level of course content: what exactly constitutes the discourse and emerging canon of electronic art theory? Which applications are appropriate for this level? Second, as the students entering the course have a diverse range of computer experience, questions arise about the skill level to be addressed. Since many students have been using e-mail, surfing the Web, and working on computers at home and in school for years, it can be difficult, in one classroom, to challenge the advanced students without leaving the beginners behind.

We all agreed readily on the importance of the theoretical, critical aspect of the course—the "electronic culture" component. It is crucial that students understand the relationship of their practice to the ways in which technology is becoming central to all aspects of our lives. An interesting paradox has also emerged—while many students are very computer savvy, many of them still have prejudices about the role of the computer in artistic practice, believing work produced digitally to be not as "high" as painting or sculpture. The theoretical aspect of the course, therefore, needs to address technology's relationship to art, art history, and society. Yet, even given this seemingly simple goal, there is a range of approaches in determining what constitutes the discourse best suited to address these issues. Those of us teaching the course found that the readings we chose to use to address these issues ranged from post-structuralist theory to the *New York Times* "Circuits" page to discussions of Napster in the technology section of Salon.com. In my section, I begin with Allucquère Rosanne (Sandy) Stone's essay "Split Subjects, Not Atoms; or How I Fell in Love with My Prosthesis" in order to engage the students in an examination of their attitudes toward technology. I then screen the Stanley Kubrick film *2001: A Space Odyssey* (1968) as the centerpiece for a discussion of the cultural fear of the computer developing its own consciousness and "taking over." Walter Benjamin's "The Work of Art in the Age of Mechanical Reproduction" follows, and we discuss it in relation to the Charlie Chaplin film *Modern Times* (1936). This enables us to further our discussion of fears of the machine/computer run amok, while also giving us a starting point from which to examine the history of the reception of "machine"-based media in visual practice, as well as Benjamin's and Chaplin's attitudes toward the political ramifications of a technologically driven society. Toward the end of the semester, we read William Gibson's short story "Johnny Mnemonic" in order to get a glimpse into the imaginings of a futuristic society. In my readings, I address popular culture in a serious manner in order to engage the students in issues that surround them in their lives, and to show them that the computer can be useful in integrating their lives with their art-work. I choose readings that will be accessible and will facilitate productive discussions.

In order to judge which applications are appropriate to the course, it became important to determine if we really should be offering the same course for all students. In other words, would graphic design students need the same basic computer skills as would photography majors, or sculpture majors? If the course were divided this way, we could teach 3D-modeling programs to sculpture majors and page-layout programs to graphic design majors. This approach could also address the diversity of the faculty, creating sections around an individual faculty mem-ber's experience and interest. What readily became apparent was that to teach the course in this way would be incredibly limiting; to imply that a graphic designer would not need 3D mod-eling, or that a sculptor wouldn't need Photoshop, would be a parochial approach to a medium that has, by its nature, integrated disciplines in unprecedented ways. Additionally, the beginning computer class might provide for a productive mix of students, which would further encourage interdisciplinary learning. Therefore, we agreed early on that we wanted one course for all of our students.

As a result of considering the needs of the upper-level courses and balancing them with an open framework, we decided that every section would start with Photoshop, have some instruction in page layout (QuarkXPress), and have a multimedia component (i.e., animation, video, or HTML). In my course, I organized the semester around one continuous assignment. On the first day of class, students pick a piece of paper out of a bag with a word on it. Each piece of paper has a different word; all words are broad concepts that relate to technology: digit, control, emerge, use, etc. For the first assignment, the students are asked to produce a series of images in Photoshop that address their concept. Next, I teach basic Quark and an introduction to typography, and the students create a poster using the images from their first series, their word, the dictionary definition of their word, and some other piece of text (such as a quote) about their word. For the final part of the term, students are asked to create a Web-based text/image piece that deals with their concept. For this last HTML-based portion, they may either incorporate their previous work, or move on to a totally different approach to their word. This approach to the semester allows me to show students how a concept can move from single images to complex, sequential projects, and it allows students to become deeply involved in the conceptual development of a project, while learning many new technical skills. This assignment is challenging to students with a range of skill levels, and I address these indi-vidually. For example, some of the students never go beyond making simple Web sites consist-ing of linked pages written in SimpleText, while others may get into rollovers and image maps in Dreamweaver. Regardless, it is by no means the most technically advanced projects that are the most successful.

Dealing with this range of skill levels is increasingly challenging, as the overall computer competence of our students increases. This past semester, I had two students in the course who had worked as Web designers, several video game aficionados, three or four students who were not adept at saving files, and everything in between. In some ways, this has always been an issue (I recall an older man in my first computer class who didn't know that if you continued typing at the end of the line, the cursor would automatically go to the next line, and therefore had created a new text box for each line of type in a Quark file). I had long anticipated a moment that came this past semester, when most of my students had a good bit of computer experience behind them. Of course, the arrival of this moment will vary greatly with different demographics. At MICA, the Spring 2000 semester was the first one where every student in my class had had an e-mail account for some time, and all had used computers in high school to write papers and conduct research on the Web. As time goes on, we will have less and less need to teach the most basic skills, as these will be covered at the high school level and even in the home.

Nevertheless, even given the increasing level of computer experience, there still is, and will likely always be, a range to the students' abilities when it comes to learning new software. For some, an instructor need only open the program and show them where to find the various functions; others require extensive instructions and repeated exercises to remember the steps involved in a given process. Additionally, certain programs have a much steeper learning curve than others (such as Macromedia Director versus Adobe Photoshop). On the other hand, any classroom in any subject will have a range of students, and the more advanced students help raise the bar for the rest of the group. Occasionally, I give the advanced students independent projects to keep them challenged. In other cases, I have an advanced student sit next to a beginner in a technical demonstration, in order to answer that student's questions.

The variety of skill levels, as well as the questions of which software and which theoretical concepts to cover, will always exist. Clearly, the curriculum of the introductory-level computer course will change every year. More importantly, what will remain constant is the idea of teaching students self-reliance. My main goal in this course is to teach students to be self-sufficient within the computer environment. Of course, teaching students how to learn, rather than teaching them rote memorization or mindless repetition of knowledge, is the hallmark of all quality education. These issues come to the fore in electronic-arts education in very interesting ways, where the professor is truly no longer a master of knowledge, but a facilitator of learning, and where the field and its discourse change so rapidly. Most of us currently teaching electronic media did not learn to use computers in school, but found ways to educate ourselves. I make my students aware of the fact that I am usually learning some new software on my own even as I am teaching them some other software, and often when they ask a question I cannot answer, I respond by saying, "let's get the book and figure that out together." Or, increasingly, there will be another student in the room who already knows the answer.

Celia Pearce calls this pedagogical approach "autodidactic communalism," by which she means the practice of people teaching themselves and each other. She writes that "the World Wide Web is the ultimate undoing of traditional education and the impetus for the autodidactic communalism revolution" because it makes information widely accessible, so that it has become easier than ever to teach oneself. If the student sees the teacher as a role model, and sees that the teacher is always learning, then the student will learn the confidence and self-reliance needed to move forward in the digital world. As in any course, my best students are the ones who figure out what they need to know on their own and then actively pursue that knowledge. In the basic computer course, these goals become even more important, and will continue to be so through any other changes in the curriculum.

The Design Technologist: Creating Interactive Experiences

NATALIE ZEE

Y2K BROUGHT ITS share of hopes and fears on the impending dominance technology will have on the human-computer experience. Movies such as *2001* and *The Matrix* paint a dark picture where computers control our world, our environment, even our thoughts. The dawn of the millennium has bombarded us with not just computers, but the promise of broadband high-speed networks, wireless access, enhanced TV, WebTV, cellphones, handheld and smart devices. What was once deemed "new media," is now evolving into media "convergence." The evolution of media and technology into our everyday lives is this defining transition period we are going through now. Designers are now faced with a whole new set of problems to solve. How should information be viewed and organized on a tiny cellphone screen? What kind of ideal shopping experience should a user have on a broadband connection? Digital designers, those that are designing the screen-based interfaces and interactive experiences, will be facing these and a myriad of newfound challenges. How can a digital designer balance the creation of innovative, interactive experiences without compromising the fundamental principles of design?

In essence, a digital designer is the sum of these parts: artist, technologist, innovator, architect, and student. To be a digital designer is to understand technology, the digital medium, and to forecast its progression into the future. True interactivity is going beyond the computer, the screen, or the handheld device, to find the human at the other side.

The core of this concept revolves around an overarching theme of designing an "interactive experience." As we are moving past the infant phase of Web design, we are expanding our design palette of tools to include more rich media content—animation, sound, text, graphics, 3D, and video. And, at the same time, we find ourselves being introduced to a bevy of new design canvases—handheld devices, cellphones, and set-top boxes, in addition to computer screens. No longer are we simply designing "pages" of content, we are designing interactive environments. By following this key concept, digital designers will be better prepared for designing and defining the heart of this evolving design discipline.

Understanding Technology

I'm not saying that digital designers need to go out and get a degree in computer science in order to design for the Internet or devices, but there is a general level of technical understanding a designer must have in order to be a true digital designer. The reality of it is, those that fail to grasp technology, will get lost as we move forward. Digital designers need to be known also as design technologists.

All too often, creative and technology teams aren't communicating, and each team is working in its own insular environment. Interactive experiences can involve anything from simple code to complex databases to back-end infrastructures. New issues in user interface and human-computer interaction are just part of this new interactive design process. In order to move the discipline as well as the industry forward, creative and technology teams must be in harmony with each other. One design concept can be executed in a number of different ways depending on platform, browser, application, hardware, and connection speeds. HTML or WAP? GIF or JPEG? Flash or Shockwave? Mac or PC? 56K or T1? As we develop and grow this digital design discipline, it is imperative that technology be given its necessary room to be not only understood, but also explored.

Start Simple

It's easy though to get overwhelmed and bombarded with all this new information. When I teach designers who are new to digital design, the first thing I tell them is that they need to learn the basics of technology. Start with HTML. Don't be intimidated by the technology. Embrace it. Learn it. Understand it. Read more about it. Be empowered.

Any sort of general understanding of technology will help to make sure that a designer's concept stays true through execution. The reality is that the digital design profession is dependant on the development and growth of the technology. And this technology is developing at a rapid pace. As designers, we need to be flexible in our ways of thinking, so that we may figure out innovative ways to work around some of technology's shortcomings to bring our ideas to fruition. Digital designers are thus also constant students, learning new things as they redefine their profession.

I hear the argument all the time: Designers design. They should be free to go crazy with ideas and not be constrained by technology. True. Innovation and inspiration come from places that may not necessarily relate to a computer. Yet, how do you explain the fact that the digital designers who are at the forefront of the industry, those that are helping to define the discipline, and those that are creating all the innovative interactive experiences, are the ones who have the ability to do both? They are Design Technologists.

Rich interactive experiences need to be researched and explored to find the right balance and combination of design and technology. As design technologists, we will be better equipped to handle the challenges and new design problems that the future will most certainly present us.

Voice Lessons: Design, Technology, and the Myth of Intention

ANNE BUSH

WHEN I ANNOUNCED to my colleagues on the East Coast that I had accepted a teaching position at the University of Hawaii, they had two standard responses. The first, usually accompanied by a knowing wink, was, "good luck getting any work done." The second, similarly influenced by visions of small umbrellas in Gauguin-colored cocktails, warned me of professional exile and was usually accompanied by "when are you coming back to the states?" (a choice of words whose irony would not be lost on the native Hawaiian community, a part of which actively resists its assimilation into the United States). In all fairness, I had my own concerns beyond distance from my family, two-day overnight mail, and $7 boxes of Special K; namely, how would what I knew about design translate in a totally unfamiliar context, one so distinct from my own.

Not long after my arrival in Hawaii, I assigned a class project that examined public and private space. Each student was to choose from five assigned streets in Honolulu, walk down one for an hour, and photograph anything that they would classify as public and anything that they would classify as private. My original motivation for assigning the project was that it would reveal to students some of their own ideological biases, made evident by the way in which they determined the boundary between public and private space. When the students brought their film to class the next day, I noticed that one student had taken all his photographs inside the local Salvation Army store. I questioned him about this and he asked for my indulgence. He explained how the Salvation Army was, for him, the perfect model for the assignment because second-hand stores take intimate artifacts from our lives and return them to the anonymity of the public realm. He went on to argue that public and private spaces were not clearly distinguishable, that people were always negotiating boundaries, moving in and out of environments that we consider neat and circumscribed. The lesson was a poignant one. It not only demonstrated the student's ability to consider distinctions, but also an ability to turn on and question such definitions. It revealed an understanding of the world that was located at the intersection of description and inquiry, convention and invention.

Probably few would argue that the academy is the ideal location for such pondering. In school we are free to experiment, to question. In fact, many designers argue that school is the only place for such inquiry, as the real world demands more attention to pragmatic concerns such as clients, budgets, and deadlines. Yet, the proliferation of this distinction sends the wrong message to students, as it reinforces the notion that in school one thinks and at work one makes. More importantly, it promotes that idea that thinking and making are separate activities. As a result students are particularly anxious about learning the skills for professional practice, and place their priorities on acquiring technical aptitude rather than obtaining a larger understanding of the contexts in which such skills will be employed. What is interesting in this position today is that it is technology itself that is casting doubt on such professional circumscription. Technology is calling the question. Exactly what is it that graphic designers do? What do they offer when modes of production are increasingly automated and democratized? Are we aestheticians? Are we technicians? If the mechanics of technology and the formal nuance of its products continue to be programmed and made easily accessible to the general public, what is graphic design's contribution? Ironically, that contribution is fundamentally the same as it has always been. It is a negotiation between raw data and the communicative situation in which the data needs to operate. As the example of my student's insight shows, what defines design-thinking is the way in which it negotiates between prescribed needs and the provisions that we imagine to attend to such needs (including ones that may redefine the original parameters of a problem). This is a conceptual act, the human contribution. It is the ability to synthesize, to analyze, to question, and to suggest. Technology can manipulate the materials, but it cannot address the contingencies of each design situation as it arises in social/historical space and time. This is not to say that technology will not reach the point where it actually embraces a kind of consciousness. One look at current research in this area tells us that it is only a matter of time. Yet, in the wake of such changes, our ability to analyze the path that such developments take, to weigh alternatives, to evaluate such changes critically, will only become more important, not less. Ironically, just as it is technology that demands this understanding of the human contribution, it is also technology that frequently masks its necessity.

In as much as new technology has caused anxiety in design educators by undercutting their assumed knowledge base (will new technology change what we teach? will it change the way we teach? will it determine if we teach, at least in terms of our current notions of that activity?), it has also eased anxiety in many. It has substituted for subject matter. Certainly it is easier to teach technique than it is to teach the ability to question. Yet, the more urgent issue is how we structure an educational experience that teaches the fundamentals of visual processes, technological aptitude, and information structures, as well as the ability to doubt. To hone this ability, designers need more than technological skill. They need to be able to think analytically about current conditions as well as future changes in technology and communication. They need to understand that it is partly their thinking that will ". . . mark out what appears to be a new area of human experience . . . define its contours, identify the elements in the field, and discern the kinds of relationships that exist among them."[1] Students need to learn to ask provocative questions about what is and what could be, to consider the space between the familiar and the unfamiliar, not with some Cartesian goal of reaching a balanced synthesis, but rather, with the ability to invent outcomes for communication that aren't necessarily evident in the immediate parameters of a given situation. Such invention relies on a deeper understanding of communication as discourse, or the interplay between fact and question.

The fact that many design students misunderstand the role of discourse in visual communication is partially a factor of the history of design education, which has, for the most part, traditionally clung to two seemingly opposite definitions of its activity: one grounded in vague notions of creativity and self-expression, the other in scientific method. In the first, the designer is the source of meaning, artistically molding a message into a visual form. In the second, nature is the source of meaning, with factual data confirming the correct communicative strategy by logically linking it to some previous empirical reality. In both cases discourse facilitates meaning but does not generate it, as each of the above perspectives locates the meaning of the visual message in something other than discourse itself[2]. The French theorist Michel Foucault has called such notions about the location of meaning the "will to truth" or the desire to deny discourse its own constructive reality. Yet, it is exactly this denial that has plagued design education and much subsequent disciplinary growth. The reality is that designers work in concert with many other factors ("relations between institutions, economic, cultural, and social processes, behavioral patterns, systems of norms, techniques, types of classifications . . ."[3]). This dialogue alters and adjusts messages and, in so doing, creates communication not as some true expression that emanates from some personal or empirical source, but as an interaction between data and its context. When considered in this way, the real threat to the design discipline comes not from technological advances undercutting a designer's skill set, but rather from failing to recognize that the designer is not, and never has been, the single source where meaning is located or the expert that can justify accuracy in a communication strategy with some existing disciplinary truth. If designers are anxious about the ways in which new technology will alter the discipline, it has less to do with the technological, and more to do with our inability to understand where authority is located.

In his essay "What is an Author?" Michel Foucault examines the privileged place of the single author in society. His thesis (which aligns with others of his generation, like Barthes who proclaimed the "death of the author") is that interpretation is never about a direct correlation between an intention and a meaning in a written message. A multitude of additional factors are always at work when considering how meaning is discerned (including the environment in which it was written, the method of dissemination, the context of reception, etc.). Foucault explains that to be an author implies the holding of a certain kind of status within society. Authorship is "a projection . . . of the operations that we force texts to undergo, the connections that we make, the traits that we establish as pertinent, the continuities that we recognize, or the exclusions that we practice."[4] For designers to recognize this fact is to admit that designer-centered communication is a disciplinary projection, one that ultimately begs the question of the graphic designer's actual contribution. Rather than searching for new ways to reinstate such authority, however, designers should rethink their role in regard to this shift, to try and understand, more profoundly, how they contribute to communication and how such contributions are altered by the changing technological environment. One way design education can foster such critical reflection, is to encourage students to ". . . locate the space left empty by the author's disappearance, follow the distribution of gaps and breaches, and watch for openings that this disappearance uncovers."[5] If neither the designer nor historical precedent can be considered the major source of meaning, has that source been replaced, and if so, in what way?

In the advanced design seminar in the Graphic Design Program at the University of Hawaii, I have explored this question in the classroom by asking students to question the very notion of authority and expertise. The project has two distinct and yet mutually informed parts. In the first part, students begin by reading Foucault's essay on authorship. Following several sessions where the students discuss the essay as a group, they are then required to write their own essay that examines a piece of graphic design and two author functions, or contributing factors (social, cultural, economic, historical, professional, technological) that circumscribe the meaning in the designed message that they selected. To complete the first part of the project visually, they are asked to create a book, using the text that they wrote, and images to present their argument. It is important that the form of the book extends the ideas in the essay and does not become just a neutral container for text and image. In the second half of the project, the students work in teams of three. Having all completed the first half of the project, they are now asked to choose two of the three designs that they examined and compare the author functions. Because this stage of the project focuses on the comparison of two designs rather than the analysis of one, students are asked to consider whether the original author functions that were cited are still the most critical, or whether the comparison alters which ones should be discussed. Because students have already had the experience of completing an analysis of their own, they can bring more to the group. Unlike the first part of the project however, the final visual form for part two will be done entirely on screen in Director. The students are now asked to write an essay as a group, one that will discuss not only the author functions in the designed messages, but will also attend to the different productive and consumptive practices encouraged by multimedia. For example, what role does movement, sound, simultaneity, and indeterminacy play in the reading of the Director piece? How do such devices create a fundamentally different reading than the one possible with print? Are there aspects of print and multimedia that parallel, inform, extend, or transform the other? As in part one, it is required that students consider such questions formally as well as intellectually. Thus, the Director piece should use the possibilities of multimedia to extend the understanding of the written argument and to demonstrate its convergences and divergences with print.

The results of this project have been provocative and have served to give the students an understanding of messages as a dynamic construction, and a better insight into how such constructions are extended and altered in both print and electronic media. In one case, a student decided to analyze the design that he selected by dividing the author functions into attributed authorship and procedural authorship, or a study of the way in which meaning was interpreted in the design versus how it was constructed. In another case, a group of three students decided to consider in their Director piece how the creation of a written message is always additive and subtractive. In their solution they compared two designs where they could isolate a generative approach in one and a more editorial approach in the other. In both examples, however, the students also came to realize that the distinctions that they articulated were never neat and absolute. The final works that were presented to the class reflected this as they demonstrated points of intersection as well as distinction.

In its most basic form, this project is a debunking of the myth of "designer-centered message construction,"[6] as it asks students (both individually and in concert with one another) to examine the multitude of factors, voices, forms, and interpretations that visual messages embody. It is important for students to understand this multidimensionality. Like the author, the designer-as-author ". . . does not precede the [design] he is a certain functional principle by which, in our culture, one limits, excludes, and chooses; in short, by which one impedes the free circulation, the free manipulation, and the free composition, decomposition, and recomposition [of messages]."[7] As designers debate the implications of consumers-as-producers, a condition supposedly brought on by new media, they are ignoring the fact that this has always been the case. Certainly electronic media has changed the way we communicate. It is more economical, more efficient, more integrated (allowing the combination of sound, visuals, text, motion), more connected (to users, to information). But print should not be looked upon as a neutral medium. Do we not scan a newspaper, sampling our way through sections, forging our own paths? If we read a book, do we not move in multiple directions, from tables of contents to chapters, from sentences to footnotes, from indexes to pages, from pictures to captions to text? Such actions are hardly linear and fixed. Such activity is only further emphasized when one considers issues of interpretation, what we as readers retain from the content of messages and what we discard. As designers and readers we are always navigating, always interacting with communication. Thus, there is always a certain amount of uncertainty, of unpredictability, of interplay, and slippage in interpretation. This is not new news, but we would be better off to remember it when we consider the act of designing. The more pertinent question becomes how to make the multi-vocality intrinsic to communication relevant, compelling, and usable. Instead of being concerned about some lost notion of expertise/authority, designers should be asking more specific questions, like who is involved in the production and consumption of the message, in what way, to what end, what are the variables, and what is the designer's role in this construction? Such introspection helps students to better understand design's "points of insertion, modes of functioning, and [its] system of dependencies."[8]

This kind of introspection is not separate from new technology, but inextricable from it since the important aspects of new technology are only partly technical. The word technology stems from the Greek word *technikon,* which belongs to *techne.* The important issue in respect to the meaning of *techne* is that "it is the name not only for the activities and skills of the craftsman, but also for the arts of the mind."[9] As such it was linked until the time of Plato with the word *episteme,* which underlines the fact that both words are "names for knowing in the widest sense."[10] In the wake of changing technology, designers have a lot to gain from such an understanding, as they can begin to see their contribution as a collaboration between their own perception of the facts and a critical analysis of such views; between this reflection and the cultural, social, economic, political, professional, and technological factors that alter such thinking; and between the designer's initial perspectives and those of the client and audience. Although we can now admit that such a dialogic approach to design has always been the case, our notion of this interaction is being expanded today as new technologies challenge our notions of "where intelligence lives."[11] More and more our interaction with electronic media will approach real dialogue, rather than the mere navigation of existing dialogue. It will become more than variances in interpretation as digitalization provides for the development of machines that will be personalized to our most intimate needs and wants. Such smart machines will be able to suggest as well as respond and, in so doing, create real interactivity. Under these conditions, designers will need to move away from an understanding of invention as innovative style, or as the development of designs that work through a series of prescribed actions. In looking toward the future, it would be useful for designers to think about innovation as "a change in the distribution of intelligence or, more precisely, the movement of some intelligence, from the transmitter to the receiver."[12] Electronic communication is moving in this direction, and designers need to be prepared to be participants in such an environment, a place where designing is a dialogue rather than some creative accident or vocational skill.

Perceiving design as a dialogue has been a useful lesson in my own work as both a teacher and a designer. If I revisit my initial apprehensions about moving to Hawaii, I understand how my thoughts about designing had not yet translated fully into how I viewed my role as a teacher. Living in a place as diverse as Hawaii has helped to clarify this discrepancy and, in so doing, helped me to grow as a teacher and a designer. Hawaii is not about polarities, but rather about the intersection between many voices. These voices do have their own identity but are always dynamic in that definition. In almost every case, perspectives in Hawaii are predicated on intersection rather than static distinction. As the writer Epeli Hauofa points out in his essay "Our Sea of Islands," this difference is exemplified in the distinction between Pacific Islands and Oceania (Pacific islands being finite and contained, Oceania being more inclusive). "People of the Pacific are at home with the sea. They played in it as soon as they could walk steadily, they worked in it, they fought on it . . . theirs was a large world in which peoples and cultures moved and mingled unhindered by boundaries of the kind erected much later by imperial powers."[13] In Oceania, "boundaries were not finite, but rather points of entry that were constantly negotiated and even contested. The sea was open to anyone who could navigate his way through."[14] The issue of navigation here is a key one, both metaphorically and literally. One could argue that the ability to navigate perceived boundaries (between perception and question, between perception and outside factors) is the defining issue in graphic design as it is in communication itself. Advances in new technology will only make such realizations more urgent, as it continues to automate and replace the tasks that designers have traditionally seen as their singular expertise.

Ironically, given these conditions, I believe that these are exciting times for design. Finally, design as a profession (and more generally education) is forced to define its contribution, a contribution that has not changed, but has frequently been misinterpreted or masked by vague notions of professional/vocational expertise. The challenge for design education is how to structure an educational experience that, simultaneously addresses the immediate concerns of the profession and attends to potential shifts in those concerns, an experience that helps students navigate between fact and question. Such an education, in my opinion, is not solely about technical expertise or about the varied contexts in which such expertise is defined and demonstrated, but rather about the capacity to balance convention and invention, to understand that communication is interactive and requires our best critical analyses as well as our skills. In an environment where technology is changing exponentially, the ability to see design as a discursive construction will allow students to understand both what is possible now and what is potentially possible in the future.

N O T E S

1. Hayden White, *Tropics of Discourse: Essays in Cultural Criticism* (Baltimore: Johns Hopkins University Press, 1978): 1.

2. *The Rhetorical Tradition: Readings from Classical Times to the Present*, ed. Patricia Bizzell and Bruce Herzberg (Boston: Bedford Books, 1990): 1,126.

3. Ibid., 1,127.

4. Michel Foucault, "What is an Author." *Textual Strategies: Perspectives in Post-Structuralist Criticism*, ed. Josu V. Harari (Ithaca: Cornell University Press, 1979): 150.

5. Ibid., 145.

6. Paul Stiff, "Stop Sitting Around and Start Reading." *EYE*, No. 11, Vol 3, (1993): 4–5.

7. Michel Foucault, "What is an Author." *Textual Strategies: Perspectives in Post-Structuralist Criticism*, ed. Josu V. Harari (Ithaca: Cornell University Press, 1979): 159.

8. Ibid., 158.

9. Martin Heidegger, "The Question Concerning Technology." *The Question Concerning Technology and Other Essays* (New York: Garland Publishing, 1977): 12–13.

10. Ibid., 13.

11. Nicholas Negroponte, *Being Digital* (New York: Vintage Books, 1996): 19.

12. Ibid., 19.

13. Epeli Hauofa, "Our Sea of Islands." *Asia/Pacific as Space of Cultural Production,* ed. Rob Wilson and Arif Dirlik, (Durham: Duke University Press, 1995): 92.

14. Ibid., 93.

Digital Humanism

CHARLES H. TRAUB AND JONATHAN LIPKIN

AS MEMBERS OF a thinking community, we must accept this premise: we are no longer antici-pating a revolution. It has already happened. It is time to build on its promise, transcend the inevitable losses, and become more comfortable, more human, with the change now wrought.

This revolution has created the possibility of reinventing ways lost in history of interacting, thinking, and creating. This is manifest in the advent of the digital computer, and its accompa-nying methodologies, giving unprecedented new opportunities for working in ways that empha-size relationships between bodies of knowledge and human minds. The computer is valuable in its ability to enable us to reconceptualize our relationship to knowledge, and to organize it, rather than merely accumulate information. The methodologies of the computer allow us to share a commonality of human expression that crosses disciplines. If approached openly by thinking people who hold the humanist tradition dear, they allow a means for creativity which will enable us to reinforce that which makes us human. The great achievements of man lie in the quest to expose the unseen, and the computer's value lies in its ability to further these achievements.

The ways of working in the digital world, however, are not new, as we shall see. Indeed, precursors of multimedia and hypertext have been around for centuries. The present strength of the computer, its speed, flexibility, and strength in retention of fact, only enhance what has already been embedded in the constant course of human intelligence—the desire to create new meanings through relationship.

We posit a new creative individual, the "creative interlocutor," a navigator of associative trails of thought and resource, who enables others to freely and creatively manage their human interests. This individual is one who is integrated: his creativity functions as an organic part of society, and he acts to connect for the common good. The creative interlocutor is also an inte-grator in his ability to negotiate the disparate fields of human knowledge and bring them together in previously unimagined ways. In so doing, he enables others to further their creative potentials.

Herein we will make the case that technology has always aided, rather than hindered, human expression and creativity. Human beings, however, have always had to overcome an initial hesitancy, whether it be telegraph or the computer. Henry David Thoreau remarked: "We are in a great haste to construct a telegraph from Maine to Texas. But Maine and Texas, it may be, have nothing important to communicate." Clearly, today one does not doubt the humanity of a grandmother in Maine who talks to her granddaughter in Texas. What we lament is the loss of content in that conversation.

We seek to negate the self-fulfilling prophecy engendered by entrenched interests that lament the loss of their primacy by blaming the inhumanity of the technology. You can't touch it, you can't read in bed, it hurts my eyes, and so forth. These regrets and fears, like all others, are inhibiting. All too often they segregate the minds of humanists and artists whose creative input is vitally needed in the implementation of this new technology. The irony is that this feeling unnecessarily reinforces the power of the technocrats who then direct the design and implementation of the technology in a self-promoting way. Ask not what the computer can do for you, but what you can do for the computer.

Humanism and the Liberal Arts

The computer has value only as it enhances that which makes us human. Most likely this is our ability to learn, or rather to learn how to learn—the knack to order, manage, and reconfigure that which we know. Our humanity lies in our ability to transmit from one to another, allowing others to gain access to successful formulations and articulations that further our notion of being. This is what builds culture—the accumulated conceptual riches brought through the history of civilization.

We use the Liberal Arts[1] to understanding these riches. They treat the fields of knowledge in a balanced and equal manner, emphasizing the commonality of human experience and its expression within its diverse fields. A student of the liberal arts creates meaning by weaving a nurturing blanket from the common threads that hold the fields together, rather than focusing on the seams which set them apart. This balance between fields of knowledge, and search for commonality is precisely what is furthered by a judicious use of multimedia digital technology.

Thinkers of the Enlightenment rediscovered patterns of thinking that today are embodied in this technology. Francis Bacon followed the Renaissance masters as a model of the creative interlocutor, connecting the spirit of the Enlightenment with the great Age of Reason. Through his methodology of inductive reasoning, he sought to free intelligence from dogma that constrained and limited our understanding of the greater rational scheme of the world. In *Novum Organum* in 1623, he argues not only for scientific methodology, but for its integration with the arts and the humanities. In inductive reasoning, which is the accumulation of information and the detection of patterns therein, is the commonality of procedures that dispels notions of a priori preconception. His philosophies opened the field of human inquiry to an ever-expanding body of knowledge. Francis Bacon's life, rooted in philosophy, politics, and the creative art of writing is exemplary of methodological inquiry furthering the connectedness of our human interest.

Maria Sibylla Merian (1647–1717)[2] was the visual arts analogue to Bacon. Through her use of the evolving technologies of optical magnification and mechanical reproduction, she was able to further humanist values and the ideals of the Enlightenment. Born to a family of bookmakers, she took at an early age to observing and sketching insects. She would take the observational skills learned as a child and go on to publish two major works: *Raupen* and *Metamorphosis*, both editions of copperplate prints. In these works, she depicts the insect and plant life of Europe and Surinam to the emerging intellectual class of the period. Merian was unique among botanists of her age. She depicted insects and plants not as specimens, but rather as creatures intricately and intimately involved in the cycle of life. She was not interested in then conventional classification schemes or in "cabinets of wonder" that present sterile specimens. In fact, she told one potential collaborator to stop sending her dead insects—she was only interested in "the formation, propagation, and metamorphosis of creatures."[3]

Prior to the seventeenth century, our understanding of the world was formed by a combination of myth and doctrine. During the Enlightenment, the West found a new fascination with the real, and developed ways of thinking and the technology to explore the world. Merian was inspired by the new optical technologies of her time; the compound microscope came about in the 1660s and Athanasius Kirchner published his book *Ars manga lucis et ubmrae*, which discussed the camera obscura as a tool for observation and illustration. In her imaginative use of these tools, Merian was an artist who responded to Enlightenment discourse about knowledge and the natural world, and effortlessly crossed boundaries. The fruits of scientific methodology fathered by such as Bacon, Merian, and the great thinkers of the Age of Reason brought forth the Industrial Age. In this new age, the ever-expanding fields of knowledge required specialization at the expense of more universally learned individuals.

Cross Fertilization

The idea that one field might enrich another is also not a new one. Though it seems to be forgotten by the over-specialization emphasized in our learning institutions, the concept and practice of what is currently termed multimedia is an age-old notion. Multimedia is not suggested merely by technological advancement, but rather it is grounded in fundamental human practice that predates the invention of the computer by thousands of years. Early uses of multimedia were cross disciplinary in an unself-conscious way. The advent of the computer did not create the technical tangle of multimedia, but rather manifests a pre-existing need in our culture for a more democratic, universal, and diverse way to communicate.

We can see multimedia in the burial rituals of the ancient Egyptians who made no demarcation between media employed in the great technology of the pyramids and their elaborate burial rituals. These burial sites combined elements of architecture, writing, sculpture, and during the rite, even music and performance, all for the purpose of captivating and mystifying the laity under the dominance of their rulers.

In the Middle Ages, the prevalent form of multimedia was at the same time a form of mass communication. The cathedral communicated the awe-inspiring Christian spiritual doctrine, which was the dominant means of rationalizing human existence. The message was made stronger by its embodiment in a variety of media stimulating the senses: visual (stained glass and statues), sound (music and hymn), touch and taste (performance and mass), and smell (incense and myrrh). Writing itself was the means for codifying the knowledge held in the cathedral, the knowledge to sort out the patterns of our existence, to know the unknowable.

All of these technologies were beyond the reach of the ordinary man, since books were tremendously expensive to produce and few could read. The expense and duration of constructing a cathedral made it an option only for the wealthy. It was of course not portable, so it remained in a central location, accessible only to those in its immediate vicinity. Due to these inherent, and perhaps intentional, constraints, knowledge and, thus, power were concentrated in the hands of the theocracy. It was not until the advent of the printed book that the quest for knowledge could become a part of a universally inclusive culture. Yet, printing came with a price: a devaluation of multimodal communication.

Victor Hugo comments further on the advent of printing, its narrowing of our field of expression, and the dominance of the word over the image in his nineteenth-century novel *The Hunchback of Notre Dame*. A character in his novel, a priest in fifteenth-century France, directly after the invention of movable type, compares the newly invented book to the cathedral and states, "this will kill that"—the book will kill the cathedral. Yet, it did not. Hugo's phrase also refers to the conflict between the text of the book and the multimedia imagery of the church. By the nineteenth century, the text had become dominant as a means of discourse. For a century to follow, the word, through the great dissemination of the written text, was the primary source for creative inspiration. If nothing else, it allowed for the distribution of description pornography and a stimulation that gave rise to Modernism.

But all was short-lived: in the twentieth century Marshall McLuhan, in his book *The Gutenberg Galaxy*, foresaw the rise of the image, empowered by global visual media such as television. He envisioned "the civilization of imagery" wherein the word is no longer the sole stimulating force to the imagination. Today there is an unanswerable conundrum—which is it that stimulates the imagination first or more, the word or the image? The computer doesn't care, because it's a multimedia cathedral!

Predictably, the phrase "this will kill that" was repeated with the invention of photography, and is all too often heard again today as we experience the digital revolution. Much in the same way that the text of the book threatened the multimodal cathedral, or photography's imagery that of painting, the computer now threatens the book. Likely there will be a co-existence in the media. The book will likely not disappear, but will inevitably change in function and meaning, as did painting. Furthermore, the computer offers us another Renaissance in our extensions of creative possibilities through the coequal distribution and interconnectedness of age-old multimedia. The Web is an ever-expanding territory of thought, commerce, and entertainment.

Obviously, there is no doubt that technology relieves us of burdensome tasks, whether it is the welding of metal or of numbers or of images, or of all of them together. But have we allowed it to free us in the greater pursuits of our humanness? Perhaps the blame lies not with technology but with our systems of learning.

All too often today, intellectual ideas are treated as chattel property whose purpose remains locked in the discourse of the "knowing" rather than serving the common good. This notion segregates us from our commonality of intelligence and unravels with technobabble and jargonization the very fiber of our humanity. Pre-Enlightenment myth returns in these forms.

Specialists sequester themselves in monasteries of learning, untouched by the great unwashed masses. Something Medieval is happening again.

Is it not astounding that at Harvard University, as recently as 1989, the late great Italian poet Italo Calvino needed to remind his audience of what should have been evident in the liberal arts ideal: Creative visualization is a process that, while not "originating in the heavens," goes beyond any specific knowledge or intention of the individual to form a kind of transcendence. Calvino stated that not only poets and novelists deal with this problem, but scientists as well. "To draw on the gulf of potential multiplicity is indispensable to any form of knowledge. The poet's mind, and at a few decisive moments the mind of the scientist, works according to a process of association of images that is the quickest way to link and to choose between the infinite forms of the possible and the impossible. The imagination is a kind of electronic machine that takes account of all possible combinations and chooses the ones that are appropriate to a particular purpose, or simply the most interesting, pleasing, or amusing."[4]

John Dewey: Pragmatic Visionary

Earlier in the twentieth century, John Dewey, in his pragmatism, advocated an educational system which would recognize the common humanist thread within experience, communication, and art. In his analysis of the Greek Parthenon he noted:

> The collective life knew no boundaries between what was characteristic of these places and operations and the arts that brought color, grace and dignity into them. Painting and sculpture were organically one with architecture, as that was one with the social purpose the buildings served. Music and song were intimate parts of the rites and ceremonies in which the meaning of group life was consummated.[5]

We ought not to have to remind today's thinkers of his philosophies, and yet find we have to over and over again. Dewey sought to recover the continuity of aesthetic experience and normal processes of living through proper education. All art is the product of interaction of living organism and environment and an undergoing and a doing which involves a reorganization of actions and materials.[6] Aesthetic understanding must start with and never forget that the roots of art and beauty lie in basic vital functions. Herein is a mimic of Bacon's earlier notion that all pattern is of the "machine of God."

Marvin Minsky, one of the founders of modern computer science, in a like manner has portrayed the mind as a society of tiny components forming a magnificent puzzle of evolving imagination. In his book *The Society of Mind* he cites Papert's principle, the notion proposed by Seymour Papert regarding mental growth, wherein Papert theorized that intellectual progress is based not simply on the acquisition of new skills, but on the acquisition of new administrative ways to use what one already knows.[7] Our conception of the computer as an art-making and communication device is just that—a tool which fosters and encourages the creative re-administration of information.

Dewey envisioned an educational system which imparted pragmatic information without elitism. In order to allow education to become a tool that enables humanity to cultivate and reorganize our work and culture, we must abandon authoritarian methods of educational practice, where the teacher is the endowed disseminator of privileged knowledge. Humanists must remember that the computer is a tool of multimedia communication between the source of information and the user, without giving authority to the selected few. This communication becomes an ongoing ebb and flow of escalating meaning/communication which engages and empowers the inquisitive user. As a tool for art-making and scientific thinking it is unique, and allows us the potential to realize Dewey's vision. More than at any other time in history, it is important to educate students with tools, both technical and intellectual, to formulate new patterns between the details of knowledge rather than to expect them to accumulate information like books on a shelf.[8] Cyber communication must be made to be the intelligent extension of human capability for new discovery. *Communication is education.*

Dataset: All Art is Image

Whether communication takes the form of vocal utterances, ink on paper, or modulation of radio waves, the intention has always been the transfer of meaning from one individual to another. This creates an *image* that will convey idea. It is in our humanism that we attempt to make manifest some facet of experience/content and communicate it to another person or persons.[9]

Until now, the medium has determined both the audience for the message and its destination. Thus, oil paintings were destined for the museum, text for the printed page, music for the radio. Subcultures have grown up around these destinations, and these subcultures have become insular and self-referential. Yet, the separations are artificial, imposed by the restraints of the technology and mostly by the lack of vision of those working within politically defined fields. These boundaries between media also forced a separation of audiences, creating the artificial divides of high and low culture. Evolution of media allows an evolution of audience. With its virtual writing spaces,[10] the computer positions us to transcend these restraints, and to reunite all experience, within its algorithms, to recognize the common humanism within all communication.

The digital computer, when combined with the optical scanner, the music sampler, and a myriad of other computer input devices, allows us to reduce all physical media to a virtual binary digit. At this point, when we have digitized sound, or photographs, or film, it is all equal in the cathedral-like space of the computer, without dogma. Images become reduced to a dataset, merely a sequence of numbers—nothing more, nothing less. Every digital movie, every digital image, every digital sound is nothing more than a sequence of zeros and ones stored in the memory of the computer. These numbers can now be seamlessly combined and juxtaposed. In the computer's virtual spaces, all forms of communication are equal.

The computer, in its use of multimedia, merely reinforces common and historic human themes. In order to communicate in the interest of evolving the human condition, there must be access to the creative tools—the computer network—to all interested. The computer has the ability to structure all communication to the common and accessible level implied within the language of the dataset. Hence, it empowers the user to also reorganize any message in new ways that allow for pattern thinking, trans-disciplinary intercourse, and the visualization of the unseen.

The Memex's Associative Index

The idea of making a large body of information available to others is not new. In 350 B.C., the Athenian Speusippus created an encyclopedia that purported to contain all human knowledge, as did Lu Pu-Wei in China in 239 B.C., who gathered 3,000 known scholars and assembled their knowledge into a work of more than 200,000 words. One of the limitations of these encyclopedias was their mass: Pliny the Elder's encyclopedia, *Natural History*, compiled in A.D. 79, was said to comprise thirty-seven volumes containing 2,500 chapters. The next limitation was cost: At a time when books were reproduced by hand, works of this magnitude were fabulously expensive. The final limitation was more of a cognitive one: When large bodies of information are put together, some organizational scheme must be used. Modern encyclopedias are organized more or less alphabetically, with one entry following another from *a* to *z*. This is a fairly arbitrary, modern, and limiting system. Diderot's *Encylopédie*, a text meant to further the Enlightenment by bringing out the essential principles of art and science, was organized by tasks and preoccupations.

Vannevar Bush, science advisor to Franklin Delano Roosevelt, has been somewhat forgotten, yet stands as a remarkable creative interlocutor. In his 1945 vision of the memex, he held out the solutions for the limitations of human mind and dexterity. The memex was an unrealized tool that a more enlightened Harvard audience, listening to Calvino, might already have employed. His machine improves memory, like an encyclopedia, while allowing the mind to operate "by association. With one item in its grasp, it snaps instantly to the next that is suggested by its association of thoughts."[11] His vision of its ability to scan information allows the user to recombine art and knowledge, to become a creative interlocutor.

He talked of new organizational schemes—ones which can be customized to the needs and interests of the particular users. His device combines two of the liberating capabilities of the digital computer: reduction of images, words, and music to a dataset, and networking in what was meant to be a personal device. He foresaw both the internal network of hypertext and the possibilities of the external network.

Remarkably, today Bush's mechanism is as common as the desktop computer, and yet, his essential idea of the memex—that users can be empowered by hypertextual trails through information—is unfulfilled. Why, we ask? It is not the fault of technology, but rather a failure of entrenched values and limited vision. The Web, the most prevalent implementation of hypertext, is essentially a one-way distribution system, where the user has little facility to be creative. We foresee the use of the computer networks to facilitate and empower the creative interlocutor.

The creative interlocutor uses hypertext and hypermedia to create trails; these trails transform data into knowledge to be redistributed to others, thus feeding the network. The memex, and, likewise, the computer create a miniature network within the data they hold in their memory. When linked to a larger network, such as the World Wide Web, their ability to create new meaning is increased almost infinitely.

Our ability to nurture and engage our own genius is stifled by an education that fails to recognize the value of associative capabilities inherent in this network. Clearly, this is the task of the redefined humanist and visual education, or what we once referred to as the classic Liberal Arts. It must engage us all, as scientists, engineers, artists, and scholars. Technology has failed us in accomplishing this goal because it has been segregated from humanist activity.

The Computer and the Creative Interlocutor

A new artist, interlocutor-designer, should be a product of an enlightened engagement fostered by a new educational system which is trans-disciplinary in nature.[12] The creative interlocutor is one who facilitates the exchange of ideas and information between one human need and another. This person is the producer, director, the organizer-navigator. More specifically, this person is the curator, editor, and collector, then the maker, weaver, welder, builder, and distributor. History reminds us easily of such as Leonardo da Vinci, Frances Bacon, and Thomas Jefferson. But one must also ponder the great stretches by multidisciplinary minds such as the weavers of the Bayeux tapestry, Anna Sibylla Merian, Samuel F. B. Morse, the Roeblings, Booker T. Washington, Laszlo Moloy-Nagy and countless others whose reach across boundaries changed civilization for the better. Creative interlocutors are: programmers, producers, inventors, researchers, teachers, scholars, and volunteers. The creative interlocutor negotiates revolutionary associations, a kind of new genius.

We see a budding of the creative interlocutor in the collaborative spaces of the Internet. The language of the computer is a shared language that allows participation by those who so choose. In the examples to follow, there is no longer a single creator, but rather a collective genius, a web of creative nodes that weave together previously disconnected pieces of information.[13] As innovators, creative interlocutors use their art in a manner which facilitates others to find and define their own creative meaning in the interrelationship of ideas and forms.

In 1979, the inventors of the RSA encryption scheme (the one currently used by Netscape Navigator) put forward a challenge.[14] They encoded a message, and offered a $100 reward to anyone who could crack it. They felt that given the computing resources of the time, and even granted advances in chip speed with a factor of millions, nobody would be able to break their code in the foreseeable future. They were wrong! Instead of thinking of a single computer as a self-contained and limited system, Derek Atkins, a twenty-one-year-old engineering student at MIT, realized that while one computer would take a long time to crack the code, he might harness the power of the Internet and distribute the computing load over many computers. And that's exactly what he did: In 1991, he directed his friends to use a recently discovered mathematical method to devise a program that would crack the code, and had it ready to go by mid-1993. The program was distributed over the Internet to more than 1,500 computers on six continents to create an expanded computer that churned out 5,000 MIPS[15] years. The code was cracked in the spring of 1994 by looking beyond the boundary of the individual computer, and thus consolidating the power of the network.

Another example of imaginative administration to enlarge our sphere of possibilities lies in the development of a computer operating system. The operating system Linux was not so much invented, as evolved through creative re-administration. It is a prime example of the networked aesthetic of the expanded public sphere of individuals working in concert. It began with Linus Torvalds. He was in school in 1990, and owned a PC that ran Minux, an operating system designed mostly as a UNIX tutorial. UNIX is a powerful operating system, which at that time, could only be run on more powerful computers. So, he imaginatively worked within his limitations, and wrote a few programs—a terminal emulator and a disk driver—so that he could save files to disk. He posted these initial programs, and generously shared them as freeware—software that is distributed primarily over the Internet, and for which there is no charge. From there it took off. As a result of Torvalds's *interlocution*, the operating system evolved in a democratic and Darwinian manner; anyone could contribute code to the operating system, but only the most evolved would become part and parcel of the final released version. He presided over the development, but was by no means entirely in control of it. He provided the seed idea, and the guidance, but left the mechanics of its development up to the community of creative users. Today, Linux has an established base of nearly ten million users in 120 countries, and is composed of millions of lines of code. All of this primarily because Linus didn't follow the usual notion of creating software through the confines of a defined proprietary scheme—hundreds of hackers around the world wrote it, collaborating over the Internet.

These examples serve to help define the notion of the "creative interlocutor," a multimedia universal designer, engineer, artist, socially responsible person whose mandate is to help negotiate the crossing of boundaries. While they reside in the field of technology itself, their parallels must be generated within the humanities and arts.

N O T E S

1. Beginning in the Middle Ages, the traditional fields of the liberal arts were defined from classical studies in order to reveal obscured meaning in the text, symbols, doctrines, icons, and mysticism of the Church. The ancient seven branches of learning included grammar, logic, rhetoric, arithmetic, geometry, music, and astronomy. All were means of deciphering the hidden codes of the Biblical text.

    Since the Renaissance and its enlightenment, the core of this traditional education held that all areas of human endeavor are suitable topics for inquiry, regardless of their nominal concerns. An integrated individual versed in the liberal arts loves learning and is directed by intellectual curiosity, rather than by disciplinary guidelines.

    The Renaissance dawn from the a priori methods of the Dark Ages revealed the various facets of diverse fields and the common rays of humanism's enlightenment. Educators such as Vittorino da Feltre of Mantua taught men to be well-rounded individuals. In his boarding schools, princes and poor scholars mixed in a classical education. Character was shaped, along with mind and body, through frugal living, self-discipline, and a high sense of social obligation. All was done with an eye to the practical: philosophy was a guide to the art of living, along with training for public life. "Students were expected to excel in all human existence."

2. Natalie Zemon Davis, *Women on the Margins* (Cambridge: Harvard University Press, 1995).

3. Davis, 181.

4. Italo Calvino, *Six Memos for the Next Millenium* (Cambridge: Harvard University Press, 1988): 87–91.

5. John Dewey, *Art as Experience* (New York: Perigree Books, 1934, 1980): 7.

6. Dewey, 16.

7. Marvin Minsky, *The Society of Mind* (New York: Simon and Schuster, 1985).

8. Johann Wolfgang von Goethe, the nineteenth-century thinker, is said to have been the last man to have known everything. This fact was remarkable for two reasons: first, there was much less accumulated human knowledge at that time, and second, Goethe's capacity to retain even this. Today, the genius of Goethe is supplanted by the convenience of the ability to communicate to all knowledge.

9. "As a photographer, I don't care about photography, and have always been irritated with those who are concerned exclusively with f-stop and stop bath. For me, it is the communication of idea to another that holds the true excitement. Photography is merely a means to an end, and if I could achieve that end in another way, I certainly would." Jonathan Lipkin (1993) *One Family's Journey*, MFA Thesis, School of Visual Arts, New York.

10. Jay Bolter, *Writing Spaces (*Hillsdale: Lawrence Erlbaum Associates, 1991). Here, Bolter traces the history of the effects of technology on writing. He discusses the book, the scroll, and pictographic and logographic alphabets. The computer is seen as merely the next step in a long series of technological advances that interact with the culture of the time.

11. Ibid.

12. Charles H. Traub "The Creative Interlocutors: A Creative Manifesto." *Leonardo*, Vol. 30, No. 1 (MIT Press, 1997): 389–390.

13. Moholy-Nagy supported our notion of genius in his description of education at the new Bauhaus (Institute of Design) by structuring education there to place emphasis on "integration through a conscious search for relationships—artistic, scientific, technical, as well as social. The intuitive working mechanics of the genius gives a clue to this process. The unique ability of the genius can be approximated by everyone". From *New Education*, p. 9. See also Minsky's reference to Papert's principle.

14. Steven Levy, "Wisecrackers." *Wired Magazine* (March 1996): 128.

15. MIPS is short for millions of instructions per second, a measure of computational power. A MIPS year is the amount of computing power produced in a year by a computer capable of a million instructions per second.

Design as Technology OR Technology Schmechnology

LOUISE SANDHAUS

LATELY, SOME EVENTS have occurred in my academic and professional life that have caused me to reconsider my own techno-evangelism, as well as my errant philosophies and public diatribes about design as a mutating profession in the context of "new" technologies. In other words, I'm reconsidering my idealism in thinking that computers are the greatest things in the last millennium. At the same time, I am evaluating my quasi-dystopic view that because graphic designers' roles are seemingly changing so dramatically in the context of new technologies, perhaps we're no longer *graphic* designers. This, therefore, is an initial attempt at making sense of the relationship as I now see it between *graphic* design and technology.

What has led me to newfound thoughts? The first, is the interactions with colleagues at CalArts (where I teach and co-direct the Graphic Design Program). In our combined efforts to formulate where we are going with the Program, and thus where we'd like to see this profession in the next millennium, I have been provoked into thinking about the cultural and technological moment in which graphic design as a practice and profession exists. This examination observes and compares the practice and profession against the circumstances that cause it to permutate and splinter, but never quite go away.

The second—an event that occurred on the professional front—was that in 1998, I was chosen (along with my project partners, architect and interface designer Tim Durfee and architect Iris Regn) to design a 47,000-square-foot exhibition. After we were notified that we got the job, I kept waiting for a call to tell us there'd been a terrible mistake: "Oops, sorry." But the call never came. Now, the reason for this paranoia was that neither my partners nor I had ever designed an exhibition, not even a teeny-tiny one, and here we were hired to do the mother of all exhibitions. But ultimately, it was through this project that I was able to see why and how hiring us made sense, and through that to understand in a more complex way what it is I do as a *graphic* designer: I invent and innovate technology for communications.

Before I go too far in describing what I'm suggesting—in particular, what I mean by "technology"—it seems important to convey the significance of "invention" and "innovation" in the first place, and why in the larger scheme of things I think these matter. And that means that, for a moment, I'm going to bare the breast of my social and political concerns.

Untitled painting by Francis Alÿs (small original work) with copies by Juan Garcia and Emilio Rivera, 1996. In interpreting Alÿs's original work, the ideas, as well as the poetics of the works, shift and are altered. Comparatively, these works convey how form informs—not content alone—and invokes meaning and emotion. Courtesy of the artist and ACME, Los Angeles, photo credit: Robert Wedemeyer.

These concerns have to do with a tension that I perceive between the multi-nationals as they more aggressively attempt to interpret life as simple, manageable forms, images, experiences, and desires—and, all that "messy" stuff—the other forms, experiences, knowledge, and perceptions that offer a richer, and more interesting, diverse, and splendid world of existence. I'm interested in invention over homogeneity. In turn, I see innovation as ultimately allowing us to connect to each other in more meaningful ways. If this isn't the larger point, I honestly don't know what the point *is* of all this crap we keep creating. But one last note on this before I leave you with the impression that I'm either a way-out-of-step utopian or a hackneyed Marxist; I actually *love* capitalism. Plenty of truly provocative things and ideas have been chauffeured into the world on the wings of capitalist enterprise: the lightbulb, the telephone, the phonograph, and the car, to name a few. And I wouldn't forget Disney or Las Vegas either.

What is Technology?

So to continue, what do I mean when I say that I "innovate technology for communications": You thought I was talking about graphic design, not engineering. The answer lies in how I'm defining "technology"—the fancy schmancy term often used to mean "computers," as in "I've got a Pentium 9 with a 2-billion-megahertz processor, what's your technology?" Yet, somewhere in the back of our over-extended, multi-tasking brains, we know it's not that simple; a quick trip to even the most common of dictionaries reveals that technology has to do with the application of knowledge and that machines aren't even specifically mentioned. While technology may include a material component, more important is the immaterial. The point I'm trying to make is that there are lots of things that are technologies: the way we think is a technology—in other words, the mental systems that classify "computers" in our minds as "technology" *is* a technology; the language in which we think is a technology. We don't generally perceive the form in which we write as technology (whether that's the Semitic alphabet or the typeface Times Roman) nor the tools with which we write—a pencil or Word—but these are *all* technologies. Because technology is whatever it is that I utilize which allows me to manipulate, make sense of, and engage with my experiences and surroundings. It allows me to engage with the world in productive ways.

So rather than talk about machines, I want to break down these technologies I've just described as "applications of knowledge"—into three types. (Or to put it another way, I'm going to create a technology to probe deeper into technology.)

The first type of technology is Modes of Perception—in other words, ways of classifying and making sense of our experiences; the second type is Technology as Forms—the shape or the mode through which something exists; and third, Technology as Tools—by which I mean devices used in the performance of an operation. This is what we may more commonly think of as technology: such as hammers, paintbrushes, and computers—or what we don't: tools can also be organizational systems that serve as devices.

I want to look at these technologies, or "applications of knowledge," more closely—first, to clarify how I see them *as* technologies, and then ultimately to observe how as technologies they *have* or might inform design practice.

Elaboration of the Three Examples of Technology

1 | TECHNOLOGY AS A MODE OF PERCEPTION I have a Japanese friend who happens to be a Zen Buddhist priest. When I first met Hiro, he told me about how difficult it was when he came to the United States to attend University. Rather than the rationalist system of education established by General MacArthur during the occupation of Japan after World War II, Hiro had been educated at the temple where he had grown up, becoming versed in fables, myths, crafts, and the natural world.

When he came to the United States to "further" his education, he discovered that knowledge and ideas were classified and segmented into strange alien groupings—ideas were either science or art, mathematics or humanities, etc. Not only were the subjects strange, but the fact that consciousness was sliced up and packaged seemed totally weird and disorienting.

I found myself dwelling on this revelation, trying to imagine how the world might seem if the whole mode through which I knew and understood it was altered. As if having been abducted by aliens, I could no longer look at life in the same way. ET was no longer a fairy tale, but a testament to our times. What would be revealed to me through this altered experience? What would I now understand? Find of interest? Engage and connect with?

Previously, what I had taken for granted—that cognitive perception was inherent and required no special training (like being able to discern hot from cold)—now appeared like a device—like rose-colored glasses or a telescope, filtering and framing my vision and therefore shaping my knowledge and experience. Or, as the saying goes, "if you have a hammer, the whole world looks like nails." The forms through which we perceive don't just shape the experience—they *are* the experience: in other words, how we think is *what* we think.

Coathammer Jut by Henk Stallinga, 1997. Coat hanger designed to install in one easy blow.

2 | TECHNOLOGY AS FORM In an article that arrived at my doorstep through a curious set of circumstances, the following quote shined forth: "In their hands, picture-making was becoming a pictorial language that, with practice, could communicate more information, more quickly, and by a potentially wider audience than any verbal language in human history." This quote, which comes from a scholarly article by Samuel Y. Edgerton, argues that the scientific revolution born of the Renaissance could not have happened without pictorial invention. He demonstrates his argument with two images.

The first image shows a late sixteenth-century engraving of a windlass pump by Agostino Ramelli. Perspectival representation and chiaroscuro—*inventions* that already existed, allowed for the illusional representation of three-dimensional space—considerable innovations to begin with; but it was the additional pictorial conceptions of the rotated view, the exploded view, and the transparent view that Ramelli utilized that allowed for further observations and understandings about how this complex piece of machinery operated. I know it's easy to take these technologies of form for granted. But imagine trying to understand how to build one of these, or explain how this pump operates using verbal language alone. The second image of the two that Edgerton discusses shows the same drawing "copied" by Wang Cheng in the early seventeenth century. The drawing has lost all significance because of the lack of pictorial devices that communicate the required meaning. The artist, unversed in these formal innovations (such as the exploded view), is therefore unable to translate Ramelli's vivid explanation.

To return to Edgerton's statement about the impact of this pictorial development, it's important to note that this progression is tied to the proliferation of the printing press spreading throughout Europe at this time. This meant that these technologies of form could convey ideas to a broader populace. And, in turn, these ideas—or "knowledges"—were utilized by a more varied public to build pumps, modernize communities, and develop even better pumps and maybe even down the line—a toilet. From here we can begin to imagine the explosive political, industrial, and scientific development in which this technology of form played a significant role.

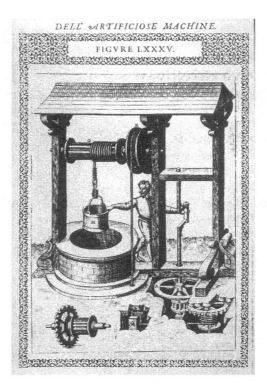

Engraving of windlass pump, from Agostino Ramelli, *Le diverse et artficiose* machine, 1588. This image uses cutaways and exploded views to enable viewers to see relationships of parts and, therefore, understand construction and operation. Originally from Houghton Library, Havard University.

Another example of knowledge as form (and form's relationship to meaning-making) can be drawn from the work of Francis Alÿs, a contemporary Belgian artist. Alÿs paints a somewhat surreal depiction of a simple domestic scene, which he then passes on to a collective of Mexican sign painters who then "copy" the original work.

This process results in something that demonstrates the remarkable relationship of representation to understanding and interpretation; or, to put it another way, the qualities and uncanniness of all that a form possesses in its entirety as a vehicle of meaning.

Using the elements of color, shape, line, proximity, relationship, spatialization, etc., form communicates in complex ways. The sign painters are left to make sense in every respect— from the intention of the painting, to the intention of the content of the painting, and in interpreting it can't help but transform the meaning and significance of the work.

There are a breadth and depth of inventive technologies of form, each of which allows us to visualize different kinds of ideas and information, but a few worth mentioning are:

- Perspectival rendering
- PROJECTED drawings—those that show how physical space is arranged, such the plan view but also charts and diagrams convey cognitive space
- AXONOMETRIC drawings, which allow relationships within volumes to be conveyed

Woodcut copied from Ramelli's windlass-pump engraving, by Wang Cheng, Ch'i Ch'i T'u Shuo, 1627. This copy of Ramelli's drawing by comparison, although formally inviting, doesn't accurately depict the pump operation. From Harvard Yenching Library, Harvard University.

- COLLAGE, which offers transformed experiences of the represented world
- Depictions as apparatus have long been used by mathematicians to give shape to thought, allowing them to test their theories, as well as describe them
- Time-based forms, such as film, and the representation of time through seriality, such as comics
- Configurations, such as El Lissitzky's 1932 invention of the tab, which created a means of interaction, as well as allowed parts to relate to a whole

3 | TECHNOLOGY AS TOOLS Now we get to that technology which seems more familiar as "technology": things or devices used in the performance of an operation—more commonly referred to as tools. Again, to point out, however, these "things" may be implements that do not exist in the material world, which makes them a bit harder to recognize, particularly when these implements may be in the form of "code." Or, as I remarked earlier, tools can also be organizational systems that serve as devices.

Tools mediate between the mode of perception and form, and allow for the figuring and refiguring of relationships, such as the relationship between construction and the hammer and nail. This simple relationship in making possible a dwelling draws upon an entire history of logic and experience, which in turn influences these very systems of logic. Mark Tinkler's Visual

Plumb Design, Visual Thesaurus. *www.plumbdesign.com/thesaurus*. This example demonstrates Thinkmap, a software "tool" that allows certain types of databases to become useful and valuable, by allowing the relationship of data to dynamically shift according to user need. The Visual Thesaurus utilizes of Princeton University's WordNet database.

Thesaurus is a prime example. To briefly describe it, the Visual Thesaurus utilizes an engine called Thinkmap that can depict data as dynamic, complex connections of related information. The Thesaurus offers a more elegant and understandable way to represent and utilize Princeton University's WordNet database, which is essentially a dictionary based on "sense relationships."

What you see is a word surrounded by a Web of associations that exist in the WordNet database. By manipulating the Part of Speech controls on the interface, the term can be viewed as a noun only, verb, adjective, or adverb.

Another tool is "Atom in a Box" created by Dean Dauger, a graduate student in physics at UCLA [*www.apple.com/education/hed/aua101/atominabox*]. Atom in a Box models or visualizes quantum physics as it pertains to hydrogen atoms. The purpose of the project was to enable students to visualize, and thus, it was hoped, more complexly understand, the relationship of an electron bound to an atomic nucleus.

How the Three Examples Collapse into Each Other

Finally, despite all attempts to neatly package these "applications of knowledge" it seems increasingly clear that these technologies can't be separated. While Dauger may have created a tool, he was, at the same time creating other technologies: modes of perception and form. In fact, for Atom in a Box to be of value all three aspects have to be conceived and arrived at almost simultaneously.

And here's where we get to graphic design.

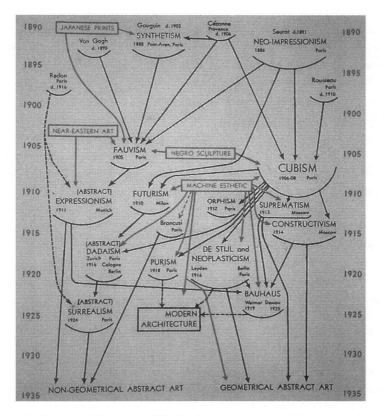

Alfred Barr, Jr. for the Museum of Modern Art, 1936. This diagram shows a cognitive projected view—a formal invention that conveys relationship of ideas—in this case the relationship of cubism to other Modern-art movements. (From cover of catalog, *Cubism and Modern Art*, MoMA, 1936.)

How the Three Examples Collapse into Graphic Design

A few years back, Apple's head of the Advanced Technology Group, Dan Russell, offered me a glimpse at a project he described as "dynamic typography." An engineer doing typography? Now that was a scary thought. But, as it turned out, this was an engineered system that "read" a text and redisplayed the data according to user-established parameters. (For instance, the user would tell the system: "Reduce this 20,000-word article to a 50-word synopsis.") How was this typography I wondered? It seemed more like . . . engineering and maybe editing.

Then, in a bonk-in-the-middle-of-the-forehead moment I remembered that typography, and for that matter, graphic design, was about the graphic display of thought. Duh. After all, this was what letterforms and the arrangement of textual matter had to do with. And through this I began to recognize the familiar role of graphic design in something that at first glance was wholly alien. Typography, born of that earlier revolution in the display of thought—print technology—was being reconsidered in the contemporary terms of *Daily Me* customizable digital data.[1] Only now the conditions for the display, which included the typography, were integrated into the meaning-making process of tools. They were all part of the form-making or form-giving process.

In the Dynamic Typography project the question was: What does this need to be in order to do what it needs to do? In other words, I have this lengthy text and I need to get what it is about without the details, for the moment. Here, function is the driving force. How can that happen? And that's where you end up having to create technologies: the mode of perception is whatever values are assigned to make sense of the longer text, then there's the shape it needs to be delivered in, and what kind of tool makes this happen. But each aspect instigates and influences the other: the minute you ask how does it happen, you're forced to conceive what it is and vice versa.

Books, as we know them today, resulted from the transformation from oral culture to print culture in response to the question: what does a reader, as opposed to a listener, need? Books are the answer to what it means to physically embody ideas and convey them to a wider audience. And what types of ideas can be embodied flows from the current technological—as well as the conceptual—circumstances for realizing a representation, or the means required to communicate understanding. Invention and innovation, mentioned earlier, flows in and out of need, desire, and possibility, conversing with and determining bodies of knowledge and the subsequent form through which they are known. Design can be thought of as the infrastructure of the meaning.

What now seemed evident to me was that Modes of Perception, Form and Tools, or to put it another way, content, form and function, aren't separate from one another—they're symbiotic, like dancer and dance or DNA and chromosomes—you can't consider one without the other. Or, as the legendary computer scientist Alan Newell put it: "As anyone in computer science knows, the boundary between data and program—that is, what is data and what is procedure—is very fluid. In fact . . . there is no principled distinction in terms of form or representation of which is which."

The three modes of technology that I have just described meet in graphic design: Because graphic design is the crucial link between what is being said and *how* it is being said. It makes what is being said meaningful. Graphic design renders thought visible and therefore experiential.

In other words, without the perceptual apparatus of form, whose shape may be generated by a tool, there is no meaning. The shape embodies or articulates a point of view. The key questions for the designer are: what needs or wants to be communicated, how can it be communicated, and what can or needs to be invented to enable the communication—and how does or could that invention further, or transform, or make possible what can be experienced? The ways in which we understand and make sense are vitally interconnected. What I'm suggesting then is that we reorient our thinking about how we conceive what we make as graphic designers.

Technology isn't computers. It's about inventing and innovating applications of knowledge in order to make sense of our experiences. Sometimes this is a way of classifying experience—finding a form to convey the experience or the means to convey that experience. Graphic design as a practice needs to understand its role in communications by working with all of this in mind, harnessing and utilizing the possibilities by inventing and creating technologies for communication.

Before I close I'd like to leave you with one last idea that connects back to the question of

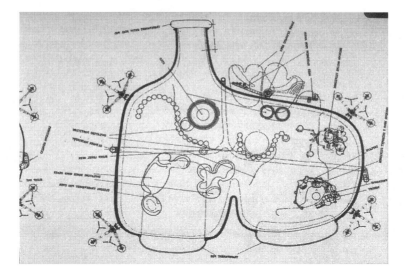

Archigram, Living Pod. This projected plan view for Living Pod shows relationships of objects in space.

why *Graphic* Design and not Information Design, or Information Architecture, or Interaction Design, or any of the other dozens of monikers graphic design has splintered into. We've been talking about really smarty-pants, elegant design without ever mentioning what I believe is that other crucial contribution—sexiness—in other words we haven't covered the terrain of making something that *looks* as compelling as it is. We've been talking about cake, and now I want to mention icing. As graphic design educator, historian, and practitioner Lorraine Wild put it, in arguing about the very particular values of graphic designers if they are going to survive beyond the competition for great and meaningful ideas: "Is graphic design only a conceptual process? . . . [then] where are all these design 'conceptualists' . . . going to find the 'commercial artists' of the future to translate their "big idea" into beautiful or remotely interesting forms that anyone else will want to look at?"

Something can be elegant, smart, sophisticated, and efficient—and graphic design can provide all that, but there still needs to be one more link between thought and experience: the bridge between thinking and experience is engagement—and engagement *is* sexiness. And this I'd like to think of as the very special domain of graphic design. Hail smart 'n' sexy graphic design *as* technology.

N O T E

1. Nicholas Negreponte, founder of the MIT media lab, refers "The Daily Me" as the personally edited newspaper of the future made possible by digital filtering systems. Page 153, *Being Digital,* Alfred A. Knopf, New York, 1995.

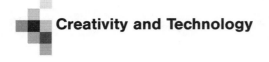

Creativity and Technology

RED BURNS

Let us not follow where the path may lead,
let us go instead where there is no path and leave a trail.

—Japanese proverb

THE INTERACTIVE TELECOMMUNICATIONS Program (ITP) in the Tisch School of the Arts is a pioneering graduate center for the design and study of new media forms and applications. The program, now over twenty years old, has come of age in a time of turbulent upheaval where the speed of technological change and the sheer grandeur of the possibilities are awesome. The siren song has us in its grip. We are living in a maelstrom—communications breakthroughs parallel the creation of the printing press in the fifteenth century.

Art, technology, and experimentation are a part of our root system. In the early days of film the action took place in front of a stationary camera—D. W. Griffith, the director, moved the camera and changed the face of film forever. Eisenstein juxtaposed scenes with editing and disrupted temporal relationships. Both men were artists. In Gregory Bateson's words, artistic innovation will be the "difference that makes the difference." The very human qualities that are responsible for art and music and literature are not logical. Imagination is required and imagination is a unique human quality.

Art reminds us to ask questions, to look at the world in new and different ways. Art makes room for the magic of discovery and the mystery of not knowing. Art makes obvious what was not obvious before. Artists have a role to play in developing a digital culture.

ITP's hands-on approach to learning relies on collaboration rather than competition, fostering an environment where exploration, analysis and risk-taking are encouraged. The program challenges the students to apply their creativity and use the tools of computers, video, audio, graphics, animation, and text in new and imaginative ways.

Who We Are

An artistic sensibility remains our defining cornerstone, but as you will see from the list of almost contradictory attributes, we need to draw from a diverse set of preparatory backgrounds. There are equal numbers of women and men in the program. The 230 students in the program come from a rich mix of disciplines, cultures, ages, and experiences. They enter the program from such diverse fields as music composition, sculpture, painting, writing, biology, law, cultural theory, industrial design, electrical engineering, architecture, dance, and computer science. The ethnic and geographic range is equally wide—from Eastern Europe to East Asia, from Canada to Scandinavia, and from South America to Africa.

A key structuring element is collaboration. At ITP, we see a blurring of disciplines all the time. The artist and the computer scientist are one. C.P. Snow's two cultures are moving closer together. Students build projects: artists collaborate with engineers, computer scientists with writers and musicians, sculptors with electrical engineers, industrial designers with biologists, architects with lawyers, urban planners with graphic designers, composers with theologians. The students are selected for the unique talent in their respective fields. The result is a vibrant community that has the ability to tackle and analyze problems from many directions simultaneously.

Each class at ITP deliberately includes an enriching cacophony of styles, habits of thought, and approaches to problem solving, so students adjust, stretch, and learn from one another. Such an environment is not always easy, and must be cultivated. But it allows a creative process that is opaque, a mix of strengths and weaknesses that defy rigid rules. The technology, as exciting as it is, does not create relationships, nor does it create compelling stories to tell and instructive experiences to relate. It does not widen the mind. It does not question faulty thinking or opinions. Human experience does that.

Our outstanding roster of adjunct and full-time faculty provides a dynamic teaching/learning environment. Our students are well served by this group of talented working professionals who keep abreast of fast changing developments as a matter of course. New York City crackles with so many creative media makers. They provide an interesting, engaging, and lively debate about the opportunities and potential problems created by a digital world. New media is media in transition.

Sense of Place

Our labs are set up in large flexible spaces to encourage students to experiment, exchange ideas, take risks and try out their ideas using digital tools. We operate with an adaptive design, a solid framework within which is a virtually blank canvas. So we welcome the unexpected, tolerate false starts and failures; but often as not we uncover the truly new.

We live in a world of formative research—learning what goes on and what is. It is not a matter of teaching a particular body of knowledge, but rather developing in our students the skills to explore their environment. They "learn how to learn."

The framework defines the limits, but the canvas varies, from student to student, from time to time, and from technology to technology. Partly this is because the field changes so rapidly that teaching students how to learn is the best strategy to ensure that they will always be able to change and grow. But it also relies on the nature of imagination and creativity. We want to train, not constrain our students.

We want to nurture a new kind of communications professional who is at once artistic and analytical, moral and questioning, concrete and imaginative, able to recognize patterns, and whose knowledge of technology is informed by a strong sense of aesthetics and ethics.

A professional with an edgy mix of the confidence to try new things and enough self-doubt to question.

In a field that moves so quickly, making today's innovations obsolete tomorrow, students need more than technical skills. They need to know the difference between learning "how" to think rather than "what" to think. They need an understanding of the culture we live in and the underlying structures that fuel the dynamism between technology and creativity.

Technology doesn't make community—people and relationships do. Without recognizing the people part of the equation, there is no sustaining value. Technology for technology's sake is empty.

In 1895, the Lumière brothers showed the arrival of a train in a Paris café—the Grand Café—I can imagine what the experience was of seeing moving images on the wall. Over the next several decades, filmmakers changed a recording technology into an expressive medium. And now, in this century, powerful computing is added to the mix. The inaccessible 2-ton ENIAC of the 1950s with 16K of RAM has morphed into the a 3 lb. PC with 1 billion bytes, and sits on a desktop or in your pocket—with a networking range to the farthest reach of the globe.

What Does It Mean?

Blips race down networks at incomprehensible speeds—benefits are promised beyond our wildest dreams, and potential implications are difficult to predict. We know there will be unintended consequences—can we maintain a balance between technophobia and euphoric optimism? It is a Faustian bargain. How we think about it and how we create applications is critical.

ITP's Beginnings

ITP's genesis was the experimental work of the Alternate Media Center at New York University's Tisch School of the Arts set up in 1971. At that time, there were three television networks in the United States. Electronic mass media was centrally controlled and it dominated the communications landscape. Two new technologies were introduced into this environment: cable television, which offered a means of originating and distributing signals, and the Sony Portapak, the first portable, low-cost video camera that made instant moving pictures on videotape. When I first picked up a Portapak, it was an epiphanous moment. Why couldn't people make their own documents and distribute them on cable television?

These developments presented new avenues for disparate voices. Our passion for discovery led us to consuming questions about the potential for new forms of communication. Could we use these new media technologies to hold a mirror to ourselves, sharpen our senses, examine our sacred cows, challenge ourselves, enjoy our differences, understand and respect one another? Was decentralized communications in a networked world a possibility?

Much was unknown in a field that wasn't defined.

During the 1970s, the Alternate Media Center developed large-scale telecommunications projects with significant funding from the federal government. We created a two-way television system with and for elderly citizens in Reading, Pennsylvania; telecommunications options for the developmentally disabled in Vermont; and a field trial of Teletext using the vertical blanking interval of WETA in Washington. We learned to focus on the needs of the users.

It was during this period that the idea to create a graduate program was explored and finalized. Initially, research was the focus, but in the early 1980s the emphasis shifted to production. Our experience with people and new technology informed us over and over again—that the most profound technologies are those that disappear, that weave themselves into the fabric of everyday life and resonate with human experience.

Pedagogy

The work we did at the Alternate Media Center provided the basic foundation and the governing pedagogy of the present transmutation of ITP. Since the program began in 1979, the tools have changed and will continue to change. Our philosophy and mission remain unchanged—and that is our strength. Our commitment is to people, not to technology.

We take deliberate steps to create a community that is a rich mix of discipline, cultures, and experiences. Only when there are differing perspectives, different backgrounds, different sources of ideas, can we expect the unexpected to occur, the bland, commercial blanket of culture to break apart. The rush to novelty that characterizes the modern marketplace is to be avoided.

It is exhilarating to see students from diverse cultural backgrounds and wide-ranging disciplines come together with differing points of view. They stimulate one another to question stereotypes, create new forms, and take imaginative leaps in an environment that is driven by a sense of adventure and the anticipation of discovery.

Imagine and Invent

Our philosophy is our engine. We hold to no dogma. Our sense of place is very important to us. We have spaces that present opportunities to improvise, where creative things can happen spontaneously and unpredictably.

Education itself might be looked upon as mainly the assimilation of experience—the content of education is more than the college curriculum. Education has no beginning or ending. We hope to graduate an integrated person—informed, intelligent, talented, knowledgeable, curious, and imaginative.

ITP has been built slowly and carefully over two decades. It is an ongoing creative endeavor. The department is an organism. It grows and changes continually. It responds to its inhabitants and its environment, an environment firmly set in an ethical foundation.

The program is conscious and continually assessing our society, the media business, and the larger field. But over the years it has been consistent in interweaving media and social concerns into activities that employ technology.

The moral and ethical issues that surround how we create new media in this time of profound social change are of paramount importance. We expect our faculty to speak with a moral authority that encourages ethical behavior and nurtures a whole, responsible person.

We believe this is particularly important because we are not technologists and indiscriminate users of machines. In professional schools, the tendency is to stress craft and skills. It is a continuing battle to remind students that there is no poetry in skills alone.

It is good to remember that the best software/hardware ever designed by human beings cannot calculate even a tiny fraction of all the relationships that exist in the ecosystem of a simple pond.

But in the end it is about enhancing the human spirit, using the power of technology to respond to the human need for communication and expression.

The Tao of Self-Support

IT'S THE MIDDLE of the night and the project is due first thing in the morning. Your Mac, however, just crashed. When you restart it, a blinking question mark has taken the place of the usual computer smiley face and the damn thing won't boot up. All your work is on *that* hard drive and you have no backup. You sit there trying to decide if you want a blunt instrument or a bottle of Rebel Yell to put you (and the computer) out of misery.

Sound familiar?

Over the past fifteen years, many graphic designers, illustrators, and writers have all seen their jobs take on a radical new dependence on technology—specifically, desktop computers loaded with page-layout, illustration, image-editing, and word-processing software. And when all the stuff works, it's great. Projects can be completed more efficiently and quickly than ever before with these handy electronic tools.

But technology is not infallible, and like a political campaign or a New York Jets game, something is bound to go wrong sooner or later. Computers are machines, susceptible to mechanical quirks and failures, and the software that runs on them isn't foolproof either. (If you don't believe me, ask anyone who's ever used QuarkXPress for more than a week.)

Having worked in the production departments of national magazines for ten years, the technical support department for a major newspaper for three years, and as a freelance technology reporter and Macintosh consultant for four years, I have had ample opportunity to observe up close the relationship between creative people and their computers. I have worked with designers who know the Mac so well that they could build one of their own in an hour from spare parts while eating lunch. On the flip side of that coin, I have also gotten frantic calls from graphics professionals on deadline, flipping out because the computer is suddenly "TYPING IN ALL CAPS AND IT MUST BE BROKEN AND I AM ON DEADLINE AND—what? There's a . . . *Caps Lock* key on this keyboard, you say?"

Creative people go into creative work to create, not to reinstall their operating systems at two o'clock in the morning, so the question is begged: How much technical knowledge about the inner workings of the computer should a designer, illustrator, or writer have to know to get by in the world? The answer will vary from artist to artist and studio to studio. If you work in a place where there is a crack team of tech-support professionals dedicated to keeping all the computers in the office running at peak performance, and catering to your every electronic whim and need at a moment's notice, I would say the answer would be, "Not much."

The reality is that most places, particularly home offices, do not have such a dream team of hardware helpers and software saviors. There's usually someone in the office known as "the computer guy," or maybe a small collection of cranky, overworked tech people doing both telephone support and the occasional desk visit, but there are bound to be gaps in the coverage. Raise your hands, those of you who have blown a whole day waiting for a member of the tech team to come figure out why the scanner won't scan or why that Illustrator 8.0 file crashes every time you try to open it.

I have personally found that Joseph Pulitzer's nineteenth-century advice for newspapers— "Always be drastically independent"—is also good rule of thumb for anyone using a computer for his or her livelihood. The road to independence, however, is a long one, especially if one is scared of the technology. But if the thought of installing a RAM upgrade by yourself, or loading a new font spooks you, remember an even older maxim that dates back to Roman times: "Knowledge is power."

Computers may have gotten their bad reputation for being cryptic boxes of pure evil from their early days, when arcane commands had to be typed onto the screen before the box would do anything, and computer-science majors and guys who thought *War Games* was the best movie *ever* were the only ones who could remember what to do. The language used to write about computers was thick and impenetrable as well, and some of this carries over today.

But things got better for the rest of us when Apple Computer released the Macintosh in 1984 and set the desktop-publishing boom in motion. Most designers I know still use the Mac, as do I, since it is my platform of personal preference. Windows has come a long way in the past five years—despite having error messages written by the Pod People of Planet Garble, and a somewhat convoluted interface compared to the Mac—and is starting to offer designers and artists more software opportunities. But the Mac still reigns supreme over most studios, and quite frankly, is much easier to troubleshoot in general than a Windows machine, once you know what you are looking for.

Regardless of which platform one chooses, a decent familiarity with the system is deeply beneficial for both productivity and a general sense of well-being. This includes being able to recognize common hardware and software problems, and how to tell the difference between the two. For example, a person who loads some new software on her Mac, restarts the machine and then has a panic attack when the computer hangs every time during booting, is probably going to have a higher stress level than someone who recognizes an Extension conflict when she sees one, restarts the Mac with the Shift key down, and removes the new program's components from the Extension folder to get the Mac back on its feet, and figure out why it did what it did.

Installing new programs, loading fresh fonts, and regular maintenance of the computer and its operating system (things like defragging the hard disk, rebuilding the Mac's desktop, trashing unneeded files to free up system space) are typical chores that computer users should be able to do successfully by themselves. Some may argue that designers are getting turned into computer jocks instead of using their time for visionary work, but it all comes down to taking care of the equipment one needs to get the job done. Upping one's RAM allocation to allow Photoshop to open that 75-megabyte TIFF image may seem a more complex task than replacing Xacto blades or wiping up a waxy mess with Bestine, but it's all part of keeping your new tools of the trade sharp.

The idea of learning how the computer works may seem staggering, but there is a very simple concept to keep in mind. Come close, Young Grasshopper, and I will impart the most important thing I have learned in this business:

If you don't know all the answers, at least know where to look them up.

There are many places to learn the Tao of Self-Support. The manual that came with the machine is probably not the best-written or coherent piece of literature ever composed, but it may be good for a basic overview. Much better, however, are the scores of books written by people with a better sense of both pedagogy and English. When you get that brand new gleaming Mac, pick up a copy of *The Macintosh Bible*, *The Mac Demystified* or one of those easy-to-read books—with pictures. Get one with lots of pictures, because visual aides help tremendously when trying to poke your way around a computer. Windows users can find similar materials, like *Master Windows 98 Visually* and let's not forget the popular and ubiquitous series of "Computers for Dummies/Idiots/Morons/Republicans," tomes that can also be quite informative.

Computer magazines, available in most bookstores and newsstands, can also provide a respectable education, although that tends to be more like learning on the installment plan as opposed to getting a giant book of information all at once. Computer publications also tend to have ads for even more books to buy, as well as instructional videotapes and other learning materials for the novice user.

Those boring README files that come on the disks with new programs and hardware devices that you may buy are also good to look over before adding new things to your system. A README file can tell you late-breaking news about the product you are about to install, if it has any known conflicts with other programs that you might have, and also how to install it properly.

The Internet is also your friend, and a wide-ranging friend with plenty of connections at that. Both Apple Computer (*www.apple.com*) and Microsoft (*www.microsoft.com*) keep links to a vast database of technical information on their Web sites. And best of all, you can type in pertinent keywords and search for specific answers to your problem. The Web sites run by the companies from which you buy your software and hardware can also be invaluable. Almost every one of them has a tech support area with a Frequently Asked Questions section, and places to download things like new drivers, program patches, and software updates.

If you don't have the wherewithal quite yet to even get on the Internet, or prefer to do your learning from a person, do not be ashamed to take a class, ask a ten-year-old video-gamer, or join a local user group. Computers have become a solid part of the landscape and there's no escaping them, but this also means there are a lot more resources about them then there were fifteen years ago. It's also a good idea to know the phone number and address of your nearest authorized repair shop, just in case the problem is beyond your scope.

It's not easy at first, but the more you work with computers, the more sense they begin to make. And while time is money and few people want to spend the time to learn about the machines they use as part of their jobs, a good working knowledge of one's operating system and hardware devices can be an investment that pays off. Instead of having an apoplectic attack at the sight of that late-night blinking question mark, just grab up your Apple system software CD-ROM or copy of Norton Utilities (or a similar fix-it program), boot the Mac from the CD, run a diagnostic and repair program, and see if you can get your old friend healthy again.

Because—as all designers know—if you want something done right (and right NOW), you have to do it yourself.

The Information Building Boom

# Unfolding Identities

ANDREW BLAUVELT

F.Y.I.

I attended the 1995 AIGA National Conference and was quite surprised to feel something other than anxiety about technology pervade the crowd. All those years of reading and listening to designers condemn the computer, followed by their anxiety about learning to use it, had finally given way to something bordering on anticipation of the opportunities (a.k.a. profits) of digital media. Of course, there were skeptical neo-Luddites in attendance, as well as a few critically conscious and socially motivated naysayers, but the opportunities unleashed by this new technological genie far outweighed their pessimism. Now that the protocol-driven Web site has displaced the template-driven newsletter as the de rigueur choice of corporate communications these days, designers (and others) have a much more sunny outlook on the technological maelstrom. Accompanying this forecast is the increasing extension—some say disintegration—of the profession of graphic design from print to electronic media, and with it a proliferation of folks who practice design, even if they don't call it that.

Even Massimo Vignelli—guardian of design orthodoxy—recently and publicly declared that he is no longer a graphic designer, but rather an "information architect," and in the process was feeling "much more relaxed" than he had ever been. For Vignelli, the information architect ". . . means to organize information in a way that is essentially retrievable, understandable, visually captivating, emotionally involving, and easily identifiable" (Vignelli, 5). This change of professional identities for Vignelli is certainly more important than any change in his practice. On the side of information, he has claimed quite a roster of traditions—"history, typography, semiotics"—while leaving graphic designers in the unmentioned but residual role of persuasive stylists, who are "rooted in advertising, pictorial arts and trends." Vignelli, following Richard Saul Wurman, invokes the title of architect to further enhance the social standing afforded by such a claim: the undisputed status of a licensed profession with aspirations of planning, order, and control. In light of the social realities of most architectural practice today, Vignelli might have claimed the more appropriate title of "information developer." After all, there is no sphere of pure information or an untainted practice that is somehow beyond, or above, the messy realities and compromised complexities of contemporary life—whether graphic design or architecture.

While I find that the dichotomy Vignelli presents is problematic—a concern that I will address later—what seems worthy of consideration is the ease with which these "camps" are articulated. The field of information design does seem to exist as an entity within graphic design practice, with its own leading practitioners, publications, conferences, courses, and journals. This kind of autonomy is bolstered by the rhetoric of an "Information Age," and the ever-expanding communications networks (e.g., "information superhighway") that support the transfer of data among far-flung places and people. When cast in a particular light, the rationalist aspirations of information design stand in sharp contrast to most celebrated forms of contemporary graphic design, particularly the kind of design produced in the 1980s and 1990s, defined as it is by individual styles. This is the kind of juxtaposition that leads Vignelli to his conclusion. I would like to examine the two camps that Vignelli proposes, information architects and graphic designers, in order to illuminate an underlying philosophy I believe is at work for each type of practice.

For proponents of information architecture there is a clear emphasis on organizing information for perceptual retrieval. Following the tenets of information theory, the focus is on the reduction of "noise" in the communication "channel" by eliminating extraneous content, simplifying formal options, and narrowing possible interpretations. The general economy of this kind of thinking leads from the many to the few. Information architecture allies itself with a certain pragmatism and utility, striving to be "useful." Contrast this with a practice of graphic design that adopts a general economy of excess, leading from the few to the many: one solution produces a variety of interpretations. Following the tenets of literary theory, the tendency is additive, not reductive; whether enlarging the message by adding "something" personal to the arguments made for multiple readerly interpretations, or the visual vocabulary of collage, montage, and other layering techniques. Following the language games employed by post-structuralists (e.g., puns, linguistic inversions, double entendres, etc.), this form of graphic design embraces the concept of "play" as its philosophical economy. It seeks the unending plenitude found within the concept of "repetition-without-exhaustion," which is the basis of all game playing, even games of the most serious kind. In this way, information is not so much a commodity that can be consumed as much as a resource that can produce new information. All institutions and practices have a survival mechanism for self-perpetuation. Information architecture achieves this by the propensity of the world toward constant disorder (that it must reorder), while graphic design relies on the constant lack of interpretive closure in communication. Both circumstances ensure that new design problems are produced that require new solutions.

Both types of practice place great rhetorical importance on how design is received by audiences: information design speaks of users, while graphic design speaks of readers. Whether cast as "users" or "readers," both terms belie a need to construct models for audiences that reinforce their respective professional ideologies. Both are types of design practice and, therefore, place great emphasis on the process of encoding messages (i.e., determining message content, giving visual form, selecting modes of distribution, etc.). However, it is in the act of decoding (i.e., how audiences interpret, respond, and otherwise receive information) that we discover two different models for audience action. It might be stated rather crudely, but accurately, that information architecture employs a "deterministic" model for audience action, one that limits options and *determines* user response. On the other hand, graphic design adopts a "liberal-pluralist" conception of an audience by claiming varied interpretations on the part of readers/viewers. Such a conception is considered pluralist because it supports diverse possibilities, sometimes infinite, for interpretation, and is liberal in the sense that readers are accorded the freedom to choose their interpretive positions. Both models share the same overly determined approach to "designerly" encoding, albeit for different ends: one tries to limit response, the other tries to expand it. Despite differently perceived outcomes, both approaches are a function of the same control by designers to produce desired effects. Both camps share an equally mechanistic view of the communications process as a closed circuit of senders, messages, and receivers. Despite the fact that this transmission model has been displaced in communications theory for decades, it is still embraced by design (*both* graphic and information) because it unquestionably reproduces the unequal power positions of senders and receivers. Namely, it conserves power on behalf of senders, even when those senders seek to "give" power to otherwise "passive" receivers. What such a linear system neglects, is the complex social contexts in which communication routinely occurs, including how meaning is actively constructed, mediated, produced, and circulated—even how common meanings are not routinely arrived at; in short, the failure of communication.

Like Vignelli, I had been thinking of the schism in graphic design between so-called information design and the rest. But unlike Vignelli, I was interested in questioning, not reinforcing, such boundaries because, as I see it, the distance between such categories has already disappeared.

Hybridity and the Information Product

Information is in a way the opposite of garbage, although in our contemporary commercialized world they may at times appear identical. . . . As a rule, information is something to preserve, garbage is something to be destroyed. However, both can be looked on as a kind of waste product, a physical burden, and for contemporary society both are among the most pressing problems today. —Bill Viola

During the recent political conventions, both Republican and Democratic, the media concluded that such gatherings had become "scripted," "programmed," "infomercials," and consequently not newsworthy. How these conventions differ from other types of news that is broadcast quite happily everyday by the same networks, including political "photo-ops" and sporting events, even coverage of "spontaneous" events like terrorism, is confusing. The problem seems to be the role assumed by convention organizers, who felt compelled to program their events to fit the allotted hour time-slot, thereby appropriating the function of news producers, reporters, anchors, and editors, who normally orchestrate such events. It seems the conventions had crossed the thin line between loosely contained events *to be narrated* and prepackaged performances *to be seen*. They had moved from the information space of a televised *event* to the information space of a television *program*. Even the most spontaneous event of either convention—the resignation of a Clinton political advisor in the face of a sex scandal—was viewed suspiciously by some news media because of the timing of the story (the day before Clinton's acceptance speech) and the source of its announcement (the *Star* tabloid).

The separation between information and persuasion exists only in an analytical abstraction. When given form, or otherwise represented, information enters the realm of rhetorical persuasion. And information demands representation in order to be useful. Information, like every other commodity, is exchangeable, but not exhaustible. Therefore, information is regulated in the marketplace on the basis of abundance, and gains value by controlling its access and intelligibility. This problem of information abundance can be seen in the shift by analysts who used to define their jobs on the basis of providing more information to enhance decision-making, and who now defend their jobs by managing too much information (Melody, 266). When gauging the claims of a so-called Information Age, it is helpful to remember that every society has been an information society. It is the amount, intensity, and circulation of information that makes this age different from others. While the role of the contemporary information professional is to regulate access and interpret information (the historic function of such people, whether priests or intellectuals), designers—as purveyors of symbolic languages—are among the most likely people to give form to, and thereby enhance, information *products*.

Needless to say, the kind of information found in the public sector of yesteryear is not likely to be the kind of information product in the private sector of today. Information used to be seen as fulfilling particular needs, but information now exists to stimulate demand. This is how information is made productive (i.e., "useful") in today's economic marketplace. I'm concerned that Massimo's happiness may be short-lived as the realization dawns that his carefully constructed divisions between useful information graphics and useless cultural garbage infiltrate each other. Of course, this is already happening. The Ross Perot of 1992—charts, graphs, and pointer in hand—may have been the poster boy of this phenomenon, but the advent of things like info-mercials, docu-dramas, and edu-tainment had already captured the public imagination. The success of these hybrid products testifies to their ability to generate some sort of pleasure in the audience. The pleasurable components of these products are found in the lowly status accorded to the second term of each coupling, whether the escapist fantasy of the commercial, the narrative engagement of drama, or the delight of entertainment. In fact, it is this aspect of pleasure that is surely missing from most envisioned forms of information design—for both designers and audiences. We need to recover the idea that information design can be both enlightening and entertaining, illuminating and delightful, practical yet fanciful.

We can understand how information technologies are themselves hybridized forms by looking to Wim Wenders's film *Until the End of the World*. Wenders unites the cartoonish look and humor of a video-game interface with a powerful imaging and database-search program to identify the film's main character, Trevor McPhee. A similar interface is also used to track the film's characters as they traverse the globe by following the information trail of their financial transactions. Wenders uncovers and juxtaposes the ironic parallels between information and imaging technologies developed for military uses that mimic the graphic language and terminology of video games (and vice versa). What makes this collision of forms so appealing, and frankly more believable than the more futuristic visions of other sci-fi movies, is the way in which information forms have blended together. The video arcade has displaced the virtual office of desktops and windows as the interface metaphor of choice. Interestingly, Wenders uses an animated "Bounty Bear," whose head twirls and hands gesture during the waiting period of extensive database searching, turning "real time" downtime into momentary leisure time for its users, as a spinning head replaces the Macintosh clock. In his analysis of *USA Today*'s info-graphics, J. Abbott Miller discusses the hybrid nature of the everyman figures that populate the charts and graphs of the newspaper, a fusion of "Otto Neurath's severe 'information man' and the more approachable Elmer Fudd: they are info-toons for the infotainment age" (Lupton & Miller, 149). Both serious statistical figures and cartoon characters share a similar reduction: the simplicity of the pictograph as a figure reduced to its bare outline *and* the simplification of the cartoon as a character reduced to the exaggerated expressivity of caricature. What the picto-graph lacks—personality and specificity—the cartoon supplies, but I wonder if these two sides of visual reduction and expressive exaggeration are not, in fact, the same side of the coin? If so, what does this portend for a design of reduction versus a design of expression?

Mutant Identities for Mutable Media

This scene from Wenders's film is merely the technological updating of the traditional sur-veillance roles performed by information technologies. The policing function of the nineteenth-century photographic archive of criminals and the work of the sketch artist are "sped-up," but still perform the same function of picturing "true" identities. The high-tech apparatus of the Bounty Bear program runs counter to the latest trends for identification, that match not external or surface appearances, like people's faces and fingerprints, but the internal genetic markers of DNA. The question of identity parallels the shifts in information theory from its belief in the pres-ence of things as visible markers of what is true, to the understanding of pattern and probability as the basis for what is intelligible and likely. It is the code of internal genetic markers (a pat-tern) that is displacing eyewitness accounts (a presence) in verifying truth claims in today's legal system.

Contained within the idea of presence is a belief in the fixed, stable nature of information markers. Such markers are fully and visibly present, no different than the "immutable" ink marks you are now reading. In the binary world of presence and absence, it's either there or not there; things are this *or* that. However, within the dialectical world of pattern/randomness, things are much more fluid and are always in the process of becoming (changing); things can be both this *and* that. Recognizing patterns makes things intelligible. Pattern recognition depends upon conti-nuity and predictability, in essence, stability. But stable systems are susceptible to change, either purposefully imposed or through the effects of entropy. The introduction of new information into a system disrupts its existing pattern, thereby changing that system. It is randomness—a muta-tion—that interrupts the pattern. The mutation is an important event or defining moment when a system is undergoing change, because it marks the threshold from one state to another:

> Mutation is crucial because it names the bifurcation point at which the interplay between pattern
> and randomness causes the system to evolve in a new direction. Mutation implies both the repli-
> cation of pattern—the morphological standard against which it can be measured and understood
> as a mutation—and the interjection of randomness—the variations that mark it as a deviation so
> decisive it can no longer be assimilated into the same (Hayles, 78).

It is the indeterminate nature of the mutation—the point at which it is neither completely pattern nor entirely randomness—that the either/or logic of presence and absence cannot readily incorporate. Hybrid forms, such as info-mercials, edu-tainment, and so on, represent a kind of mutation as they mark the threshold or boundary point between two different systems. The notion of hybridity threatens the stability of any system built on a foundation of mutual exclusion. The hyphen used in a word such as "docu-drama" serves both to separate and join two different forms: not documentary, not drama but documentary *and* drama.

Michael Jackson's 1992 music video, *Black or White*, provides a complex site for understanding the interaction of digital technologies and mutable identities. The famous and influential morphing sequence in the midst of that video, where men and women of different color transform gender and race, provided Jackson with a potent image of a fluid, seamless, multicultural experience. Each individual's identity yields and succumbs to the next as transformations possible with morphing technology produce a continuous stream of difference. This fluidity is an extremely important factor in the handling of such disparate physical characteristics. Every transformation is comprised of several in-between, or hybrid, states. The introduction of motion preserves continuity and acts as a kind of glue to hold the heterogeneous fragments together. In his analysis of *Black or White*'s morphing technology, Greg Lynn compares it with Jackson's own bodily quest to be both "black *and* white, male *and* female," and concludes that Jackson's "physical morphing . . . is monstrous because smoothness eradicates the interval between . . . discriminant characteristics without homogenizing the mixture" (1993, 12). The bodily image of the indeterminate hybrid—much like Jackson's facial surgeries—exists devoid of distinct origins, fixed for observation, while the act of morphing strives for continuity and smoothness, thereby *easing* us into the idea of indeterminacy, while allowing for a certain kind of narrative logic to unfold before our eyes as we watch one thing become another. Flow is the narrative. The idea of a contaminated purity that hybridity exemplifies—the debasement of purer forms—is at the heart of pejorative reactions. Historically, hybrids were first created as crossbred plants or animals that exhibited traits or characteristics of both origins, but were sufficiently distinct to create a new entity. Barbara Stafford, writing about hybridization during the Enlightenment, taps into the historical roots of the unacceptable nature of the hybrid:

> The aesthetic claims of clarity and distinctiveness were more insistent as one mounted the evolutionary ladder. Elaborate theories abounded concerning the virtue of pure strains, the detection of good and bad combinations, and the presence of blazes or marks thought to denote inner constitution. All were predicated on the judgment that mixtures abstracted from normal procreation easily led to the monstrous (Stafford, 1991, 265).

The mutable nature of digital media, including, and especially, morphing technology, allows us to envision the seemingly impossible (social harmony), visualize the ineffable indeterminate (not-man/not-woman, not-black/not-white), and flirt with the thrill of fantasy and terror (to be the other). The mutable nature of information in digital form means that it is not only more profoundly open to change and alteration, but that it is expressible in many different ways and modes. This is, of course, the raison d'être of multimedia. The time-based, interactive, and sound possibilities found in multimedia dramatically extend the expressive range of choices for delivering information. This possibility of "manyness" contained within the digital oneness of binary code, is more than the battle between terminology (multimedia versus "unimedia"). It is the inherent multiplicity of digital media that must be considered. Part of this multiplicity is to be found in the recognition of the *information event* as something more than the place of information, and instead suggests a performance where information is both staged and experienced.

Unfolding Information / Unpacking Meaning

Since movement creates the event, the real is kinedramatic. The communications industry would have never gotten to where it is today had it not started out as an art of the motor capable of orchestrating the perpetual shift of appearances. —Paul Virilio

It's not just the space and place of information (its punctuation), but its *unfolding* and *becoming* in time (its mutation) that needs to be considered. The concept of punctuation (from the Latin, *punctum*, or point) as a space or placeholder, a shaper of meaning and emphasis, is ultimately tied to the idea of presence, fixity, and closure: an endpoint. But with motion and time as added properties, the idea of punctuation can be expanded from the static idea of endpoint, or space marker, and reconceptualized as a dynamic point of departure: a mutation, a fold in the surface of information, a spatiotemporal marker. The dominance of space as the constitutive fabric that regulates meaning in graphic design has to be radically augmented by the possibilities of time to regulate meaning. Therefore, it is necessary to speak not of static objects and mute figures, but of performative events. Peter Eisenman speaks of the same contemporary condition to which architecture must respond:

Architecture can no longer be bound by the static conditions of space and place, here and there. In a mediated world, there are no longer places in the sense that we once knew them. Architecture must now address the problem of the event. . . . This is a new type of environment, comprised of light, sound, movement, an event-structure in which architecture does not stand simply against media, but is consumed by it (Eisenman, 423–4).

Eisenman realizes that architecture cannot accomplish the dematerialization of physical space the same way that certain media can; however, because graphic design is a media form, it has the potential to address these problems directly. But before addressing these problems and opportunities, it is necessary to revisit some recent grappling with the spatial containment of information found in the very kind of contemporary graphic design that sent Vignelli packing in the first place.

Just as Robert Venturi was arguing for a semantic dimension to architecture in his 1966 book, *Complexity and Contradiction in Architecture*, where built form could express "meaning," graphic designers were (and still are) similarly interested in how form can express meaning. Rejecting the reductive or subtractive approach favored by Swiss modernism, corporations, and information design, and instead employing an additive process of numerous layers in designs that rely heavily upon a collage aesthetic, certain designers seek, in theory, to link different layers with different levels of meaning. This layering theory frequently strives for a hierarchy in the information usually resolved by dividing the space into foreground, middle ground, and background, and assigning various functions to these layers. The finished results favored a richly textured, dense fabric of images and text that signals a more complex, even contradictory, approach to presenting information. The tightly organized field of information found, for example, in many grid-based forms of communication, gave way to a "reader-syntaxed" page where the audience actively "constructs" meaning from the available fragments. The layering process can be considered more inclusive than exclusive, and in this way parallels what Venturi had described in *Complexity and Contradiction* as the concept of "both-and":

> If the source of the both-and phenomenon is contradiction, its basis is hierarchy, which yields several levels of meanings among elements of varying values. It can include elements that are both good and awkward, big and little, closed and open, continuous and articulated, round and square, structural and spatial. An architecture which includes varying levels of meaning breeds ambiguity and tension (Venturi, 23).

Venturi goes on to state the virtues of such an architecture, which we might consider in the context of such graphic design experiments:

> Most of the examples will be difficult to 'read,' but abstruse architecture is valid when it reflects the complexities and contradictions of content and meaning. Simultaneous perception of a multiplicity of levels involves struggles and hesitations for the observer, and makes his [*sic*] perception more vivid (Venturi, 25).

I would like to suggest a re-reading of Venturi's *Complexity and Contradiction in Architecture*. In the early validation of Venturi's concept of "both-and" used to explain or guide the use of layers in graphic design work, another concept he discusses was largely ignored: the *double-functioning element*. Venturi describes the distinction between "both-and" and the double-functioning element as follows:

> The "double-functioning" element and "both-and" are related, but there is a distinction: the double-functioning element pertains more to the particulars of use and structure, while both-and refers more to the relation of part to whole. Both-and emphasizes double *meanings* over double *functions* (Venturi, 34).

The double-functioning element in architecture performs two different tasks. For example, a series of columns in a room has the more obvious function of structural support, but could function to articulate the space of that room. Of course, it seems easier in architecture to differentiate between functions such as structural support or shelter, and communicative aspects such as "enter here" or "this is a gathering place." In graphic design it is difficult to separate function from communication. Whether by sheer novelty or some inherent property, digital media appears to foreground issues of use, function, and structure more readily than most genres of print media. Digital media demands attention to defining and assigning specific functions, as well as to planning user experiences and program structures. One could make a case that the overwhelming concerns in digital media are about function and structure, not meaning. It is necessary to join the possibilities of multiple functions with the desire for multiple meanings.

The two dominant modes of information organization in print media (information architecture and graphic design) run parallel to the previous discussions about the logic of "either-or" and "both-and." Explicit organization of information, say for example in a grid system, encourages *separation* of elements and specialization of functions, because spatial placement and articulation are thought to be essential for both perception and understanding. Explicit organizational schemes favor the exclusionary logic of "either-or." Implicit organization, for example in layers, discourages separation and encourages *integration* through the superimposition of elements and their simultaneous presentation, all of which tends to emphasize meanings over functions. Implicit organizational schemes favor the inclusive logic of "both-and." In contrast to both explicit and implicit forms of information display, the double- or even multiple-functioning element in digital media encourages *juxtaposition* that fosters the act of comparison, between this and that, in managing the complexity of information events. "This or that"—as distinct, even contradictory, moments—is possible in what we might call "switchable" or interactive elements that can express different functions *and* meanings through the time-based properties of digital media. In conventional print media, a designer must choose in advance what typefaces, what images, what texts are available to any potential reader, and these must be presented simultaneously on the surface, or perhaps successively in a series of pages. Digital media can organize the same elements and present them alternately and immediately. Meaning can be tagged to temporal occurrence rather than spatial placement or layer. This prioritizes issues of time over arrangements of space. Position is fixed not as much by space as by time. What is also unique in digital multimedia to graphic designers, but not to film or video makers, is the time- and sound-based possibilities of narrative construction from multiple perspectives. Formerly constrained to two dimensions, graphic designers now have ready access to the fourth dimension and the properties of the visual, the verbal, and the audio. What was previously relegated to layers of meaning and information, to text and image, can now be deployed in moving images and sounded text. In this scenario, it is *channels*, not layers, that are important. Curiously, very little has been done by graphic designers to utilize the possibilities of these various channels; rather, most graphic work for and about digital media, especially in print, still features layers.

Graphic designers must move away from thinking in solely simultaneous, static, and visual terms, and consider the multiplicitous, dynamic, audio-visual confluence that is the complex and contradictory nature of information. Digital multimedia has a potential to express the hybrid nature of information whether explicit or implicit, demonstrative or suggestive. Information can move from being displayed to being *performed*—and not just animated—but rendered as the complex phenomenon it represents.

In(ter)active Displays and Performative Play

The event, being itself impassive, allows the active and the passive to be interchanged more easily, since it is neither the one nor the other, but rather their common result. . . . —Gilles Deleuze

The performance of the information event demands its staging (display) and interaction. Active audience engagement is crucial, which means considering anew the assumptions of "passive viewers," "active readers," and "interactive users." The entire spectrum of viewers/readers/users needs revision, as these formerly distinct audience practices (or modes) are collapsed in the single medium of multimedia. The dynamics of the information event—who or what is active, passive, and interactive—could learn much from current research about cultural identities. Not only are identities much more hybrid and mutable—just like information—they are also understood to be both performed and narrated. This kinetic dimension is echoed in Paul Gilroy's comment that identity is a function of *becoming* more than one of *being* (Gilroy, 24). Or, as Edward Ball states:

A constructed ethnicity is a national, regional, sometimes racial identity produced in the presence of, and for, a spectator. This performative dimension within ethnicity is based on the presumption that culture is not written, as theorists of language might build their metaphor, but staged (1995, 144).

The staging of identity means that the dynamics of looking have been reconfigured, as the formerly static, passive object under observation becomes *a subject to be seen*. Craig Owens reminds us that ". . . to *pose* is, in fact, neither entirely active nor entirely passive . . ." and reflects a choice on part of the subject as "the subject poses as an object *in order to be a subject*" (Owens, 214–15). The "true" nature of information, preserved as it is in visual, two-dimensional form, can be disclosed and even disguised in masquerading performances of multidimensional perspectives. Such collusion between the deceptive and the apperceptive occurs in the complicitous dynamics of "passing," in which individuals trade on their ability to appear "true" while trespassing categories such as sex and race (Ginsberg, 1996). Passing "succeeds" through "misrecognition" and misinterpretation, in essence, through miscommunication.

Dustin Hoffman, cross-dressing in *Tootsie* (a precursor to the gender-bending themes in vogue during recent years), passes as Dorthy Michaels—a performance that allows the performer access to another world, another culture, and even another career. As a performance, passing is always subject to exposure—the danger that the impostor will be revealed. Although many people in *Tootsie* suspect something is "not quite right," they inevitably recognize and accept Dorthy as a woman until she is revealed or chooses to reveal her "real" identity. Dorthy exhibits the hybridity of being between cultures. Others perceive Dorthy as neither a man nor a woman; sometimes a man, sometimes a woman. Identity for Dorthy Michaels/Michael Dorsey is context-specific and time-dependent. Although the elaborate physical transformation of actor to actress is accomplished through makeup, wigs, and costumes, it also encompasses the verbal, gestural, and behavioral attributes of a caricatured gender. Each item in the ensemble functions to create the illusion as well as to break it. Gendered voice is used strategically by Dorthy as she chooses to reveal her "true" identity to her manager (Sydney Pollack); which is to say, Michael Dorsey chooses to drop his voice rather than his pants in order to "prove" himself.

The hybrid world of info-tainment is predominately read as entertainment passing for information. But what if information performs "in drag," masquerading as entertainment? Do we have what Edward Tufte calls "chartjunk" or, following *Learning from Las Vegas*, ugly "graphical ducks?" (1990, 33). Certainly Tufte favors the "self-effacing" or transparent reflection of information over the data distortions and visual excesses of "chartjunk":

> Chartjunk promoters imagine that numbers and details are boring, dull, and tedious, requiring ornament to enliven. Cosmetic decoration, which frequently distorts the data, will never salvage an underlying lack of content. If the numbers are boring, then you've got the wrong numbers. Credibility vanishes in clouds of chartjunk; who would trust a chart that looks like a video game? (1990, 34).

In his case against chartjunk, Tufte quotes Venturi, et al. from *Learning from Las Vegas* in order to support his thesis: "In promoting Space and Articulation over symbolism and ornament, they [Modern architects] distorted the whole building into a duck" (1990, 33). Venturi, et al. support the case for a symbolic, communicative architecture of interpretation, and thus read Modern architecture's buildings, designed as transparent expressions of their "content," as monolithic icons of "Space and Articulation"—symbolic "ducks" no different than the kitsch Long Island Duckling (a building shaped like a duck) that Tufte reproduces along with the quotation. Tufte could have only misused this quote to support his arguments because he does not see how his "self-effacing" diagrams—just like Modern architecture's "glass boxes"—are loaded with symbolic meanings. Tufte's functionalist aesthetics are thus exposed; who would trust a video game that looks like a chart?

Common ground may be found in the desire for a variety of positions through which a more complex understanding of information can be arrived at. The display of information is not a linear narrative and therefore allows for multiple pathways, and when complex enough, multiple positions from which to analyze the data. Each of these paths and positions performs a distinct function. The rich complexity of information is a direct product of the multiple *functions* that provide a variety of vantage points from which to experience the data event. This moves the idea of multiplicity away from the "liberal pluralist" declaration of infinitely diverse audience readings of one text (or display) and toward the kind of multiplicity found in the double-functioning element: a number of critical vantage points that serve to construct the complex, sometimes contradictory, nature of "true" information.

These acts of display extend beyond the reversal of the roles of observer and observed as they implicate the act of looking in a much larger web of actions, expectations, and functions. The implication of a complicit, and active, audience has been provocatively addressed by Néstor García Canclini, who argues: "insofar as [identity] is a narrative that we are incessantly reconstructing, and reconstructing together with others, identity is also *co-production*" (Canclini, 39). The passivity normally associated with viewing film, for example, can be quite engaging (and therefore active) not only because of content, but also because it is an "immersive" form (to borrow a term from virtual reality). Conversely, the activity most associated with interactive media comes not from choosing but from clicking. Consequently, our notions of what constitutes activity and passivity as (co-)participants in information display and spectacle need to be rethought with more attention paid to the complex dynamics that actually govern the processes of perceiving, interpreting, and experiencing information.

An Erotics of Information?

Design historian and critic Robin Kinross, in a letter to the editor, commented: "Meanwhile, dried-out information design—so far not considered in the pages of *Eye*—has to struggle on, the possibility of pleasure denied to it." Kinross's comment resonated with me, but not in the way he would have intended. Where *is* the pleasure of information design? Part of the problem, as I stated at the beginning of this essay, is the implausibility of information *with* pleasure. In fact, it is the dichotomy between the informative-as-serious and the entertaining-as-pleasurable that needs to be uncoupled. Ien Ang, a media scholar of television, notes how such an oppositional system between information and entertainment helps to shape and reinforce distinctions in the minds of viewing audiences:

> Of course, this doesn't mean that audience preferences are only directed toward programmes which fall into the category of "entertainment." Indeed, the institutional categorization of televisual discourse, which constructs an opposition between what is serious (= what really matters) and the popular (= easy pleasure), obscures the fact that, from the point of view of audiences, "information" can also be pleasurable. The problem is that in televisual discourse "informative" programmes, especially when they are about "serious" politics and culture, are too often constructed as the important—and thus unpleasurable—which viewers are supposed to watch because it is "good for them" (Ang, 31).

The revision of such a dichotomy is particularly important at this moment in the development of digital media networks and products, which are, each day, battlefields for various interest groups (corporations, schools, entertainment industries, the state, etc.), that would like to imprint their particular consumption patterns and information preferences on this "marketplace." Each of these constituencies brings to the new media a predisposition of how they formulate, regulate, and even negate aspects of pleasure in older media forms. These older forms— whether predominately televisual, filmic, aural, or print-based—must negotiate the specific contexts, limitations, and possibilities of digital media products, networks, and environments.

Another part of the problem is the association of pleasure with audience duplicity or "mass deception," rather than examining its capacity for engagement. In this line of thinking, media forms themselves are debased, particularly if they are predominately visual, such as television, film, video, and now digital multimedia. These media are characterized as the harbingers of depthless spectacles, leaving viewers mesmerized. However, viewer engagement in forms of spectacular display are characterized and categorized by Stephen Greenblatt as instances of "exhibitionary" *wonder* and *resonance*:

By *resonance* I mean the power of the displayed object to reach out beyond its formal boundaries to a larger world, to evoke in the viewer the complex, dynamic cultural forces from which it
has emerged and for which it may be taken by a viewer to stand. By *wonder* I mean the power of
the displayed object to stop the viewer in his or her tracks, to convey an arresting sense of
uniqueness, to evoke an exalted attention (Greenblatt, 42).

Greenblatt's reciprocal merger of a "wonderful resonance and resonant wonder" is but one
possibility for acknowledging the power of display to both arrest the viewer and engage him or
her in reflection, reflexivity and contemplation (Greenblatt, 54). Perhaps even Tufte can agree:

The best designs . . . are *intriguing and curiosity-provoking*, drawing the viewer into the wonder
of data, sometimes by narrative power, sometimes by immense detail, and sometimes by elegant
presentation of simple but interesting data (Tufte, 1983, 121).

Of course, with Tufte it's always the data that does the talking and has the last word.
Another revision might be what Barbara Stafford has noted as the historical use of spectacular
displays of "sensationalized knowledge" in the Enlightenment as a means for "informed looking" in her concept of an *artful science*, "lying somewhere between entertainment and information, pleasure and learning" (1994, xxiv). Stafford sees the spectacle as a pedagogical tool, an
instrument for knowledge, through what she terms the "performative gaze." It is also necessary
to acknowledge the power of special effects, as Scott Bukatman does in his analysis of the
"technological sublime" in science-fiction films, to induce awe as well as "balance sensory
pleasure and cognitive play" (Bukatman, 289).

Not only must the supposed duplicity of pleasure be countered, but the repertoire of
devices used in display needs to be recovered from its consignment to Hollywood mastery.
This means a critical, strategic use of rhetorical devices and special effects such as framing,
cropping, positioning, sequencing, montaging, morphing, slow motion, fast-forward, instant
replay, juxtaposition, superimposition, split frame, freeze-frame, voice-over, jump cut, and so on,
that need to be brought to bear on the problem of representation in kinetic and interactive environments. Ella Shohat and Robert Stam provocatively argue for what they call "pedagogic jujit-
su," using the tools and grammar of media against itself to reveal suppressed information, articulate alternative viewpoints, and engage spectators in a more active form of viewing they call
"spect-actorship" (Shohat & Stam, 1995). Similarly, we need to rethink notions of "interactivity,"
understood mainly as "options," and exchange it for positions; differing perspectives and
conflicting points-of-view.

The problems of visual display demand that attention be paid not only to the heterogeneous mixture, but also to the possibilities of unfolding meaning and unpacking content. This
means speaking less about layers and more about channels of information, not so much for a
fashionable eclecticism, but for an eclectic self-fashioning. It means using both the mechanics
of display and the pleasure of play to communicate information in mediated experiences. It
means fusing the exclusions of "or" with the inclusions of "and." It means looking at the fusion
of categories such as edu-tainment and info-mercials, as well as things like ficto-criticism, as

possibilities for engagement rather than signs of debasement. It means asking if there is an erotics of information display, a seduction in the art of performance.

B I B L I O G R A P H Y

Ang, Ien. *Living Room Wars: Rethinking Media Audiences for a Postmodern World* (London & New York: Routledge, 1996).

Ball, Edward, "Constructing Ethnicity." *Visual Display: Culture Beyond Appearances,* Lynne Cooke & Peter Wollen, eds. (Seattle: Bay Press, 1995).

Bukatman, Scott, "The Artificial Infinite: On Special Effects and the Sublime." *Visual Display: Culture Beyond Appearances,* Lynne Cooke & Peter Wollen, eds. (Seattle: Bay Press, 1995).

Canclini, Néstor García. "Rethinking Identity in Terms of Globalization." *A.D.* (*Art & Design*), 10:7/8 (July/August 1995).

Eisenman, Peter. "Unfolding Events." *Incorporations,* Jonathan Crary & Sanford Kwinter, eds. *Zone 6* (1992).

Gilroy, Paul. " '. . . To be real: The dissident forms of black expressive culture." *Let's Get It On: The Politics of Black Performance,* Catherine Ugwu, ed. (London: ICA & Seattle: Bay Press, 1995).

Ginsberg, Elaine K., ed. "The Politics of Passing." *Passing and the Fictions of Identity* (Durham, NC: Duke University Press, 1996).

Greenblatt, Stephen. "Resonance and Wonder." *Exhibiting Cultures: The Poetics and Politics of Museum Display,* Ivan Karp and Steven D. Lavine, eds. (Washington, D.C. & London: Smithsonian Institution Press, 1991).

Hayles, Katherine N. "Virtual Bodies and Flickering Signifiers." *October,* No. 66 (Fall 1993).

Lupton, Ellen and J. Abbott Miller. "McPaper." *Design Writing Research* (New York: Kiosk Books, 1996).

Lynn, Greg. "Architectural Curvilinearity: The Folded, the Pliant and the Supple," *A.D.* (*Architectural Design*), No. 102 (1993).

Melody, William. "Electronic Networks, Social Relations and the Changing Structure of Knowledge." *Communication Theory Today,* David Crowley & David Mitchell, eds. (Palo Alto, CA: Stanford University Press, 1994).

Owens, Craig. "Posing." *Beyond Recognition: Representation, Power, Culture.* (Berkeley, CA: University of California Press, 1992).

Shohat, Ella and Robert Stam. "The Politics of Multiculturalism in the Postmodern Age." *A.D.* (*Art & Design*), 10:7/8 (July/August, 1995).

Stafford, Barbara Maria. *Artful Science: Enlightenment Entertainment and the Eclipse of Visual Education* (Cambridge, MA & London: MIT Press, 1994).

Stafford, Barbara Maria. *Body Criticism: Imaging the Unseen in Enlightenment Art and Medicine* (Cambridge, MA & London: MIT Press, 1991).

Tufte, Edward T. *Envisioning Information* (Cheshire, CT: Graphics Press, 1990).

Tufte, Edward T. *The Visual Display of Quantitative Information* (Cheshire, CT: Graphics Press, 1983).

Vignelli, Massimo. "A Masterpiece," *AIGA Journal of Graphic Design.* 14:2 (1996).

Venturi, Robert. *Complexity and Contradiction in Architecture* (New York: Museum of Modern Art, 1966).

Venturi, Robert, Denise Scott Brown and Steven Izenour. *Learning from Las Vegas* (Cambridge, MA & London: MIT Press, 1977).

Portions of this essay were presented in lectures at Cranbrook Academy of Art and the Jan van Eyck Akademie.

Outside and Inside in Print and Online Publication Design

STEVEN HOSKINS

THE OUTSIDE OF a magazine, much like the exterior of a package, or of a building, and as I will argue, of a Web site, can be thought of as a shell that encompasses its contents. There are as many different classes of magazines as there are kinds of Web sites (and packages, and buildings). For all of these designed artifacts, this shell is both functional and conceptual in relation to that which it encompasses. This is more than the physical cover, and more than the conceptual shell communicated to the audience. It is a relationship between these to the information on the interior. This relationship between outside and inside exists in both print and online publication design. Some surprisingly similar methodologies—some of them intentional—can be observed in how print and online publications are created and ultimately understood. However, the relationship between the outside and inside from the designer's point of view of creation, and users' point of view of interpretation is undergoing a metamorphosis that may forever change its nature and value.

Visual communication design for the Internet presents a distinctly different set of variables that e-designers are still coming to terms with. We understand this to be an extension, or an evolution, of multimedia by affording a combination of time- and static-based media on a single platform. The World Wide Web adds a dynamic variable of networking—real-time connection to information. Internet applications that network and actively serve databases of information allow audiences a truly interactive communication, supplanting the broadcast of a finely tuned message with point-casting to individuals. This is, arguably, the new context for design. E-designers in this environment find themselves defining the medium as it itself continues to evolve.

This is frustrating news for those of us, particularly design educators, who would like some degree of quantification of these variables. However, because it is a new context for design, and because of this newness, there are several observations that might help us come to terms with it.

Whenever anything "new" becomes available for the transmission of information, the way that creators of technology formulate it, and consequently the way users will understand it, is in terms we already know. The original developers of the World Wide Web used the metaphors of publication design to structure our understanding of its functional use. Thus, we refer to a Web *page*. We divide the parts of the Web page HTML into its *head*, *title*, and *body*. We find linear book-like aspects such *as beginning to end*, moving *forwards* and *backwards*, retaining our place with *bookmarks*, as well as the concept of the cover or *front page*. These developers also understood the dynamic relationships that could exist between these pages, and attached spatial metaphors largely foreign to publication design: That a Web site is a *location*, an *address* that exists in a vitual*space*, where one can *navigate* through it. With these metaphors, exhibit designers, city planners, landscape and architectural designers can (and do) easily migrate. However, the persistence of developing the Web site based on a model of a printed publication has handed designers several ideas that are widely accepted, have an impact on the relationship between a Web site's outside and inside, and deserve scrutiny. One is the plan of publication design itself; the other is the function or purpose of the front page.

The Plan

For publication design, this has often meant developing a flexible framework for a publication that can contain changing, as well as unchanging, information. Typically expressed visually through the publication design grid, the hierarchy of type and the relationship between type, image, and color, this is a *plan* for multiple issues; its observable result is the issue itself.

The challenge in publication design is to create an interpretable sense of order, and in the special case of magazine design, to allow for change within this order. Thus, a magazine may be divided into editorial sections (feature stories, columns, and letters) in such a way as to give each issue the freedom to make it separate from all other issues, and yet impose certain structures, making them consistent *across* issues and *within* the issue. The objective of the plan is to insure that readers don't think they change magazines each time they turn a page, and, especially in popular culture magazines, allow them to experience a controlled degree of variety.

In publication design, the designer always considers this a linear experience. Although conscious that the possibility of reverse-order experience (back to front) and information shortcuts (via the table of contents or indexes) may undermine this linearity, designers still approach this in one direction: front to back.

No single designer has contributed more to how designers still approach magazine design than did Alexey Brodovich. His view of the whole of the magazine issue—that the narrative visualization of this linear process could be planned from above, and its pages spread out on the floor—is still a great model for planning magazine issues today. By organizing the entire issue simultaneously, and by designing it in a manner distinctly different from the way in which it was experienced, he showed subsequent designers how to "map" the magazine experientially, not by thinking about it, not by modeling it on a diagram, but by experiencing it.

One could criticize Brodovich for this methodology. We observe the inherent limitation for users not being able to *experience* the magazine as a whole in this way—going from one spread to any other—let alone being able cut up individual pages as he did and build a narrative from one page to any other. But we need to remember that part of any methodology is keeping functionality in mind. The publication designer cannot disconnect from functional limitations.

It is also important to underscore that this is a process of integration. The manner in which communication comes together—the way it is designed—is the reverse of how it is read or viewed. Designers use a whole view to select and organize parts in a particular way. The reader or viewer encounters the parts in this particular way to reconstruct that original whole view. This has significant implications for the functional and conceptual shell of the magazine, and of a Web site.

If we were to examine an issue of *HotWired*, an online publication, we could reasonably reverse engineer, via Brodovich's model, the entire issue from beginning to end, figuratively from front to back. *But how can I say that?* There is no spine; there is no back cover. There is a front page; there is a table of contents. But we can barely find any linearity aside from that built into the contents (from top to bottom, from left to right, from biggest to smallest on the hierarchy of its information).

If we were to lay these out on a virtual floor, we could no doubt accomplish a loose linearity based on the table of contents. But unlike Brodovich's whole view of a linear narrative, the reader *can* go from almost any section to any other. As is often the case for Web sites, the reason for going from one place to another will be less a matter of serendipity than of the actual relevance of going there. The whole view is still applicable, and valuable, but we need to reconsider the linearity implied by Brodovich's 2-D surface of the floor.

Website designers do this, but in a manner that flattens the multiple linear narratives into buckets of content. They are more likely to develop a strictly functional site map. At best, this will describe the interaction of going from one bucket to another: a largely undifferentiated visual description of how it works. The rich visual and verbal content we saw on Brodovich's overview isn't here.

One reason for this is dynamic content. Unlike online magazines where it is possible to orchestrate static content, most Web sites are not magazines, but set on top of databases from which the site draws information. This information must be organized along generalities of types of information (pictures, dates, facts, and discussion), since the content may be dynamically generated in any combination deemed relevant by the user.

This largely undifferentiated plan for "types of content" would have significant implications for the functional and conceptual shell of a magazine, as it does for a Web site. The plan for the Web site tends to become a plan for a plan.

The Cover

A magazine cover is the entrance to the magazine. Functionally, it is the outside sleeve of an issue and acts to define not only the issue inside, but also the concept of the magazine as a whole: a variation of the whole view. Language markers on the cover—the masthead, the images, the text, and their composition—contribute to the conceptual shell for the magazine's culture. This cover is typically the page that has the fewest visual elements performing the most connotative communication. The front page must do these things:

➟ Denote the identity of the magazine via the masthead, type, color, and composition
➟ Separate the issue as unique from all other issues of the same magazine, by denoting the contents

➼ Connote what the magazine is about, in an aggregate sense: a generalization about the reader who needs this information, the social culture that the reader identifies with, and how the editors fashion that information toward this end

The last item is obviously the most intangible requirement, but also the most important from the perspective of outside and inside, and we can observe the result in the substance and prose of copy, the choice and use of images. The denotative task of defining issue contents is cursory. Like packaging design, the cover must represent what is inside, not just specifically, but what it means to use the product.

One can look at this as a set of language "filters." The leveraging of existing language attributes of a social culture; the choice of images and typographic form, the manipulation and cropping of images and type, and the organization and color on the page in the service of establishing relevance to the audience. Of course, more happens as the choice of words and images relate to what is found on the inside—to the plan—but without this first filter operating correctly, there is little purpose in going further.

The front cover of a Web site, the (choose your term) home page, main page, splash page, is a traditional publication feature that Web sites continue to find useful. But to what ends? Given the dynamic information environment of the Web, its function as a conceptual shell is changing. It is less like the orchestrated entrance to the content and more like a highway marker denoting a city limit.

The conceptual entrance on the Web is less stable than in its print counterpart. The actual entrance to the interior may not be from the front page at all, but from an external hyperlink to the page of relevance, or from one of the internal sections to another, bypassing the front page altogether. This means that the conceptual attributes of the outside have no choice but to migrate inside to header graphics: a pseudo outside—as if the outside and inside are presented simultaneously. Perhaps more significantly, the table of contents has taken on both denotative and connotative tasks, often at the expense of both. In fact, the table of contents *is becoming* the front page.

The Dilemma

The designer's development of, and the users' experience of the Web site is more fragmented than its print counterpart: The sense of the whole (the outside) is less stable. For the print version of a publication, the reader encounters the whole conceptually via the cover. On its inside, this conceptual entrance characterizes every story, every image, each piece of type, and the text. On a Web site, the whole is more likely to be built from the encounter of the individual parts. The designers of an undifferentiated plan do not account for this experience for the interaction. The outside, in fact, is an unknown quality in Web site design.

It is ironic that the best pathway to developing a Web site, of being above and outside of it, to plan and coordinate the dynamic narrative pathways within it, is now entirely out of line with the experience of using that Web site. The challenge for designers is to decide if the outside and inside is a viable perspective in Internet design. If it is not, what is?

The Baseball Projects: A Step-by-step Approach to Introducing Information Architecture

HUGH DUBBERLY

OVER THE LAST five years, the rapid growth in the number and complexity of Internet Web sites has created a demand for designers with skills and experience in Web site design and Web application design. The increased demand has bid up designers' salaries. The public spotlight on the Internet, and the job opportunities it presents, has increased demand from students for classes that will prepare them for the Web-design market.

Often, students believe that they need skills in using specific software applications, such as Photoshop and Flash, or familiarity with mark-up or programming languages, such as HTML or Java. Design faculty generally recognize the limited value of specific application skills. Applications are likely to change as the technology surrounding them changes. What's more, application skills have little to do with actually designing Web sites—or anything else.

Faculty, then, face a problem: how to satisfy demand for courses that will prepare students for the Web design market, while also preparing students for a world that will change greatly over the next five years—and even more over the forty or fifty years a graduating student might expect to practice.

A strong thread in design education has been the real-world-project approach to teaching, for example, the exercise that has students design a music CD cover. This approach can be popular with students, and even with employers, because it builds a portfolio.

Applying the real-world-project approach to teaching interaction design is tempting. Why not ask students to design a music Web site, for example? Teaching with real-world projects carries risks. The outcome or product can overshadow the process. Time spent working on the product can crowd out time spent understanding principles. Applying the real-world-project approach to Web-site design can carry practical risks as well. Web sites are complicated and students have relatively little experience with them, compared to books or television. Introducing students to information architecture or interaction design by asking them to design a commercial Web site, is like teaching people to swim by pushing them out of a boat in the middle of a lake. The students may learn, but the process can't reasonably be called teaching.

One way to approach the problem is to ask how it can be broken into smaller, more digestible pieces. I visualize the problem as a large step function. The x-axis represents time. The y-axis represents skill level. A lot of time passes before the first skill level is obtained. Scott Kim, who introduced me to this model, uses it to describe the process of learning a difficult and (initially) unrewarding game. Juggling might be an example. Scott contrasts that kind of game with what he thinks of as a good (or well designed) video game that is easy for users to begin playing and then offers a succession of more challenging levels. The user receives positive feedback for mastering one level by being allowed to move to the next. Mastery of the next level is always close at hand. A second example can be envisioned, a series of small steps building a set of stairs forming an easy path to the top; it contrasts with the large step function of the first diagram, which illustrates more of a barrier than a path.

How Can We Apply the Multiple Small-Step Approach to Teaching Information Architecture?

The rest of this paper describes a step-by-step approach to introducing information architecture. It is an outline for an introductory course on the subject. The course is heavily focused on various aspects of information design and touches on issues of interaction design. It describes a series of related exercises that build on one another over a semester. My hope is that other instructors will find the approach useful, and will borrow and build on the sequence of assignments.

I have designed the course for college-level seniors (or first-year masters-level students) in graphic design programs. The course assumes students have had introductory and intermediate 2-D design and typography courses, and that they have some familiarity with design systems and the design processes—though the course offers ample opportunity to elaborate on those subjects. No specific computer skills are prerequisites. In theory, students can successfully complete all the assignments using conventional tools such as pencil and paper. In practice, I find an increasing number of students, even those in high school, have taught themselves the rudiments of using Photoshop and Illustrator. These skills can be helpful in the class—not for improving the quality of design, per se, but for increasing the number of options considered, and speeding the process of creating a high level of finish.

In organizing the course, my strategy was to put off consideration of the computer (and interaction) until the last section, and to focus on understanding a body of content. That process involves:

➤ Gathering data
➤ Structuring and representing the data in multiple ways
➤ Synthesizing the data, structures, and representations

Through this process students come to own the content and create for themselves a set of content assets (texts, photos, illustrations, and diagrams). They learn to look at the content from different points of view, and begin to understand how methods of structuring and representing information affect content and influence perception.

Now, we come to the problem of what content to use in the course. I use baseball and how to play it. More specifically, I ask students to describe how to play baseball to an adult speaker of English (someone over twelve) who is unfamiliar with the game.

Why baseball?

- It's a system—it consists of elements and their relationships
- It's discreet—we can define (or agree on) its boundaries
- It's complex—we can't hold the entire system in mind at once
- It's finite, even relatively small—approximately sixty terms suffice for a description
- It's a fun subject—rather than a serious, technical subject
- Students have different levels of domain expertise
- Most students have easy access to qualified reviewers
- Information about the subject is easily and widely available

I worry that some people might see the subject as having inappropriate gender, cultural, or other biases. In the classes I have taught, I find students who have never played or even seen the game alongside avid fans and players. I have students from the United States as well as other countries. The students with knowledge of the game help those unfamiliar with it. Students new to the game have an important asset: a beginner's mind. These students are more easily able to put themselves in the shoes of the intended audience. In fact, they begin as the intended audience; they sometimes have an advantage because they can see what's really important, while an avid fan may get lost in the details.

Course Structure

Before launching into specific assignments, it's a good idea for you to set students' expectations and describe the entire course—the goals, the general sequence of assignments, your method of grading, and your expectations.

1 | **SECTION 1: GATHER DATA** The first section of the course focuses on gathering data in order to understand the subject. Do that by asking students to participate in an actual game, read the official rules, read other explanations, and summarize a specific game.

- 1.1 | PLAY A GAME The best way to begin the project is to go out and play a short, informal game. This exposes everyone to the basic elements, and lets each student experience first-hand the flow or process of play.

    You'll need a bat and ball; a plastic whiffle-ball set is fine. You can improvise the bases. Divide the class into two teams. If there are more than nine people on a team, or less, that's okay. It's just a game. Ask one of the students to briefly explain pitching, hitting, fielding, outs, and scoring. Play a couple of innings. If space or weather interfere, play inside. The field can be quite small; you can ask base runners to *walk* instead of *run*.

    Alternatively, you might begin by asking the students to watch a game. The drawback to watching is that some students may not understand what they're seeing, or may not pay attention, or may simply not watch. If you begin with watching a game, you may want to ask the students to record what happens. (See section 1.3 below for details.)

➤ 1.2 | READ THE RULES Provide a copy of the rules of baseball. Or send the students out to find the rules. A version is available on the Web at
www.majorleaguebaseball.com/u/baseball/mlbcom/headquarters/rulesfront.htm
   Make sure they do the reading. For undergraduates, a test might provide the needed incentive. Suggest that they also find and read books that introduce and explain the game. Ask them to bring the books to class to discuss what's good and bad about the content and design.

➤ 1.3 | RECORD A REAL GAME Ask the students to record a real baseball game—using more than just video. Ask for an easily readable summary, such as a sequence of key frames grabbed from video or shot with a camera, or a text transcript, or a completed scorecard. Scorecards are available at large sporting-goods stores and on the Web. A great, short introduction to scorecards and their use is available on the Web at
www.baseballscorecard.com/
   The scorecard provides a way to introduce the general idea of scoring—notation for recording all sorts of things. Scoring is an important branch of information design.

2 | SECTION 2: STRUCTURE AND REPRESENT THE DATA IN MULTIPLE WAYS The second section of the course focuses on analyzing the data and internalizing it—on really understanding it. We do that by organizing the data into different structures and re-presenting it.

➤ 2.1 | LIST RELATED TERMS The real work begins with the class as a group, listing terms related to baseball. The instructor acts as a facilitator for this brainstorming session, writing down all the terms suggested by the students (none are "wrong"). I like to write the terms on sticky notes (Post-Its) so that we can rearrange them later. The facilitator has three main tasks: (1) Involve all the students, making sure no one dominates, (2) Remind the group of the focus on how to play the game, and (3) Ask questions to elicit more terms should the group get stuck.

   The goal is to come up with fifty to seventy-five terms. This takes only ten or fifteen minutes.
   The next task is for the class to edit the list, deleting terms not relevant to the explanation of how to play the game, for example, names of players or specific teams. Then, discuss which terms are related and how they might be grouped; point out that there are several possible groupings, and that a term may be used in more than one group. Finally, discuss how the terms might be ranked—the most important concepts to the least important.

➥ 2.2 | WRITE AN ESSAY Assign each student the task of writing an essay describing how to play the game of baseball. Divide the exercise into a series of steps: (1) List terms to include, (2) Define each term, (3) Rank the terms, (4) Write an outline, (5) Write a first draft, (6) Edit the draft to create a final draft, and (7) Format the text using the tools of typography to make it clearer.

Ask the students to begin with the terms from the previous exercise and determine which ones need to be included in the essay. Suggest that they write definitions of all the terms before organizing them. Having defined the terms, the students should then decide on a ranking for each term: major, minor, or detail. The ranking leads to an outline. Review the outlines for completeness and structure. Ask for a first draft. Read the first drafts and mark them up. Ask for a final version.

Logically, the essay belongs in the third section of the course, the section on synthesis. The reason for beginning the second section with the essay is that students already have some writing skills, and can focus on the content rather than on new techniques. The essay also establishes a foundation for further work by making sure all students demonstrate a basic understanding of the subject. The outline of the essay may also serve as a basis for the concept map. Of course, the converse is also true: the concept map and the process flow diagrams might well serve as bases for the essay.

Unfortunately, my experience is that many design students are poor writers. Reviewing and copyediting outlines and drafts can be a substantial amount of work for the instructor. I am interested in experimenting with small group development of outlines, and with peer review of both the outlines and the essays.

➥ 2.3 | CREATE A CONCEPT MAP Ask the students to create a concept map of the game of baseball.

A concept map is a picture of our understanding of something. It is a diagram illustrating how a set of concepts is related. Concept maps are made up of webs of terms (nodes) related by verbs (links) to other terms (nodes). The purpose of a concept map is to represent (on a single visual plane) a person's mental model of a concept. See *Learning How to Learn*, by D. B. Gowin and Joseph D. Novak, for a more detailed description of concept mapping. It's available on the Web at *www.amazon.com/exec/obidos/ASIN/0521319269*

Concept maps provide a useful contrast with essays. With a concept map, a viewer can see both the forest and the individual trees. The big picture is clear because all the ideas are presented on one surface. At the same time, it's easy to see details and how they relate.

Examples and a good description such as Gowan and Novak's are essential for learning concept mapping. Students may benefit from an exercise in which they quickly (perhaps in class) make a simple concept map (with eight to twelve terms). See *Designing Business*, by Clement Mok, and AIGA's journal, *Gain*, volume 1, issue 1, for examples of complex concept maps [a model of the Internet, a model of search, model of experience, and a model of brand].

Begin the baseball concept map by going back to the list of terms and their definitions. A useful exercise is to create a matrix listing all the terms down one side and repeating the list across the top. In the boxes where a row and column intersect, write the relationship between the terms. The resulting matrix of relationships provides a checklist for building the concept map.

Review the ranking of the terms. Review the outline of the essay. Consider the main branches from the primary term (baseball). One approach is to ground the primary term within a sentence that also contains the other two or three most important terms. A first sentence might set context; a second sentence might define the main term branching out at ninety degrees from the first sentence.

Figuring out the structure of a concept map is a significant amount of work, but not necessarily the end of the task. A second phase is giving the map an appropriate typographic form—to make the typographic hierarchy support the structure of the content.

Divide the exercise into a series of steps: (1) List terms, (2) Edit the list, (3) Define the remaining terms, (4) Create a matrix showing the relations of terms, (5) Rank the terms, (6) Decide on main branches or write framing sentences, (7) Fill in the rest of the structure, (8) Use color and the tools of typography to clarify and make the content more accessible, and (9) Create a final version.

Format: 22" × 34", full color (11" × 17" is generally not large enough for a readable map of 50 terms).

The concept-map assignment works well for individual students (its origin is as an assessment tool for individuals). I have also found that it works well as a team project for groups of two to five. Groups are able to create richer maps in a given time period than are individuals. The experience of developing shared understanding through the process of co-creating a concept map is valuable in and of itself. And it can also be quite valuable in the "real-world" development of Web applications. The assignment may also make an interesting and useful team-building exercise. As a practical matter, critiquing and grading five or six maps is easier, and allows more detailed feedback than is possible for twenty or thirty.

If undergraduate students work on the project in teams, they will probably benefit from a discussion of team dynamics before they begin. Encourage them to discuss roles, disclose their availability, and map the process they plan to follow. They also need to know how you will grade team projects. Asking the students to evaluate each team member is a way to understand who contributed and who shirked.

➤➤ 2.4 | CREATE A PROCESS FLOW DIAGRAM Concept maps are good for defining a set of terms—for defining rules. Essentially they are descriptive. But understanding involves both description and prescription. Rules gain meaning when applied to an activity. One way to represent activities is with process flow diagrams (sadly, a technique not only ignored, but actively eschewed by Gowin and Novak).

More advanced students may come across the problem of describing the process of playing baseball in their concept maps. Sometimes they will present concept maps with partial process flows embedded. Such mixed diagrams are great points of departure for the process flow assignment and should be discussed with the entire class.

Ask the students to create a diagram mapping the process of playing baseball. When the diagram is complete, it should be possible to trace the sequence of steps in any play, in any game on the diagram. Most of the game lends itself easily to a decision tree. The simultaneous action of fielding and baserunning is more difficult to map.

Students may be unfamiliar with process flow diagrams. Show them examples. Explain the basic building blocks of events and decision points—a question (often represented as a diamond) to which the answer must be yes or no. Describe feedback loops. A good introductory exercise is to ask students to make a process flow diagram describing the operation of a simple system such as a thermostat and heater.

In creating their diagrams, ask the students to consider: (1) The divisions of time within the game, (2) Nested and repeated sequences, (3) Counting—how the system/diagram tracks the state of the game, and (4) Decision points.

Divide the exercise into a series of steps: (1) List operators (players) and their roles, (2) Define things to be counted, (3) Define boundary conditions (beginning and ending), (4) Begin with a walk through sketching each step, (5) Fill in the rest of the structure, (6) Reorganize to create a coherent overall structure, (7) Use color and the tools of typography to clarify and make the content more accessible, and (8) Create a final version.

Format: 22" × 34", full color (11" × 17" is generally not large enough).

Students with experience in programming should be challenged to apply it. Tracking state involves creating variables; repeated sequences and nesting is similar to creating and calling functions. Students with no programming experience can complete the assignment, though less mature or less analytical undergraduates may find it difficult. Like the concept maps, process flow diagrams lend themselves well to development by team.

3 | SECTION 3: SYNTHESIZE THE DATA, STRUCTURES, AND REPRESENTATIONS The third section of the course focuses on synthesis. Having worked with the information in a number of forms, students are now prepared to produce more finished work—work directed toward end users. I must acknowledge (and you should point out to the students) that the concept map and process flow diagram are tools to help the design team think about the subject; they may prove poorly suited to explaining how to play the game to a naïve audience (though they're quite useful for discussions with experienced audiences). The assignments in this third section (as with the essay) focus on communicating with our original audience of adults unfamiliar with the game.

➤ 3.1 | CREATE A POSTER (DIAGRAMMATIC FORM) Ask the students to focus on explaining how to play baseball using primarily visual means. Use diagrams, illustrations, and photographs. Organize the information on a single surface to create a "poster." Use a minimum of text. Suggest that the students review their concept maps and process flow diagrams and think of them as points of departure for the poster, as check lists for concepts to include, and as direct sources of content.

I call this project a "poster" in order to emphasize the importance of a strong organizing principle for the content, the need for a strong visual hierarchy, and to set an expectation for a high level of finish in the final result.

Divide the exercise into a series of steps: (1) Sketch at least five alternative main concepts or organizing principles, 8.5" × 11", (2) Sketch at least five alternative organizational structures for the selected concept, (3) Create a full-size pencil rough showing all information for the selected structure, (4) Create a tight comp showing all information, probably in "Illustrator" format, and (5) Create a final poster.

Format: 22" × 34" (so that 11" × 17" printers can be used for comps). Final poster in full color.

Often students ask whether they must create their own illustration and photography, or whether they can find and appropriate other people's work. The main focus of this assignment should be diagrams—which the students should create themselves. Allowing appropriation of photos and illustrations for use in details or examples (with appropriate attribution) saves time, and focuses students on the structure of the information. Requiring students to create their own illustration and photography may mean that more time must be allotted to the project.

I first saw examples of work from the baseball diagram project (3.1) in the portfolios of students from Krystof Lenk's classes at Rhode Island School of Design (RISD). A few examples are printed in *Graphis* magazine, number 238, July/August 1985, page 50. I am indebted to Krystof for the original idea, which I've borrowed to form the basis for this sequence of assignments. Krystof is a partner in the design firm Dynamic Diagrams in Providence, Rhode Island.

⇥ 3.2 | CREATE A BOOKLET (NARRATIVE FORM) Ask the students to explain how to play baseball using a combination of visual and verbal means. Ask them to build on the assets of the essay and poster to produce a sequence of double-page spreads bound in a booklet. They should also consider the organizing principle for the booklet—the idea that ties the spreads together. And, as always, they should consider visual hierarchy and quality of finish.

An interesting variation on the assignment is to require the students to layer in a description of a real game—individual plays, a summary, or the whole game. Weaving the story of a particular game together with a description of how to play provides an extra challenge and may yield a richer result. By the way, the use of examples from a real game can make parts of the poster clearer, or even serve as an organizing principle in the poster.

Divide the problem up into a series of steps: (1) Text description and thumbnail sketches of two options for organizing principles, (2) Outline describing the main topic of each spread and the main image, (3) Pencil sketches of each spread (show headlines and indicate placement of text and images), (4) At least two options for grid structures, (5) Tight comp showing all information, probably in Illustrator or Quark format, and (6) Final booklet.

Format: At least ten pages (five spreads) plus cover; each page 8" × 8" (so that 11" × 17" printers can be used); bound (accordion fold or codex form).

➤ 3.3 | CREATE AN INTERACTIVE SYSTEM At last we come to the interactive version of the content. Students now understand the content, have seen it organized in several structures, and have seen those structures represented in many forms. They've also developed a set of content assets. The earlier assignments form a strong foundation for moving to the interactive world. By taking these early steps first, the last step is much smaller. And students are able to focus on what an interactive system can provide that might not be available in other media—rather than on understanding the subject and creating content.

Ask the students to create an interactive (computer-based) system to explain how to play baseball. Challenge them to consider what an interactive medium allows that was not possible within the constraints of the earlier assignments.

With the interactive project, it's important to introduce students to the idea of usability testing. Of course, user feedback can improve the poster and the booklet as well. Encourage or even require students to show their work to users and present a summary of feedback to the class. Explain the process of usability testing with rough paper prototypes—how the team can simulate the operation of a working system. One member of the design team acts as facilitator, one as note-taker, and one plays the software system responding to the user's decisions by presenting the appropriate parts of the prototype.

Divide the exercise into a series of steps: (1) Paper prototype (low fidelity, rough), (2) Usability test, (3) Rough screen flow diagram, (4) Detailed screen flow diagram, (5) Functional prototype (low fidelity, scanned sketches), (6) Usability test, (7) Graphics design of templates, and (8) Final graphics in a working system.

An interesting variation on the assignment is to require the students to layer in animation, a simulation, or even a game for users to play. Weaving together the game and the description of how to play baseball will yield a richer result.

The project is a great deal of work for one student. Students working alone are not likely to generate such rich results. The project is better suited for teams.

Students can design the interactive system entirely on paper. This option is especially attractive if access to computers is limited, for the classroom or for students, but it's not a bad idea even if computers are available. However, students are usually quite eager to work on the computer. Hypercard, Director, and HTML are all good development environments and require little learning from students. John Maeda's programming language, DBN, described in his book *Design by the Numbers*, is also a potential development environment—though the learning curve might be somewhat steeper.

Schedule

The amount of time needed for each exercise can vary depending on the experience of the students, other demands on their time, and the level of finish the instructor accepts. Below I've offered estimates for senior-level graphic design students:

SECTION 1: GATHER DATA

- 1 class   1.1 | Play a game
- 1 class   1.2 | Read the rules
- 1 week   1.3 | Record a real game

SECTION 2: STRUCTURE AND REPRESENT THE DATA IN MULTIPLE WAYS

- 1 class   2.1 | List related terms
- 1 week   2.2 | Write an essay
- 2 weeks   2.3 | Create a concept map
- 2 weeks   2.4 | Create a process flow diagram

SECTION 3: SYNTHESIZE THE DATA, STRUCTURES, AND REPRESENTATIONS

- 3 weeks   3.1 | Create a poster (diagrammatic form)
- 3 weeks   3.2 | Create a booklet (narrative form)
- 3 weeks   3.3 | Create an interactive system

The total is about fifteen weeks.

The complete sequence of projects is probably too much work for a fifteen-week semester—but should fit easily in an eighteen-week semester. The interactive system project, especially, could benefit from more time. On the other hand, you can tailor the course in a number of ways: You might give less emphasis to the second section, asking for less finished results, or leave out the process flow diagram altogether. Another option is to cut the booklet project; while it has value, you may wish to emphasize the second section more, or dedicate more time to the interactive system project.

Conclusion

I have outlined a semester-long introduction to information architecture for senior-level (or graduate-level) graphic design students. My focus has been on creating a sequence of steps through which students can build an understanding of a body of content in preparation for designing an interactive system. The course touches on a whole range of information design problems, but I have not organized it as an introduction to information design. That is to say, the course is about the structure (architecture) of information, rather than about methods of diagramming. It assumes some familiarity with information design methods, and it also assumes 2-D design and typography skills. The course also touches on aspects of interaction design (or user experience design), but that is not its focus.

I have taught the exercises outlined above at Art Center College of Design in Pasadena, San Jose State University in California, and the Institute of Design, IIT, in Chicago. I am indebted to those schools for the opportunity to teach, and to their students for teaching me. I'm very grateful for what I've learned from them.

I hope other teachers will find the course useful and begin to adopt (and adapt) it. I welcome comments, suggestions, and examples of student work on the projects.

Designing Experiences

Making the Invisible Visible

HILLMAN CURTIS

SO I'M SITTING in this conference room. It's one of those rooms you find in modern glass buildings . . . way down in the guts, through the mazes of cubicles, all pumped air and fluorescent lights. And I'm surrounded by the enemy: Two soulless corporate execs and the creative services team that does their bidding. I've just presented my comps for a Flash motion graphic advertisement, and I'm sitting back sipping hazelnut flavored coffee, thinking to myself, "Why do they try to flavor coffee? It's already got a flavor." Just then, one of the execs leans forward to speak. It's kind of strange how much power a slight lean can have in the hands of the right person. The room quickly falls quiet and all eyes turn . . . except mine. I'm looking at the pastry tray at the center of the table.

"What are we trying to communicate here?" the exec asks. Silence. "Hillman, I love the look of these designs, but I don't know if they support our message." More silence.

I was eventually able to speak up, and with help from the members of the creative team, make it through the meeting. Later, back at my office, which at the time was a rented desk in someone else's office, I thought about what had happened. I realized that I had made two key mistakes. I had not presented a design based on a strong theme or concept, and I had identified my clients as the "enemy" to creativity, and not as allies in the work of clear, cogent communication. Not wanting to repeat these mistakes anytime soon, I came up with a systematic list of solutions to those problems, and this list became the basis for the process I use to this day to conceptualize, design, and implement new media.

I call this process, "Making the Invisible Visible," which means that there should always be a theme that will power your project. The difficulty inherent in such a concept is that central themes are rarely obvious. In fact, they are usually invisible at first. Once identified though, the theme will define every design decision you make for the course of the project. And the process isn't only about identifying the theme; it's also about developing a strong concept to support that theme, and about following three simple steps to ensure that the theme is maintained throughout the project.

Targeting the Theme

All of our design projects start with identification of theme. Whether it's a ten-second Flash ad, a full site design, or a broadcast commercial, there's usually just one word that can be used to define the project's purpose. Think of it this way: You design to communicate and at the core of that communication is an emotional center. You want the viewer of your work to feel something, as well as absorb whatever marketing messages are presented in the work. And that emotional epicenter is the theme. Our job as designers, I think, is to identify the theme, build a concept around it, and do everything in our power to support it . . . both before and during the design and production phases. The process begins with a target.

It's very simple. When we meet with the client, we draw a three ring target on a piece of paper, and as we discuss the requirements of the job—the client's desires, and the project's purpose—we listen for words that could be potential candidates for the theme—words that are repeated, or emphasized throughout the conversation.

At the end of the meeting, we usually have five to ten words. At this point, we decide which of those words deserves placement at the center of the target, our core theme, and which two or three belong in the second and third tiers.

Once we have identified the theme, we examine how we can support it. For example, if the theme turns out to be "community," as it was in a recent project, you would avoid the use of black or white as base background colors. Instead, you would choose warm tones that are more welcoming. You also wouldn't choose motion that was frenetic or chaotic, but alternatively, would utilize soothing, smooth motion. In addition, elements might draw toward one another on the screen, or build upon one another. Every element ought to convey "community" . . . a place where you feel welcome, a place where people come together. The rule we live by in my design shop is that theme defines style. In fact, we often tape our theme targets on the wall next to our monitors before we begin designing. That way when experiencing uncertainty about a design decision, you can glance over to your target, using it like a map to keep you on course. It's a very basic concept, but having a tool, in this case the three-ring target, really makes the difference.

Concept

After we've targeted the theme, we concentrate on building a concept around it. For example, we recently designed a Flash spot for 3com. The company was releasing a new product called "3Com HomeConnect," which is a DSL service aimed at the home Internet user. The product offered high speed Internet connectivity in a package that was simple enough for any member of the family to use. Although we met with the client only once—and then only for about an hour—by using the target we were able to identify the theme of the spot very quickly. In the center of the target was the word "fast," and in the second and third rings were the words "simple" and "family," respectively. Using this target we were able to build a concept for the spot. The spot would revolve around three prototypical family members: the novice Internet user, the casual Internet user, and the "work from home" user. We would show these three demographic types in various poses. At the same time, we would display core messaging around them. We wanted the audience of this spot to "see themselves" in the ad and to react to the messaging. We chose a simple white background on which to place our three "types," and animated four one-word messages, supplied by the client. These words—freedom, vision, possibilities, and connections—then zoomed in from very large and in the foreground, to small and fading out of the background. We concepted a spot that was in itself very "simple" and "fast." It lasted less than twelve seconds from start to finish, and every animation was fast, with the zoom-ins communicating "fast download." The messaging supplied by the client was, it's fair to say, basic market-speak, but by developing a solid concept, we were able to create a spot that used motion and layout to transcend that uninspired corporate talk. What I always tell my designers is that with a strong concept you can lead the client, and with a weak one, the client leads you.

Eat the Audience

My mother-in-law teaches English as a second language. As part of the course, she asks that her students give presentations to the class. One of her Japanese students, when asked what he did to prepare for public speaking, replied that he "eats the audience." I think this is fantastic. What he meant, I think, was that he takes the audience into himself and acknowledges their importance in his preparations. We've taken this phrase and added it to our process. It demands that we consider and include our audience in our concepting, design, and implementation. The 3com spot mentioned earlier is a good example of eating the audience. We included that audience in our process in a number of ways.

First, we knew that our audience, in this case, was going to be on the Internet already, since that's the only medium where the spot played. We also knew that most of our audience would be connected to the Internet by 56.6K, and that most would probably have computers powered by CPUs of 200 or higher. So, by including the audience first, we're able to get a clear picture of the technical environment we'll want to design for. We also acknowledged that most people, while on a computer, are going to be multi-tasking . . . maybe surfing the Web, while at the same time talking on the phone, listening to headphones, or talking with a co-worker. Therefore, we had to grab their attention quickly and then deliver the message just as quickly. With the 3com spot we were able to achieve that. The piece downloads after a couple of seconds, streams consistently, and plays smoothly across 56.6K modems, and is over in eleven seconds. By "eating the audience" we were able to design and implement a stronger spot.

Filtering

I mentioned earlier that I had identified my client as "the enemy," and not an ally of the creative process. This early mistake led me to include what I call "filtering" in our process. Filtering employs the idea of using limitations, whether you see those limitations in terms of clients who might cramp your style, or the inevitable environmental limitations such as bandwidth, browsers, or slow CPUs. The savvy designer simply must come to understand that these limitations or "enemies" can serve to act as your best friends, forcing you to "filter" out unessential design elements. Again, using the 3com spot as an example, our early comps had substantially more graphic design in them. By that I mean that we had a lot more cool text effects and graphic elements spread throughout the spot. But when we tested these early comps on slightly less powerful computers, and on different bandwidths, we found that they performed poorly. The animations would redraw slowly and the download of the file was inconsistent, often freezing in the middle. This performance certainly detracted from the central theme of the spot, which was "fast," so we had to go back and filter out the unessential elements. Most of the "cool" stuff had to go, and that can be hard because you get attached to all of that "wow" and you assume your client will too. But to me there's nothing better than editing out unessential elements, whether visual, audio, or motion, and watching as the theme becomes clearer and more effective as a result. You usually end up with a far more focused spot. And that was certainly the case with the 3com spot.

Clients are another wonderful "filter." There is a tendency among new media designers to play clients as fools who are ignorant of both the technology and the proper way of presenting their companies to maximum effect within these new media. No matter what you might want to believe, your client knows the product or service better than you do, and can be a big help in working toward tight, sensical communication.

Justify

Our final step in the process is justifying. When we get close to completing a project, we'll gather around a monitor and present the work. At this point anyone on the team can point to anything on the screen and say "justify." In other words, we impose a final filter upon the work . . . this time our own. We are all aware that every element, every move, every color should support our theme. While we can let a few unjustified elements slide, for the most part, nothing should in any way obstruct that theme. We want to communicate clearly, and unjustified elements in the design distract from effective communication. Of course, this final stage usually ends in fistfights, but it's well worth it.

Conclusion

I'm kidding about the fistfights, though the "justify" step can get pretty heated. The point though in all of this, is to take design seriously. We are designing for new, constantly changing, and often very limited media. It can be easy to overlook the possibilities within those limitations, focusing perhaps more closely on "bells and whistles" and the latest software, than on the theme and message of any given project. Dispelling the notion that clients are stupid, and corporations full of soulless drones is a good first step in recognizing that what we are doing essentially is talking to each other. And we are having those conversations across new media. Emotions still matter . . . themes still matter. Having a process in place that reinforces that reality, has helped me, and the designers who work for me, evolve.

Thinking About the Audience

DAVID VOGLER

IF YOU'RE READING this book, there's a darn good chance you're an art student or a so-called e-designer just breaking into the Internet business. (If you're not an art student or a young e-designer trying to break into the business, then please skip this writing and advance to the essay immediately after this one. I've read it and I can tell you it's a lot more entertaining.)

If you're anything like *my* students, you're probably an insufferable punk with a pierced tongue, painted pinky nails, and an unjustified contempt for "traditional" media, like print, packaging, or broadcast.

At the risk of sounding preachy, I'll let you in on a little secret. It doesn't matter what medium you choose to work in. Good design transcends *all* media. Regardless of whether you're an e-designer or a "traditional" designer, your core mission is smart communication. Whether you work in print or pixel, successful design solutions begin with knowing your audience. Below are three anecdotes that come to mind.

Get in Their Head

Many years ago when I was an insufferable punk like you, I was fortunate enough to work for The Grand Master of Parody. His name was David Kaestle and he initially made his mark as art director of the *National Lampoon* magazine. Kaestle and his team created some of the industry's most brilliant satire.

Specifically, Kaestle was the man behind the *National Lampoon*'s high-school yearbook parody, which is considered to be the gold standard for print humor. (Kaestle's project actually led writer Doug Kenny to create a little movie called *Animal House.* That film launched the career of John Belushi, and essentially changed the course of mass humor and pop culture. I submit that if it weren't for the likes of Kaestle and the *Lampoon* in the late 1970s, we wouldn't have humor Web sites, like *Onion.com*, in the late 1990s.) Kaestle's design direction was spot-on target and amazingly accurate right down to the smallest detail. You'd swear it was an actual high-school yearbook made by actual high schoolers.

I once asked Kaestle what the secret was to creating such accurate parodies. He told me

Nick.com is clean, intuitive, intelligent, and fun. A modern design based on visuals relevant to today's kids without being trite. Reminiscent of skateboard graphics, rave flyers, and youth fashion.

to think of the target being spoofed and simply "get in their head." In other words, to art-direct a parody of a high-school yearbook, you had to think like a high-school yearbook art director (and like the high-school audience it was aimed at). As painful as it might have been, you had to fully assume that person's point of view, art style—and in the case of an amateur yearbook designer—lack of talent. By being true to the host and the audience, you could easily emulate their approach and converse in their language. Essentially, you would be "in their head" and the results were nothing short of pure genius.

Be an Actor, Not a Star

A few years later, an actor friend of mine attended a theater workshop held by veteran Shakespearean actor and starship captain, Mr. Patrick Stewart. (Since this friend—who shall remain nameless—was a crummy actor who never really hit the big time, I always questioned the validity of his tales. Nevertheless, there's a moral to this story that supports my point, so please bear with me.)

On the first day of class, Stewart confronted the group with a chilling question: "Do you want to be an *actor* or a *star*?" Stewart's question was loaded. He then angrily demanded that any of those in attendance who wanted to be "stars" were unworthy of his time and would be banished from the workshop. Stewart then went on to explain the difference between an "actor" and a "star." A Hollywood star was not a true actor, but rather a vain publicity-monger whose purpose was to maintain a persona. "Stars" are people who essentially play one role—themselves—regardless of where they are cast. An example of this would be someone like Jean-Claude Van Damme. He can only play one thing: the doofus kickboxer heavy. The "star" is creatively insubstantial and is just concerned with the surface.

An "actor," however, is very different. A true actor is concerned about *his craft*, not his sur-

MaMa Media's site has very poor production values and a confusing design. The graphics and editorial slant is condescending and treats kids with disrespect.

face appeal. An actor is a chameleon capable of morphing into a variety of diverse characters with each one being wildly different than the next. Think of Alec Guinness or Gary Oldman or Tom Hanks. These are true actors who "get in the heads" of their given characters.

That being said, I've always found that the best designers are the ones who approach their craft like "true actors." The good ones can adjust themselves to serve a variety of clients without defaulting to one single surface style or trend. This ability to emulate the mindset of the target audience can be the key to effective communication. And that holds true for both old or new media and everything in between.

Listen to the Audience

For the past decade I have worked at Nickelodeon. Most recently as a vice president and creative director, helping them launch their online division. It was here that I met Scott Webb who taught me the "art of knowing your audience." Scott was one of the founding fathers of Nickelodeon and was a mentor to me; he was "Yoda" to my "Luke Skywalker." When it comes to branding, creative direction, and relating to the audience, Scott taught me everything I know. In the business of branding, he's a true Jedi Master.

Nickelodeon is the number one brand for kids in every medium they get into. Nick dominates in television, magazines, consumer products, and, more recently, online. How do they do it? They talk to kids. They listen to their audience and respect them. This sounds rather obvious, but no other entertainment company listens to kids with the passion, devotion, and sincerity that Nick does. Every script, product, and design is tested and approved by kids. Nickelodeon has a massive research department devoted solely to communicating with its audience through carefully engineered focus groups. No idea is realized unless a kid says he likes it.

Disney.com uses a theme park "map" metaphor as a content organizational device. This is an approach considered to be outdated and embarrassingly amateur. This antiquated navigational logic breaks down quickly and usually produces frustration for the user.

Scott Webb taught me to listen to the kid audience, as well as the kid inside me. This was especially helpful when I re-launched *nick.com* in the summer of 2000. This was a serious refreshment of the "look and feel," navigation, and content direction of the entire site. We also upgraded our publishing systems and server solutions. It was the single most ambitious re-launch in Nick Online's history. But before I touched a single pixel, I talked to the audience.

From what kids told me, they found most kid Web sites to be "babyish" and insulting. After I studied the competition, I couldn't help but agree. (See sample screen grabs.) Naturally, Web design conventions for adults are different than for children. Kids have different motor skills, reading levels, and a profoundly different relationship with a computer than grown-ups. The new *nick.com* needed to be more than pretty eye candy; it had to be fun, navigationally clear, intelligent and kid-friendly. As a result, I directed my team with these five informing design principles:

1 | RESPECT Unlike most kid Web sites, the Nickelodeon interface respects the audience. There are no cornball environments as seen on the Fox, Disney, and JuniorNet sites. Nick offers intelligent menu systems that work for all ages and all skills, without the creative crutch of real-world metaphors such as houses, maps, dashboards, and spaceship windows.

2 | TEMPLATED All the *nick.com* pages follow a strict program of design guidelines and layout templates. This ensures consistent site packaging and enhances user clarity. This clear design program also ensures cost-effective page maintenance. I'm a strong believer that an interface should take a back seat to the content. The UI should be "invisible" and unobtrusive. The interface is there to help you *access* content, not overshadow it.

3 | SURPRISE, MOVEMENT, AND PLAY The *nick.com* site packaging is lean and functional, yet maintains a uniquely Nickelodeon sense of play, fun, serendipity, and discovery. It's loaded with "easter eggs" and undocumented surprises. All the pages combine smart utility with animation and sound. In a sense, each Web page is a cool "digital toy" unto itself.

4 | CONSISTENT NAVIGATION The tabbed navigational bar is devilishly simple and appears consistently on every page. This navigational solution is intentionally "unclever" and does not pretend to entertain. The content is where the cleverness and entertainment is found, not the signage. Basic color-coding provides clear, consistent visual themes that unify each area. Even non-readers can navigate based on appearance alone.

5 | GRAPHICS WITH ATTITUDE The *nick.com* Web site uses modern design elements based on visuals relevant to today's kids without being trite. It's reminiscent of skateboard and snowboard graphics, rave flyers and youth fashion. Fonts, colors, and layouts promote a hip, "bubblegum techno" style. It's a site design that suggests a "junior varsity MTV" rather than *Barney*.

By talking to the audience we were able to launch a new site that better serves their needs and increases our traffic. In a sense, the kid audience helped design the new *nick.com* as much as I did. And judging from the hundreds of letters that we get each week, the kids say they love it.

Whether it's through creative arrogance or innocent over-enthusiasm, designers sometimes assume the audience they serve is just like themselves. Only on rare occasions will you embark on a project where the end user shares your own tastes, insights and opinions. For all other times, I suggest you check your ego at the door and ask the audience for input. They'll thank you for it.

On-the-Job Training

LISA WALTUCH

CREATING A SUCCESSFUL Web site is not easy. This is an obvious conclusion when looking at sites that are difficult to use, understand, find information from, or transact with. As users, we are victims of poorly conceived, designed, and implemented sites. As developers, we need to tackle the problem in a new way.

The Internet landscape has changed significantly in the past few years, with businesses embracing the reach of the Internet and understanding the potential of high-powered computations. Basically, sites have evolved from simple "brochureware" to sophisticated "megasystems," and this logical progression has led to the challenge to successfully develop hugely complex Web sites.

It is important to understand that the onus falls in the lap of the development company and, therefore, that company is responsible for making a site that is not only functional but usable, appropriate, and compelling. This is a tall order.

Taking on this responsibility has implications far beyond a good concept, successful branding, and company image. It has an impact on the revenue stream, production, sales, and the bottom line. These are issues that exist mainly in the real, practical world and rarely in the university environment or the academic space. Both worlds have important components to contribute to the process, and they should be utilized appropriately in the development cycle.

One provides a sound thinking and approach model that accommodates the utilization of abstract ideas and concepts. The other supplies a context, constraints and a specific measure for success. Too often the burden of "time to market" (or unrealistic deadlines), budget, schedules, and client needs obfuscate the real challenge at hand, and ultimately the solution is uninspired, unimaginative, and relatively unusable. Similarly, it is difficult to duplicate the business context in the classroom. The financial pressures that drive a project don't exist, and neither does the team-oriented infrastructure required to complete a project of great magnitude typical in the current environment.

It is with this revelation and understanding that a new and smart approach is to bring an educational curriculum into the workplace, into the corporate environment. With the right thinking models, we can equip real practitioners with tools to not only do their jobs well, but to push beyond the ordinary or obvious solution to new inventions, efficient interfaces, and brilliant ideas. This is how we can directly improve the user experience.

An Experiment

I work at Icon Medialab in New York City as a creative director. Our company develops Web sites for clients from Sony and Motorola to the Metropolitan Museum of Art and Carnegie Hall. We are a full-service firm with two thousand people in twenty-four offices in eighteen countries. In June, I attended a gathering of sixty art directors from our offices around the world. Each office presented its work, and I realized that many of the usability issues were the same no matter where the sites were developed or what their goals were. The designers did not discuss their work in terms of the intended audience, the interaction between a system and a user, or more specifically, the user and a task. Instead, they focused on the presentation of information. There was no emphasis on user profiles, how a user might approach or access information, and how he or she would feel when interacting with the site.

After the art director's presentations, a Human Computer Interface (HCI) specialist explained the HCI role in a project as understanding user needs, translating those needs into a prototype, designing the interface in an iterative process, and evaluating the prototype in user tests. The art directors responded with curiosity and interest and a sense that we, in fact, do the same thing, but that our process is not well defined. What we do is perhaps more organic and intuitive, but it is clear that we can use the same information and interpret it from a designer's point of view.

User-experience design is the practice of creating a meaningful or valuable interaction between a person and a system. The nature of that interaction can be many things, from short, one-time functions to prolonged sessions and frequent use. In every case, users have an "experience" to which they attach meaning. Their experience is "loaded" in that it elicits a response, for instance: "convenience." If they were able to purchase movie tickets on the Web instead of having to dash out to wait in a long line; or "frustration," if they were so confused by a checkout process that they abandoned their shopping cart; or "entertainment" because they were playing a game; or "utility" because they were able to look up the weather in Kansas City before flying out for a business meeting. Efficiency, delight, aggravation, and stimulation are feelings that someone may associate with an interaction. In some cases the best experience is one that is unnoticed—the interface transparent with the focus on the result instead of the method. For example, when you read a story in the newspaper, you focus on the subject matter of the story; the fact that it was on the upper-right side of the page in times roman print neither registers, nor does it make a difference, if it is designed well. If the print is blurry or too small, then you are unable to read the story and the experience is annoying. The same is true for an interface. If you want to purchase your groceries online, and it only requires a simple task, you are satisfied; the experience of actually interacting online becomes irrelevant. You are pleased because your house is freshly stocked with groceries, not because they were easy to order.

The designer's interest in the HCI approach inspired the idea of building a curriculum around user-experience design for everyone involved in creating interfaces, including art directors, designers, HCI experts, information architects, copywriters, and producers. I wanted to build a methodology that had immediate application within day-to-day practice. I knew this would be an experiment, and Icon seemed like a good laboratory to start with in terms of having an impact on the usability of the Web.

I collaborated with Katie Salen, a design professor at the University of Texas in Austin. We decided to take on the challenge of teaching usability and user-experience design at Icon with a short-term goal of changing employees' approach to projects, a mid-term goal of improving the quality of our projects, and a lofty, long-term goal of making the Web more usable.

Together we wrote a proposal that included our goals, a time frame, and a budget, and Tom Nicholson, the chief creative officer of Icon MediaLab recognized the need for this type of internal education and gave us permission to test our ideas. He specified that we experiment in, and get support from, the interface teams in both New York and Stockholm, where we have some of the largest creative communities in our company.

The initial phase of our work took the form of a four-month experiment in which we tested, modified, reworked, and developed curricula for workshops in our New York and Stockholm offices. Our plan was to first develop an approach and get feedback in New York. Our efforts in Stockholm would be the final part of our testing phase. We would then reevaluate. If our work was successful and promising, we would plan the next phase.

We began with the premise that our employees are smart, motivated people who are committed to collaborative work in interface design. We defined our process as educating a multidisciplinary group of people in user-experience design, and creating a methodology that participants could take back to their teams immediately to work more effectively as Web site developers.

The Hamptons: Workshop I

Our first New York workshop was two days away from the office with eleven people from the same project team.

We began the User Experience offsite with the notion that through a set of activities, discussions, and exercises we could instill in the participants the responsibility for creating optimal user experiences.

We wanted to integrate the idea of usability in everything we did that weekend, to bring these ideas to all levels of consciousness. Issues around usability can be found everywhere from getting out of a car (was the handle easy to reach? Did it require a natural action, or a contortionist maneuver to make it work?) to cutting a piece of steak (is the knife too dull? Is there a good surface under the meat, or could you cut right through the paper plate and scratch the table?). Ideally, the group would pay attention to their surroundings in terms of how usable or workable they were.

We wanted our group to understand that as developers they can determine a general structure for someone to use. A user can make personal choices within that structure and therefore have an experience that is customized to his or her specific needs. Our job is to not so narrowly define an action that the user has no choice, but to offer the user freedom in a well-designed system—where they can get what they want. Developers can determine how a user fulfills an objective if they understand what is of most value to the user. This is the primary role of the developer.

In the following exercise we wanted the group to explore a narrative method of concept generation through the steps below.

❶ Develop a user profile. They were given sample user-attitude statements (i.e., "I am very happy with my job, but if the "perfect" job came along I will definitely consider it.").

❷ Create a persona. Each group wrote a short "character portrait" of the user (i.e., wishy-washy boyfriend).

❸ Tell the story of the site. They composed a short narrative that characterized the site attitude based on qualities of the user profile (i.e., This is a site that feels noncommittal, that won't give me its full attention, that spends a lot of time roving the periphery.)

❹ Determine concept architecture. They distilled the essential qualities of the persona profiles and the site narratives into a clear, concise concept statement (i.e., The driving concepts for this site are "focus" and "temptation.").

❺ Develop interface proposal. They developed proposals for an interface that met the objective of the concept architecture (i.e., storyboards for a site that has a small, centrally situated interface and an opposing peripheral structure of ever-changing, ever-tempting information).

We established criteria for evaluating the finished projects. We discussed the benefits of critique and how to effectively and constructively talk about the work. One of our goals was to incorporate critique into the workshop, so teams would be encouraged to practice it in the office regularly and, to an extent, formally during the various stages of their projects.

In the exercise, the "user attitude" was essentially a source of inspiration that led to an interface solution. The process was about a unique approach to creating an interface rather than developing a user experience.

After the first workshop, we decided that it was more important to emphasize usability and user experience instead of a general creative approach to designing a usable system. So we added another New York–based workshop before taking our ideas to Stockholm.

Again, we focused on the idea that usability is everywhere, but this time we wanted it to be at the core of our workshop. If we devised an experience that was common to everyone, we could incorporate the notion of usability easily. Our choice was a restaurant, a dining experience. Everyone knows how to go to a restaurant and eat, especially in Manhattan. This context served as the perfect backdrop to an analysis of usability. The participants experienced something relatively familiar, not abstract, and therefore were able to clearly identify what was easy or what was difficult, things that made sense and things that didn't.

We met with Patrick and Abby, chef and owner of CamaJe, a bistro north of Houston Street and a few blocks away from our office. We told them about our workshop and our goals of teaching usability. They were intrigued and agreed to participate as "developers" of the restaurant experience. We wanted to have breakfast, lunch, and appetizers, but it was important that

Patrick and Abby decide how and what they wanted to serve. We asked them to create a dining experience for us.

CamaJe: Workshop II

We invited eight people to the restaurant for a day to participate in a workshop on usability and asked everyone to "come hungry."

People trickled in at nine and, either eagerly or lethargically, ordered coffee or double espressos. It was a beautiful day and there were many seating options: outside on the sidewalk tables, indoors on the couches clustered around a big coffee table with magazines, and the indoor tables set with tablecloths and napkins. Eventually, everyone migrated either to the couches or the outdoor tables. They ordered their coffee from a waitress, but helped themselves to a variety of fruit, muffins, and juice set up buffet style around the restaurant.

After an hour, we asked them what they did. They said they had breakfast, and we asked more specifically about their experience. The discussion went from macro-observations such as "I ate a banana muffin" to micro-observations: "I was a little embarrassed that I ate my muffin with a fork when I saw Claudia eating hers with her hands." We continued to dig and found that Johanna ate her muffin with a fork because the forks were placed next to the muffins. Abby put the forks next to the muffins, a misstep perhaps on the part of the restaurateur. They should have been next to the fruit, a clear example of ways in which developers can "guide" users.

Once we made the list of their actions that morning as a group, we asked each person to write down fifty observations they had that morning. Then they coded each observation into three categories: physical, emotional, or contextual. For example, some physical observations were: "Picked up a plate," "waited for crowd to thin before getting food"; emotional observations: "I was worried about being late," "I felt happy to sit outside"; and contextual observations: "observed who was present," "wouldn't eat like this if I was in the office." They coded their list with colored dots and we analyzed the results. Some lists were covered with red dots for "emotional," while others were mixed. They were able to see that people perceived the same experience differently. Patterns emerged that identified a variety of personalities, expectations, and approaches, and it accentuated the fact that we need to understand and be highly aware of human behavior in order to design effective solutions. We learned that it is imperative that we gather information about the people who will be using our systems and recognize that it is impossible to anticipate an individual's reaction to a system without researching the user and testing assumptions based on that understanding. The exercise made these ideas concrete and explicit because of the shared breakfast experience, where they observed the variety of reactions among their peers, a fairly homogeneous crowd. They noted that if there were more variables in the demographics of the participants that morning, the range of reactions and observations would have been even greater.

This approach was more successful and in line with our goals of creating awareness around the user. We reinforced these ideas with exercises that translated information about a user to a design approach for usable systems, and ultimately felt ready for the next step.

Johanna Ullman, the HCI lead from Stockholm, spent five weeks in the New York office and participated in the CamaJe workshop before returning to Sweden. She took on the responsibility of coordinating our week in her home office, and we began to strategize about the best approach.

Together we decided that an exchange of information would be informative and beneficial to their office and our endeavor. They have a rich history of running and participating in workshops, especially in the HCI discipline. HCI is new to the New York office and, unfortunately, is neither well understood nor is it part of the project teams currently. Whereas in Stockholm they play a significant, if not major, role in creating user interfaces.

An exchange was an appealing idea because we were curious about how designers and HCI worked together on projects. We understood the benefit, but not the process or the collaboration. I met with David Pohlfeldt, a creative lead from Stockholm who described the working relationship between HCI and designers as good, but not maximally beneficial to the projects. In his mind, HCI dictated what designers made. They basically handed off the requirements, and the designers churned out interface designs without contributing to the driving concept or inventing original solutions. He said that their art directors were extremely creative and talented, but had no codified methods or techniques for explaining their solutions, or why they made certain visual decisions and how these ideas were relevant to solving a problem. This handicap compromised their credibility with other team members and with clients.

In the same vein, they wanted to understand more clearly the creative director's role in the conception and implementation of a project's "vision" since this role was relatively new to the Stockholm office.

And finally, we were interested in the new "gamelab," a brainchild of David Pohlfeldt and under the leadership of Kim Nordstrom and Annica Englund. We were interested in exploring the relationship between game play and usability, game design and interactive design.

Stockholm Exchange: Multiple Workshops

Based on this information, we focused on three main topics:

- Sharing experiences and knowledge with a goal of gaining a clear understanding of how art directors, HCI and editorial/content work together on a project
- Defining the creative director role in terms of a project's "vision"
- Bringing the concepts of game design into a discussion of user experience, usability and interactive media development

Stockholm Workshop I: The Creative Director Role

We presented two projects and described the "vision" behind the projects in terms of "design knowledge." We explored the idea of design knowledge, which involves an understanding of how the driving concept for a project must be supported within four areas: user experience, technical innovation, utility, and aesthetics. These areas are taken into account in all phases of a project, from initial ideas and philosophical approach to making and implementing.

We did an exercise in which they quickly chose a topic, a context, articulated a vision, and then developed a system with the components of design knowledge in mind. Our goal was to impart a methodology that they could apply to their project work. They were enthusiastic and thought the process was valuable as a starting point. Their main challenge was to incorporate creative directors into the projects at the very beginning, so they could have an impact on the overall direction and development of the site.

Stockholm Workshop II: How HCI, Art Directors, and Copywriters Work Together

The spirit of exchange was most evident in this particular series of workshops. We asked each discipline to provide answers to the following questions:

➥ What is the definition of user experience within your discipline?
➥ Where, within the overall process is your discipline's contribution the most important?

Overall, the answers from the HCI teams were more consistent, well defined, and more specific than the designers' answers.

HCI defined the user experience as a quality of interaction that addresses utility and usability, and the ability to communicate a message, a feeling, and a sense of trust. In response to the second question, they said their contribution to the project was most important for the entire life cycle of development, from inception to implementation. The copywriters said that their definition of a user experience was to present users with the right content in the most communicative and appealing way, and that their contribution was the most important through-out the entire "communicative process." The designers defined user experience in their discipline as "awakening emotions," which involves developing ideas of how best to "reach" people. They said their contribution to the project was most important at the very beginning.

Each group that wasn't involved from the beginning of the project felt that they were included too late. The copywriters described themselves as "text monkeys" called in to check spelling in the final stages of a project, and the designers saw their job as putting visual form to an already established idea. They all had confidence in their own ability to fundamentally con-tribute to the conception of a project, but said the current project structure didn't support their early and complete involvement. They seemed to get along and respect one another, but felt that their process didn't allow adequate time to collaborate, that the technical aspects of the project took precedence over the creative research and development time, and as a result, they were relegated to superficial implementation and cleanup.

As we gained an understanding of their situation, we offered suggestions that could be incorporated immediately into their process. We knew that it was impossible to make a major shift in process overnight, so we focused on specific fixes that would have a positive impact in the short term. For instance, we suggested that the HCI specialists invite an art director and copywriter to a user test so they could observe for themselves the problems a user encoun-tered, and the subsequent reaction. Then they could take that raw data from their own observa-tion and put it through the filter of their discipline to invent an appropriate and innovative solution. This is a more efficient production cycle because all disciplines are being used to the fullest extent of their talent and expertise. Better quality solutions are almost always the result of successful collaborations.

It is important to recognize that all disciplines are trying to understand the user. Each competency has specific and valuable contribution to make toward that goal by adding significantly to the things they can affect. For instance, HCI experts fundamentally contribute to an understanding of specific user behavior, while designers contribute to an innovative interpretation or an inventive solution that supports and enhances the identified user behavior.

Art directors, HCI specialists, and copywriters presented case studies from the point of view of each discipline. We asked them to describe how they worked together. What was their process? What were their deliverables? Who presented to the client? How did the client perceive the team? How did they work with the client? Did they have any rough spots or difficult moments with the different disciplines? We wanted them to concentrate specifically on their process instead of on the project in order to understand, troubleshoot, or imitate their approach. It was quite interesting to listen and then identify when an HCI directive trumped a designer action, or when a deadline, budget, or client request took precedence over both the HCI specialist and the designer.

Ultimately, we wanted to understand successful, existing models, or define new ones, aimed at creating effective collaboration between competencies and across offices. We wanted to identify concrete methods/processes and deliverables that bring everyone on the team to the same level of understanding.

Stockholm Workshop III: Gamelab and Usability

The gamelab in Stockholm intrigued us, and we were curious to find out what they were doing, how HCI was involved, and how we could learn some lessons and apply them to creating compelling user experiences in traditional interface design projects.

We explored five questions:

- What aspects of game design are useful for interactive designers?
- What are games' particular relationship to issues of interactivity, user testing ("playtesting"), prototyping methodologies, and the creation of meaningful user experiences?
- To what extent is it possible to work with usability when it comes to game design?
- What does it mean to say that a game is usable or useful, and how can usability in games be studied and then applied to non-game contexts?
- What can the HCI community specifically, learn from game design?

After several discussions and a planning session for a joint presentation with Gamelab principals and HCI representatives, we began our final session with participants from the HCI, design, and copywriting disciplines. Playtesting and analysis using traditional HCI methods of user participation and observation were at the core of our workshop. We divided into two groups and took turns playing or observing two different games with contrasting structures. We played "Pennies," a card game that is based on speed and matching, and "Pictionary," which involves drawing and guessing. Both games are goal oriented and have an element of competition.

As we watched the game players, we recorded our observations and then translated them into "qualities of use," with the idea that these could most easily be used in creating stimulating user experiences. The participants identified qualities such as competition, constraints, goals, familiarity, connection, engagement, rules and structure, time limits, and active versus passive participation. Not only was it clear how these qualities could be incorporated into their current projects, but it was gratifying to see them embrace new ways of looking at their own process. At the end of this session, an HCI specialist exclaimed, "I didn't realize that HCI could have a sense of humor!" In fact, games were an appropriate, unexpected, and important source for behavior analysis. This discovery was exciting for us, and the response on the part of the participants was enthusiastic. We had completed our final workshop, and our last day in Stockholm, but felt that we had just scratched the surface of exploring "gamespace" as it related to user experience. The conversations via e-mail have continued since our departure, and we feel confident that we will collaborate on new discoveries in this realm.

What's Next?

We concluded our experiment upon our return to the United States. It was an interesting and thought-provoking journey, and we are poised for the next step. We are committed to teaching and learning, as they say in the realm of education, or research and development, in the corporate lexicon. We would like to continue to straddle both worlds because we believe that it is the most effective way to do the best work and have a significant impact with direct application. We know that we would like to expand our learning base from current practices of employees to research organizations and university programs; from Icon Medialab–based workshops and emails to publications and lectures; from internal discussions to industry meetings.

These efforts are positive, but perhaps, not tangible. It is true that an article about creating enhanced user experiences is tangible, but the impact or effect of that piece is harder to evaluate. This is where it gets tricky. We work in a commerce-based economy. Our effort is measured in billable hours and seen in the increased traffic and revenue on a site that we designed. If we dedicate ourselves to learning and teaching, how do we judge our success? By what means do we measure it?

Up to now, encouragement came in the form of a good reception. In all cases, the workshop participants felt they learned something valuable. We were well received and, by extension, the competency coaches and the people who measure employee satisfaction were pleased with our work. But as we move forward, we need to define a set of criteria for evaluation. The biggest goal we set for ourselves was long term: to make the Web more usable. Clearly, this is nebulous, because the evidence is a user's comfort level. It gets even more complicated when we realize that the easier or more transparent the Web becomes, the less we'll notice. For instance, we get annoyed when we are stuck in traffic and miss an appointment, but if there are no problems, the drive is smooth, the appointment made, we don't think twice about it. We tend to remember the bad, and the inconvenient, rather than the good or the easy, especially when the task is utilitarian. According to Don Norman, an expert in usability, it takes twenty-five years to see a shift in behavior, adaptation, and adoption. That's a long time to justify what we are trying to do. Understanding this has allowed us to focus on the process of gaining and imparting knowledge in user experience design. The end goal still drives us, but we want to concentrate on the path that eventually gets us there. As teachers and researchers, we can influence developers to make things better, easier, more enjoyable, and more usable; as users we can witness gradual improvement and nod our heads with satisfaction. Perhaps that is the measure of our success.

AIGA Briefing Paper on a Curriculum for Experience Design

PREPARED BY MEMBERS OF THE ADVANCE FOR DESIGN,
MEREDITH DAVIS (DEPARTMENT CHAIR, NC STATE UNIVERSITY)
AND HUGH DUBBERLY (VICE PRESIDENT, NETSCAPE/AOL),
COMMITTEE CHAIRS

THE FOLLOWING PAPER was prepared to inform the National Association of Schools of Art and Design, AIGA members, educators in general, and design practitioners of the key knowledge and competencies necessary for the practice of experience design. By necessity, descriptions of competencies cannot be based on software or technology-related concerns that may change over the ten-year period of accreditation. Instead, they must focus on those aspects of design that will transcend any given invention and that are fundamental to communication problem solving. Further, language used in the description of key competencies must be understandable to individuals who have no background in design.

There are approximately 50 industrial design programs, 110 architecture programs, and more than 500 graphic design programs in four-year colleges and universities in the United States. It has been estimated that nearly two thousand two-year colleges also teach design in some form. Industrial and graphic design programs generally reside in schools or departments of art that exhibit certain curricular priorities and instructional biases. Students in these programs may or may not have access to course offerings in the technical or social sciences; generally speaking, there is no national history of collaboration between faculty members in these programs and design professors. Electronic media–related study may occur under the course titles of computer art, computer graphics, multimedia design, Web design, information design, interaction design, and animation, and may be taught in programs of design, art, computer science, mass communications/journalism, or technical writing.

As a result of this educational landscape, two dominant descriptions of interaction design study have emerged in many American colleges and universities: (1) resourceful students from many fields piece together relevant coursework from an array of offerings inside and outside design programs, and apart from any planned curriculum; and (2) design faculty offer what they believe to be interaction design, usually in the absence of professional experience and advice from practitioners of the field. Under the latter profile, much of the student work resembles print layout or filmmaking. While there are exceptions to these two profiles, in the majority of programs students are unlikely to acquire substantive knowledge of programming, human factors, or business practices, and will focus on software mastery and inventive form.

Industrial and graphic design programs are accredited by the National Association of Schools of Art and Design, which reviews its members every ten years for compliance with a group of general and disciplinary standards. The industrial and graphic design standards each occupy one 5½" × 8" page in NASAD guidelines. Recently, the AIGA affiliated with NASAD to rewrite standards, train qualified graphic designers to serve on accreditation review teams, and publish white papers on issues of importance to design that require more extensive discussion than can be accommodated in standards manuals. This is one in a series of papers for designers, faculty, and college administrators.

Introduction: Designing Experiences, Not Objects

The historic focus of most design education has been on objects and the skills necessary to produce them; on communication and products that have physical form, from which certain relationships with audiences and users arise, and on the skill-set for developing that form. Courses in college design programs are generally titled and described by the products that result from design activity (e.g., typography or photography); by the processes employed by the designer (e.g., design methods or production); and/or by the critical framework that serves as a means for analyzing and critiquing objects after they are made (e.g., semiotics, human factors, or various approaches to communication theory). "Object and designer centeredness" is a natural outgrowth of graphic and product design programs in American colleges and universities as extensions of fine arts curricula, where the artist and manifestation of his or her expressive intent and technical execution are paramount.

This strategy for teaching design has been applied more recently to instruction in interactive media. In schools where faculty and technological resources permit development of courses in computer multimedia, interface, and interaction design (to use current terms referring to these areas of design practice), the focus of teaching and learning is frequently on the invention of form and mastery of technical skills. Motion and sound are acknowledged as new variables for graphic designers, but usually amplify visual concepts.

With respect to interface design problems, where dynamic user interaction with information is at the heart of the problem, many solutions and teaching strategies still maintain an object-centered approach. The designer's primary attention is focused on building a virtual object inside the real object (the computer monitor with its own navigation devices), refocusing the designer's attention on the physical attributes of interactive products, rather than on the interactions themselves. Designer dependency on computer programmers or software, whose tendencies are toward machine-centered rather than human-centered solutions, exaggerates this problem.

While few will argue that the agendas of design and design education should disregard form and objects, what drives choices about these issues is called into question by the nature of the contemporary communication environment and emerging technological opportunity. In three meetings from 1998 to 2000, leading interaction or experience designers (design professionals who develop interactive, technologically mediated communication) met under the leadership of the American Institute of Graphic Arts (AIGA) to discuss the changing nature of design responsibility in a networked economy. The conclusion reached by this group is that design is increasingly less about creating objects and more about creating conditions that support user experiences, and that this experiential nature of interactive communication and products will only accelerate under rapid technological development that reduces the need to be in a particular place at a particular time to accomplish a task.

This position has implications beyond simply refocusing designers' attention on users, although that is a significant outcome. While the physical and cognitive interactions of people with information and objects at the time of use remains important, how these interactions are nested within the larger array of human experiences becomes central to design. What we know about how people converse, negotiate, and collaborate in their interactions with the world in general can have implications for how designers construct specific interactive experiences for commerce, learning, work, play, and decision-making in and among various social and political communities. And despite the demand on designers for speed of production and short-term outcomes, what individual interactive experiences mean in the lifetime of people's relationships with clients for design, should guide decisions about the design of those experiences.

The Purpose of This Paper

The purpose of this paper is to raise discussion among design educators about what should constitute an education in "experience design," and how that education serves the growing need for leadership and insight in this area of design practice. It also calls into question certain educational traditions that have been taken for granted in their emphasis on objects and designers, rather than on audiences and their experiences. Lastly, this paper identifies the growing need for research related to experience design and the traditional role of universities in building and disseminating knowledge.

It is important to assert that commerce is not the only application of experience design, nor is the Web the only form it takes. While designing business interactions (and more specifically, buying-selling relationships) may constitute a high percentage of today's work in interaction design, it is only one kind of experience users have with interactive communications, products, and environments. Interactive experiences increasingly characterize learning, work, recreation, community, and access to the privileges of democracy.

The following curricular objectives for the study of experience design describe learning outcomes that should result from any academic program intended to produce experience-design professionals. This statement of objectives avoids specifying particular curriculum structures, course descriptions, and hardware or software expertise; these program characteristics should arise from institutional contexts and the technology available at any given time. The listed objectives attempt to transcend issues that might change quickly in favor of those at the core of designing conditions that support user experiences, and that are likely to withstand social and technological invention over a longer period of time.

It is also an underlying assumption that the knowledge, skills, and attitudes described in this paper are most appropriate for graduate-level study. However, undergraduate design programs can prepare students for later study and practice by embedding some of these concerns in studio projects and theoretical discussions, and by recommending general education courses that build students' knowledge in related inquiry (anthropology, psychology, computer science, management, marketing, semiotics/linguistics, etc.).

Learning objectives for a curriculum in experience design:

➻ Students will understand the difference between designing objects and designing experiences, opportunities, and self-organizing systems.
➻ Students will analyze and synthesize the relevant aspects of meaningful human interactions in a networked and mediated environment, including:
➻ the physical, cognitive/emotional, social, political, economic, and cultural dimensions of these interactions; and
➻ The relationship of such interactions to commerce, learning, work, play, community, and gaining access to the privileges of democracy.
➻ Students will explore the technological mediation of experience in terms of:
➻ Representing/simulating/visualizing/transforming

This objective refers to the representation of perceptions, events, and ideas in some medium other than the one in which they originated, and to the abstraction of information to eliminate extraneous and distracting aspects. It includes the use of modeling and diagramming to explain and explore relevant relationships in the communication process. It also refers to designers making judgments about the appropriateness of form in facilitating the understanding and use of information by particular users/audiences, and accounting for the contribution the medium makes to the meaning of the representation. This objective should not be regarded merely as the locus of formal invention, but as describing how designers make judgments about the "goodness of fit" between form and context. It also addresses the nature of human-centered (as opposed to machine-centered) representation in a rapidly changing technological environment.

➻ Structuring and positioning information/managing complexity

This objective refers to determining and accounting for structures that influence the nature and meaning of interactive experiences. It addresses designers' understanding of the structural conventions embedded within users' previous experiences (e.g., the expectations of information hierarchy established by learning to read in a particular language, or the practice of browsing when shopping in a store), within or against which new interactions among people, and with information, will be designed. This objective also encourages a systems approach to design that views the design of interactive experiences as having consequences in contexts larger than their immediate applications. It acknowledges the intervention of technology in social relationships, and that such intervention carries with it a values dimension about which people can make choices.

➻ Responding/clarifying/providing feedback

This objective addresses shaping the social characteristics of technologically mediated experiences to meet users' emotional, cognitive, and functional needs. This objective calls for students to assess patterns of social interaction (e.g., human conversation, interpersonal negotiation, or coaching), and to make use of these patterns when designing technological interaction.

» Validating/empowering

This objective refers to the attitudinal and critical assessment aspects of human interactions with information and its authors/sponsors (e.g., users'/audiences' perceptions of credibility, authority, or reliability; the role of self-determined paths and choice in navigation strategies; or the structure of persuasive arguments that activate critical thinking). This objective also addresses the cultural human factors that define how users/audiences are different in their interaction skills and attitudes. In this context, culture refers not only to nationality or ethnicity, but also to groups that share common skill-sets and values or interests.

» Students will master the "techniques" used to create interactive experiences, including:

» Visual, audio, temporal, and kinesthetic elements and principles of design

Students will explore the full range of human sensory reception and use them in the information environment. The use of these elements and principles should facilitate user understanding, enhance meaning and the quality of interaction among people, and mediate the relationship between people and technology.

» Language structures

Students will employ language structures (e.g., storytelling) that enhance understanding and support users' objectives in a variety of contexts, including commerce, learning, work, recreation, and social and political decision making. Students will understand the construction of verbal messages and the roles they play in defining experiences.

» Technological affordances

Students will understand the characteristics of technology and select appropriate forms for the creation of specific experiences. They will account for the contribution technology makes to meaning, and the role it plays in defining contemporary culture and communication.

» Collaborative/team-oriented project management

Students will develop processes that are appropriate to the communication task, recognizing that a variety of specialists contribute to successful solutions. They will learn to participate in and manage multidisciplinary teams.

» Students will understand the history of design and the history of communications technology.

Preparing Undergraduates for Later Study

While the complement of skills and knowledge necessary for high-level experience design practice requires more study than can be accomplished in four years, relevant practices and attitudes can be fostered at the undergraduate level. The following pedagogical approaches by faculty encourage the development of such attitudes:

- Centering faculty-defined student projects around users' experiences, not around designers' expressions.
- Articulating the full ensemble of issues that define project contexts (cognitive, physical, social, cultural, technological, and economic).

- Engaging students in some projects that demand the structuring of content across time.
- Engaging students in some projects that require managing complexity, especially those for which there are many possible hierarchies among information components.
- Encouraging students to diagram and model relationships among information components spatially, before designing communication products.

Legozeit: Creating User Experiences

"**THE KEY CRITERION** of a system's usability is the extent to which it supports the potential for people who work with it to understand it, to learn, and to make changes. Design for usability must include design for coping with novelty, design for improvisation, and design for adaptation."[1]

1 | 11:30 A.M. I blithely disregard the easy-to-follow instruction guide provided only to reviewers—I want the real experience—and load up the CD-ROM–setup program. Piece of cake. I put batteries in the RCX, and get the motors to run. "You are amazing," the computer tells me.

2 | 12:00 P.M. I am rummaging through the box, trying to find a tiny piece with two holes and four bumps, to build the basic robot necessary for the training program. I cannot find the piece amid the 726 other blocks. Tiny chunks of plastic go flying and disappear into the crevices of my desk as I paw through the box. This, I suddenly recall, is what I hated about Lego when I was growing up.

3 | 12:30 P.M. I have assembled the robot, and walked through the first programming demo: Make a robot that moves forward in a straight line. My robot goes in circles. I start swearing.

4 | 1:35 P.M. I figure out that I haven't rigged the motors to the RCX properly, causing one motor to rotate in the wrong direction. I fix it, and the robot goes forward. I cheer.

5 | 3:00 P.M. I've built a robot that looks somewhat like a dune buggy, and I've managed to get it to go forward, hit a wall and stop without breaking. I can't figure out, however, why it won't then turn in a circle.

6 | 3:30 P.M. Welcome to Mechanics 101—I realize that wheeled machines need axles to turn. My robot works. I'm brilliant.[2]

Design Knowledge

In a famous lecture at M.I.T. in 1968, Herbert A. Simon outlined a program for a science of design, and a curriculum for training professional designers. He concluded that "the proper study of mankind is the science of design, not only as the professional component of a technical education but as a core discipline for every liberally educated man."[3]

Simon was aware of the growing communication that was taking place among intellectual disciplines around the modern computer, a situation magnified exponentially within the contemporary field of interactive design, where disciplinary knowledge from fields such as information technology (IT), human computer interaction (HCI), graphic design, engineering, and copywriting sit in close (and often uncomfortable) proximity. The ability to communicate, via shared processes, has become one of the critical issues facing development teams. Toward this end, Simon argued that the ability to communicate across fields comes from the need to "be explicit, as never before, about what is involved in creating a design and what takes place while the creation is going on."[4]

This requirement to "be explicit" found an interesting (and rather concrete) application in the course, "Legozeit: Creating User Experiences," a design course I recently taught at the University of Texas. This course asked students to explore the myriad ways in which designers create systems of interactivity, from point-and-click interfaces to complex game-play scenarios. Over the course of the semester the students designed and programmed interactive objects, scripted scenarios for the use of these objects, and constructed containers to house them. While these objects varied in size and application, they shared a common material of production, a system of programmable plastic building bricks known as Lego Mindstorms.

Broadly speaking, the course "Legozeit" engaged primary connections between design, interactivity, and the use of Mindstorms as a playful conduit between making and thinking practices. Three questions shaped the curriculum: How could the process of playtesting (rapid prototyping and user testing) be integrated into the design of interactive, programmable objects? To what extent could issues of user experience and usability be made evident in the design of these objects? What did it mean to create "meaningful interactivity"? In practice, the use of the Lego Mindstorms facilitated a design method based in iterative testing of physical, interactive objects. Through the construction and direct handling of artifact and associated code, the students' design processes were literally made visible, and as a result, knowable, within the context of a specified design scenario. Over time the students gained a clear command of "actionable" design methods, or ways of working that made their disciplinary knowledge explicit.

For those unfamiliar with Mindstorms, a brief description of the product might be helpful here. Mindstorms is a new lego system that incorporates computer chips to enable users to build and design their own programmable devices. The electronic brick (RCX block) at the heart of this system is able to perform various robotic activities: moving across a surface, reacting to light or sound, turning, flipping, or jumping. Users program the interactivity and movement of their lego creations on a PC, using software designed specifically for Mindstorms. Programs are then downloaded to the RCX block via an infrared transmitter, and off the devices go!

Due to Legozeit's practical emphasis on procedural and behavioral prototyping methods, it is important to note that the use of the lego blocks and the creation of the computer programs that drove the inventions were interwoven activities: the Mindstorms creations, with their mixture of engineering and programming, combined pretech mechanisms and high-tech software, celebrating the union of making and thinking. The programmable blocks provided an opportunity for the students to "play" with software and basic programming languages, flipping back and forth between open exploration and focused research. "Our goal," said Mitchell Resnick, one of Mindstorms' creators, "is to bring back a craft spirit. We think of computers as a new kind of material used to create things in the world."[5] The computer, he suggested, should seem more like modeling clay or finger paint and less like television. This celebration of material manipulation via digital technology allowed students to move seamlessly between the object and the object-in-use, two sides of the same coin that are often overlooked in the classroom setting.

The decision to use Lego Mindstorms as the applied model for a study of interactive design came about for several reasons, not the least being their ability to evoke an almost immediate and deep engagement on the part of any user. As mentioned above, Mindstorms offers an important mixture of visual design, engineering, and programming. It represents a dynamic, self-contained design system that can be isolated by students as a model for the study of interactivity. On a technological level, Mindstorms offers an introduction to basic programming skills, which can be immediately implemented and tested. Finally, as an open design tool, Mindstorms allows for the sharing of knowledge through collaborative learning, a principle that formed the foundation for many of the projects developed in the course.

Rules of Engagement

In addition to an investigation of interactivity and play, students were introduced to several design models drawn from the field of human computer interaction, as a way of deepening their understanding of user experience issues. The first model was intended to facilitate an understanding of how designers use different kinds of knowledge within their process. It consists of three non-sequential steps or modes of operation: conceptual, constitutive, and consolidatory. Developed in an article titled "Conceptual, Constituent, and Consolidatory Phases: New Concepts for the Design of Industrial Buildings," I quote the authors at length:[6]

- The conceptual step is guided by the designer's vision, which is typically not very distinct: unclear in parts, hard to communicate. To clarify the vision, the designer matches it to a repertoire of known structures, which are called formats. The matching process is a physically tangible activity, in which externalization of different kinds are used to guide the work and to communicate with users.
- In the constitutive step, the concept from the conceptual step is confronted with typical use situations in order to raise questions about requirements and constraints. The concept is modified and extended, and possibly abandoned in favor of a new wave of conceptual activity.
- The consolidatory step is concerned with refining a proposed solution in terms of simplicity, elegance, and appropriateness for long-term use. Value-based judgment and experience are crucial components of consolidation.

While this model found application within a variety of contexts throughout the course, its value can best be seen in the course's very first project, where students were charged with the design of a container to house the over 720 lego components that came with their Mindstorms kits. This assignment focused on the issue of "utility," and required the students to design a container that a) supported their system of organization (general versus granular), b) supported their mode of transportation (bike, bus, motorcycle), and c) supported their style of building (desk versus floor). These three criteria demanded that the students experience themselves as the system's primary users.

During the first week of class a range of organizational and building techniques were identified: on one end of the spectrum were the "rummagers" who sorted their pieces on the fly, rejecting the tidy module approach favored by many of their peers. Then, of course, there were the students for whom the term "organize" demanded granular, or "anal retentive" articulation. These students' elaborate taxonomies of shape, color, and scale were best supported by container designs that shared a structural affinity with card catalogs or tool chests. Because these containers were to be used throughout the entire semester, the students had a unique opportunity to refine their designs, as knowledge of their use situation grew. Many of the designs that initially favored multiple levels of sorting were modified once their users realized that returning the pieces to their original location after a building session was, quite frankly, no fun. The recognition that the container design had to support a user's needs throughout the entire process, from setup through breakdown, was revelatory to many. In addition, because the project was considered a "perpetual prototype," the students constantly reworked their solutions, testing and refining their ideas. Perhaps most importantly, the students realized they were participating in a design problem where their own experience as users was what counted most of all.

While the value of these results can be seen in very general terms, their specificity to the field of interactive design lies in an approach that focuses on the use situation rather than the user per se. Implicit in this approach is an understanding of design as a creative activity that is concerned not only with the development of artifacts, but also with the shaping of situations of use. As the container project demonstrates, the ability to learn from observations and experiences of systems in use, and to operationalize this learning in new formats, was supported by the conceptual-constitutive-consolidatory model. The model also had implications concerning the value judgments being made by the students throughout their development process. They learned to ask: Is this a good choice of format? How serious is the constraint that we have discovered? Is the solution appropriate for the actual user?[7] Each of these questions helped to shape the students' understanding of the effectiveness of their designs, and served as vital tools in the assessment and evaluation stages of their process.

Quality-in-Use

A second model, that of "Quality-in-use," was introduced in the latter half of the semester as a means of reinforcing the need for interaction designers to look beyond the object in order to locate the "design ability" of an object within specific contexts of use. As a model, quality-in-use addresses the value of artifacts-in-use as the appropriate balance between technology

proper (structure), the contextual social utility of the artifact (function), and the subjective experience of using the system (form).[8] I first learned of this idea during a research exchange with a
designer from Sweden whose disciplinary expertise was in human computer interaction.
Together, we had been looking for models that might be shared by designers working in Web
development and game design; the quality-in-use model he introduced me to resonated with
the "Legozeit" course curriculum, as it related the form of a system directly to the relation
between system, context, and user.

While the initial course projects emphasized the objective values of artifacts, later projects
focused on the social and subjective dimensions proposed by the quality-in-use model. Rather
than limit our study of usability to a structural perspective, we turned our attention to the contextual aspects of function and form. Because the quality-in-use model came from a discipline
(HCI) outside of our own expertise, we established a set of working definitions. These definitions
were taken from the article "What Kind of Car is This Sales System?", a research paper written
for the IT Design Quality Project:[9]

➻ The structure of a system is its material or medial aspects, the technology in terms of hardware and software. The structural aspects of the system are objective in the sense that
   they are inherent in the construction of the system, and less dependent on context and
   interpretation.
➻ The functional aspects of a system concern its actual, contextual purpose and use.
   Typically, different users have different purposes and usage of a system.
➻ Finally, the form of a system expresses the experience of using the system. Form is not a
   property of the system, but rather a relation between system and user.

With these definitions in hand, the students were charged with creating a "play scenario"
that brought together a set of users with a group of interactive, lego-based objects. The goal of
the project was to create a context of use where the interaction between objects and users
could be documented from the point of view of both designer and user. Students worked in
teams; building and programming objects that supported play activities such as drawing ("doo-
dlebots"), breakdancing ("Electric Boogaloobots"), sparring ("battlebots"), and running-jumping-
skipping ("gauntletbots"). They then spent an afternoon participating as users in one another's
scenarios. A team of objective observers took notes on the events (written, audio, video, still
image formats), recording details of the users' interaction with the objects, one another, and the
situating context. This observational data formed the foundation for the next component of the
project: The Experience Cube.

In The Experience Cube, students were asked to analyze their play scenario from the three
different perspectives outlined by the quality-in-use model: structure, function, and form. This
analysis, which took the form of mind-maps, visual schematics, and narrative descriptions, was
first translated into a list of values that best described the qualities of interaction between the
users and the lego devices. These qualities-in-use—concepts such as transparency, conflict,
anticipation, and mimicry—were values associated with the user experience. Next, each student
selected one of the identified values (conflict, for example) and designed a 4" × 4" × 4" cube

that mapped the interactivity of the event as an expression of this value. As singular artifacts, the Experience Cubes helped the students to visualize form and function. In sum, they represented a concentration of use experiences, articulated as a system of aesthetic qualities. The students then went on to design a series of products—from backpacks to children's furniture—informed by this rich analysis.

Run Program

While there is not room here to detail the full results of the Legozeit course, it is possible to draw some general conclusions. First, the use of the Mindstorms system allowed the students to explore issues of interactivity, user experience, and usability while supporting an iterative design methodology. The seamless transition between making, thinking, and testing practices reinforced the necessary relationship between designer, use, and user. Second, the incorporation of models drawn from the field of human computer interaction provided specific frameworks for contextual assessment and evaluation. These frameworks became powerful tools by which relevant values were brought to bear on the problems at hand. Third, students walked away from the course with a critical understanding of the requirements for situations of meaningful interactivity, as well as a deeper appreciation of the need to "be explicit, as never before. . . ."

N O T E S

1. Ehn, Pelle. Jonas Löwgren. "Design for Quality-in-use: Human-Computer Interaction Meets Information Systems Development." *Handbook of Human Computer Interaction,* M. Helander, T. K. Landauer, P. Prabhu, eds. 1997.

2. Brown, Janelle. "I, Robot? My, Robot?" *www.salon.com/21st/reviews/1998/10/02review.html*

3. Ehn, Pelle, Jonas Löwgren. "Design for Quality-in-use: Human-Computer Interaction Meets Information Systems Development." *Handbook of Human Computer Interaction,* M. Helander, T. K. Landauer, P. Prabhu, eds. 1997.

4. Ibid.

5. Abrams, Janet. "Bricks With Brains." *If/Then,* Jan Abrams, ed. (The Netherlands Design Institute, 1999.)

6. Ehn, Pelle. Theis Meggerle, Odd Steen, Micke Svedemar. "What Kind of Car of this Sales System? On Styles, Artifacts, and Quality-in-Use." (Department of Informatics, Lund University, Lund, Sweden. 1995.)

7. Ibid.

8. Ibid.

9. Ehn, Pelle, Jonas Löwgren. "Design for Quality-in-use: Human-Computer Interaction Meets Information Systems Development." *Handbook of Human Computer Interaction,* M. Helander, T. K. Landauer, P. Prabhu, eds. 1997.

R E Q U I R E D   C O U R S E   R E A D I N G

Dave Baum's *Definitive Guide to Lego Mindstorms.* Dave Baum, 2000.

"Bricks With Brains," Janet Abrams. *If/Then.* Jan Abrams, ed. (The Netherlands Design Institute, 1999.)

"Discovery in Digital Craft," Malcolm McCullough. *If/Then*, Jan Abrams, ed. (The Netherlands Design Institute, 1999.)

"Meaningful Space," Yuri Engelhardt. *If/Then,* Jan Abrams, ed. (The Netherlands Design Institute, 1999.)

"The Heresy of Zone Defense," David Hickey. *Air Guitar*. 1998.

"Games as Structure," Elliot Avedon and Brian Sutton-Smith. *The Study of Games*. 1971.

"The Definition of Play," Roger Caillois. *Man, Play, and Games*. 1961.

"Play and Ambiguity," Brian Sutton-Smith. *The Ambiguity of Pla*y. 1998.

C O U R S E   M O D U L E S

1. Rules module: robots + container project 1 (utility)

2. Translation module: robots + interface design (interactivity)

3. Play module: constructing user experiences + play mapping (the experience cube)

4. Container module: container project 2 (context of use)

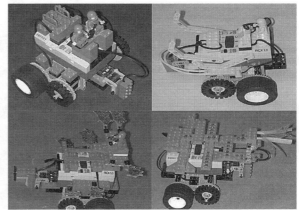

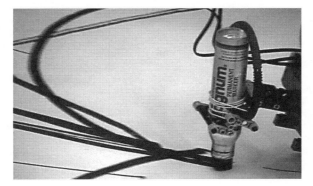

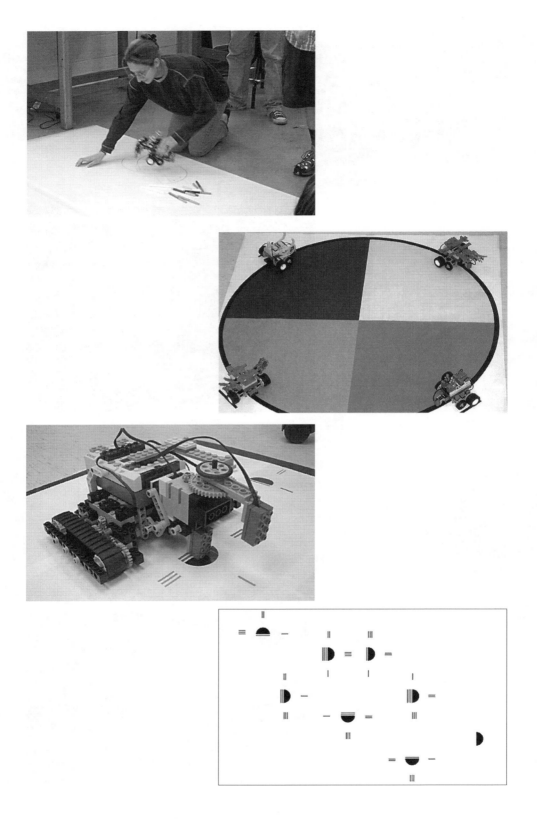

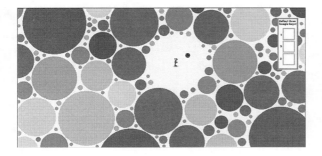

Strange
Bedfellows

Design by Committee

KATHERINE NELSON

ONCE UPON A time, a designer's work was fixed, static, and timeless. Today, design has undergone a traumatic, seemingly irreversible shift. Design products have moved off the page into the digital realm and are flexible, interactive, and virtual. The definition of design now incorporates business and brand strategy, information architecture, as well as old-fashioned creative decision-making. Contemporary designers work in production teams of up to thirty or forty people, and are barraged by demands from almost every discipline: social sciences, engineering, business, and management. But how much is too much? Have the demands of research-intensive, marketing-driven design superseded the humanizing, cohesive sensibility that an individual can bring to a project?

In response to this question, a majority of digital design firms *and agencies* are actively addressing the nuances of communication between their designers and the increasing number of *people from* other disciplines who now contribute to the design process. Whether the firm is a global corporation or a small design hot shop, digital companies have found that creating a common understanding between departments like research, strategy, and design is a core company concern. And while committees *are now the industry standard*, the good news is that this trend does not have to mean the dissolution of a consistent and cohesive design message.

While print designers may be uncomfortable with the idea of working in large teams, much of the history of the field has been one of collaboration, according to Richard Buchanan, head of the school of design at Carnegie Mellon University. "The designer as artist or lone wolf is more of a style and less a definition of design," says Buchanan. "It harks back to an older art-school model that may not be so effective or relevant today. In fact, designers have been generally very good at working together." Buchanan notes companies such as Herman Miller, Dreyfus, or Loewy as organizations with long histories of groundbreaking design collaborations. The challenge of incorporating other areas of knowledge into product development is less about losing the "purity" of design and more about reaffirming the field's increasingly central role in the process. "The question is not whether social science research should be incorporated into design," he says. "The question is more about how you go from a scientific understanding to design-making. A scientific understanding will not give you the particular features of a product. It may confirm some things. It may give ideas. But the actual precise working out of the details, that's a design challenge."

Discovering a richer, more flexible definition of design—one at the crux of many disciplines—is now a way of life for today's designer. And while designers at ad agencies have traditionally had more team experience, the increasing numbers of specialists involved in design decisions continue to make the process a challenge for agencies like Red Sky. At Red Sky, whose clients include Slim Jim, Altoids, and Absolut Vodka, two to three designers work on teams that can contain as many as fifteen people. "From the design standpoint, we are able to handle the majority of jobs that we do with a design director and two designers," says design director David DeCheser. The other members of the team comprise researchers, business strategists, information architects, producers, and representatives from engineering and development. Within these large teams, DeCheser says, one of the best ways to facilitate understanding about a project is to avoid a "hand-off" situation. "Collaboration is a staple of how we work at Red Sky," he says. "Sometimes at other organizations, designers aren't included in the project until the design phase begins. They are simply handed storyboards and business objectives and they have to work against that. Over here, everyone collaborates on what we call a 'better blueprint' for everybody to work off of." One of the keys in putting together this "blueprint" is to have the design teams sit in on user research at its earliest stages. Katie Holihan, a senior experience planner whose job it is to develop creative strategy, agrees, "We have a team approach from the very beginning. We like to have creatives with us observing [our research] and some like to get more involved. And when I do a briefing, every team member is there because we are all interdependent." This collaborative methodology enables a fuller design solution because it engages participants not just professionally, but also personally: "What we've found is that regardless of the position they are in, everybody is interested in more than just what they do," says DeChesser. "Designers love design, but they also want to participate in strategy. They want to meet the client. They want to influence the information architecture. And it's not just because they want to be in control or they feel like they are out of control. It's because they are genuinely interested."

DeCheeser claims that giving everyone a "voice" on the project contributes to a feeling of ownership, which is good for the entire team as well as the client. Understandably, there are always refinements being made in team structure as Red Sky, the result of a recent merger between San Francisco–based Red Sky Interactive and New York–based Nuforia, grows along with its industry and new technologies. Before the merger, Red Sky Interactive had approximately eighty-five employees and Nuforia had approximately three hundred fifty. Now, with over five hundred employees, the new company has the need for team members who are increasingly specialized. And in a collaborative environment, transitioning from general to more specific job descriptions has created some confusion as to just where the boundaries should be drawn. "When we were a smaller company, the information architecture, for example, was done by the producers, design directors, and strategists," says DeCheser. "As we've grown and projects become more complex, there's more detail that we've needed to keep track of so a new discipline is introduced. Because we have such an extremely collaborative environment, one difficulty is actually who owns what. It's something that we are in the process of refining."

Scient is one company that has collaboration down to a science. It is a global e-business consultancy with approximately fifteen hundred employees, twelve offices worldwide, and clients like Chase, First Union, and *Sephora.com*. Scient is respected industry-wide for the detailed projects the company undertakes, as well as for its forward-thinking user research. Currently, the company is working less on individual Web projects and more on general business consultation. "At Scient we don't really design sites; we design businesses," says Shelley Evenson managing director, customer experience architect. The massive scale of Scient's projects can incorporate huge teams of up to thirty or forty people. Therefore, communication between team members is an issue that the company takes great pains to address. "I think the thing that makes Scient different is that it truly integrates the disciplines," says Evenson. "That is crucial. You can do great design and have great technology but if it doesn't make business sense it doesn't matter. You need strengths in all three domains to make it work."

One technique used at both Scient and Red Sky is to begin an engagement with what is referred to as a group of team "leads"—approximately five to ten representatives of business, technology, and experience—who meet with the client before the larger team sessions take place. "Each lead brings a different perspective to the business design. To have a truly integrated solution, you need to have people bring that perspective to the table from the beginning," says Evenson. Another way to facilitate communication at Scient is the creation of a business design model called a "framework." Beginning with the initial research, team members do a series of "mapping exercises." During these exercises, groups of user "needs" will be clustered into categories; then, a project framework is developed out of these initial clusters of information and observations. "The framework becomes a map of the design criteria," explains Evenson. "You can point to a specific element in your design solution that addresses a specific cluster of needs." This framework grows as the team refers to it over time, creating a shared vocabulary about a project that can be used by all team members, as well as by the client. "You have a shared view or common ground among team members," continues Evenson. "And it's a simplified view that the client can also refer to. So when a particular situation arises, it gives the client a way of grasping onto the idea and seeing where it fits." This process of building a modular, flexible framework brings an overview rather than a detailed view to a project and avoids last-minute changes or surprises. And the presence of the framework also allows for fluid transitions from one phase of the project to another, bringing disparate team members quickly up to speed. "Things are so complicated when we are creating these experiences for people and designing these businesses that you have to have a gestalt before you create a detailed view," says Evenson.

While a gestalt view of a project or business is an essential part of design strategy, the new media industry does have its share of specialists. Arc, a firm that has worked with Citibank, Disney, and WeightWatchers, provides strategy, design, and architects Web applications, but—unlike Red Sky or Scient—doesn't actually build or implement them. Chief strategic officer, Jack Templin, and his partner, CEO Ian Kerner, created the structure of Arc to address some of the difficulties that they experienced personally while working at larger new media companies, including iXL, where they met. "The companies that try to do everything, from the most strategic activities to implementation, involve so many different types of people," says Templin. "It is frequently difficult to create a compelling culture around that." Templin claims that while his team members have varied interests, backgrounds, and wear many hats; the company is purposefully very focused. Teams at Arc are kept small, averaging about five or six people. Unlike at most design firms, the teams are also dedicated, meaning that members work on only one project at a time. "We try to bring together like-minded people who are truly performing as consultants," says Templin. "At a lot of other companies, only 10 to 15 percent of the workforce is performing in a consulting capacity and the others are back at the ranch implementing. And right there is a cultural rift that I think can be very challenging."

Another conflict at larger firms, Templin says, involves the objectivity of in-house research. "One can argue that there should be a natural tension between user testing and information architecture," he says. "Because if user testing is essentially critiquing work that has been done in-house there is a lot of pressure for it to be validated. Imagine a project running over budget and over schedule and then it goes to user testing and user testing says that the users hate it. And then the client hears that. That's a tough situation." While Arc may experience fewer internal communication challenges than either Red Sky or Scient, the company also works with a wider variety of outside vendors. Collaboration skills at Arc, as well as at the larger companies remain key. "We have to be careful that our methodology and ways of talking about things don't only work for us internally, but that we can also communicate effectively to our clients and third parties." One of the ways Arc encourages communication between vendors, the client, and team members is by having all of the functional specifications of a project put into what Templin calls a "knowledge management database," which can be customized for a particular viewer. "[This database] allows us to have a central repurposable pool of data that can serve a number of audiences," he says. Considering Arc's focused approach, one might consider that it's easy for the company to lose control of a project as it "hands off" its design and strategy blueprints to outside developers. However, Templin disagrees. "I think there is much less danger of losing control than at a number of other places because our scope is fairly contained," he argues. "A lot of these I-builders sign up for six-month projects. We have long relationships built on short, action-oriented engagements like six to eight weeks."

With the explosion in new technologies have also come numerous new design approaches and methodologies. Companies can be large or small, creative- or research-driven, highly specialized or richly generalized. One thing is certain, there is no single right way to approach design for new media. And the field is changing at such a rapid pace that design firms and agencies will be reinventing themselves for years to come. Design's place within this interdisciplinary, digital mosh pit is hard to fix. On the one hand, design has become more integral to product development than ever before. On the other hand, design now incorporates the perspectives of so many different disciplines that it's hard to get a handle on where it fits into new media, if at all. Says Richard Buchanan, "In one sense, design has come forward as a great hope for the future. At the very same time that is happening, we are losing the sense of what design is. I think it's a short-term problem. I think we will come out of it in good shape, but right now it's a tricky situation."

Us Versus Them

NANCY NOWACEK

THESE SHOULD BE the best of times for graphic design, a second golden age to rival only the invention of the printing press. A time pregnant with possibility, made muscular and radiant with sustenance and fortification of a new medium, the Internet. The World Wide Web has created a whole new space, immaterial but performative across a thousand-million computer monitors. Incredible. It offers sound and motion, interactivity and informational linkages, scalability and reproducibility the likes of which have never been seen on a poster, or a brochure.

Every day newly designed Web sites are launched, and old Web sites are being redesigned. In addition to e-commerce and business-to-business start-ups, there are scores of bricks-and mortar-businesses that in their reluctance to invest their brand on the Internet three years ago, are rushing to design their own Web presence, and claim validation and credibility through a URL.

Despite the market's great expectations, these very well may be the worst times for graphic design. The Web, still in its relative infancy, has given birth to Web site design, which seems, from the experiences and observations of the author, to be forging a schism in what we used to call "design," diluting, degrading and disengaging all those who called themselves "designers."

What Was Design?

A dry cleaner cleans clothing. A firefighter fights fires. Medical doctors heal bodies. The practice of design eludes such concise definition. Design is a complex and vague process conjoining information analysis and aesthetic intuition. It is at once rational and inarticulateable. Objective and subjective. It makes objects and communications that are both beautiful and useful. "Graphic design—which fulfills esthetic needs, complies with the laws of form . . . which speaks in semiotics, sans serifs, and geometrics; . . . is not good design if it is irrelevant. Visual communications of any kind, whether persuasive or informative, from billboards to birth announcements, should be seen as the embodiment of form and function: the integration of the beautiful and the useful" (Paul Rand, *Thoughts on Design*). Design is both problem seeking and problem solving. Will a four-color brochure best serve a client's needs or would a billboard be better? If a billboard, then what should the billboard look like? What should it say? Who should see it? Where should it be located? And should it be one billboard or a series? And so on.

Design is also understanding cultural signs and human behavior to create resonant, clear, and intuitively usable objects. Will those who see the billboard understand the relationship between the image and the tagline? Will viewers be able to read the entire billboard as they pass by, and remember the telephone number to call? Design, too, must understand and engage its context: how does a billboard function differently than a T-shirt? And, what are the ramifications for locating a billboard for hamburgers atop an animal rights office space? Syntactically, design is color, line, scale and texture. Semantically, it is word, image, and text. Taken together in the consumer landscape, the syntax and semantics of design can create powerful messages capable of altering popular behavior and re-forming opinions.

Once designers have been trained in syntax, semantics, and context, they should be able function across a continuum of applications and operate in every capacity to creatively solve their clients' problems and address their clients' needs. The idea that design is a multimodal activity has roots in Bauhausian idealism, the legacy of the Eames office, and the practices of Massimo Vignelli and Bruce Mau. The Bauhaus education cultivated the correspondences between textiles and photography, sculpture and design, and supported their students' work across media and discipline. The Eames office created the cross-pollinating studio model, working in architecture, product design, exhibition design, and filmmaking. Massimo Vignelli and Bruce Mau's studios have continued this model, taking projects in signage design, wayfinding, furniture design, typeface design, exhibition design, book design, filmmaking, and corporate identities.

Before the Web, designers with an education in typography, layout, color, image utilization, and production techniques could move fluidly between book design and corporate identity or environmental signage without titles or specialization. It was regarded that a variety of project types provides a constant recontextualization of problem solving and cross-pollination of methodologies and experiences to each discrete pursuit.

Since the Web, however, the climate seems to have changed. Now every designer goes out of his or her way to define a specialty and work narrowly within that segment. Niches abound. There are now branding specialists, annual-report designers, motion-graphics design-ers, broadcast designers, book-cover designers, and retail designers. Web site designers, in particular, seem to travel the farthest to differentiate themselves from those who are not Web designers—namely, those who work in print. If you're not in New Media, you must be old school.

I have been working for the Web for two years—my business card titles me an "information designer" (which sounds strangely redundant). I worked in other media for four years (nine years including undergraduate and graduate education), and referred to myself as a "designer." These past two years I have been creating Home Pages, Splash Pages, Sub-level Pages, and Consistent Navigation. I dream in 72 dpi and 256 colors. I have pushed more pixels around the page and set more type in Photoshop than I ever thought possible.

I came to cyberspace to learn more about it, to extend my design skills into a new medi-um, and learn more about Internet technology, just as I had learned about paper and ink, screen printing, pre-press, letter press, and a variety of other technologies, as required by design jobs (e.g., high frequency rubber molding, linticular, embroidery, engraving, soap milling). When I started in Web site design, I was unaware of my outsider status and apparent design handicap because I didn't understand why HTML can only really set text at ten and twelve points. It was unclear to me, in my excitement to join cyberspace, that it would be anything but the informational utopia that had been described by *Wired Magazine*. In fact, it's far from utopia, of any sort. Although Web site design suggests challenging problems and unfettered opportunities, it is frustrating, demoralizing, and downright disappointing. There are two obstacles to creating good design on the Web: the Web and Web-site designers. From these two obstacles branch an array of hurdles.

New Business Director, Producer, Programmer, Interaction Designer, CEO Versus Web Designer

Web site design is inherently a team activity—it feels more like making a film than a book—and design is just one discrete segment of the project. There are proposals, there are program statements, there are technical program statements, content surveys, and interaction design schematics—all of which are accomplished before the design process even starts. Web Designers are responsible for what's called "look and feel." The graphic designer on the team rarely has the opportunity to analyze the client's content and objectives, and give input on behalf of visual communication and meaning. The rest of the team has already done that for the graphic designer, so it's up to the designer to make the Web site look good, regardless of the appropriateness of the proposed ideas. The Web designer is the hands of the team, and sometimes the eyes, but not the head, heart, or ears.

Consequently, because Web designers are more laborers than collaborators in this field, they are second-class citizens who, for as much expertise as they may have in communication design, have little influence on the client. Furthermore, in some cases the Web designer does not even present the work, and those responsible for presenting it are not well-versed in design, and lack the vocabulary and translation skills necessary to elucidate the visual solutions to the client.

Client Versus Web Designer

Design is normally collaboration between designer and client—a productive push-pull, an intellectual and creative dialogue. This dialogue requires listening, communication, compromise, and most important, trust. In Web design, the client and designer have little opportunity to have such a dialogue. Rather than listen to the informed opinions of experienced designers, Web site clients prefer to place their trust in themselves. They come to the project with a list of URLs of Web sites they like ("*Drugstore.com* has buttons that are really easy to use") and, despite their lack of practice, experience, and critical knowledge of information organization, whittle away at the Web designer's original ideas, until they have a potluck of a home page pirated and cobbled together with elements from the myriad sites they've visited. Moreover, it has become de rigueur in commercial Web site design for the clients to seek designs that most resemble those of other Web sites in their market or industry. Differentiation and originality are eschewed. Derivative is good; mediocre even better. No matter what Web designers may do to convince their clients to believe in a more intelligent, more elegant, better-structured site, clients will trust the low standards and precedents already set by other sites. (And then there are clients who consider themselves experts because they are neophytes: They have never surfed the Web, they don't know how to scroll, and they believe that all their users are equally uneducated—but that's another article, for another time.)

Web Designer Versus Web Master

Have you ever had a suit custom-made, but decided once you got it home, that despite the deliriously perfect fit, the luxurious fabric, and the staggering craftsmanship, it would be better to make the sleeves or legs slightly shorter, and hem them with a stapler? Of course not.

This happens all the time in the Web. Companies often hire a Web-design studio to do the initial development of their Web site (not cheaply), then have their in-house Web department administer the finished product over time. The Web site is designed and launched, and Photoshop files are transferred from consulting studio to in-house department. Within weeks, the launched site has different typefaces, the layout has been reconfigured, the navigation reordered, and the buttons have been replaced. Within months, the original site is unrecognizable.

And nothing makes for a more awkward and frustrating design process, than to have used one's problem-solving skills and creativity and worked hard to fulfill the client's objectives, only to start receiving ideas, input, and criticism from an in-house designer who clearly wasn't hired to be part of the process. Like jilted stepchildren (and rightly so), in-house designers can often derail a productive client relationship, and meddle with what is already an ephemeral object, rarely for the better.

Educated Web Designer Versus Software-Savvy Web Designer

I spent almost six years in design education, tracing letterforms, making hypothetical exhibition design and theoretical book design, and reading and writing about design. David Carson didn't. He was born with the design gene, and has incredible innate talent. Lots of well-known designers have that. The rest of us learn through art school or apprenticeships. We learn the nuance of letterforms, we learn about readability, we learn the history of our profession and the wealth of experimentation and study that has come before us. We practice our skills and acquire craftsmanship and methodologies to use in professional practice. While this is true of some Web designers—and more, one hopes, as art schools, universities, and colleges around the world graduate New Media design students—this is not currently true of the majority of Web-site designers. More commonly, Web designers received their design education from software manuals and Photoshop filters. Many were liberal arts majors who, for lack of a more immediate career, bought a computer and mastered 3-D buttons and drop shadows. There's merit in self-education, and many a brilliant designer has been self-educated, but the Web design industry, in it's rapid expansion, is less finicky about designers, portfolios, and qualifications, and has lowered its standards as its need for workers has increased. Consequently, many Web designers suffer from a poverty of knowledge, practice, history, critical evaluation, and crafts-manship, and this is ultimately reflected in their work. Instead of rigorous self-evaluation and a well-trained eye, anything goes and everything does. The derivative, the clichéd, the unusable, and the confusing are launched everyday on commercial sites. But by golly, the buttons look so real you could touch them.

The Fallout

First of all, there's a great communication breakdown and it's breaking down more every-day. It's an *us versus them* situation. Print designers think Web designers only know the tech-nology, and Web designers think print designers are outdated dinosaurs. Aside from missing out on the experiences one could share with the other—like swapping typesetting tips and inter-esting interactivity solutions over a roaring campfire—the factions are so suspicious and deroga-tory of one another that collaboration is often a stalemated affair.

It is becoming common for a company to hire a print or branding studio to develop its corporate identity, and a Web studio to develop its e-commerce or Web presence. Sometimes, an advertising agency is also contracted to develop an ad campaign to promote the new iden-tity and/or Web site. The client assumes that all efforts will be coordinated and that their new image will be seamless from advertisement to Web site to product. Meanwhile, the branding firm has developed a logomark that is virtually untranslatable onto the Web; on screen it loses its spirit and immediacy. Or the logo has been made in just those colors that don't really exist in the 256 palette. Or, as frequently happens, the branding firm will just not answer requests from the Web studio to share materials, so that the Web efforts may reflect the print efforts. And often, halfway through Web development, the advertising agency decides to finally send over their media campaign materials, and wouldn't you know it, they're totally different from the Web site that's almost finished! We're become a dysfunctional family of divorce where our familial grudges are getting in the way of our professionalism, and the one who loses most is the client. And when the client loses, we lose.

Yes, our profession is suffering, and it may well be divorcing itself. Fragmentation and self-imposed segregation is destroying our credibility and confusing our potential clients. It's difficult enough to educate clients about the necessity and value (monetary and social) of our work, without having to explain ourselves in contrast to another kind of designer. Furthermore, in our industry-based grudge match, we lose the cross-pollination that has typically fed our practice, because we have stopped trusting in and communicating with one another. Making connec-tions between different sorts of projects and problems offers new perspectives on old problems, and valuable insights, and it sparks inspiration and innovation. Without that, we stand the chance of depleting our own resources. A fallow practice draws nearer and nearer.

A Reconciliation?

At this particular stage of Web-site design—neither infancy nor full maturity—we have the opportunity to address these dichotomies, and call off the grudges. We need to identify the sources of these attitudes and issues, and counterbalance them with inclusion and integration. We must start with design education and the forced segregation that comes from tracking students into a specialization after their first year. Medical students spend two years in basic sciences and then two years in general rotations before choosing a specialty. Design education might consider the same model, and work to build stronger foundations and give equal exposure to all specialties, while reiterating the common denominators of design practice. Design also needs to teach more collaborative methods of working, between teams of designers and non-designers, and between various design specialties—making sure to focus on critical listening and communication skills. In short, we should train designers who have a sense of breadth and depth; designers who can work well with others, and be their own best advocates; but most important, designers who can relate to one another with a sense of integrity, trust, and community.

Additionally, we should question design editorial that segregates print and interactive media. Separate design annuals, competitions, and conferences for print and interactive design, send the message loud and clear that these two fields can't share the same criteria, page space, or panel topic. We should demand integration in design awards and publications. We should request conferences concerning all sub-practices of design, with programs specifically designated to generate dialogue between print designers and Web designers. Much dialogue is needed. And most simply, we need to cultivate a definition of our practice that includes all media and all manifestations of design. We must self-consciously cultivate a "we" to overcome the "us" and "them."

The Web Versus Design: "Usability" and the Homogenized Future

GUNNAR SWANSON

A WHILE BACK, one of my graphic design students took a salary of almost 30 percent less than he was offered elsewhere to go to work for Razorfish in San Francisco. "Why would I want to work for a middle-of-the-road Silicon Valley design firm when I could work for the hottest Web design company in the world?" he asked me. I couldn't argue. A few months later he recruited a classmate.

The second student moved on after a few months. The first student lasted about a year before moving to New York to work for RG/A. That adds up to a wonderful résumé, but my students' experience with the experienced designers wasn't quite as wonderful. They expected to work long hours; that was no problem. They didn't expect the glory jobs; that was no problem. They expected to work for the team and for clients' needs. . . .

What my erstwhile students didn't realize was that the cool work that attracted them there had also attracted a lot of new, better-paying clients who wanted e-commerce sites. These young Web designers found themselves doing more and more static, formulaic work and being less and less happy.

If Jakob Nielsen had his way they'd be doing nothing that resembled graphic design. Web site owners are listening to what Nielsen has to say. Is mundane and pedestrian work under the flag of "usability" the future of the Web?

A year or two after my graphic design student took lower pay to follow his Web dreams, several of my multimedia students declared to me that they were not interested in the Web. They looked at most of what was out there and saw nothing that made them want to have anything to do with this boring, ugly, plodding monster. I suggested that they go listen to the radio for a few hours or watch "Total Request Live" on MTV and then tell me whether they like music.

What is it that makes the Web, that place that seems to be the future of graphic design, so boring? Part of the answer might be found in the radio analogy: The medium is dominated by people who copy one another's formulas. The same can be said for print graphics, though, and the moments when designers say, "I don't want any part of graphic design because it's all junk mail and underwear ads" are fewer and farther between. The Web has something else that haunts us. What evil lurks in the hearts of DHTML and Flash animations?

Despite our rhetoric about form following function (well, maybe it's just the old folk like me that bother making those noises anymore), print graphic design is often a veneer of style. In most cases, non-designers make the basic choices about structure and the like, but somehow designers find some level of autonomy by adding visual spice to the pot. On large Web projects, teams or team leaders make basic decisions about the nature of the project, including how style issues play out (and graphic style doesn't define the fell of a Web site as much as it does a brochure). Graphic designers often feel helpless when they find themselves in the role of visual dishwashers for the Information Architect chefs.

What does that do for graphic designers or, perhaps more important, what does it do for graphic design? It depends, of course, on who runs, leads, or guides the teams. Leaders will be people with an understanding of the overall process, but that could be someone with a background in design, computer programming, business administration . . . you name it. As the man said, go to an architect with a problem and you'll get a building as a solution; the background of team leaders will greatly affect outcomes. As a graphic designer, I can't help but hope for someone with a design perspective in charge.

But what happens when a graphic designer gets that broad understanding needed to lead the team? Does she lose an important point of view, co-opted by technological and bureaucratic forces or does she find new ways of dealing with design? Can designers retain an advocacy for design standards while dealing with a team of people who may have no sense of or interest in aesthetics, or deep user experience? When faced with functional ("That won't work on 28 percent of browsers"), statistical ("13 percent fewer people click through if we do that"), and aesthetic/experiential problems, can a project manager maintain an advocacy for design standards, or will the things that are easy to quantify and explain always dominate?

How can designers gain experience in dealing with varied points of view and complex projects? What are the potentials of new technologies from a design standpoint? The way we answer these questions will shape the future of the Web and the future of graphic design.

What happens to designers when so much of graphic design has dematerialized? If one can't fall back on the joy of the object because the point is another's experience, what does that do to our joy in the process? Does all of this require a new kind of designer? How do we make sure that doesn't mean a designer in name only? Does doing meta designer—designing what will happen when a database meets a unique request generating a different (and unpredictable) "object" 250,000 times a day—require a different mind than that of a graphic designer?

Part of the problem may lie in thinking that large team projects are the singular future of design, or even of the Web. When Jakob Nielsen and others talk about the Web as a singular thing, I wonder if they'd make the same claim for print. Should all print material aspire to be the *Wall Street Journal*, a car repair manual, paper-sample brochures, or a rave flyer? Why shouldn't screen-delivered design be just as diverse as paper-delivered design? The Web is not just the home of giant sites; it's the place where all sorts of sites abound.

Where is the interesting future of the Web? As tools for the Web change, how will that change opportunities to design for the Web? Things that would have required writing (or appropriating) some rather obscure code a short time ago are now as easy as the routine work of preparing print files for publication. The dream of animation that works over a slow modem and vector graphics is fulfilled with Flash and LiveMotion and Scalable Vector Graphics is an official standard.

We think of new design on the Web taking place at the cutting edge of technology, but the cutting edge of print design isn't usually at the limits of press technology. Hasn't ease with the tools allowed new opportunities for aesthetic advancement in print? Will designers embrace technical limitations and find a new aesthetic there—a sort of "technoRetro?" Is it time for the crudeness of "vanilla" HTML to be embraced as an aesthetic as punk graphics did for bad Xerox, or Zuzana Licko's early typefaces did for crude bitmaps?

Or will we be trapped into thinking of the Web as one narrowly defined thing instead of seeing it as a universe of experiences? Will we misunderstand the Nixon-era advice and "follow the money" and lose ourselves in the process?

I seem to be asking many more questions than I have answers. Where should Web design go? All I know is that I'm not waiting for Carson to play it for me on TRL.

A previous version of this article was published on the Web site "Elusive Arrangements" at the University of Missouri, Columbia *http://web.missouri.edu/~artdh/ElusiveArrangements.*

Engineers Are from Mars, Designers Are from Venus: Creating Peace through Collaboration

MARIE KACMAREK

TECHNOLOGY AND DESIGN have gainfully coexisted in architectural and industrial design for decades. Traditional print-based design centers itself in the notion of "The Great Idea" with a more paternalistic, top-down approach to process. Which path does design for the Internet take? As the need for collaboration shifts from a vertical to a more horizontal approach, designers are often finding themselves ill-prepared to handle the barrage of technical specifications, intricate user-interface functionality, and transactional data streams, not to mention the more fundamental issues with the edge-case musings of Engineering. In essence, designing for the Web is becoming a marriage between pure design and application design, simply because Web design must *work*. If there truly is a need for left-brained/right-brained partnerships, how can designers come out of this shotgun marriage without becoming disillusioned in the process? What are some of the pitfalls to avoid along the path and some of the strategies for success?

Two Sides of the Same Problem

Imagine a fictitious multi-office Web shop that just within the past year or so began offering integration services to its customers. Let's say it's a shop that was a combination of what were many other smaller, independent shops at one time, companies that had nothing to do with one another in the past, and some of which had limited Internet experience. Now this newly formed group is providing an intricate and vast service that runs the gamut from online advertising to PERL scripting, broadband consulting to PHP programming, site design to e-mail marketing. Now, imagine two young employees of the Boston office, Leigh and Adrian. They were working on a Web site together for one of their clients, a relatively new tech-savvy start-up with second-round funding and a client-supplied functional spec for their e-commerce site, code-named "Robotnik."

The Robotnik founders, Glen and Rob, loved Adrian. In fact, it was Adrian's whip-smart technospeak during the pitch sold them in the first place, rather than his usual enthusiasm for solving a complex problem. Once the contract was signed, Glen and Rob gave Adrian a skeletal site map, and told him to "run with it" (they felt comfortable with Adrian, a fellow engineer), which is exactly what he did. Adrian was fascinated with how the thing worked. What he didn't realize was that instead of running with it, he was being chased by something way out of his control. Which programming language would he use? Which dynamic publishing system? How would he fill up all the holes in the site map? How would he architect the site? It was easy: once he figured out how it worked, then he could figure out how to use it!

In the meantime Leigh was continuing to teach herself Flash because she really thought it was neat. This is what the Web is all about: movement and energy. She was secretly coveting the use of Flash for the Robotnik Web site. If people could just glimpse the expressive nature of Robotnik, they would flock to it in droves! Plus, imagine how cool it would look! During the kick-off meeting with Glen and Rob, she asked them several questions about their business model and their various partnerships. She asked them about their likes and dislikes. What colors did they love? What colors did they hate? What were the most important aspects of their brand? What was their main marketing message? She was envisioning different designs for the site halfway through the kickoff, even though she didn't really like their company logo. Since the deadline was so tight—only three weeks until the big design presentation—she had better get going right away on thinking this through.

The Beast is Ugly

After about two weeks of going back and forth with Glen, on the phone or in his offices' beanbag-laden conference room, about how the e-commerce engine talked to the various databases, or what to do about the limitations of the middleware, or how to add collaborative filtering at this stage of the game, Adrian had (finally) what he considered to be a pretty leak-proof information architecture and technical spec, even though the site had grown so much in complexity in just two weeks. Christ, he had basically given up everything (even his weekly ulti-mate Frisbee games) to finish this. There was virtually no one he omitted when it came to figur-ing out how the site worked. *Everyone* would be able to use it. There was a reason they call engineers "stinking gods among men."

Leigh had taken to practicing yoga much more regularly in the those two weeks. She had been designing and redesigning, ad nauseam, some sample comps for the client presentation, based on Adrian's work. Every time she thought they'd nailed down a good design, Adrian came sidling over to her desk with another change to the interface or another button on the navigation, which made her feel as if she needed to start all over again. He was also becoming more and more impatient with Leigh, especially when she made suggestions to him. She decided to continue focusing on the Flash intro for the site and on which of the four acceptable hex values of yellow she would pick for the background of the logo flyby.

The night before the presentation, Leigh and Thomas, one of the production designers, were up until 3:00 A.M. preparing the various design directions for the site. Adrian left around midnight, right after he had finished the functional prototype he had been noodling with for that past week. Leigh would present to Glen and Rob what the site would look like, while Adrian would show them a snippet of how the content-management system functioned with his code, minus the visual design. By the time Adrian left that evening, he was pretty ragged from the hours and hours of complex coding required for the next day's presentation, and a little sick from the pizza he had eaten at his computer. Leigh, frantically working in Photoshop, had her headphones on when he left and barely nodded at him.

It's a Lot Easier to Keep Fooling Yourself

Leigh thought the first presentation to Glen and Rob actually went fairly well, even though Adrian talked too much. She felt left out at times, and it was hard to reel the "Robot Brothers"— as she called them—back in when Adrian took them way out there with his tech-talk. She was here to talk about design. They loved the Flash animation and, both in agreement, hated the yellow. They thought that blue or grey would work much better. Once they saw all of Adrian's work in context too, they started "seeing" the information for the first time. Leigh knew what this meant: back to the drawing board.

Adrian was pleased that Glen and Rob saw the vastly different tasks he factored into the design of the site. Because he has a mathematician's abstract view of complex systems, he was cognizant of every possible scenario in using the Robotnik site. If it is probable, then it must be designed for! He took Glen and Rob's absence of criticism as a compliment. For Adrian, this project was textbook "implementation model," meaning that as long as he understood how the site operated, he would mirror its internal workings with the way it functioned from the outside. As long as he continued to do this, he would be designing the most powerful Web sites in the world.

Over the next several weeks, both Adrian and Leigh kept plugging away at iterating both the design and the functionality of the Robotnik site with much feedback from Glen and Rob. Of course, the week they launched was insane. Rob was getting married the following week and was not around that often. Glen was overcompensating for Rob's absence or preoccupation by checking in every few hours on the progress of the coding. By the time the entire site had gone live after a couple close-calls with the code, both Adrian and Leigh could barely look at each other without wanting to fly into an internal, personal rage toward the other; Adrian thinking that Leigh was flaky and self-absorbed, and Leigh feeling that Adrian wasn't on her side and had helped ruin the design of her site.

Why Everything Broke Down

Like any relationship, the one between Leigh and Adrian was built on power shifts and balances. These may be slow glacial movements or quickly shifting crevasses, but because both people were so closely tied to the outcome of the Web site, the power struggle was there. It had become very personal. Add Glen and Rob into the mix, and like a paternal pair, Leigh and Adrian felt as if they were in the midst of a family melodrama where each and every one of them had something at stake. What went wrong here and when?

Probably the single most important element of a successful design/engineering working relationship has to do with the order of events in the development process. As long as software development has been around, the mantra has been: develop, test, iterate. The engineer writes the code, sorts through any issues by running it through a variety of "smoke tests," and then finally turns the bad code into good. Next, the visual designer is tiptoeing a couple of steps behind, doing her own thing based on what the client told her because that's all she can do. The result is almost always a bad product, in that it doesn't make sense to the people who use it—they have trouble figuring out what the host company is all about and what they are supposed to do there.

The truth of the matter isn't pretty. Like feudal lords during the birth of the industrial revolution, engineers cannot relinquish their territory after they've occupied it for so long. Their desire to control the design process is based on their own assessment of their performance; they also want control over things they find interesting, things that are complex and deterministic. Controlling humans is not as interesting as controlling a computer. Po Bronson's study for *The First $20 Million Is Always the Hardest* had programmers choose between playing practical jokes on their peers and having their computers jump to attention at their mercy. Of course, the computer is more appealing, since it is a finite system, unlike a human being.

To make matters even worse, there are myriad Web sites out there that look good—sites that are aesthetically pleasing and abuzz with eye candy—but are a source of frustration to the user. With the Robotnik site, Leigh's adoration of cool, new technologies such as Flash add a faster and more powerful system that may or may not work even though the player is well distributed. Unless the person using a site is adept at getting around the inefficiencies of the design (longer load times, strange error messages, and confusingly designed animated interfaces), he will likely abandon it if there are other options. If not, he will quickly learn to hate the Web product itself, and eventually develop a grudge against the company for making him jump through flaming hoops.

Just as children suffer the hardships of their keepers' indiscretions and battle of wills, site users tolerate the grim, drama-ridden relationship between the visual designer and engineer. If you are using a site designed this way, you are probably being made to feel like you are one of their least-favorite stepchildren.

Now What?

With any relationship problem, the direction from which you approach it makes all the difference. In the situation of Robotnik, both Adrian and Leigh were focused first on pleasing Glen and Rob, then on satisfying their own complex personal agendas. The second you either abdicate control of the product design or hand it over to your client (which is what Adrian and Leigh did), you immediately cease thinking of the Web product as a cohesive whole. When pressing Rob on what the core of their business model was, Leigh was actually surprised at how difficult it was for Rob to put it into words. Imagine that a muddled viewpoint now *shifts drastically* to your own business, the business of designing their site. *If they are telling you how to design their site, then you are not designing their site.*

Design should be written down and firm before the coding begins. This means that no changes (feature creep) begin to appear as the production process begins. The word "design" here is not related to visual design, but to interaction design. This is very high-level, goal-oriented design. By helping to determine what is most valuable for the user in the first place, overarching goals come to the surface. Amazon recently discovered, by re-examining its user-base and redesigning its site, that it is in the business of selling books. Amazon discovered that it's what most people do at its site, even though the site may also be offering lawn chairs. It took an awful long time to make this discovery and Amazon is still considered one of the most user friendly sites out there. This says that there is much room for improvement.

Designing for the user means that all who are involved in the conception and production of the site must remove themselves from its design. The user doesn't care what the CEO's color preference is, or if the programmer prefers ASP to CGI scripting. Imagine a surgeon operating on a patient with her own goals or the goals of the hospital or the HMO in the forefront. I would hope the patient is self-preserving enough to get a second opinion. Since building a Web site is not (to my knowledge) a situation of life or death, we easily forget that we aren't the center of the universe; the person using the Web site is. So, we need to develop a precise description of the potential users and what they may wish to accomplish. Developing a cast of characters by creating Personas is tremendously powerful (this is explained in *The Inmates Are Running the Asylum* by Alan Cooper). He calls these people "hypothetical archetypes" of actual users, and they are by-products of one-to-one discussions with potential and actual users of Web products.

The conceptual design is also focused on only *one* of the entire cast of characters, because it is much easier, and more effective, to please 25 percent of all the people rather than making all the people 20 percent satisfied. It simply doesn't work any other way. Every time you attempt to shoehorn another type of user into the equation you get a more malformed product. Eventually you are designing for a non-existent user: what I call the "überuser." This person is a pastiche of varying users, stitched together in such a ramshackle fashion that *it* no longer resembles anything human at all. The goals of the überuser are nothing like the goals of a real human. If you want to design a Web site that makes people happy, then you must have a single individual in mind, the person with the most overarching and challenging goals.

What this means for the Adrians and Leighs of the world is that in exchange for relinquishing a little control to an interaction designer, they gain the ability to focus with clarity on what people need to accomplish at the sites they design and build. Product design has been doing this for decades. If a pitcher has a badly designed spout, you can be sure you will hear about it via the manufacturer's sales channel. Since the Internet has evolved to such an extent that most sites are expected to provide function, and no longer serve as just "brochureware," they must work, and their creators must know what their purpose is. Instead of dressing up existing or organically built functionality by, as Alan Cooper states it, "putting lipstick on a pig," they are creating something cohesive that looks great and functions naturally, and allows both the designer and the engineer to craft and extend what they are good at.

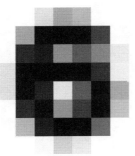

The *ABCs* of e-Commerce

Everything That Can Be Digital, Will Be!

TUCKER VIEMEISTER

ONE NIGHT IN early in 1996, the two founders of Razorfish were sitting in a restaurant talking about the inevitable advance of digital science. They thought it made almost everything better: digital machinery is cheaper, stuff can be done faster, it's more dynamic, connectable, interactive, smarter! "Everything that can be digital, will be!" exclaimed Craig Kanarick. The notion goes beyond VDT screens and all the new computing power that Moore's Law is fueling; they were thinking about how new electronic technology is like a snowball rolling down a mountain picking up everything in its path, transforming everything whether it rolls over it or not.

That doesn't mean everything *will be* digital. There are a lot of things that shouldn't or can't be replaced with some digital substitute: like food, air, or sex for example . . . (well, maybe sex). Designers are instrumental in the creation of this new technology, although not as distinctly as scientists. We translate clunky technology into useful and desirable experiences. We use our talent and our emotions to try to satisfy our inner needs and those of the people who use our designs. This new e-technology is testing all our abilities across lots of media—and the stuff on the computer screen is just the beginning. Soon computers (or at least chips) will be embedded in almost everything around us.

Digital versions of many things are better than their low-tech equivalents because they are cheaper, easier to use, more readily available, more shareable, more sustainable ecologically, or they do more than the old stuff they supersede—just like Jeff and Craig thought. Getting the latest news is faster and more personalized online than waiting for the paperboy. Digital technology enables us to invisibly stay connected to a family separated by miles of real space. Stock trading on line is easier, faster, and cheaper than calling your real human broker.

This is not the first time new technology has dramatically transformed our world. The invention of writing revolutionized the way we remember and it allowed us to pass ideas around more easily than ever. More than 60K years ago, even before humans harnessed fire, the new technology of words and speech put the most powerful technology in our "hands" and separated us from all the other living things. These kinds of technologies have totally changed the way we live.

Digital technology will be even bigger—it's like adding a new dimension. It can redefine everything because it is a new universal medium. The electronic binary code of yes/no, on/off can be translated into many "languages;" it is a very low common denominator for data exchange. Because it is a common medium, it can be used to transfer data from one machine to another and/or from one platform to another. With it, you can encode musical analog sound waves into to digital samples, record them on a CD, then decode the data stream back into analog electrical signals that drive some speakers, re-creating sound waves to enjoy. When the data has been translated into a universal medium, that information can be used in lots of other ways by other machines. Digital binary code can be used to connect almost everything in the world by translating everything into simple bits of data. Information devices, interactive TVs, PDAs, police departments, insurance companies, and nuclear power plants could talk to one another. With digital sensors attached, all kinds of things can communicate—a rock can tell the farmer when to water the corn as easily as my daughter can ask me for a cup of juice.

The new media are blurring the distinctions between services and products—between physical and virtual. Now, with our Physical Design team, Razorfish not only can design what's on the screen, but what the screen is on—coupling integrated digital technology and digital change management with the ability to cast the vision into real physical objects. The seamless integration of digital and physical media demands a new kind of designer, that's why *Metropolis Magazine* called me "the last industrial designer."

So far, the Internet has been about transferring information from one computer to another. With the addition of wireless protocols like WAP or IR connections, computers will no longer need to be physically attached together to network. Meanwhile, TV is merging broadband broadcast entertainment data with personal interaction of the PC—ITV. Moore's Law is packing more and more data into that digital experience. Soon we'll be using more specialized information appliances—e-books or Java toasters. Connecting them all will be cool; my coffeemaker will check with my calendar on my PDA to figure out when to start brewing in the morning, or my car will contact the airline to rebook my flight because light traffic allowed me to get to the airport early. By connecting the sensors and little chips everywhere, the net will become something that will exhibit intelligence, transforming education, reforming our social structures, reconstructing entertainment, overthrowing the economy, and revolutionizing the biosphere. Interconnecting all our gizmos so that they can automatically take care of us will be a great connivance. Digital Technology is the latest attempt of humans to control nature. We believe that through this network humans will be able to harness the power of reason to avert wars and famines, prolong our lives, sustain the environment, and supply everyone with all the goods they desire.

Digital technology and global cultural movements are merging in market trends that put the individual at the center of all business. The "experience" the customer has is the main target, and information is the currency of the new economy. Digital technology allows companies pinpoint accuracy—multifaceted profiles detail all kinds of needs and desires, making it possible to tailor services and products to exactly fit the individual. Personalized service delivers user contentment, which should engender loyalty to the business. Gratification coupled with a good brand presentation should build market share. Normally, a strong market position is easy to translate into profitability. Having all these ducks in a row should ultimately impress investors, thus satisfying business objectives by raising the stock value. In the new economy, customers make their own products, leaving the employees to add value to the user, not the products. Satisfaction merges with commerce. Digital technology means we all profit.

Like the user, Razorfish measures success based on the user's experience. This definition has always been critical in the industrial design field. The reason "experience" has taken on a new importance is that in the digital environment, the product, brand image, and delivery (distribution) may all happen in the same place. Designers will need to create the shape of the hardware, the feel of the interface, and desire for the service! This will demand new roles for designers and strategists. From designing plastic packages for electronic devices, physical designers will revert to creating experiences through the design of natural, unobtrusive objects, because in the future, wooden tables may be able to display information, or teacups will predict the future. You won't need a phone when you'll be able to telephone your Mom by simply calling her name.

"Communication is the economy," exclaims Kevin Kelly in *New Rules for the New Economy*. Business cultures are so much larger, and popular culture is in constant flux, making a consistent message much more difficult to deliver. That is why Razorfish is so concerned with integration. The convergence of content across media platforms makes for a more coherent message. Or conversely, a message that hits more of our senses will trigger more responses, adding up to a deeper meaning that users will associate with higher value. More layers or platforms, engaging more senses, will give more touch points, giving a fuller, richer experience that means a more meaningful experience that should be more valuable to the user, the commercial endeavor, and the rest of society too! The goal now is to manage the dramatic changes so that we make sure it makes a better world!

The Print Versus Internet Smackdown

DAVID VOGLER

DO YOU DREAM of the prestige, comfort, and respectability of a contemporary print design studio, or perhaps the adventuresome, trail-blazing "lets-roll-the-dice" excitement of a new media start-up?

I am often asked by my students for advice about the job market. Up until the past few years, almost all graduating designers were faced with relatively easy job-hunting decisions. The world of graphic design was rooted in the print medium and the rules were reasonably clear. But with the emergence of the Internet, a newly minted designer can be faced with the perplexing choice of a traditional print studio or a dot com company. Naturally, there are pros and cons for both disciplines. Both media can provide wildly creative opportunities and personal gratification, yet both have intrinsic qualities that put the other to shame. In the "celebrity death match" of Print versus Internet, it's tough to decide which medium is worthier.

This handy chart compares the top issues. You be the judge.

	PRINT	DOT COM
If company were run by a "Sopranos" character	Beleaguered Prozac-addicted mob boss Tony Soprano	Arrogant wise guy nephew Christopher Molitsanti
Publication most often read	*The AIGA Journal*	*The Wall Street Journal*
Office decor	Pricey Herman Miller chairs and Steelcase workstations enhanced with the sophisticated aroma of freshly snipped tulips.	Rickety flea market tables and Mom's mismatched mildewy chairs from the basement permeated by the aroma of naked, bowel churning fear.
Compensation packages	Salary, benefits and a reseasonably nice Christmas bonus.	Lots of dubious stock that's "sure to make you rich when we IPO."
Company's business strategy	"We leverage our core competencies to deliver world-class graphic design and branding solutions that enable our clients to gain a competitive edge in the ever-expanding global marketplace for the new millennium and beyond."	""What business strategy? If we miss our launch date we're royally fucked!"
Caffeinated drink of choice	Starbucks grande, skim, no-whip cappuccino	Flat Mountain Dew
Inane question asked by your Aunt Ruth every Thanksgiving	"So explain this to me again, do you actually draw the pictures?"	"So explain this to me again, do you actually draw the pictures?"
Point at which youthful idealism is flushed straight down the toilet	You've happily signed up to design the corporate identity program for the NRA.	The value of your options has sunk so low, they are known around the office as "Laughing Stock."
Person you suck up to	High-paying, dumb-ass client	High-paying, dumb-ass VC's
Redeeming qualities	Projects can be viewed without the need for convoluted plug-ins or "fat" bandwidth.	Riding your Razor scooter in the hallways is considered acceptable behavior.

e-Design: Speculative Art or Experimental Business?

ERIK ADIGARD

GRAPHIC DESIGN HISTORICALLY exists both as art and business disciplines. Until recently, the polarity between these two sides was very clear: Typically, art was creator-centric, experimental, exploratory, based on singularity, and it had a long-term value; while business was consumer-centric, pragmatic, exploitative, based on multiplicity, and it had a short-term value. Today, however, these two notions are more interdependent than ever before. The main cause has to do with our reliance on technology, especially in the past ten years, since graphic design in particular has gone through a profound revolution of media and processes. No communicator can afford to ignore the whims of the economy, the technological novelties, or the artistic trends of the moment. It is a relentless right brain-left brain pong game in which each side tries to colonize the other.

Historically, it is business that has maintained a close proximity with technological innovations, and artists have followed and sought ways to make their art more relevant to their contemporary culture. In the case of e-media, it is artists and designers who have enthusiastically explored the new possibilities before business could find ways to exploit them. It is this relatively long period of experimentation that has given the medium such an aura of creative possibilities. Today, most graphic designers concerned with communication must take into account the factor of changing technologies and its impact on our profession.

Designing with new technologies means that communication also happens at a meta level. When we base our design on a new technology, we also bring in the resonance or the semantic baggage of this technology. We design with and for innovation and, therefore, become actors in the current transformation of the modern world. In that sense, communicators and their clients, as we have seen with Ebay, Razorfish and the like, use the mystique of technological innovation as a communication strategy, and the media become an audience that may be as important to us as are clients, employees, customers, or investors.

Speed and longevity become interdependent: Both corporate designers and their clients need to maintain a constant state of preparedness. Developing e-design solutions often depends on the latency factor of technology, since it typically takes a short amount of time to learn the new tools, but learning how to apply them and learning how to make users adopt them has proven to be very difficult. The need for our clients to be prepared for changing land-scapes entails an early adoption of new technologies, even when these technologies are rid-dled with problems and limitations, and even when the adoption of these technologies proves to be a short-term economic drain. Because this new environment is very unstable and degrades quickly, we often need to adapt the design specs to these limitations.

Today, R&D (or "art&D") often exists as an important component of large organizations, if for nothing more than to learn and integrate the new tools and languages of communication that will guarantee tomorrow's competitive advantage. But there remain many scenarios that cannot be charted by very structured organizations. I am convinced that no one who does busi-ness in the "new economy" can ignore the possibility that new paradigms can emerge out of nowhere and neutralize one's hard-earned achievements. In a sense, the "Love Bug" is a reminder of this climate of unpredictability.

Could graphic designers be rendered obsolete by something like the "Love Bug," which in the spring of 2000 caused billions of dollars worth of damages worldwide with its ILOVEYOU message? In many ways, yes. Technology is like a "Love Bug." Professions such as typesetting, retouching, and stripping disappear, and many others are introduced: information designing, interface architecture, programming of all kinds, etc. And these often threaten the authority of highly trained graphic designers. During this period, we have gone through many generations of computers and software, and it seems that we never had the time to master any of them. Learning to design today is not a matter of learning to master either tools or aesthetic values, but it is a matter of learning to adopt and integrate new methods. I believe this new talent is a combination of analysis and intuition, playfulness and rigor, and experimentation and historical perspective. Doing design today is an activity of research, reflection, and translation. It is an activity that is very mechanical, but that demands that we include a voice or a gesture to bring the design solution into the realm of culture, as some sort of emotion of the moment should always attach itself to the message. The need for graphic designers to exist in a cultural and historical context is combined with a new need to exist in the context of unstable technologies and business methods. The Web is a particularly challenging environment for graphic design-ers, given the nature of the medium: limited screen resolution and real estate combined with limited bandwidth demand that we constantly work with an economy of means when designing sites. The relative difficulty of using the medium from the consumer's point of view also demands that we simplify site architecture and navigation. Once all medium-centric demands have been met, there is typically very little space left for graphic expression. And then, user testing is often added to the process. The challenge of graphic design on the Web is by far the most frustrating and most important design problem of the day. It is a problem of interpreta-tions, definitions, and redefinitions of each innovation that will enter our field.

This need to adapt experiment with new technologies has brought in the possibility of "design hacking," which is an area of great artistic expression. By "hacking" I mean the activity of playing with and subverting any accepted notion, whether it is in the way of doing business, or the way of using typography or iconography. It is also in the way we think of functionality. It is the breakup of grids, of fixed forms, of continuity, of logic, and of other notions that have held graphic design in one place since Bauhaus. And, of course, Bauhaus was the hacking of the day as it worked to free design from archaic traditions, and allow better things into people's lives.

New technologies have come to us with a lot of mystique—one could say "with a graphical interfaced mystique" and, of course, mystique and art are always close neighbors. We have the impression that a hyperbolic excess of self-expression has rooted itself in the design world as it is becoming increasingly show-business-like. Perhaps more than ever before, people want new styles and attitudes in every day of their lives, and these styles and attitudes arrive—at home, in the street, and at work—in the form of highly gestured magazines, tattoos, typefaces, restaurants, laptops, and desktop icons.

But self-expression is no longer a sign of art; it is really more an "expression" of the new tools rather than that of true exploration. In that sense, we can think of design in similar terms as our tools: Design 1.9 has just been upgraded to Design 2.0. Times come with their own expressions, and new generations of designers are implicitly asked to adopt these pre-defined ways. Photoshop, Quark, and other tools have given their specific spins onto graphic design. Today, Flash is used as an alternative to the limitations of Web site design. Flash is often very artistic-looking, but it only is a temporary cover-up to Web design limitations. When art becomes a status quo and, therefore, the business model of the day, one needs to bring art back to the flip side of business.

In my mind, the role of today's art is to break away conceptually from technology to redis-cover the relationships between humans and the things that they live with, as well as the things that they invent. These things may in fact be digital, or virtual, but in any case, one needs to create them and see them not in terms of their novelty ratio, but in terms of their contribution to humanity, not just to industry.

In e-design, the role of art is to go where business cannot afford to go today: to master and outgrow the technological issues. Art exploration today needs to bring the organic, the eco-logical, the emotional, and the spiritual out of technology. And it needs to explore the future technologies, especially biotech, before they become conceptually frozen by business objec-tives. And it seems evident today that this "Fourth Wave" has begun and that it will have an impact on graphic design, as graphic design, in turn, will need to explore, question, and rephrase the place of these new inventions and discoveries in our lives, and in our practice as designers. This challenge is both one of contributing artistic substance to culture and one of maintaining our position of strength in the new economy. The game goes on. . . .

Of Bonding and Bondage: Cult, Culture, and the Internet

DENISE CARUSO

BECAUSE OF THIS newly huge, mainstream, and extremely lucrative cult that we've created around technology, American culture has uploaded pretty much its whole palette of weird, obsessive-compulsive proclivities onto the Internet. And more often than not, it has found five, or a hundred, or a couple thousand people around the world who share them. That's what the Internet is really good at. It's a cult machine.

So, what exactly is a cult nowadays?

The standard definition usually describes a group of people with some kind of extreme point of view, and the rituals and ceremonies they use for worshipping the object of their obsession. Basically, you can type *anything.com* into just about any search engine today and come up with a match. In fact, it only took a couple hours whacking around the Web to find . . .

science cults,

conspiracy cults,

religious cults,

game cults,

technology cults,

business and financial cults,

celebrity cults,

mass-murderer cults,

TV-show cults,

movie-director cults,

fountain-pen cults,

hairless-dog and reptile cults,

amusement-park cults,

sex and eclipse and millenium cults.

Pretty much you name it. So, let's look at a few of them. . . .

Okay, here's a science cult: Nanotechnology—according to its proponents, the next big thing. Well, actually the next very small thing. Nanotechnology is the design of machines the size of atoms.

Then you've got your conspiracy cults . . . now this is a "debunk" site, but trust me, there are hundreds of conspiracy sites on the Web, and all the conspiracies you see on this page are legitimate, quote unquote, within the conspiracy community. (And yes, there is a conspiracy community, too.)

Then there are the cults of entertainment, which of course are great news for companies like Sony, but which can have some nasty side effects.

A science-fiction author friend of mine, Bruce Sterling, sent me a glum e-mail telling me about what he considers to be one of the biggest online cults—the thousands of people who are addicted to playing Ultima Online.

One of his best friends is getting a divorce because he's literally spending all his time in a virtual world, with virtual people.

As you might expect, technology cults abound on the Internet—cypherpunk sites devoted to the arcane science of encryption, incredibly rabid We Hate Microsoft cults, and you'd probably have to call devotees of Linux programming something of a cult, too.

And now, with Apple's apparent resurgence, there are actually several sites devoted to the very earnest Cult of Steve, and others, like the Church of Virus, that I don't even want to know what they hell they're talking about.

And we should not underestimate the effect of business and financial cults on the wild popularity of the Internet as a get-rich-quick scheme. There are people who spend all their waking hours day-trading stocks and trolling for information and typing endless e-mails to one another about what they find, what to do with it, how much money they made/lost, rumors about the CEO and what he does with hairless dogs, blah blah blah.

And, as you might suspect, the Internet is thick with celebrity cults of all stripes, both the expected—such as Ricky Martin—and the unexpected, like Jeffrey Dahmer.

On the Dahmer site, creepily called "The Lair," y'got yer Dahmer pictures, Dahmer quotes, Dahmer awards (!), Dahmer fetishes, crimes, rumors, art, photo album, house, life story. Kind of redefines "too much information."

I don't know how much sites like The Lair have contributed to it, but the connotation for cults on or off the Internet has become progressively uglier as people have escaped from suicide cults like Heaven's Gate and homicide cults like AUM Supreme Truth in Japan.

Cult-education organizations say they've gotten reports about more than three thousand individual cults—most of them small, but some, like Scientology, with tens of thousands of members. One statistic says that 5 to 10 million people have been involved with cult groups at one time or another.

But nowadays what defines a cult, particularly on the Internet, depends on your point of view. It is the "I know it when I see it" phenomenon that some people use to describe art. But unlike art, we tend to brand cults if we *don't* like them, rather than if we do, or if they make us uncomfortable or challenge our worldview or somehow fly in the face of cultural norms, like the Goth movement. These kids got a really bad rap during Columbine—and anyone who knows a Goth or used to be one knows it.

So what is it about the Internet that makes it a cult factory?

The most simplistic explanation is that the Internet is both broad and deep. It is the first medium in history that allows us to both publish and communicate, often at the same time. We can publish our ideas globally on the Web, and people can find us just by typing a few words into a search engine. And at the same time, we can communicate in a deeply personal way by e-mail, to have conversations that are impossible in any other medium that we traditionally think of as publishing.

A broad-and-deep communications medium is perfect for cults because, for one thing, it automates the recruiting process—anyone who hates Jews or collects Beanie Babies, or worships Trent Reznor, or believes that the lost years of Jesus were spent in India, can find their people, in the privacy of their homes, and at the click of a mouse.

This is a manifestation of what you might call "the verticalization of everything"—and in this context, it allows cults to proselytize globally via the Web and use e-mail to personalize the bond. And because it's become so affordable, at least by our outrageously decadent Western standards—even Alan Greenspan has admitted it's driving the economy—the Internet is a celebration of self-indulgence taken to the extreme.

Finally—and this may be of particular interest to you—technology can be designed to be a subtle persuader, to impel people to actions they wouldn't necessarily undertake on their own.

In fact, there's a new discipline being taught in Stanford's computer science department, called "captology," which stands for "computers as persuasive technology," and the guy who came up with the idea focuses on the intentional effect of certain kinds of technology to persuade us to do their bidding. One of the most relevant chunks of his research looks at how product designers use these methods of persuasion.

For example, nagscreens built into shareware programs to persuade people to pay up. Or the computerized "Baby Think It Over" doll, that tells you when your "baby" needs to be fed, and changed, and bathed, and played with—clearly designed as a propaganda tool in the fight against teen pregnancy.

Captology is a subtle science. It's new enough that most designers don't know enough to use the concepts mindfully, and consumers aren't connected enough to make them widely useful. But the people who are connected, especially our parents and grandparents and our kids, are much more vulnerable than you and I. They tend to believe stuff because "it's on the computer," just like they believe it because they "saw it on TV." And why shouldn't they? Public relations agencies get paid a lot of money to sell us on computers as repositories of the world's knowledge, knowing and anticipating all our needs, largely infallible, and absolutely indispensable.

Microsoft, of course, is the classic example. Why wouldn't cults on the Internet bill themselves the same way? When the mass suicide of the Heaven's Gate cult hit the news a few years ago, sociologists started publicizing what they believe are the characteristics of a cult. But, clearly, those definitions need to evolve for the Internet age. Because if we're judging cults from the context of the culture in which they exist, then we have to re-examine culture in light of the changes the Internet hath wrought upon culture in the past decade.

The question is whether culture—that homogeneous, unifying social structure that's defined our identities until now—still exists, in the shadow of a global network that caters, simultaneously, to such incredibly narrow private interests and such incredibly broad commercial ones. In other words, is there really much difference nowadays between cult and culture?

For example, how do you draw the distinction between the real scientific endeavors of SETI, the Search for Extra Terrestrial Intelligence group, and the kind of conspiracy-thinking, TV-driven obsession of *X-Files* fans? At what point does our culture's obsession with celebrity, with exhaustive knowledge about the lives of people we'll never know—encourage cyberstalkers?

What is a cult and what's just a mirror of today's culture? It's a matter of perception, of what you know and what you already believe. It also depends on whether you're looking at the question from inside the culture or outside. And on whether we're willing to question our own worldviews, even if the answers make us uncomfortable.

So this is what I think.

Even though Heaven's Gate got all the chickens clucking about wacko online cults, the truth is that in terms of how they work and what they're trying to accomplish online, they aren't all that different from any successful foray onto the commercial Internet.

Eek! you say. How can *that* be true?

Well, the big cash-cow mantra buzzphrase of the Internet is online community. And successful online communities, in order to be successful, have to provoke and encourage and reward exactly the same kind of addictive, obsessive, insular, self-referential behavior as any standard-issue religious cult of years gone by.

So you've got your iVillage Parent Soup, designed to create a "community" around the issues of parenting—complete with advertising and shopping opportunities, of course. And then you've got the Southern Baptists. The difference is that these—well, let's just call them "commerical" cults like iVillage—are economically, thus socially, acceptable.

Internet companies cultivate cultish behavior. For them, it's the classic "sticky" application—basically the Roach Motel of the Web. You log in but you never log out. You surrender your personal information, you commit your money to buy more stuff, or more services. You can always get what you want, right here. You find and commit to the one true Web site or service that meets all your needs. And, of course, in the perfect world of these commercial cults, that is where you live.

It's good for you to keep pumping your money into this Big Long Boom Economy! Consumerism is really the One True Religion for the millenium. It is the quintessential global cult.

Now let me just say, this analogy means no disrespect to anyone who has suffered through the real horror of having a family member or friend indoctrinated into a cult—and a surprising number of my friends have had this experience. But I do believe that the way people look at the commercial Internet today—and the Internet's skill at breeding obsession—has almost completely erased the line between cult and culture. And if cult is culture now, we ought to wake up to that reality, and make sure that we proceed with caution.

For example, I was shocked to read a *Wall Street Journal* editorial that really nailed librarians—calling them pornographers, basically—because they refused to filter public access to the Internet. It trotted out the same old arguments about protecting our children from cults and pornography and everything else that's yucky about humanity.

But if we're *really* concerned about the role technology plays in promoting cult behavior, we have to keep in mind that particularly on the net, what's a cult is really open to debate. We'd be far better off cultivating the courage to allow all points of view on the Internet, without censorship.

If we really want to help our parents and our kids understand this peculiar, persuasive power of technology, it's a much better idea to educate them—and ourselves—about how the Internet really works, and prepare them for whatever they might find there. For example, I've been working on a project with the Pew Charitable Trusts for nearly a year now, drafting credibility standards for Web sites.

The idea is to get people—*you*, people who use the Internet—to demand that anyone who publishes on the Web tell the truth, whether they're individuals, organizations, or companies. To disclose who they are, where they get their money, and whatever biases and ideology are behind the screen.

Disclosure standards have the potential to take the steam out of recruiting efforts by cult groups, and hit commercial cults, too, by—for example—making Amazon.com and drkoop tell us when their reviews were paid for by publishers or product manufacturers.

Fear is the real enemy here, not cults. Sometimes, when people get scared, they forget that the very same features that make the Internet a cult factory also make it the most powerful tool for free and open discourse that we've ever known.

A friend of mine who used to work at Disney said he had an experience ten years ago that made him realize the net was the perfect place for cults. He'd stumbled onto a cult of people obsessed with Disney World—who were so into it that they listed wait times for rides—by the half hour. And listed all the music they played at the park, by time and date. And argued amongst themselves about different performances of the Main Street Electrical Parade—which, as you may know, is actually the same parade every day.

His final pronouncement on the subject pretty much sums it up for me:

"Thank God these people have somewhere to go," he said "And the best part is, they're all out there, hiding in plain sight."

Making
Motion

Convergence Doesn't Matter

KYLE COOPER

TODAY, THE GOAL in the education of a designer has shifted to accompany a multitude of opinions. The ideas of universal aesthetic and geometric forms are challenged. Regardless of contemporary standards, the most simplistic goal still remains—to understand how image, typography, and space function in a controlled environment.

Design excellence stems from process. It is initiated with the abstract, and forms the concrete. It begins with a problem and ends with resolved communication. Method is process, and process determines that you have undoubtedly arrived at the best solution for the problem.

Overall, the most significant article in visual communication is the transfer of information. You must first ask yourself: What is the idea and how do I express that idea? If a clear voice is heard amid hysteria and the information is understood, the design is a success. The beauty of motion and new media is that informational content can be both staged and experienced.

The development of technology has certainly forced a shift in educational practices. In my second year at Yale, we were the first class to be given Macintoshes. It was a big moment when we made our first Photoshop storyboard, printed out on slick paper with real photos integrated, rather than presenting something that was made out of Xeroxes, colored with a Magic Marker, or hand-drawn things. The computer continues to evolve, and motion and video are overtaking the Mac.

Design is definitely one of the most powerful vehicles to explore emotion. To get a passionate reaction is so hard that you can't just open a bag of tricks. We need to keep pressure on ourselves to come up with new graphic languages, to do something original; modernism is a nice place to visit, but we cannot take refuge there. To create an emotional response based purely on form is not impossible, but to do it based on a concept, an idea, is more tangible.

Designing is not simply applying a solution that you'd arrived at before; it is about exploring new avenues and tailoring actions to needs. The only way we know how to stay innovative at Imaginary Forces is by not applying a stylistic formula to every job, but to let the content or the emotion dictate what it looks like.

Design is design—interactive design versus web design versus main titles versus commercials versus live action. There are different formats and parameters, but the criteria of trying to elicit an emotional response are relatively unchanging, whether you make a poster or you make a movie. I've made posters, and now I've directed my first movie. Instead of being one frame, there are many frames, but I'm still trying to do one frame at a time. Today everyone's talking about broadband and convergence. Well, convergence is something that designers have thought about all along.

And it doesn't matter! Convergence doesn't matter. I'm glad we have movies on the Web now because people will realize that Web design is the same as film directing. Maybe that sounds irrational, but I think it's true. Sure, there are more parameters with film—you have to shoot live action and think about lighting and sound. On the interactive side, you have to know about Java programming, browser compatibility, and various technical issues. But they're all just different parameters of solving a creative problem, to communicate something and evoke an emotional response from someone whom you've targeted.

Ultimately, everything is about some kind of storytelling. That is what people respond to. That's why this whole interactive world has grown so fast, because people are either telling stories or experiencing things on their own or in communities.

Technology has become an overwhelming force in design. It has given us the ability to work all inclusively as a "one man band." We can conceive, sketch, scan, design, shoot, animate, and create audio all under one roof; whereas before that was not possible. It also supplies us with faster results. Instead of waiting for others, we can decide right here and now if the treatment is something we want to pursue. It's a good thing that we're so well equipped to deal with the rapidity of modern expectations. Technology and its new achievements have only accelerated society's impatience. We're performing tasks at top speed, but it seems you still can't rush a concept or a story; it comes when it comes.

New media gives us the chance to play with what we have done; the variables are completely accessible. As far as reconciling traditional and modern technique, it's really about knowing what is the best way to get your idea across, and having the flexibility to use both modern and traditional methods.

# Screen Shots

MARINA ZURKOW

EVERY DESIGN PROJECT tells a story. Not in the conventional sense of a story with a plot, per se, but rather as an object that has (or defies) an implicit beginning, middle, and end. It assumes a point of view. It takes time to unpack its secret meanings. It talks to other stories that were told already. It talks to a viewer's set of stories. The idea of "story" is the foundation from which work can grow, and is the framework that informs the questions that follow.

Web design could be divided into two factions: the Book Camp and the Film Camp. They are not mutually exclusive, but their orientations are decidedly different. What can electronic design take from each Camp, and integrate into its own unique, non-linear form?

The Book Camp

The Book Camp treats a Web site as a set of pages. A user "reads" through a page, then makes a choice to "go to" another page. Some undefined interval occurs between the pages, usually contingent upon download time: the wait. Nobody waits between the turning of pages, or needs a "next" button; implicit in the act of reading is a spatial constraint that requires a set of pages.

The precedent for the Book Camp was set from the infancy of the World Wide Web, and was a result of the early browser limitations: Netscape 1.0 (in the Jurassic days of the Web) offered a gray background, black text, and the option to embed static images on the page. A Web designer de facto designed "Web pages." And a Web site was *merely* a collection of these things. Because the browser slowly introduced new features, and because content creators (especially producers of information-based sites) feared late adapters, the book model held.

When Netscape 2.0 introduced the Frameset, in which a browser screen is divided into separately controlled and loaded windows, there was a possibility to extend the book model into new territory. These Framesets could tell simultaneous stories—placing more than one window on a screen, each window separately controlled; now a creator could collapse narrative structure onto one plane. For instance, three points of view, which are better read side-by-side, can exist in separate scrolling frames, controlled by an overarching interface in its own frame.

Or, a split-screen experience could be made in which several specifically sized windows perform auto-advancing slide shows. But the Frameset is primarily used for traffic control (keeping users within a site by creating an "über-Frameset") and bandwidth economy (fixed items in their own frame do not have to be reloaded if you "go to" the next page). Its potential for interactivity or the simultaneous exploration of "stories" is rarely seen.

The Film Camp

The Film Camp is spatially *and* temporally differentiated from the Book Camp. It emerged out of the linear and time-based work of more established media, including film, motion graphics, and television, as well as CD-ROMs, which were already being created when Netscape 1.0 was still the browser du jour.

Spatially, when you read a book, your eyes scroll down the page like little scanners. But when you watch a movie, or TV, or play with a CD-ROM, you apprehend the screen at once, as a whole. In Web design, the recent development of pop-up windows has allowed designers to create a controlled screen area to work within. It is very difficult for print- and film-trained designers, myself included, to produce unpredictable screen composition; are you reading, or are you seeing?

Temporally, a screen-based approach means that everything that happens over time does so deliberately within the framework of the screen. In page design, you could say that what happens over time occurs outside of the browser's edges and is the interval of waiting . . . for the next page.

Two essential characteristics of film can be usefully applied to electronic design: synchronous action and diachronic motion (synchronous = simultaneous; diachronic = over time). Synchronous action refers to that which happens on the screen at once; in film, it includes superimposition, split-screens, subtitles, or simultaneous dialogue. Diachronic motion describes the act of film passing through time—not only the unfolding of a shot or a story, but the connectors between shots—the montage itself. It includes the sometimes-overlooked intervals between the edits; this could mean the moment off-screen and in-between the shots, or the visual devices deployed in transitions, such as dissolves or wipes.

The transposition of synchronous principles from film to electronic design is a fairly easy one; there are more inherent synchronous tools in e-design than in film: split screens are a matter of course, and rollovers can be used with a simple piece of Java script. DHTML offers layers of information than can exist simultaneously, or float into place. Triggered sound hot spots can suggest an aural spaciousness to an otherwise flat experience.

There are also at least two "wild card" aspects of synchronous design: the user and the browser. Her actions in the moment drive the screen, and can enact change in ways that are specific to her in that moment, specific to the configurations of her browser, her screen resolution, and her download speed. Scalable browser windows can completely unbalance a screen design. Pop-Up windows can obviate the scalable browser window issue. I would always advise: Control the window size; make the plug-ins as common as possible without compromising your intentions; and keep download time minimal. You cannot account for whether people will have the right plug-in, their Java enabled to interpret the script to launch a pop-up window, and their screen resolution set at the optimal size for the scale of your design, and if you do, you will be making lowest-common-denominator, entirely scalable, scrollable, HTML text-only designs.

In design for the Internet, the only required temporal consideration is download time—bandwidth. Even if you are designing a set of pages, what will people be doing in that waiting period? How can you alert them when it's time to draw their attention back to you from their spreadsheets? An author may consider creating flexible modules of design that fill the "wait" time— loops that may or may not play depending on the user's download speed, and impart tertiary information, create a preview for the work that is loading, or otherwise captivate the user. The author may want to create an alert sound so the user knows when the content he's been waiting for has finished loading.

Consider the experience of a Web site or Flash piece from the perspective of transitions and intervals. Not just during an initial download, but also between the pages, or between the screens, or changing frames. What's happening in there? Can you offer a more integrated experience through sound, through a formal transitional element? But then what happens when the user wants to get somewhere fast, the second time around, and has no need for lengthy transitions? Web users often don't want the bells and whistles. And that's because so often, any nod toward time-based media is purely extraneous. "Just the facts, ma'am" is often the war cry in all but pure entertainment content. But it does not have to be. If the intervals are varied, and never pure eye candy, they can be enhancements. A creator could also make these elements either "smart" (recognizing a user's prior visit) or tactically expedient, and if the motion is integrated and fluid, it won't feel like a removable component.

If the final form of a site (or a portion) will be created in Flash, then why not prototype in Flash? One designer-friendly facet of Flash is the capacity to drill down: A creator can start with broad strokes and gradually refine, embellish, and fine-edit the work. The problem with fine-designing in a static program (Freehand or Illustrator) is the Book Camp effect: You will have a series of pages that you will, as an afterthought, attempt to stitch together.

When Macromedia Flash was introduced, the Web became animated. Flash is not only used to produce cartoons. Just as many Web producers use Framesets to control site flow, Flash is still mainly used to "spice up" a Web site. But there's more to it, and this is where understanding film principles and considering them in the service of "story" becomes very useful.

Agoraphobia

The Web browser does not like empty space. Breathing room sometimes only exists for the expendable, skippable, but elaborate site intros. The screen is small, the browser window's even smaller, there's a lot to say, and no one wants to waste time and wrist clicks by adding too many pages. The result is a ghetto aesthetic: literally a small walled city in which words, pictures, stories, and submenus all live on top of one another. A sensational visual subculture (not for the claustrophobic) has arisen from this phenomenon: the use of the smallest possible type and images. They are the pixel equivalent of drawing on grains of rice.

As bandwidth widens, will the screen's visual and temporal scope do so as well? Much of the fear of empty space is reflected in the tabloid-paper approach. Fearful of losing user "hits" by creating a proper intro, sites pack their front pages with as many headlines as possible, needing to prove to the user that their content is freshly updated, that their site is full of stuff. This agoraphobia is the result of the current economic model for the Web, and is also a matter of convention.

A leaner, more elegant open space might be accompanied by tightly written copy and design principles that incorporate emptiness. Areas of the screen may develop more interesting relationships to their content than a left-hand nav bar. Transitions may bear teasers, subliminal messages, or at the very least, redirect your eye to the place on the screen you are going. There might be room for fluid, intelligent, intuitive, and pleasurable interfaces.

It's All New Media, After All

But the Web is a new medium; it's not a book, or a shopping center, or TV, or a movie title sequence. Why am I looking back at these models? Because these models will bear influence, whether you think you're looking back or not. And some conventions become conventional *not* because they are the best ones; why is the Web site's left-hand navigation bar a requisite? Do users hate clicking through *all* material, or only when page after page of badly organized content is a waste of their time?

People forget that film, television, and radio all had tenuous exploratory beginnings. The World Wide Web *is* a nascent, schizophrenic, uncontrollable medium. An expression of the accelerating speed of twenty-first-century consciousness, the Web possesses a history from dinosaur to android, *and* is a new, undefined, untested, and transitional medium. While we cannot be impatient to define, we also need to push the definitions before the status quo does the defining for us, based on at least one simple constraint: lowest-common-denominator-marketing.

The Web is rising as a new medium in a culture that is eager to meteorically create new conduits for commerce. It is in the interest of a commerce-oriented environment to come up with conventions that will make the user's experience painless and effortless—as quickly as possible.

Designers and directors need to critically question the meaning of "appropriate models" for each of the facets of business and art that the Web engages. And to look back at a myriad of art histories, not in order to emulate, but preferably to test and grow ideas in this rich medium of electronic design.

Non-linear design has already fed back into the aesthetic mainstreams. As the Christians absorbed and repackaged Pagan rituals, mainstream pop culture absorbs and reframes its "alternative" siblings. Electronica and sampling got absorbed into mainstream rock. Interface aesthetics are completely at home on sports and news shows (as if waiting patiently in the TV-screen's corner until users can click and buy). Electronic design is not an end-of-the-line repository for old tried-and-true techniques, but a medium that can and will upend conventions. It is more than just a commercial medium; my hope is that new experiences and new ways of creating stories can emerge out of electronic design that reflect a speedy and labyrinthine world.

Digital Animation: Beyond the Imagination and Back Again

J. J. SEDELMAIER

ANIMATION IN THE digital domain can be as complex as a *Toy Story*, or as naïve and hands-on as a *Beavis & Butthead*. Whether it was the visual imagery, the budget, or the schedule, that determined the digital approach, each project couldn't have been produced without the computer.

My personal involvement in animation surrounds the idea that the craft has no restrictions when it comes to a design, look or style. Each project is developed with concept, design, movement and sound, balanced and weighed for a specific effect in mind. The use of digital computers has expanded the capabilities of animation beyond what I could've imagined less than ten years ago. I'm able to deliver work in one-third the time of a decade ago, with sometimes a lower budget, in addition to being afforded more control over revisions.

While most designers might emphasize the creative fusion of mind and computer, I'm still in awe of the time-savings this technology has provided me. Probably the best example of this is the work I've produced for NBC's *Saturday Night Live*. "Saturday TV Funhouse" (conceived and written by Robert Smigel) is a short 1½ to 3½ minute cartoon vignette which airs periodically during the show. It's a self-contained cartoon complete with opening titles and end credits. They concern a variety of subject matter from political satire to social commentary and parody. Production time on these fluctuate from 1½ weeks to a month. To place this in perspective, I'll only say that a normal schedule for a 30-second commercial is at least eight weeks. The SNL work would not be possible if a traditional approach of painting on celluloid, shooting on film and transferring to videotape, had to be employed. On top of this, we sometimes made fundamental revisions on the project just 2 days before the cartoon aired on Saturday. One time we were in the final stages of production on a piece, which parodied Michael Jackson. The Thursday before the show was to air, he announced his impending fatherhood. This was too good an opportunity to pass up. What would've taken at least a week to revise ten years ago, took a day and allowed us to make our airdate.

Drop shadows, colored line work and compositing animation with live action, are all special effects that used to require a separate phase or level of production. These techniques are now generated from elements already existing in the art work themselves. Now I find myself using the digital technology available in sculpting concepts. You see this in television commercials all the time. Special effects are used to sell everything from cars to toothpaste, and sometimes the basis for the concept itself. Their use in films like *Jurassic Park* transforms the hokey 3-dimensional animation of the past into hyper reality. However, from the standpoint of a small studio, I have to make sure that my reliance on technology and in-house "equipment" doesn't find me stranded if something crashes. I have to have back-up but the investment pays for itself quickly in terms of both money and control. We're using fewer outside vendors. Even messenger and courier costs go down and once again we're saving time by keeping more work and responsibility "in-house."

There is one concern that's beginning to surface. No one seems to know yet how to effectively archive digitally produced work. Unless you generate or print out a hard copy, or output onto motion picture film, many are worried that the information or data, might be irretrievably lost. Paper, film, and even videotape decays at a rate which allows you to witness its deterioration. Simply put, digital data is comprised of coded numbers. If the data or the material that the disc is made of deteriorates through time, it may be there in all its glory on Monday and suddenly non-existent on Tuesday.

The opportunities provided by digital technology won't save bad stories or inadequate concepts. What's bad is still bad—It just becomes flashy technique with no substance. This aspect of any industry will never change, but the level of control and accessibility that digital technology affords the user makes it possible for more people to do good work and to have more control over their product.

The Digital Designer/Filmmaker: Overcoming Motion Sickness

MICHAEL SCHMIDT

CALLIGRAPHIC LETTERFORMS GLOW against an iridescent background, illuminating a human "book" as its author spreads ink over its flesh "pages."

A small colored circle containing plant forms sways against a vast black background before it enlarges to reveal itself as a rusted hole, providing an unsettling view from the inside of a boxcar in Rwanda.

And a single word enlarges to fill the interior of another rail car, in post-World War II Germany, creating a composition reminiscent of German object posters.

This isn't graphic design I'm describing; well at least that's not the label given these films at your local video store.[1] The first example is from a scene in *The Pillow Book* by Peter Greenaway. The second reference is to a documentary film on genocide in Rwanda, titled *Kisangi Diary,* by Hubert Sauper. The third illustration describes a scene from *Zentropa* by Lars von Trier. Film projects such as these reveal the growing similarities in film form and design language. Evident too is the increased relevance of a "conventional" medium, like film, to the new media dimensions of graphic design. This coupling has led to the designation of film and design as converging media.

Convergence is clearly seen in motion graphics and moving interfaces on the Web, but this merger is fueled far further by the recent advent of digital filmmaking (a.k.a. digital video filmmaking or just DV). This new brand of filmmaking is widening the doorway to new experimentation in both cinema and new media design.

Digital filmmaking, already far-reaching in its applications, means something different for practically every author on the subject.[2] For example, I will not be discussing digital effects design. While effects design is a growing area of employment for designers of all kinds, I intend to focus on the nature of film as it pertains to the nature of design for the sake of elucidating correspondences that, I hope, will promote the integration of these disciplines. Therefore, I do not advocate the Hollywood paradigm to which many current digital filmmakers aspire. This does not mean I am opposed to narrative. No, I am opposed to blind emulation and gratuitous explosions. Yet, the lure of these mainstream examples retains a stronghold on students, particularly with recurring overnight success stories from the makers of these effects-driven and standard Hollywood formula films. My reservations regarding quality notwithstanding, this is a fortunate time for both film and graphic design.

Relatively cheap prosumer digital film cameras, like the Sony TRV 900 and the Canon GL-1, and affordable editing software, like Final Cut Pro, are democratizing filmmaking. Consequently, a vast international independent film community is developing with genres and sub-genres galore.

Digital film festivals are more abundant each year and now even Cannes offers a digital film showcase. Movie theatres across the country, anxious to profit from DV, are installing digital video projectors.[3]

Of course the Web is fast becoming the dominant venue for short digital films and animation, and soon feature-length productions will be easily accommodated.[4] Far more people will view films on their personal computers—either on DVDs, through downloads, or via streaming—than on their television sets in the very near future.[5] Delivering Web video content, whether live or prerecorded, is becoming huge business.

Television networks have also set up dot.coms, and even bookstores like Barnes & Noble are transforming their static, textual offerings into a video presentation platform for books on the Web. And application service providers (ASPs) like Softcom have a mission to make video the centerpiece of Web communications. Moreover, DVDs are evolving into interactive movies, and live-action and animated shorts are evolving into interactive Web interfaces.[6]

Lest we forget advertising, there are plenty of commercials designed specifically for Web broadcast. Firms specializing in the use of streaming media write, shoot, edit, and compress "mini-mercials" solely for Web presentation.

Film delivery through interactive presentation media is now an important part of trade exhibitions, museum collections, retail stores, and business-to-business presentations. Yet the DIY movement in graphic design is far from over. In fact, digital filmmaking can only aid the proliferation of self-authored works by designers. This new medium of digital film needs poets. And experimentalists from various fields, especially graphic design, will have a lot to say about the evolution of this medium's techniques. Yet, it is presently clear that the integration of time, space, and motion—whether for narrative structures, non-linear experiences, or information architecture—is the ubiquitous paradigm.

From the inception of interaction design, film was derided as "conventional," "passive," "manipulative," and "anachronistic." Ironically, new media technology has made "film" all but a ubiquitous component to interactivity. From adjunct to interface, video is a key ingredient. And actors, who previously appeared as an extinct species in this new digital universe, are finding plenty to do for digital films, Web mini-mercials, and interface designs that incorporate everything from rotoscoped "spokespeople" to performers who interact with a typographic atmosphere.[7] To be sure, presentation and interaction—and the merging thereof—are requisites for current graphic-design and film students alike.

David Liban, filmmaker and chair of the Electronic Media program at George Washington University, states that graphic design and film are rapidly merging as practitioners in both fields create motion graphics and interactive experiences for the Web.[8] This merger will also affect cinema. As film viewers increasingly become Internet users, designers and filmmakers will discover that they can use this enhanced reservoir of collective visual literacy as a means to implement new cinematic techniques that emphasize abstract reasoning over verisimilitude.[9]

While all this convergence sounds exciting, making a film of any length is far from easy. In fact, it's absolutely humbling. But for all of film's complexity, the design student must begin to think like a director/editor hybrid every bit as much as she needs to think like an artist, social scientist, technologist, and business executive. The digital filmmaker, who often works as both director and editor, must be each of these things too.

This director/editor model is useful for design students because it describes the process of communication in two of its major stages: the process of organizing information, and the process of finding meaning by establishing relationships between those same bits of information. While the former refers in very general terms to directing and the latter to editing, these roles really aren't so clearly bifurcated even in conventional productions. The question of where the director leaves off and the editor begins is becoming moot. These roles are so enmeshed in digital filmmaking that films are often edited as they are shot. For some DV filmmakers, the process is very conscious, deliberate, and faithful to a preconceived script. For many others, digital filmmaking offers the financial affordability to be far more intuitive, experimental, and improvisational. Mood, as opposed to rational explanation, often takes precedence as a guide in both the directing and editing of a digital film. This is not to say that the intuitive filmmaker is not conscious of how he uses the principles of form, quite the contrary. Proportion, texture, symbolism, and color are as important in the construction of meaning in film shooting and editing as these principles are in graphic design.[10]

Just as film serves multiple roles in design, design can serve a wide array of functions in film. Titles, typographic commentary, transition, effect, information, and graphic/textural metaphor add to the list. Yet, the potential to invent new cinematic techniques and ways of seeing/understanding film may advance from studies in print design, interaction design, and animation, and emerge in new time-based hybrids [Fig. 1]. Graphic designers, whose roles have traditionally revolved around information, communication, publication, promotion, and advertising, are encountering new ways to participate in the artistic life of society through DV and digital media in general.

The flexibility of DV technology makes film production, particularly editing, like handwriting. The work of emerging independent filmmaker John Olivio demonstrates the versatility of digital editing software to highly specialize—and personalize—the appearance, flow, and transitions of images and meanings [Fig. 2]. His goal is to avoid the trap of employing conventional or obvious technique while simultaneously playing with—and evolving beyond—the established film lexicon; the ultimate aim to uncover a visual language endemic to this new medium.[11]

Filmmakers, such as Olivio, give credit to graphic design for enhancing the public's visual literacy.[12] The boom in short films and quick Web mini-mercials may have something to do with this acknowledgment: Both are closer to graphic design because there is far less time for a standard narrative to unfold. Time is compressed and is thus divided—spatially—into conceptual or literal "zones" in an analogous manner to print communications. Traditionally, graphic designers collapse time (e.g., multiple events occurring in one space simultaneously) and filmmakers collapse spaces (e.g., multiple spaces pictured on one screen or jumps in edits

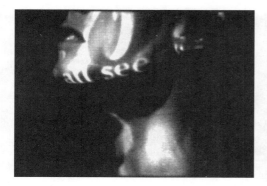

Figure 1. Still from *Friction*. Written, produced, and directed by David Liban. Production Design by Mike Schmidt. Typography by Ronny Scholz. 16 mm, 1997.

Figure 2. Stills from *Libration Points*. Written, produced, and directed by John Olivio. Feature digital film, 2000–01.

from one space to another).[13] What was once a defining distinction is now a trivial semantic difference.

Furthermore, the views of new filmmakers closely resemble those of recent type designers. Editing, like type, is not a crystal goblet for those attentive enough to appreciate the qualities of the vessel. Once an editing aesthetic and a strategy are established, a highly stylized variation on the familiar can become recognizable on its own terms and in its own context.[14] Yet film, like type, still relies on some reference to the "real" world—on an established model as both point of departure from and threshold to the familiar in an often "defamiliarized" parallel world. Typographic experiments rely on this tenuous relationship between what we know and where we have yet to go. For example, type designer Tobias Frere-Jones excels at referencing—while simultaneously advancing from—the familiar models and standards of typographic form in his experimental work. His typeface, Quandary, exemplifies the fact that experience may only open our eyes to blind us [Fig. 3].[15]

The film director/editor and the graphic designer, then, both have the task of creating a new perceptual and conceptual whole. But this gestalt exists outside or parallel to reality and is not bound by the laws of the physical world, but to the cognitive and emotional capacities of

EXPERIENCE
OPENS OUR
EYES AND
BLINDS US

Figure 3. *Quandry.* Typeface design
by Tobias Frere-Jones.

Figure 4. "Page" from *African Voices*, interactive exhibition
(*www.mnh.si.edu/africanvoices*). National Museum of
Natural History, Smithsonian Institution. Produced by Terra
Incognita Interactive Media, 2000.

the viewer. David Small, designer of interactive information environments, establishes this correspondence for interaction design: "In the visual design of information spaces it is much more
important to understand the relative and ultimately fluid relationships between shifting and
mutating information chunks than the fixed elements of the real world."[16] Small also utilizes film
language in his interactive presentation of the Talmud, relying on shifting focus and transparency as means to explore text.[17]

Bart Marable, principal and creative director of Terra Incognita Interactive Media, creates
virtual environments and exhibitions that rely on various models such as print, architecture, and
film, which combine in one overall interface structure [Fig. 4].[18] Terra Incognita's accessible yet
engaging work demonstrates the advantage of using conventional paradigms, such as film, to
establish innovative architecture for new media. It is the commingling of various paradigmatic
voices that is perhaps most telling of innovations to come.

Terra Incognita's projects for clients like the Smithsonian and National Geographic serve
the public's continued interest in documentary work. It remains important, however, to also
study the productions of non-mainstream and non-Western media artists done by and about
themselves.

In 1972, anthropologist Sol Worth called for the integration of filmmaking and film studies
with cultural anthropology curricula. Like other scholars of this period, he sensed the Web.
Worth was excited about ethnographic subjects speaking for themselves.[19] It's my impression
that we will go far in cinema and commerce as film and design conflate, but this process may
only promote familiar valuations if we forget about the postmodern critiques the design field
has left for dead.

While the formal principles, techniques, and taxonomies of graphic design and film vary,
these fields are becoming strikingly similar nonetheless—in form, process, goal, and users/audi-
ences—as new media applications continue to develop. Greater acknowledgment from design
and film educators of this correspondence would make far more likely the integration of these two
fields in process, communication strategy, and form. The resultant integrated curriculum would
open a gateway to understanding the emerging co-determinant nature of film and graphic design.
Then, I think, we will find that the way to overcome motion sickness is with a new pair of eyes.

N O T E S

1. "Graphic design" will be utilized in this essay as a term meant to encompass all the various aspects of graphic design process and practice: print and interactive. This is a tattered umbrella, so I will specify design application where appropriate to avoid confusion.

2. Film studies—the history and theory of cinema—is a crucial component to any curricular integration of film and design. Unfortunately, an introduction of this topic area is outside the already cumbersome focus of this short paper.

3. It appears at present that the theatrical experience of movie-going will remain in demand even as home viewing proliferates in options.

4. Numerous sites exist for viewing digital films. Here are a few I recommend: *D.Film.com*, *newvenue.com*, *Atomfilms.com*, and *ifilm.com*. I have one disclaimer: Don't get on the Web expecting to find great examples of filmmaking, and you won't be disappointed.

5. For example, RealNetworks offers a Web interface that provides full-screen VHS-quality Internet video. DVD quality and HDTV quality broadcasting are now being made available by 2netFX, a competitor of RealNetworks.

6. For an interesting use of actors in Web interface design, see the egomedia site (*egomedia.com*). Exciting too is the hillmancurtis site done for Contagious Pictures (*hillmancurtis.com*) where actors sneeze type in an ethnographic experiment reminiscent of Edison Laboratory movies.

7. Please see note 6 for examples. For further viewing, see *The Week Before* by Dave McKean. Excerpts from this film were shown on *D.Film.com* as recently as October 2000 and may still be available on this site. In a very different manner, digital films and "film" films since 1996 have placed an increased emphasis on acting. Most noteworthy is the Danish Dogma 95 movement ("Dogme 95" in Europe) founded by Lars von Trier and Thomas Vinterberg. I recommend seeing *The Celebration* by Vinterberg and *Breaking the Waves*, *The Idiots*, *Dancer in the Dark*, and *Zentropa* by von Trier. Von Trier's films are not technically classified as Dogma films because he never really followed the Dogma rules, with the possible exception of *The Idiots*.

8. David Liban, interview by the author, August 12, 2000.

9. OK, I have to be allowed at least one wildly idealistic statement per essay.

10. Bryce Button, "Visual Linguistics and the Editor," *Digital Video Magazine* (November 2000): 46–48.

11. John Olivio, interview by the author, 18 October 2000.

12. It would indeed be a huge oversight not to acknowledge the fact that experimentation with non-linear narrative in recent filmmaking owes a debt to our Web-bound zeitgeist. For a discussion that focuses on new media narratives, please see Anne Burdick, "Ways of Telling: Or The Plot Gets Thicker, Fragments, Reconfigures, Branches, Multiples . . . ," American Center for Design *Design Journal* (Spring 2000): 19–30.

13. *Zentropa*, a 1992 film by Danish filmmaker Lars von Trier, uses rear-projected film as a backdrop to the foregrounded actions of the cast. Through carefully orchestrated shots and edits, actors walk back and forth between the three-dimensional world of the set and the two-dimensional world of the rear-projection film screen. Perspective is thus heavily manipulated and color fields emerge as the rear projection remains in black and white and the foreground action appears in color. Peter Greenaway's films *The Pillow Book* and *Prospero's Books* utilize multiple picture-in-picture screens and text/image superimposition.

14. Erik van Blokland and Just van Rossum explain their typeface Beowolf (*Émigré*18: 1991) with the analogy of being on the phone with a sick friend. Their voice may be husky and coarse, but you still recognize this vari-

ant "font" of a voice as theirs. And Zuzana Licko repeatedly makes the point that typographic legibility/readability is dependent on familiarity and not some abstract, rational paradigm of what constitutes a successful—or optimally readable—typeface.

15. From "Quandary," a typeface and discussion of type design by Tobias Frere-Jones, exhibited in "Word as Image: A Traveling Exhibition of Contemporary Graphic Design." Curators: Sandy Lowrance, Mike Schmidt, and Wendy McDaris of The University of Memphis.

16. David Small, "Rethinking the Book," in *Graphic Design and Reading: Explorations of an Uneasy Relationship*, ed. Gunnar Swanson (New York: Allworth Press, 2000), 189.

17. Small, 190.

18. Flash™ films are shown in windows appearing alongside text in interactive exhibition Web sites for the Smithsonian's "African Voices" collection. Additionally, interactive "tours" play across the screen like a filmstrip that moves at the pace of the user (*www.terraincognita.com*).

19. Sol Worth, "Toward an Anthropological Politics of Symbolic Forms," in *Reinventing Anthropology*, ed. Dell Hymes (New York: Pantheon Books, 1972).

Ten Career Tips for Digital Artists, Designers, and Animators

ISAAC KERLOW

DIGITAL TECHNOLOGY CHANGED the face of art, design, and animation production during the last twenty years of the twentieth century. Some of these changes were temporary and kept evolving until a good balance was found between the old and the new production techniques. But many of the fundamental day-to-day aspects of design and animation production changed drastically.

Being a successful *digital artist* (we will use that term interchangeably for digital illustrators, designers and/or animators) requires many different skills and talents. Some are in the creative front, a few in the technical area, and many in a variety of other areas. The specific balance of skills required varies among the industries that use digital technology for art production: Web site design, animation for feature films and television series, and graphics and game design for platform and location-based interactive games. But there are some basic strengths that every digital artist in these fields aspires to have, or is looking for in potential employees. The ten tips offered here have been distilled from years of experience and conversations with young and old practitioners. These tips might help you achieve your professional goals faster, and make your career path smoother and more successful.

Be Prepared for Change

The daily realities of working as a digital artist, designer, or animator in a digital production environment are in constant flux. This is not a new phenomenon. Many of the factors that define the flavor of the professional practice of digital production artists changed during the 1990s. These factors—which include technical developments, artistic styles, business cycles, and professional trends—are still changing, and it is very likely that they will continue to change in significant ways for several years to come.

Technical developments, for example, have a profound impact on the realities of working in digital production because they define many of the skills that are needed to complete a project. *Artistic styles* are critical because productions often hire artists based on the style of their work. In the case of three-dimensional modeling, a difference in artistic style might be a cartoony versus a realistic approach. In the rendering area, for example, lighting scenes that are to be composited with live-action shots may require a stylistic approach different from the one needed to light scenes that define stand-alone environments where virtual three-dimensional characters engage in real-time battles.

Business cycles often determine project budgets and deadlines, both of which have a major role in defining the potential of any project. Budgets usually determine the size of the creative and production teams, the type of tools (hardware and software) used to make the project a reality, as well as the period of time that the team has to complete the project. More than anything else, deadlines define the overall pressure on the members of the production team. This pressure is a very real factor that governs the quality of the work experience in the life of a three-dimensional digital artist or animator.

Focus on a Realistic Goal

It is not uncommon for individuals who want to pursue a career in digital art and design production to have immediate goals that are clearly beyond their reach. Many who enter the field have dreams of earning fat paychecks and winning international awards within a couple of years. While some veteran digital artists and animators do make a good living and adorn their studios with awards, that is usually the result of a lifetime of effort and dedication. In many of the industries that are touched by the digital production revolution there have been periods that resemble the 1849 California Gold Rush. A few adventurers hit the jackpot and thousands follow expecting to hit it with the same magnitude and within the same time frame. You have to ask yourself whether you are interested in any of the digital creation and production fields because of the vocation or because of some sort of gold-rush fever.

A good way to focus on a *realistic goal* is by identifying a job that you both like and are qualified for. This process may start by identifying the type of place where you would like to work. Would you be interested in joining a small shop, a medium-sized one, or a large studio? Each has pros and cons that include issues like pay scale, opportunity to learn from others, scope of work, daily interaction with a more experienced mentor, and the type of projects that you would be working on. As you think about the type of place where you would like to work, you could also make a list of companies that fall within the category (or categories) that interest you. The next step would be to decide what type of positions within those companies are the ones that interest you most, keeping in mind which positions would be best suited to your skills and talents.

All this preparation may mean a significant amount of research. Whether you obtain this information from magazines, instructors, friends, or at professional events, you can be sure that in most cases it pays off to be well-informed. A few lucky ones, of course, are able to land great first jobs without following this step-by-step approach, but it is best not to assume that you will be that lucky. Once you have identified the type of job you are looking for, you can customize your portfolio, Web site, or demo reel to meet the job's requirements, and start the application process.

Know Your Digital Craft

The craft of visual artists is what allows their ideas to be expressed in the form of images. The craft includes things as diverse as knowing how to get expression out of lines, shapes, color, and composition; knowing how to navigate through the different software programs used for production; the ability to work with elements created by others and, in turn, submit your own elements to the next person in the production pipeline; and the ability to keep a creative focus through a production process that can be complex and removed from the final product. The *digital craft* of today's artists has not been around for centuries; it is still being defined, so do not be surprised if you sometimes feel like you or your team are trying a digital production approach for the first time—you might be.

In very few other creative fields is the craft as important to the work of an artist as it is in the digital realm. When creating in some of the areas that still have not gone into a fully digital production environment, the pressures on the digital artist to be in full command of the craft are usually not overbearing. In those cases the production process usually involves a single individual for each stage in the process, tools that have been around for a while (like pen and ink, or brushes and watercolor paint), and a fairly stable production process that all participants understand.

In areas that follow the digital art-production model, the creative and production team is usually made up of several digital artists. These individuals are required to use tools that are always changing: hardware reconfigurations and software upgrades are constant. To make matters more difficult, today's digital production processes are not yet standardized, because many projects present such novel challenges that the process has to be adapted to those specific challenges. Staying up-to-date in the area of your artistic craft is doubly important because digital techniques continue to evolve quickly. This rate of change will probably start to slow down at some point. In the meantime, continue to update your skills, perhaps by taking professional education workshops regularly, and by sharing knowledge with your peers on a continual basis. Your technical knowledge and creativity can always be complemented with new specific software skills.

Update and Customize Your Reel and Portfolio

It almost goes without saying that the most important thing about a digital art *portfolio, Web site,* or *demo reel* is that it represents your specific talents and skills in the best possible way. The second most important thing—for getting the job that you want—is that your portfolio or demo reel contains the types of items that the potential employer is interested in seeing. For example, your portfolio or demo reel may be of high-quality, but if the work is not the kind that your potential employer is looking for, even a high-quality portfolio will not be an effective tool for getting that job. All this basically means one thing in respect to maximizing your chances of getting the job that you want.

While you should focus your energy on developing a body of work that is of high quality, you should also spend a significant amount of energy customizing it to the specific preferences and requirements of the company that you are applying to. For example, if your potential employer is involved exclusively in the creation of Web sites. They will surely be interested in seeing and evaluating your Web site. Find out as much as you can about the specific *review requirements* of the companies that you want to submit your work to. Some companies will mail or fax their guidelines, others post the information on their Web sites, and a few will provide it over the telephone.

The fact that different companies have unique review requirements may mean that you will end up with a couple of slightly different versions of your portfolio, reel, or Web site. In the case of companies specializing in motion graphics, for example, some might prefer to review videotapes or CD-ROMs containing any kind of work of any length in any order, while others may only want to see reels that are under three minutes long, that start with wire-frame motion tests and end with fully rendered animated sequences, and that exclusively contain character animation created with motion-capture techniques. You do not have to customize your reel to get a good job, but when you do, it certainly increases your chances and your options.

Be Prepared to Work as a Member of a Team

Virtually all digital projects are team efforts. Whether the project is a Web site, a videogame, or an effects shot for a live-action show, the complex nature of these projects almost makes it a condition that the production process be collaborative.

In the case of a computer-generated visual-effects shot, for example, the sheer number of steps in the process requires a team of several individuals to handle the workload. On occasion some of the steps have to happen in parallel. For example, someone may have to build the extensive three-dimensional environments, while someone else builds a detailed three-dimensional character, while yet another member of the team paints the textures that will be applied onto the model before rendering the finished version. In the case of a Web site, even if the visual content is simple and requires only straightforward techniques, there is always the ever-present pressure of tight deadlines. Because Web sites are commonly refreshed every day or every few days, the best—and often the only—way to meet deadlines is by dividing the workload among several people.

In predigital production times many artists were able to complete their works of art by themselves. A painter working on a small painting is probably the paramount example of a traditional visual artist who can complete the work without the help of other artists. The painter sketched the composition, primed the canvas, mixed the colors, laid on the under paint, rendered the details, and varnished the finished work. In a similar vein, even many of the pioneering experimental animators or video-makers of two or three decades ago were able to complete many of their projects by themselves. But the complexity of the work often calls for a team approach; we also find examples of this in traditional media. When paintings became too complex—as was the case with murals—the master painter had assistants who mixed the colors, prepared the painting surface, and even applied the paint. As animators developed works where the action was more complex, subtle, or longer in duration, or as they strove for more realistic effects, the production model had to include several individuals who took care of specialized tasks. Today, only the simplest of short computer animations could be designed, modeled, painted, rendered, animated, and composited by a single individual. The same can be said of almost any interactive or multimedia digital project.

Traditionally, *teamwork* has not always been what we are taught in art and design schools. The emphasis there still tends to be on developing our individual artistic voices as we master a few techniques. Perhaps we will soon see the fruits of innovative art and design teachers who devise new approaches to teaching art that allow students to develop their artistic vision in parallel with their teamwork skills.

Develop an Appreciation for Preproduction

Digital productions are usually complex because they require many steps to complete the work. Many of these steps often have to take place in parallel, or in a very specific sequence. Experience has taught us that the best way to tackle *complex productions*—digital or not—is to analyze them and break them down into their simplest components. This analytical and planning process takes place mostly during the preproduction stage of a project. In a digital production environment, preproduction is not a matter of choice, it is a requirement; especially if we want to complete the digital project *within budget* and *by the deadline*.

Getting used to *planning ahead* is a key factor for success in your digital-art-production career. From the production point of view, you will be invaluable to others on your team by having a plan of action you can present to them and by sticking to the plan after you all agree to follow it. Find out what the next step in the process will be. That way you will be more likely to stay one step ahead of the action, and you will be able to be more flexible and more efficient. Finally, take the preproduction meetings as seriously as you can by contributing your best ideas to them, even if others do not realize the importance of those meetings. In the long term, this is likely to win you the respect of your peers and will contribute to the success of the projects that you work on.

Focus on Issues That May Have an Impact on Your Health

As with any other profession, the work of a digital artist has potential *health risks*. Fortunately, most of them can easily prevented by paying attention to some basic rules and work habits. A significant number of today's artists and designers who work with computers suffer from work-related health issues, ranging from simple backaches to carpal tunnel syndrome. One would think that working with computers is a greater health threat to an artist than working with other tools, but that is actually far from the truth. The real issue here is that, unfortunately, we are still in the process of learning—as a community of digital artists and as individuals—to take preventive measures in a systematic way.

Let's think for a moment of a few of the preventive measures that artists working in other media have developed to minimize the chances of physical injury. Sculptors, for example, who use power tools or who work with high-temperature metals in foundries, have learned to wear goggles, gloves, and heavy boots. Dancers and athletes who submit their musculoskeletal systems to a daily eight-hour routine take the time to warm up and to cool down, so that their bodies stay relaxed and limber. Painters who use paint with toxic pigments do not lick the tips of the brushes to make them pointy. Photographers who work in a studio with multiple flash units try to give their eyes a break as they trigger the lights hundreds of times throughout the day.

It is clear that artists throughout the decades and centuries have developed ways to preserve their health in the workplace. It is time for us to do the same, and it is up to us to not only to come up with simple health guidelines, but also to follow them every day and to share them with our peers. We should be proactive in preventing stress-related problems including repetitive stress injuries (RSI). We can easily do this by stretching before we start using the mouse and keyboard, taking breaks once in a while, keeping the right posture while we spend hours sitting down. Exercising once in a while doesn't hurt either. Use common sense.

An earlier version of "Ten Career Tips for Digital Artists, Designers, and Animators" appeared in the Second Edition of *The Art of 3D Computer Animation and Imaging* by Isaac V. Kerlow, published in 2000 by John Wiley and Sons.

User
Experiences
(Selected Syllabi)

Principles of Interactivity: Interactive Planning and Design

MELISSA NIEDERHELMAN

Professor, School of Design, Arizona State University

16-WEEK SEMESTER; 34 senior graphic-design students

Introduction

1 | COURSE OBJECTIVES This course is based on the principles of interactive design, and focuses on the planning, organization and design of content, as well as on user issues in interactive solutions. The course will cover four main areas of interactive design in order to help students identify and manage the interactive-design process: (1) Users, (2) Content, (3) Navigation, and (4) Interface/Identity.

This course is not intended to produce finished interactive solutions, but rather, to give students the opportunity to examine the organizational and planning aspects of interactive design as a unique process. In addition to addressing user issues and content structure, students will produce working (clickable) prototypes of their proposed solutions as an example of a hypothetical interactive design. The class will also consider interactive design in relation to print design in order to help students gain more perspective on the role of digital media in visual communication.

This course will be based on one project, broken down into multiple phases. Each phase will require a digital presentation of the results and investigation during that phase.

This course will also require students to work with a partner toward a collaborative solution. Use this opportunity to share ideas, help one another with technology, and learn together.

2 | PROJECT PHASES The main project in this course will be different in nature from other projects you may have worked on in the past. This is because the project focuses on the preparation of information for interactive solutions more than on the finished digital product itself. Your knowledge of these skills will help you in developing a realistic and professional approach to future interactive projects. Don't underestimate the importance of content, navigation, user needs, functionality, and information design when it comes to interactive design! At the end of each phase, each team will give a digital /oral presentation that clearly shows the team's project ideas and decisions. Each team will then be required to produce a prototype of their proposed interactive solution that shows the function, navigation, identity and consideration of user needs.

3 | REFERENCES I recommend the following books as good resources for this class:

- ➻ *Interactivity by Design; Creating and Communicating with New Media,* Ray Kristof, Amy Satran
- ➻ *Designing Web Graphics 3,* Lynda Weinman
- ➻ *Secrets of Successful Web Sites: Project Management on the World Wide Web,* David Siegel

4 | A WORD OF ADVICE When working on this project, put most of your time and effort into managing details within the content. Success on these assignments will be as a result of really understanding your users and designing content. Don't just arrange things without considering how it could be clearer, more functional, more relevant, or how it might connect to something else.

Phase 1: Definition and Content

1 | OBJECTIVES The first part of this project begins where any well-organized interactive design project begins, in the planning. This phase of interactive design involves the following considerations: Goals, Users, Type of solution, Nature of content, Understanding of content, Inventory of content, and Project plan.

There is much more to interactive design than just deciding how things will look. Perhaps more so than other areas of design, interactive design requires planning, organization, management, and collaboration with other people. This project will put more focus on the planning than the product.

2 | PROCESS FOR PHASE 1 Students will be assigned a general theme (one example is travel) as a point of departure in developing content. With this theme in mind, you must then begin the process of deciding and assessing the best sort of solution to create, and whom it will be created for. You will need to decide how it will be used and in which context. Will it be a Web site? A CD-ROM? An information kiosk? Something that involves new technology?

You will need to define all aspects of the solution and document all decisions. Remember that since you are not responsible for creating the complete interactive solution, you don't have to limit yourself. Think instead about the best way to communicate the information.

3 | WHAT YOU NEED TO COVER In planning your approach to this interactive design solution, you must address the following questions and make decisions about them:

- ➻ What are the goals of the interactive design?
- ➻ Who are the users and how are they defined? What do they want?
- ➻ What kind of interactive solution is most appropriate?
- ➻ What is the content of the design?

- Have you read, and do you understand all the content?
- What is your content inventory? Will there be other media such as sound, video, etc.?
- Who else will be involved with your project plan?
- What areas of expertise, other than your's and your team's, will be required?

4 | PRESENTATION FOR PHASE 1 The outcome for this phase of the project will be a digital presentation (Macromedia Flash is preferable) of the decisions made during Phase 1. Each team will need to walk us through what is being proposed, why the solution would be useful, whom it is for, and what research was done to support the idea.

Here are some elements that will need to be addressed in your presentation:

1. *Goals.* What are the goals of your interactive design?
2. *Audience/Users.* (a.) Who are the defined users for this proposed solution? Who are you trying to reach? (b.) What makes these users a defined group (age, profession, interests, etc.)? (c.) How would your interactive design help/benefit them?
3. *Proposed Solution/Outcome.* List three advantages and three disadvantages for the interactive design solution you are proposing in relation to your specific users and goals. Why is this the best choice for your topic and goals?
4. *Authoring Tools.* Based on research or previous knowledge, what will be the best authoring tools to create your interactive solution (software, hardware, etc.)?
5. *Content.* (a.) Provide a brief description of the kind of content your solution would provide users. What will they find in your solution? (b.) Develop a preliminary outline for the content you will be including. Create several basic categories and then a few topics under each one. (c.) Will your solution include any multi-media content (video, sound, etc.)? (d.) Will your solution include any dynamic content (forms to fill out, calculators, etc.)?
6. *Project Plan.* (a.) In addition to the designers, who else might be involved with this project (writer, Web developer, researcher, historian, industrial designer, etc.)? (b.) Provide a basic schedule estimate for this proposed project (generally indicate how much time will be needed for planning, design, testing, etc.).

Phase 2: Information Organization and Structure

1 | OBJECTIVES You will build on the ideas established in the first phase of the project in order to determine a more specific and structured organization of the content. The thoughtful organization of content and information in interactive designs has many implications for the user, navigation, and function of the solution.

2 | PROCESS FOR PHASE 2 Using the content outline you have created in the first phase, you will now expand and organize this content in order to build a series of possible structures for the information.

Your team must create three flowchart structures for your content, each one using a different organizational arrangement. Your flowcharts of information must visually, and clearly, explain the following elements: Categories of information, Levels of information, Navigation options,

Paths and links, The kind of information at each link/level, Depth of the information, and Reoccurring elements or links (like a way to return to the home page).

Each flowchart solution must represent a different way to organize and navigate through your content. At this stage we are not as interested in how this information and navigation will look visually (i.e., buttons, interface, menus, etc.), as we are in how the information flows. You will need to show us how to move around within your content, and plan for the visual process that will follow this.

3 | PRESENTATION FOR PHASE 2 Your outcome for this phase will be the same as Phase 1—a presentation of your decisions and strategies. You will need to show your three flowchart solutions (this can be in print or digital form).

Phase 3: Identity, Interface and Prototype

1 | OBJECTIVES The last phase of this interactive design project will consider visual identity, interface design, and creating a working prototype of the solution. Now that you have successfully defined the interactive product, have structured the content, and have mapped navigation, it is time to give the solution a visual form.

2 | ELEMENTS TO CONSIDER There are several visual elements that you must now address in your planning for this interactive solution:

- ➻ You will need to establish an identity. How does someone recognize your solution? How is it represented visually? You will need to consider an identity system for your proposed solution. There are, however, many unique aspects to identities in digital environments. What are these unique aspects? It should be a cohesive system that may involve color, typeface, hierarchy, images, composition, functions, and any other elements that give the solution unity.
- ➻ You and your team will also need to consider system design as it relates to functional elements within the solutions. Here is a list of just a few of those elements:
- ➻ Menus
- ➻ Buttons/navigation tools: Rollovers, Reoccurring links, Images, Multimedia, Text, and Windows. What do these things look like? How do they relate visually to your overall identity? How do they function? How will someone know where to go and what the choices are?
- ➻ Finally, you will need to consider the overall context of your solution in terms of things like environment and object. What kind of solution is it? If it is an info kiosk, is it touch screen or operated with a mouse? If it is a CD-ROM, do you also consider the packaging? If it is a technological device, what will it look like? If it is designed to be used at a particular location, what is the location?

Your goal is to have results that will help us visualize and understand how your interactive solution will look and function.

3 | PROTOTYPE You and your team will not have time to design all the possible pages or parts of your solution, so it is best to think of designing a prototype or an example to represent the entire solution. Choose one path or section, or part of your content structure to work with, and show us how it will look and function.

4 | PRESENTATION FOR PHASE 3 Once again you and your team will give a brief presentation at the end of this phase for feedback and suggestions. One week later, at a formal presentation to the class and some invited guests, you and your team will give a final account of the entire project and your proposed solution.

User Testing

Once each team has created a working prototype, you will need to show this prototype to users who fall within your defined user group. Let them use the prototype and have some questions ready to ask them, or even a survey, about the results.

Document this feedback as well as you can, and record all responses both good and bad.

Final Presentation of Project

At the end of all three phases, you and your team will give a formal presentation about your process, decisions, proposal, and prototype to the class and some invited guests from the professional community.

1 | ITEMS TO COVER IN PRESENTATION

- *Topic (what you are doing).* Give a brief overview of the topic and a basic idea of your project. Don't go into a lot of detail—just bring people up to speed.
- *Goals and Objectives.* Outline your goals and objectives for the interactive solution. Be concise, and remember to make them goals and not a list of activities.
- *Users.* Explain how you have identified your users: Who are they? What characteristics define them? Why did you focus on this group? Whom did you talk to in user testing throughout the project? What do they want? Explain any research you conducted about them.
- *Proposed Solution.* Explain briefly the interactive solution you have chosen and why you chose it. What are the benefits of this application over others? Point out any research you did to support this decision.
- *Content and structure.* Give a brief overview of your content. What kind of information your solution will contain. Show one working diagram to explain content structure.
- *Identity.* What sort of overall identity, or visual characteristics, did you choose for the solution? How did these visual choices relate to the users and goals of the solution?
- *Interface and physical product.* Show designs that outline the visual translation of all the features and functions of the interactive solution. What were some the considerations for designing for a digital/interactive environment? Show any drawings or ideas for objects

and technology that relate to the interactive solution (drawing for the design of info kiosks or handheld devices, etc.).

➤ *Prototype.* Show a working (clickable) prototype of the solution.

➤ *User testing.* How did you follow up the process of testing your solution with users? What did you learn from this testing? What comments did you receive? How would you modify your solution/direction as a result?

Try to leave five to ten minutes for questions and comments.

Web Design 1: Principles of Strategic Web Design

RAYMOND PIROUZ

THIS COURSE INTRODUCES the concept of strategic Web design and focuses on building a communication design aesthetic through a series of exercises and critiques.

Week 1: Formulating a Communication Strategy

Communication Designer Defined. The Communication Design Approach. 8-Step Communication Strategy.

ASSIGNMENT Based on what we've discussed today, the first part of your assignment for next week is to visit three Web sites that you think *do not* employ a communication strategy. Once there, take snapshots of pages you feel would help to visually state your case (or provide URLs), and write a brief paper stating why you think that these Web sites fall short.

The second part of your assignment is to visit three Web sites that you think *do* employ a communication strategy. Once there, take snapshots of pages you feel would help to visually state your case (or provide URLs), and write a brief paper stating why you think that these Web sites are successful.

Week 2: Measuring Effectiveness in Communication Design

The Four-Phase Strategic Design Development Cycle. Establishing Effectiveness Standards.

ASSIGNMENT Based on what we've discussed, your assignment for next week is to visit two Web sites that you have *never* before visited. That's not such a hard thing to do seeing how there are millions of Web sites on the Internet.

Please make sure to visit "design-wise" Web sites that will challenge you. An ugly and pointless Web sites are easy to criticize.

Once you have spent at least a half hour going through the content of each Web site, write a paper addressing each of the above ten effectiveness standards for the two Web sites (providing any images to reinforce your statements).

Week 3: Defining the Key Purpose of a Web Site

The Mission Statement. The Key Purpose. Defining Intimate Understanding. Backwards-Definable Through Analysis.

ASSIGNMENT Based on what we've discussed so far, your assignment for next week is to do the following:

- *Dog-Grooming Service.* Name the service, prepare a mission statement for the service, and develop a key purpose for its Web site.
- *Plumber.* Name the one-man (or one-woman) operation, prepare a mission statement for the operation, and develop a key purpose for its Web site.
- *www.commarts.com.* What is this Web site's key purpose? How can you tell, or can you tell, why and why not? If you can tell what it is, do you think that it is adequate strategically, and adequately visualized in the design of the Web site?
- *www.amazon.com.* What is this Web site's key purpose? How can you tell, or can you tell, why and why not? If you can tell what it is, do you think that it is adequate strategically and adequately visualized in the design of the Web site?

Week 4: Identifying and Targeting an Audience

Target Audience and Audience at Large. Evaluating ups.com.

ASSIGNMENT Based on what we've discussed so far, your assignment for next week is to spend some time at the Lego.com Web site. One thing you'll notice right off the bat is that there is no *store* here. Up until several months ago, the Lego site had a shop link; however, it took you to a horribly designed site that looked nothing like the Lego home page. I suspect that they finally took it down and are in the process of redesigning it—maybe.

As part of your assignment, it is your duty to evaluate the present Lego Web site home page and determine if it is adequately targeting its intended audience. If not, redesign it or enhance it—you've got free reign to do with the site as you will. How would you incorporate a shopping mechanism into this site? Create a link for a store and design a home page for the Lego store.

Week 5: Applying the Visual Language

The Visual and Universal Language. Content and Context. Evaluating ups.com.

ASSIGNMENT Based on what we've covered so far, the first part of your assignment for next week is to go out on the net and locate a Web site that you feel makes good use of visual language to enhance its overall content while communicating to its target audience. Write a small paper describing why you think the site is successful, providing reinforcing visuals as necessary.

The second part of your assignment is to locate a Web site that you feel does not do an adequate job of employing visual language and perform a one-page redesign (showing "before" and "after" in your final presentation).

Week 6: Strategic Web Site Layout Concepts

Less is So Much More. Defining Editorial, Entertainment, Marketing and Promotional, e-commerce, Search Engine, and Portal sites. Establishing a Visual Hierarchy. Presenting Information within Context. Presenting Call-to-Action Opportunities.

ASSIGNMENT Based on what we've discussed so far, your assignment for next week is to design a Web-site home page for a nonprofit organization of your choice. If you like, you may redesign its current identity, and introduce a more sophisticated navigational system based on what's available at their current Web site (if any). In your design, consider information overload and minimalism, visual hierarchy and call-to-action element(s). Accompany your design with a short paper introducing your project, and describing how you arrived at your design solution.

Week 7: Designing with the Brand in Mind

What is a Brand? Defining the Brand and Branding. Taking the Brand Online How Branding Translates in the Online Experience. Maintaining a Consistent Online Brand Image. Building Long-Term Online Brand Recognition.

ASSIGNMENT Based on what we've discussed today, your assignment for next week is to write about a Web site whose brand image is new to you. What are your initial impressions, and what factors in the Web presence helped to formulate your initial impressions regarding overall brand image? If what you've visited is a commerce Web site, would you buy from them? If what you've visited is an information Web site, would you visit again, why and why not?

Week 8: The Strategic Use of Technology

Technology for the Sake of Communication. The Cool Factor. The Competitive Edge. The Press Factor. The Pushing the Envelope Factor. Beware the Hype. Stable Technology. Experimental Technology. Appropriate Use of Technology.

ASSIGNMENT Based on what we've discussed today, your assignment for next week is to visit a Web site that you feel uses technology in an inappropriate fashion. Present the Web site and tell me why you feel that its use of technology is gratuitous. Try to describe where they may have gone wrong with their strategy, and suggest possible alternatives.

Week 9: Designing Feedback Mechanisms

The Subscription Form. The Data Collection/Survey Form. The Order Form. The Contact Form. Privacy Considerations.

ASSIGNMENT Based on what we've discussed so far, your assignment for next week is to find an online example for each of the four kinds of feedback mechanisms (the subscription form, the data collection/survey form, the order form and the contact form). Write a short paper telling me what you thought of the structure, layout, design, and usability of each, and whether or not you thought the forms were effective. Please be sure to visit a different Web site for each feedback mechanism.

Week 10: Incorporating Modularity and Repeat-Visit Mechanisms

Making the Case for Modular Design. Integrating Visual Repeat-Visit Mechanisms.

Course wrap-up and final thoughts.

Digital Creativity: Designing for New Media and the Internet

BRUCE WANDS

Chair, MFA/Computer Art, School of Visual Arts, New York

THIS IS A lecture class that reviews professional creative practices as they relate to the Internet and new media. It is designed to give students an overview of the impact of digital technology on the creative process in these disciplines. It also explains how to come up with ideas, design theory, the production process, and the software and hardware used in creating new media. Samples of professional work are shown and deconstructed in class to explain how they were produced.

1. History of New Media and the Internet

The history of new media will be covered in detail from the early development to the present day, including the development of computers, CD-ROMs, the Internet, the World Wide Web, and DVD. In addition, the cultural impact of inventions like the printing press, telephone, motion pictures, and television will be discussed in relationship to digital media, mass communication, and the development of global culture.

2. Basics of Digital Media

This week we'll focus on the technical aspects of new media. What are the component parts of a computer, how do they work, how to configure and set up a system, and how the Internet functions. We'll also look at the digital implications for color, type, and video.

3. Creativity

Creativity is the most important part of any commercial or fine-art project. This lecture will cover how to come up with ideas, the nature of the creative process, keeping notebooks and sketchbooks, and other ways to increase both the quality and quantity of your creative output.

4. The Production Process

Commercial studios have refined the methods for producing new media. This class will review this process in detail, including preproduction, concept development, production methods, and postproduction issues. We will also examine the different roles of people on the production team, including the producer, director, artist, programmer, and editor.

5. Drawing and Illustration

Images form a critical part of Web sites, CD-ROMs, newspapers, magazines, etc. Drawing is the fundamental way in which most artists communicate their ideas. This week, we'll look at the process of drawing. We'll also discuss illustration, how it differs from drawing, and developing your own illustration style. The work of various illustrators will be reviewed to demonstrate the wide variety of illustration styles.

6. Typography

Typography is critical to making design projects successful. We'll look at the fundamentals of type, including fonts, type styles, kerning, leading, and other basic typographical issues. Samples of work by well-known typographers and designers will be looked at in class and discussed.

7. Web Design

The Web is the hottest design area right now. It has the advantage of allowing animation, video, and audio to be a part of the design process. It has the limitations of cross-platform issues, limited fonts, and bandwidth considerations. We'll look at Web design from both the positive and negative sides. We'll look at several Web sites and discuss how they work and what their design process was.

8. Digital Photography

Photography is rapidly moving from a film to a digital format. Like most visual media, digital will not replace the traditional, but will augment it. We'll review the traditional methods and tools of creating good photographs, such as composition, lighting, lenses, exposure, and aperture. We'll review the work of several well-known photographers, and look at the impact the digital process has had on photography.

9. Video Production

This class will explain how to produce video, both for video and for the Internet. We'll look at the video production process, including directing, shooting, lighting, and editing. Non-linear editing systems will be explained. We'll also talk about preparing video for the Web.

10. Audio Production

Sound is a vital component of most new media projects. This class will review how to record sound, microphones, digital audio formats, and mixing sound. We'll also look at making audio CDs, MP3 files, and preparing audio for the Internet.

11. 2-D Animation

2-D animation has a history dating back to the early 1900s. It has remained a vital art form. We'll trace the history of 2-D animation from early black and white through recent cel animation. We'll look at work from Disney, Warner Brothers, and other well-known animation studios. Then, we'll look at how digital 2-D animation is produced for film, television, and the Internet.

12. 3-D Animation

3-D animation really came of age in the 1990s with the development of the computer-animated feature. We'll look closely at how 3-D animation is produced, what software is needed, and how it is output to film, video, and the Internet. We'll talk about modeling, animation, lighting, and texturing and rendering. The various software applications used to create 3-D animation will be explained.

13. Professional Issues

This class will look at what it takes to become a successful new-media artist. This includes writing a résumé, developing and refining a portfolio, how to search for jobs, etc. We will have a guest lecture by a successful new-media producer, who will discuss what he does, and how he got to this point in his career. We'll also look at freelancing, exhibiting your creative work, and ongoing professional development techniques.

14. The Future of New Media and the Internet

Technology is a rapidly changing area. We'll take time during this class to speculate about what the future will bring and how it will affect current new media. Examples of future trends are broadband Internet, wireless technology, and voice recognition.

15. Review of Class, Question and Answer Session

This class will review the previous material, and provide a forum for discussion, questions, and answers.

Typespace

DAVID KARAM AND BOB AUFULDISH
California College of Arts and Crafts

HELLO, WORDS (AND LETTERS) come from a need to express ideas and describe things. A vessel is a story and its form is a reference to a concept or memory. A word or letter has a sound and form which has meaning and is interpreted in context. This course is about creating that context through typography as it functions on screen.

Course Description Don't Panic

In this class, students will explore the expressive and experimental aspects of 3-dimensional animated typography and character development. Typography will be used to discuss gesture and anthropomorphism, physical and virtual environments.

Software & C

All assignments should be linear quicktime or video presentations that simulate or demonstrate a concept. Represent interactivity when appropriate as scripted sequences. After Affects will be used for 2-D animation, and Infini-D will be used for 3-D modeling and animation. Prior knowledge of Photoshop and Illustrator is required. You will be expected to keep notes on all technical lectures and do outside reading. Please experiment with the software. Save multiple versions of your work.

An Aside

This is not a digital studio course. Programs needed to execute projects will be demonstrated, but are not the focus of the course. The computer is the tool, not the subject.

Policy

You are required to be familiar with and follow the School of Design student contract. To summarize, students are expected to be on time and prepared for class, and to stay for the entire class period. If a student is late for class four (4) times, it will count as an unexcused absence. Three (3) unexcused absences will result in lowering the student's final grade one letter. Missing six (6) classes for any reason will result in failing the course. Deadlines missed will result in lowering the project grade by one letter for every day late. No grade of "incomplete" will be given.

Grades

Grades are determined by evaluating the student's work against the objectives of the project and against the work of fellow classmates. Also entering the equation are work habits, craft, and class participation. Grades move above and below C based on the above criteria.

Course Outline

➻ demonstration: after effects
➻ project 1: character emotion
➻ demonstration: infiniti-d
➻ project 2: navigation space
➻ presentation: critical essay
➻ project 3: narrative structure

Reading

1 | SUGGESTED TEXT *Type in Motion, Innovations in Digital Graphics,* Jeff Bellantoni, Matt Woolman, Rizzoli, 1999. This is a good source of general information on the interaction of form and content. It's available at the Art Store in Oakland.

2 | SUGGESTED GENERAL READINGS
➻ *Dimensional Typography: Words in Space,* J. Abbott Miller, Kiosk/Princeton Architectural Press, 1996.
➻ *Envisioning Information,* Edward Tufte, Graphics Press, 1990.
➻ *The Liberated Page, An anthology of major typographic experiments of this century as recorded in* Typographica *magazine,* Herbert Spencer, ed., Bedford Press, 1987. *Typographica* was published from 1960–67; it was the *Eye* of its day.

3 | NON-DIGITAL SOURCES OF EXPRESSIVE TYPOGRAPHY AND LETTERFORMS
➻ *American Wood Type: 1828–1900, Notes on the Evolution of Decorated and Large Types,* Rob Roy Kelly, Da Capo Press, 1977.
➻ *130 Alphabets and Other Signs,* Julian Rothstein, Mel Gooding, eds., Thames and Hudson, 1991.

4 | **ON ATTACHING FORM TO MEANING** *Point and Line to Plane,* Wassily Kandinsky, Dover Publications, 1979 (originally published 1926 as Bauhaus Book #9).

Specific suggested readings will be given throughout the semester.

5 | **REQUIRED VIEWING** A CD of projects will be available for you to copy in the next few weeks.

Project 1: Character Emotion (due: 2.2)

Animate a letterform so it expresses the emotional state you have been assigned. You may use only one letter. A successful project will communicate the emotion without additional explanation.

Consider carefully your working methodology: When time is short, planning is essential before moving to the computer. Investigate typefaces, make sketches by hand or in Illustrator of key frames for presentation of your ideas. Sound, color and duration, along with animation, are crucial ways of communicating your concept.

1 | **NEXT** A storyboard of your concepts

2 | **FORM** 2-D animation

3 | **SUGGESTED READING** *Dimensional Typography: Words in Space,* by J. Abbott Miller.

4 | **EMOTIONS** ennui, foolishness, joy, depression, anger, delirium, love, exuberance, hate, courage, fear, sadness, rage, hysteria, calm, nervous, languid, sanguine, dread, angst, anxiety, jealousy, embarrassment, contentment, and alienation.

Project 2: Navigation Space (due: 3.8)

The intersection of text, meaning, interpretation, structure, space, and navigation. Choose a haiku, short poem, or a word. Create a space that reveals multiple meanings and annotates the text.

Use of limited imagery is allowable, but the project should work primarily in the typographic realm.

Consider how your space will be constructed and how that space might relate to the form of the text.

Consider how the space can allude to meaning or connections between meanings.

Consider how the typography can function as a navigation device.

Consider how interactivity can be communicated to the user.

Build a 2-D diagram that communicates how the space is constructed.

Present your project as a fly through animation built in Infiniti-D—depending on complexity, the animation may be of only part of the space, but should nonetheless demonstrate how the navigation works.

The project will demonstrate how interactivity will work in your space, but the project itself need not be interactive.

1 | **NEXT** Your selected text and research into its meaning.

2 | **FORM** 3-D animation

3 | **SUGGESTED READING** Reference MIT Media Lab Work: Visible Language Workshop
   www.infoarch.ai.mit.edu/jair/jair-space.html

Project 3: Narrative Structure (due: 5.3)

How can narrative structures be translated into space/time? There are two options to consider: (1) Create an animated sequence that translates a story into an abstract typographic environment. (2) Create an animated sequence that retells a story using typographic elements.

Some background information with examples of different narrative structures will be provided. An interim presentation consisting of key frames is an important part of the working process; deadline to come.

1 | **FORM** 3-D modeling and lighting

Presentation Critical Essay (presented 4.17–26)

How has typography changed with the emergence of motion and interactive media?

Make a five-to-ten-minute presentation that references at least two sources as well as your opinion on the subject of dynamic typography. Include dynamic media (Web pages, QuickTime movies, etc.) as part of your presentation.

Having a coherent point (and a point of view) is important.

1 | **FORM** Speaking and clicking

Project captions

➡ Francesca Bautista, Fall 1999. *Exuberance.* A letter *S*, the color of bubblegum, bounces, flies, and duckwalks to express exuberance.

➡ Jason Botta, Fall 1999. *Contentment.* A letter *X* breathes deeply, stretches, and sighs to express contentment.

➡ Adam Kirshner, Spring 2000. *Poem.* The viewer selects words out of a blurry cloud of text as a method of navigating the meaning of a poem.

➡ Francesca Bautista, Fall 1999. *Bee in the only rose.* The viewer flies out into space until the text of the poem is sighted. The text then rotates to reveal a second, interwoven text.

➻ Ragina Johnson, Fall 1999. The navigation device is a sentence used to generate non-sense words. The viewer selects a letter and a new sentence is generated using the non-sense word. The process continues in a circular fashion.

➻ Adam Kirshner, Spring 2000. *Moby Dick*. Ahab is visualized as a maelstrom that inhales the crew of his ship.

➻ Michael Courtney O'Connell, Spring 2000. *Metamorphosis.* The letters in "Gregor" swell and deform, much to the horror of his family.

➻ Francesca Bautista, Fall 1999. *The Shadow.* A retelling of a radio play, with the Shadow performed by a pair of parentheses.

➻ Jeroen Mimran, Fall 1999. *Mezzanine.* A typographic interpretation of Nicholson Baker's "Mezzanine." The viewer moves through typespace as mental space.

➻ Makiko Tatsumi, Fall 1999. A sequence of Duane Michals photographs is abstracted into a typographic environment. The internal visual logic of the photographs is used to generate a spatial typographic logic.

Interactive Design: Play with Signs

RACHEL SCHREIBER

Coordinator of the Master of Arts in Digital Arts program
at the Maryland Institute, College of Art

Course Objectives

This course explores interactive forms, focusing on computer-based media. We will look at old as well as new models in order to think about how interactive modes of viewership affect the work. We will also consider various issues pertaining to "interactive media" in cyberculture, including (but not limited to) issues of distribution, access, novelty, convention, mediation, interactive gaming and gaming communities, and more.

Course Format

Most days will start with a discussion, lecture, or critique, and continue with technical instruction and lab time. This course will focus on Macromedia Director as a tool for producing interactive works.

Assignments

1 | ASSIGNMENT 1: INVITING INTERACTION Make an interactive piece using the "cootie catcher" as the form (sometimes these are called "fortune tellers"). Focus your ideas on trying to make a piece that will invite the user to interact with it.

2 | ASSIGNMENT 2: SUSTAINING INTERACTION Using Macromedia Director, make a word game. The game may take any form, but you are limited to the following options in Director: the action "go to frame" and simple animations. Your other limitation is to use text *only*. You may create text from within Director, or any other way (Photoshop, Illustrator, or scanning made or found text). Think particularly about what keeps a user involved in your piece. What keeps them interested? What makes them want to keep playing your game?

3 | ASSIGNMENT 3: CONVENTIONS For this assignment, you will work in groups in order to research navigation alternatives—can we rethink conventions, while providing an autodidactic alternative? That is, how can we improve upon current conventions, while making the functionality inherent and evident?

Each group will present two kinds of navigation alternatives: one set that is realistic, and one set that is fantastic. The realistic set must be able to be implemented within current technology. The fantastic set could be any kind of imaginative solution, no limit and no constraint in terms of ability to be produced.

Groups will be assigned the following conventions to investigate: cursors, forward and back buttons, home and help buttons, waiting icons, and text/image links.

4 | **ASSIGNMENT 4: SOUND, IMAGE, NARRATIVE** For this assignment, you will make a Director project that uses only sound and image to create a narrative. This time, there are no constraints on what you may do in Director. However, you may not use text, either written or audio.

The dictionary defines "narrative" as: the representation in art of an event or story.

Consider the following for collecting sounds:

- You may: download a sound off one sound-effects Web site, download a sound off any other Web site, use SoundEdit to edit a portion of a sound from a CD track, experiment with the speech function in Simple Text, record a sound using the Apple system microphones, or record a sound using any other means available to you.
- You may not: use voice-over or use music that someone else has written, unless you edit and alter it considerably.

5 | **ASSIGNMENT 5: RESEARCH ASSIGNMENT** Breaking into the same groups from the conventions assignment, find three Web sites to present to the class that exemplify experimental approaches to your given convention.

6 | **ASSIGNMENT 6: FINAL ASSIGNMENT** The final assignment is open. Students may begin a new project or pursue further one that you have started in this class. Students must submit a written proposal, which is subject to my approval.

Syllabus

1 | **WEEK 1** Course introduction; play computer games, find games on the Web

2 | **WEEK 2** Screen: *Tron*. Critique: cootie catchers

3 | **WEEK 3** Reading: selections from *The Interactive Book* by Celia Pearce. Technical demo: introduction to Macromedia Director.

4 | **WEEK 4** Reading: selections from *Hypertext: The Electronic Labyrinth* by Ilana Snyder, and "The End of Innocence, Part I" from *The War of Desire and Technology at the Close of the*

Mechanical Age by Rosanne Allucquère Stone (history of the Atari gaming company). Show: artist's CD-ROMs. Technical demo: more on Director.

5 | **WEEK 5** Reading: "The Death of the Author" by Roland Barthes, "What is an Author?" by Michel Foucault, and "The Creative Act" by Marcel Duchamp. Lecture: Roland Barthes, Jacques Derrida, and notions of the open text.

6 | **WEEK 6** Critique on assignment 2

7 | **WEEK 7** Technical and lab day: sound and behaviors in Director

8 | **WEEK 8** Groups present conventions assignment (assignment 3)

9 | **WEEK 9** Individual meetings—final project proposals due

10 | **WEEK 10** Critique on assignment 4

11 | **WEEK 11** Spring Break

12 | **WEEK 12** Reading: "Burning Chrome" by William Gibson. Screen: *Bladerunner.*

13 | **WEEK 13** In-progress critique of final assignment

14 | **WEEK 14** Research presentations (assignment 5)

15 | **WEEK 15** Final critique

Course Reader

1. Selections from *The Interactive Book.* Celia Pearce, *The Interactive Book* (Indianapolis, IN: Macmillan Technical Publishing, 1997).
2. Selections from *Hypertext: The Electronic Labyrinth.* Ilana Snyder, *Hypertext: The Electronic Labyrinth* (Carlton South, Victoria, Australia: Melbourne University Press, 1996).
3. "The End of Innocence, Part I" Allucquère Rosanne Stone, *The War of Technology and Desire at the Close of the Mechanical Age* (Cambridge: MIT Press, 1995).
4. "The Death of the Author" Roland Barthes, *Image/Music/Text* (New York: Hill and Wang, 1977).
5. "What is an Author?" Michel Foucault, from *The Foucault Reader*, Paul Rabinow, ed. (New York: Penguin Books, 1984).
6. "The Creative Act" Marcel Duchamp, online: http://members.aol.com/mindwebart3/marcel.htm
7. "Burning Chrome" William Gibson, *Burning Chrome* (New York: Ace Books, 1994).

Advanced Digital Imaging

RACHEL SCHREIBER

Course Objectives

This course will explore the effects of the current possibilities for manipulating photographs digitally on the status of the contemporary photographic image. The thesis for the course is to draw a grand comparison between the effects of industrialization on the aesthetics of Modernism (focusing on the photomontage work produced between the Wars), and the effects of technologization on postmodernism.

Course Format

Class time alternates between lab days and discussion/lecture days. On lab days, students are expected to be working on the current assignment in the computer lab, and I will assist with technical and/or conceptual questions. On most discussion/lecture days, there is a reading due from the course reader. Students are expected to have the reading completed by the start of class and be prepared to discuss the reading.

Studio Assignments

1 | ASSIGNMENT 1 As we approach the end of the millennium, we realize that in Western civilization, technology is part of all of our lives. For this assignment, you are asked to make a series of four images that respond to the question: How does technology affect your daily experience?

2 | ASSIGNMENT 2: SIGNIFICATION Photographic images contain both connotative and denotative aspects. Denotative aspects include the elements that are "objectively" in a photograph: a tree, a house, a person. Connotation is about the communicated meaning of these elements. This communication relies on a previously agreed-upon cultural meaning of an image. Signification is the process through which meaning is created; it is the net result of the connotative aspects of a photograph.

Choose one of the following themes: Wealth, Beauty, Death, Horror, Sexuality, Love, or Knowledge.

Create a series of images that signify the chosen theme, while having nothing in the image that is typically thought to signify that idea.

3 | ASSIGNMENT 3 Choose one of the following concepts to be the formal basis for a body of work: Repetition, Montage, or Anachronism.

Repeat: to say or state again; to say over from memory, to say after another; to make, do or perform again; to go through or experience again, to say, do, or accomplish something again.

Montage: the production of a rapid succession of images in a motion picture to illustrate an association of ideas; a literary, musical, or artistic composite of juxtaposed more or less heterogeneous elements; a composite picture made by combining several separate pictures; a heterogeneous mixture.

Anachronism: an error in chronology, especially misplacing of persons, events, objects, or customs in regard to each other; a person or thing that is chronologically out of place.

4 | ASSIGNMENT 4: FINAL PROJECT The final project is open, but students must write a proposal, which is subject to my approval.

Writing Component

One of the requirements of the course is that each student writes a two-page, typed response to three of the readings. Students may choose which readings to respond to.

Guidelines

The operative word is response. Response differs from criticism. You are not writing criticism. Hints:

➼ I am not interested in whether you thought it was a "good" or "bad" reading. Let's assume that all of the readings were chosen for a reason, and that they have something useful to offer. Let's also assume that, given the fact that all of the writers are highly regarded, well-published authors, that none of them are "bad" writers.

➼ Avoid statements about whether or not you liked the reading.

➼ Avoid comments about the writer's style of writing.

➼ Avoid comments about whether you thought the reading was easy or difficult.

You are writing a response. Hints:

➼ Write about how a given reading might have an impact on the way you think about something, such as the way you approach making or thinking about art. Be specific.

⇥ Write about the specific ways in which a reading has changed the way you think about something.

⇥ Write about how this reading relates to other readings we've done, other topics of discussion in the class, other ideas you've learned about elsewhere, the work of a particular artist, or aspects of your own art practice. These will make particularly interesting topics for an essay.

Essay Test

Answer any two of the following questions:

⇥ Many artists working with digital imaging employ photomontage techniques. Other than this obvious reason, what relationship exists between the history of photomontage and contemporary digital imaging? In your answer, make reference to at least two of the readings from the semester.

⇥ On page 27 of his Introduction to *Iterations: The New Image*, Timothy Druckrey writes: "The relationship between interactive, multi- and hyper-media and the breakdown of 'master narratives' . . . is not coincidental. Rather, the links between the development of digital technology and that of postmodern culture are becoming clearer." Elaborate on what Druckrey means in this statement, and make reference to at least one more reading from the semester.

⇥ Druckrey writes: "The merging discourses of creativity, technology, scientific visualization, experience, and art have reached critical mass. Theories of interactivity must be joined with theories of discourse. Without this, the affiliations between representation, intention, and technology will remain mired in outmoded presumptions about the 'two cultures.' *Images can no longer be dissociated from the tools used to produce them.*" (p. 29).

What does Druckrey mean by this, and how does this statement relate to either of Benjamin's essays that we read ("The Work of Art in the Age of Mechanical Reproduction" or "The Author as Producer")?

Syllabus

1 | WEEK 1 Course introduction.

2 | WEEK 2 No class; Martin Luther King, Jr. Day.

3 | WEEK 3 Reading: "The Work of Art in the Age of Mechanical Reproduction" by Walter Benjamin. Screen: Charlie Chaplin's *Modern Times*. Lecture: Marxist theory and its impact on artists during the industrial revolution.

4 | WEEK 4 Reading: "Communication through Photography" by Frank Webster (introduction to semiotics, connotation and denotation, sign, signifier, signified. Lecture: Introduction to

Semiotics. Walter Benjamin stated that montage rips the signifier from its signified; in order to pursue the study of montage these terms are addressed.

5 | WEEK 5 Reading: "The Rhetoric of the Image" by Roland Barthes. Discussion of reading.

6 | WEEK 6 Reading: Selections from *Photomontage* by Dawn Ades and *Cut with the Kitchen Knife: the Photomontage of Hannah Höch* by Maud Lavin. Lecture: Introduction to the history of photomontage; focus on Hannah Höch.

7 | WEEK 7 Reading: Christopher Philips's Introduction to *Montage and Modern Life*. Lecture/screening: Continuation of photomontage, view clips of Eisenstein, Vertov, and Riefenstahl.

8 | WEEK 8 Reading: Interview with Gran Fury from *Discussions: Conversations in Postmodern Art and Culture*. Lecture: Special topic: The art of AIDS activism—Gran Fury, Tom Kalin, David Wojnarowicz. Comparison is made between the political agenda and aesthetic strategies of these artists and the Berlin photomontage artists, particularly John Heartfield.

9 | WEEK 9 Spring Break.

10 | WEEK 10 Reading: "The Author as Producer" by Walter Benjamin. Lecture: Benjamin's ideas about the role of everyday life in art practice.

11 | WEEK 11 Individual meetings, proposals for final project due.

12 | WEEK 12 Reading: "Postmodernism and Consumer Society" by Frederic Jameson. Lecture: slide lecture on postmodernism.

13 | WEEK 13 Reading: "A Cyborg Manifesto" by Donna Haraway. Discussion of reading.

14 | WEEK 14 Reading: Timothy Druckrey, "Revisioning Technology" from *Iterations*. Discussion and essay test.

15 | WEEK 15 Final critique.

Course Reader Contents

1. "The Work of Art in the Age of Mechanical Reproduction" Walter Benjamin, from *Illuminations*, Hannah Arendt, ed. (New York: Schocken Books, 1969): 217–251.
2. "Communication through Photography" Frank Webster, *The New Photography* (London: John Calder, 1985): 17–37.
3. "The Photographic Message" Roland Barthes, *Image/Music/Text* (New York: Hill and Wang, 1977): 3–19.

4. "Introduction" and "The Supremacy of the Image" Dawn Ades, *Photomontage* (London: Thames & Hudson, 1976): 1–36.

5. "Introduction: Representing the New Woman" Maud Lavin, from *Cut with the Kitchen Knife: The Photomontages of Hannah Höch* (New Haven: Yale University Press, 1993): 1–12.

6. "Introduction" Christopher Phillips *Montage and Modern Life: 1919-1942* (Cambridge: MIT Press, 1992): 82–127.

7. "Interview with Gran Fury" from *Discourses: Conversations in Postmodern Art & Culture*, Russell Ferguson, et al., eds. (Cambridge: MIT Press, 1978): 196–208.

8. "The Author as Producer" Walter Benjamin, from *Reflections: Essays, Aphorisms, Autobiographical Writings* (New York: Schocken Books, 1978): 220–238.

9. "Postmodernism and Consumer Society" Frederic Jameson, from *The Anti-Aesthetic: Essays on Postmodern Culture*, Hal Foster, ed. (Seattle: Bay Press, 1983): 111–125.

10. "A Cyborg Manifesto: Science, Technology, and Socialist-Feminism in the Late Twentieth Century" Donna J. Haraway, *Simians, Cyborgs, and Women: The Reinvention of Nature* (New York: Routledge, 1991): 149–181.

11. "Revisioning Technology" Timothy Druckrey, *Iterations: The New Image* (New York: International Center for Photography, 1993): 17–38.

Visual Communications Fundamentals

STEVEN HOSKINS, *slhoskin@saturn.vcu.edu*

Virginia Commonwealth University, Department of Communication Arts + Design

. . . we must remember to always look for the storyteller, for the person or society behind the narrative; for that is where the power lies. The power to change political and social opinions and values is inherently a narrative power. —Hammett Nurosi

Overview

What makes a string of events a narrative? What is not a narrative? What can we say about narrative in literature, television, or film that would be useful to narrative in graphic design, or human-factors design, or architectural and urban planning? Does interactive media design pose a different case for narrative structure?

For three credits devoted to visual communication fundamentals, you will be asked to explore the creation and experience of visual communication from the explicit perspective of narrative. We will cover some fundamental concepts of narrative structure, technique, and form, though not in an explicitly structural, or technical, or formal way. Rather, as needed (as your pace and the projects may require).

My intent is to have you delve into traditional media narratives (that is, where the form of the media is basically linear, even though the narrative may not be), and nonlinear, interactive media.

Course Structure

1 | **MEETINGS** Group meetings can only occur on Tuesday or Thursday, 1:00–3:00 P.M. Typically, our group meetings will be scheduled for the Floyd conference room.

Individual meetings may be scheduled during those times when group meetings are not scheduled, and will occur as needed in the graduate studios, the Floyd conference room, the grad computer lab, or my office. I will do my best to announce changes in our group meetings beforehand, in person or by e-mail. If you don't know what's going on, please contact me.

2 | PROJECTS You can anticipate two to three projects dealing with visual narrative; some or all may break down into project assignments.

At the outset of this class, I am uncertain of the group's collective or individual ability to access the specific resources and tools needed, so I anticipate amending or extending some projects. This might include devoting certain group meetings to technology usage, or perhaps scheduling non-class time specifically for this task.

3 | GRADING AND ATTENDANCE Mid-semester and final only. Please familiarize yourself with the information in the CARD handbook on grading and attendance. I (must) support and follow this policy.

The Four Hundred Blows, a Review of the Narrative Language of Truffaut's Movie

CARD 611 Spring 2000. Steven Hoskins, slhoskin@saturn.vcu.edu

The establishing shot from opening scene defines the visual language of the film (including objective treatment, long takes, and use of tracking); the main character (Antoine); and the sub-plot of authority and conflict. The entire scene was composed with only four shots.

Truffaut's scenes consistently use tracking with subject in center, as the camera moves with the subject, often across background.

The persistent framing of Antoine (confining our view of him within and through objects) is a major symbolic device of film, as is the fragmented (mirror) composition in his parents' bedroom.

As in the ride sequence, rather than use a quick montage to merely suggest most experiences, Truffaut shoots the whole thing, partly from Antoine's swirling POV, to allow us to feel what his young hero does—this combination of glorious joy and frustrated entrapment that is also his life. True to his Hitchcock influence, Truffaut appears as one of the riders.

Extended, long shot, real-time micro-narratives proliferate throughout the film, as in the scene with the physical education instructor.

Several micro-narratives violate the visual language of the film, contrasting it to bring emphasis, as in the "audience" of children's expressions. This scene is also where the two main characters plot their crime.

Weaving through pillars, the slow, cautious, wide-angle-camera tracking parallels Antoine's slow, cautious movement. This is contrasted with the subsequent invasive close-up sequence that amplifies the frenzy in his act of stealing and flight.

In another violation of the film's visual language (in an improvised scene in the juvenile detention center), Antoine speaks directly to an unseen psychiatrist (and to us, of course), about his sad life.

The final scene is set up with dark figures, including Antoine, racing from one side of the screen to the other, playing football in the juvenile detention center.

In the final shot of the film, Truffaut catches him in a freeze-frame (in one of the first dramatic uses of that now overused, utterly mediocre technique), as he turns, trapped, back to the audience.

Project 1: Film Title Sequence

1 | OVERVIEW This project is about linear narrative. It will focus on the temporal and sequential aspects of typography, image, and sound. It is important to understand that your explorations—aside from advancing your typographical skills and your understanding of graphic form in general—will primarily focus on the idea of sequencing information: how to express a short story or concept within the context of time. In other words, we will spend most of our time discussing aspects of rhythm, pacing, progression, sequence, etc. We will try to influence and shape meaning in both a cognitive (reading, structuring) and interpretive manner (tone and voice).

As a vehicle for such explorations, we will design a sequence of titles for the movie *Les Quatre Cents Coups* (*The 400 Blows*). This will allow us to apply images (still and moving), typographic means, and sound, all within the context of time.

You need to be familiar enough with the movie to be able to discuss the basic story or plot of the film, its underlying concepts, as well as predominant visual details. A review of the film a second time, with emphasis on angles and movement, type of editing, and type of interaction with the audience may be enough to proceed, but you are encouraged to see the movie, in its entirety, at least one more time. This is really important for several reasons:

First, understanding the given material inside out (as is the case with any design project) is essential in your search for meaningful visual representations for your film-title design. Such knowledge of the film will play an important role in your ability to take part in discussions—you should be prepared to speak extensively of your design ideas in relation to the film—and second, third, or fourth viewings will allow you to discover subtle visual details that you might be able to carry over into your design.

Also, listen to nuances of tone of voice, look for ways the filmmaker uses sound, and silence (an important aspect of an audio-visual presentation such as this). Pay special attention to less obvious visual metaphors and abstractions. Anything you find during such screenings now, may become useful elements to adapt to your film titles later.

2 | ASSIGNMENTS There are only three parts to this project: (1) presentation of a storyboard, (2) translating and prototyping the storyboard into real time, and (3) the final film title.

3 | THINKING ABOUT FILM TITLES (Achim Wieland, designer and design educator) A film title is a special case in narrative because it resides in direct relationship to the extended narrative it introduces. It acts somewhat like the cover of a book. When designing titles for a film, we have to consider that the film already exists. We are in search of a proper representation for its "cover."

Though we have more control over aspects of time when designing a title for a film versus the cover of a book, their functions are very similar:

Film-titles act as a moment for your audience to change modes from the everyday (life outside the movie theater) into the actual film. Aside from the dimming of lights right before the beginning of the movie, film titles offer a moment of transition from the outside world to the inside; a very intimate and fragile moment created by the filmmaker. It is our job as designers to retain—possibly elaborate on—the intimacy or otherwise special characteristic of such a film. It takes more than seating people and turning on the projector to prepare the audience for the experience to come.

Film titles should create curiosity for what is about to come. Your aim is to give only a "hint" of that which is about to come. Such hints can be an elaboration on one single moment in the film as, well as an abstract visual notion of the entire story or plot; of course, it can also be a combination of both. When searching for visuals or treatments of type, keep in mind that you are not designing a "trailer" for advertising purposes. Do not give the story, plot, or outcome of the film away.

3 | CONSTRAINTS There are very few limitations with this project. I prefer that you customize your exploration and presentations to what suits your clarification of concept best.

➻ You must have a certain amount of typography in the title, and most of it must have a general sequence to its presentation. It is in your hands to decide if the titles are English, French, or a combination.
➻ The movie is black and white: You may do your titles in black and white or color.
➻ The movie is in French Dyaliscope aspect ratio (2.15 × 1). You may use this, digital TV (16 × 9), or regular TV (4 × 3). Using these screen dimensions for storyboards are optional.

Assignment 1: The Storyboard

Prepare a storyboard that illustrates your ideas for the film titles. While storyboarding varies from discipline to discipline, I would rather you present a storyboard that works well in communicating your concept, rather than dwelling on what "a storyboard is supposed to be."

When presenting your storyboard, on paper, be sure to include all necessary elements: typefaces, images, as well as possible sounds. Your presentation should be as visual, elaborate, and clear as possible. In support of your presentation, you may bring sketches, sound recordings, CDs, parts of the film; anything that helps to explain your ideas. Any audio/video material should be cued to the part you wish to present.

Linear and Nonlinear Narrative

1 | NARRATIVE STRUCTURE, MEDIA STRUCTURE, EXPERIENCE The concept of narrative as a linear construction—that unfolding sequences of a story would parallel the time-based principle of beginning, middle, and end—has dominated most forms of communication for thousands of years. The narrative structure of *Les Quatre Cents Coups* uses linear narrative as a *convention*. We do not need to understand the unfolding of events as framing the story in any particular way other than that which we readily understand: time moves from beginning to end, and so does the story (and so do the film media used). It is enough to make sense of the changes in the perception of linear time: parts of the story move in real time, other parts move in compressed time. In *Les Quatre Cents Coups*, the media of the story (film and sound) merge with the time-based story and become a transparent aspect of the experience.

Other kinds of narratives (including film, even though it is still limited by the linear nature of its media) are not linear narrative structures. In instances of nonlinear narratives time is no longer transparent. It is fundamentally related to the telling of the story. The convention of linear time is undermined to reveal an entirely different interpretation of a story when it is not in chronological sequence, or when chronology has been manipulated, or simply when chronological simultaneity is crucial. Sequences of micro-narratives may unfold from the chronological end to beginning (reverse chronology). It may fold into itself so that the chronological end is in the middle (folding chronology). They may present the same chronological story multiple times from different perspectives (perspective change, or parallax); or may present disconnected or loosely related simultaneous micro-narratives, which ultimately intertwine or, at least, become related or analogous to one another.

However, when the medium of the storytelling is still fixed, whether text or film, audio or visual, the audience is more or less held captive to a linear sequence of events. Thus, the experience of these nonlinear narratives is much like that of linear narrative; the major difference is that the progression of time is not transparent in a nonlinear narrative—it must be recognized and understood.

What about a medium that is not fixed, whereby the audience is not held captive to an experience, where the unfolding of events is under audience control?

It has been asserted by many people, from Andy Cameron: "narrative form appears fundamentally non-interactive" (Cameron, *Dissimulation: illusions of interactivity*, 1995) to George Lucas: "...by definition they are different—storytelling and games are two different mediums" (Kelly and Parisi, "Beyond Star Wars," *Wired* 3.02 UK, 1997, p. 72), that interactivity and narrative are incompatible.

However, the effects of interactivity on narrative are still not largely understood. Part of the problem may be that imposing the idea of narrative (linear or not) on what constitutes most of the task-oriented interactive experiences available today—such as graduating to the next level of *Doom*; getting money from an ATM; searching Yahoo.com; or finding the right flight gate of an airport—focuses more on the usability of a tool or wayfinding system than on the unfolding experience of events.

The premise of the next (and final) project is not to assume that it must be possible to construct interactive nonlinear narratives. Instead, we will question to what degree it might be possible.

2 | A COMPARISON The film titles cited below (some of which are adaptations of plays and novels) are not intended to be definitive examples of each type of nonlinear narrative. Some use more than one approach.

- ➡ Linear (chronological) narrative and linear (time-based) media:
  - Time-based media: 1 → 2 → 3 → 4 → 5 → 6 →
  - Chronological narrative (*Les Quatre Cents Coups*): A → B → C → D → E → F →
- ➡ Nonlinear narrative and linear (time-based) media:
  - Time-based media: 1 → 2 → 3 → 4 → 5 → 6 →
  - Reverse chronology (*Betrayal*): F → E → D → C → B → A →

- Folding chronology and chronological jumping (*Pulp Fiction, Slaughterhouse Five*):

  A → D → B → E → C → F →
- Perspective change, parallax (*Norman Conquests, Run Lola Run, Ground Hog Day*):

  $A^1 → B^1 → C^1 → A^2 → B^2 → C^2 > →$
- Simultaneity/interleaving (*Lock, Stock and Two Smoking Barrels, Night on Earth*):

  A → X → B → Y → Z/C → D →

➠ Linear narrative and directional, or multidirectional, linear media ("slide show model"):
- Time-based media: ← 1 ↔ 2 ↔ 3 ↔ 4 →
- Forward, backward: ← A, B or D ↔ C, or A ↔ D or B ↔ C or A →

➠ Nonlinear narrative and nonlinear media
- Media:

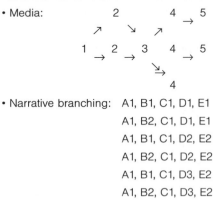

- Narrative branching: A1, B1, C1, D1, E1

  A1, B2, C1, D1, E1

  A1, B1, C1, D2, E2

  A1, B2, C1, D2, E2

  A1, B1, C1, D3, E2

  A1, B2, C1, D3, E2

Project 2: Nonlinear Narrative

1 | THE PROJECT Develop an interactive, nonlinear narrative that is open to interpretation, can be experienced in multiple ways, or otherwise does not require a strict linear sequence for its understanding. Use type and/or image and sound. Propose this as a storyboard first, and then produce this as a prototyped interactive project.

2 | THE CONTENT The content of your project is up to you. Some suggestions for this, or at least how to begin thinking about content, follow:

Content may either be based on subject matter that is expressed linearly (such as a traditional story), or it may be based on any subject matter that, by its structure, must be nonlinear.

➠ *Linear Subjects.* These (such as those that are chronological) can be re-interpreted using any of the discussed nonlinear narratives (reverse chronology, change in perspective, etc.) or, if these don't satisfy you, you may hypothesize a nonlinear structure of your own. However, unlike these examples, which are contextualized by linear media, you must transpose nonlinear narrative onto nonlinear media.

A reasonable strategy for developing linear subjects into nonlinear narratives is to use more than one subject, juxtaposing one against the other. The subjects can be similar, analogous, antithetical, or completely unrelated.

➼ *Nonlinear Subjects.* These are harder to come by, but they do afford a more natural "mapping" to interactive projects, where narrative branching can be paralleled exactly or nearly exactly in an interactive project. Thus you might consider real experiences or events that encompass choices and consequences for actions taken.

As you begin to think about nonlinear subject matter, the attached exercise may be helpful. It uses associative meaning (an excellent example of nonlinear structure). Because this is the same process as "mind-mapping," it should at least help you to jump-start your content development, if not even evolve into your final project.

3 | ASSIGNMENTS There will be three assignments in this project: (1) presentation of a storyboard, (2) translating and prototyping the storyboard into an interactive project, and (3) the final project.

You are asked to use Macromedia Director as the authoring tool for this project. Can you do this any other way? If you have a persuasive, principled argument for choosing any other media, I will consider it.

Project 2: An Exercise Using a Nonlinear Subject

Beginning with a single-word concept, *formlessness*, a dictionary is consulted for usage, synonyms, and forms of the word.

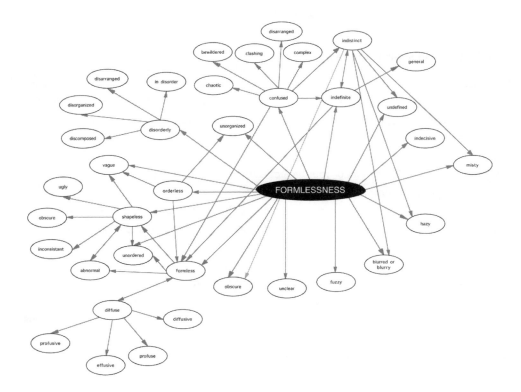

formless:*
abnormal*
diffuse,
diffusive
formless*
profuse
profusive
effusive
gushing
gushy
copious
exuberant
extravagant
prodigal
fecund
teeming
prolific
productive
abundant
superabundant
overflowing
redundant
pleonastic
repetitive
reiterative
tautologous
shapeless*
unordered*

shapeless:
abnormal, *
unnatural:
affected
eccentric
heartless
pretentious
ungenuine
anomalous
anomalistic
irregular
eccentric
erratic
deviative
divergent
different
aberrant
stray
straying
wandering
heteroclite

heteromorphic
formless*
shapeless*
amorphous
subnormal
inconstant:
changeable
fickle
irregular
nonobservant
nonuniform
transient
unfaithful
obscure *
ugly
unordered *
vague*

featureless
characterless
nondescript
inchoate
lumpen
blobby or baggy
inform
amorphous
amorphic
chaotic
orderless:
formless*
unorganized*
vague*
disorderly,
in disorder
disordered*
disorganized
disarranged
discomposed
dislocated
deranged
convulsed
upset
disturbed
perturbed
unsettled
discomfited
disconcerted
turbulent
turbid
roily

out of order
out of place
misplaced
shuffled
out of kilter or kelter
out of whack
out of gear
out of joint
out of tune
on the fritz
cockeyed
awry
amiss
askew
haywire
unordered,*
orderless
disorder
disordered*
unorganized*
unarranged
unmethodical
unsystematic
incoherent
formless
irregular
haphazard
erratic
aimless
unorganized:*
formless
inorganic
unordered
unprepared
confused:
bewildered
chaotic
clashing
complex
disarranged
distressed
flustered
formless *
indefinite *
indistinct *
shy
anarchic
kaleidoscopic
indeterminate
indefinite:*

formless*
general
indistinct*
inconspicuous
half-visible
semibisible
low-profile
unclear
unplain
indefinite*
undefined*
ill-defined
ill-marked
faint
pale
feeble
weak
dim
dark
shadowy
vague
obscure*
indistinguishable:
unrecognizable
half-seen
merely glimpsed
uncertain
confused
out of focus
blurred*
blurry*
bleared
bleary
fuzzy*
hazy*
misty*
filmy
foggy
uncertain
undefined*
indecisive
vague*
misty*
hazy*
fuzzy*
blurred* or blurry*
unclear
obscure*

An associative map of the concept is created with the aid of a thesaurus. While this map could also be done via brainstorming, a thesaurus provides an associative structure in which words are arranged and interconnected by similarity. This provides for redundant referencing, and this is visualized as an interrelated, nonlinear web with words as nodes. It is not hard to further visualize this as the foundation of an interactive architecture.

The map below represents about one-third of the list, and the list itself is incomplete. It is potentially as vast as the language it represents (all things are ultimately connected).

Project 2: Background Information

Hypertext narrative was the impulse for this project and this page is offered for those interested in learning more about it. Most search engines will give you a wealth of information on hypertext (but not much on hypermedia), including numerous hypertext projects that vary tremendously in interest and success. Hypertext seems to have become aligned as an art form within academic circles of English, literature, and creative writing. As a technology it is a fundamental concept of the WWW.

Hypertext: text that does not form a single sequence and that may be read in various orders; especially text and graphics . . . which are interconnected in such a way that a reader of the material (as displayed at a computer terminal, etc.) can discontinue reading one document at certain points in order to consult other related matter [Oxford English dictionary].

Theodore "Ted" Nelson, who first coined the terms hypertext and hypermedia, wrote in *Literary Machines* that "As popularly conceived, [hypertext] is a series of text chunks connected by links which offer the reader different pathways." Neither hypertext nor hypermedia requires the use of links.

Hypermedia is similar to hypertext but includes media other than text, e.g., a hypermedia document could include text and graphics, or sound and animation. Mark Bernstein has pointed out that, in practice, many hypertext documents have some graphical content (just as texts often include illustrations).

Note that the definition quoted above makes the same point. The distinction between hypertext and hypermedia is so blurry that some authors call them both "hypertext."

Several Web Links

➤ *Hypertext Breakdown, An Overview,* by Mindy McAdams
  www.well.com/user/mmcadams/basic.units.main.html
➤ *Hypertext narrative,* by Michael Joyce
  http://noel.pd.org/topos/perforations/perf3/hypertext_narrative.html
➤ *Bridging the Gulfs: From Hypertext to Cyberspace,* by Thierry Bardini
  www.ascusc.org/jcmc/vol3/issue2/bardini.html

Designing for Utopia

ERIK ADIGARD AND AARON BETSKY
California College of Arts and Crafts

OUR CLASS "DESIGNING for Utopia" (also known as "Future Media") was originally conceived with Aaron Betsky when our plan was to organize a collaboration between architecture and graphic-design students.

Historically, utopia seems to have been explored in all media, but mostly in architecture. My original hope was to see how this aspiration could find its place in graphic design, digital media, and especially in Web design.

My faith in this model was based on two notions:

- Utopian experiments historically happened in tandem with new discoveries and technological innovations.
- Computer interfaces and the Web in particular need the combined attention of graphic designers and architects.

As we are finding ourselves living in increasingly mediated environments, the participation of graphic designers becomes ever more possible, even necessary, in the creation of modern living spaces. Some current models to study are parks, networked computer games, online environments, whether in text or graphical forms, and online communities. These constructions allow multiple activities such as one-to-one or one-to-many communications, exchanges of goods or services, meetings, collective entertainment, etc. The forms can allow both privacy and public spaces, and they can quickly mutate in response to changing needs.

Utopia is "no where" in Greek, and we can speculate that it is the discovery Sir Thomas Moore wished we would be making in the aftermath of America's discovery. Similarly, one could believe it is the place one will discover thanks to the paths that are being laid by the "new economy." If utopia is nothing more than a fantasy, it may be an impossible design problem to resolve, but if it is indeed a possibility, then every new invention should be applied to our continued quest of discovering and inventing it—because it can only be *both* a discovery and an invention: the harmonization and the synergy between that which was already there but was not seen or understood and that which humans managed to invent.

Learning to design for new media depends on understanding discoveries and inventions. It also depends on understanding the evolution of design as it applies to changing problems, by means of changing tools and media.

Designing for Utopia is one way for students to speculate on the possibilities allowed by new tools and new environments. Corporations themselves are in search of the E-bay-like utopian model that will be weightless, addictive, and viral, so the class is also an introduction to a profession that increasingly is asked to intervene in the creation of concepts for products that are often very abstract, since speculative prototypes or "representations" are often used to "sell" these new products and services.

By asking students to identify areas of society that they believe are host to possible utopi-an core concepts, we can see the kinds of structures and values, as well as languages and interfaces that merit to be studied and integrated in our daily environments: especially the desktop and the browser. By studying historical as well as contemporary situations, students can better understand the dual role of the designer: that of observation, reflection, and that of representation, which is an exercise in organizing conceptual and aesthetic solutions in ways that are adoptable by specific audiences—or "users"—therefore making the notion of habitability believable.

My hope was to see how graphic designers, with the help of interface designers, could build a habitable virtual utopia and, in so doing, provide urbanists and architects with elements of answers to the brick-and-mortar utopias. Mostly, however, it was to show how these new environments, whether physical or virtual, require understanding and the collaboration of vari-ous disciplines. Therefore, one important aspect of the class was to invite specialists to discuss the place of new technologies and/or utopia in their professions.

These guest instructors acted as studio critics and advisors. They included:

- Aaron Betsky, who acted as art historian
- Asymptote: architects (also did some well-publicized print and Web design)
- Gary Wolf: "digital age" journalist and new-media producer
- Chris Salter: digital artist
- Mike Kuniavsky: user testing expert
- Dave Thau: creator of bianca.com, one of the first and most important online communities

Aaron Betsky introduced the class theme to the students and, in doing so, showed how utopia has appeared both as conceptual representations (especially in literature and in fine arts) and as livable spaces (architecture).

Introduction *by Aaron Betsky*

These days, the good place is what you find behind security fences, in air-conditioning, in places far away, in your mind. Perfection is something we achieve through engineering and focus groups. We gather communities in restaurants, in concerts, or by the clothes we wear. We sign utopia in the abstract symbols we tattoo on or bodies, in corporate logos, in the clothes we wear, in themed environments. Utopia is a memory of a perfect place we were once going to inhabit. Perhaps utopia exists in the electro-sphere, but how will be inhabit it? This studio will propose a new crop of utopias.

The idea of utopia has been central to design since Sir Thomas More originated it in the sixteenth century. Designers have always believed that they could create a perfect building, page, painting, or environment that would dissolve time, space, and social antagonisms into an abstract field. The twentieth century in particular has been rife with utopian impulses that gave birth to everything from standardized letterforms to the international style in architecture. These were all meant to further or bring about utopia. Now we are being promised an era in which technology will alter our bodies and perceptions to such a degree that we will transcend what makes us human, while information will be everywhere, always immediately available as the field in which these post-human subjects will live. Designers, especially those involved with the making of either those prosthetic devices or the fields of the electrosphere, are seen as the prophets and enablers of this utopia. But how can they make a utopia that will allow us to be human and live in the electrosphere?

These will be the central questions of this studio. Students will be asked to create a utopia. This "good place" that is "no place" must address the prosthetic nature of technology and the ubiquity of digital domains, but beyond that, the media each student uses is free. In the end, each student must produce a visual sign of utopia, complete with its rules, regulations, ideology, and mechanisms by which it might sustain itself. Students are urged to study historical utopias, and to research the utopian implications of new technologies. In the end, students will be asked to answer the question through their work of whether new media will bring us any closer to utopia and, if so, how.

Syllabus

The five students were given a chart of the class that was also a model for its home page. It showed the various phases of the class and the relative position of the five different projects. The chart was accompanied by the following text, which was written with team teacher Steve Jaycox, who is an architect and Web designer:

Phase 1: Historical Analysis

From a historical perspective, utopian models (although addressing different social/political/economic contexts) share a few common themes that seem to be timeless (or universal), and are augmented by more polemical themes, which are often reactionary to the context of their invention. To better understand the historical precedents of utopian models, you are asked to choose a utopia from those presented, or identify one independently for study. The study should yield a demonstration of your understanding of the differentiation and relationships between the Core Concepts of the Utopia, the Context (political/social/economic circumstances), and the Agents (vehicles by which the core concepts are "delivered").

1 | INTERRELATIONSHIP Begin by listing the above in a matrix, then create a mapping of the interrelationships found among the three categories:

2 | LOGO Continuing with the same historical model of utopia, and a greater awareness of the Core Concepts that form its basis, create a graphic representation of the essence of the utopia in the form of a Logo. Be careful to keep separate the operations of an icon and a logo, as an icon represents something external to its expression via a likeness or a symbol onto which a meaning is culturally ascribed. The logo created should be indexical of the core concepts you have identified in the utopia.

Mapping: Review the mapping you had created earlier and create a dynamic/Web publishable presentation of the interrelationships between Concepts/Context/Agents in a manner that would be useful for comparison to other utopian models being studied in the group.

3 | PRESENTATION Isolate the core concepts and create a Web-publishable presentation for each individually. Each should be represented as neutrally as possible, since the results will form a collection of utopia "building blocks."

4 | THE DYSTOPIAN IDEA The only way to take down the Master's house is with the Master's tools. Totalizing systems tend toward reversal of intent when one or more of their structural features are compromised. Utopian models are inherently totalizing systems because they seek to revise comprehensively a broad range of social relations to achieve their goal via a quite willful (and sometimes hopelessly diagrammatic) re-framing of the same. The morality of such a system can sometimes be overturned by attacking a core precept, such as in one of the following examples: LeDoux's Salt Works at Chaux, which becomes Bentham's Panopticon when the benevolent gaze (in a framework intended to clarify) becomes a disciplinary one. The function of a utopian model can be neutralized if the model can be easily commodified and shed its polemical nature.

Radical Element: Identify the dystopia within your chosen model; what is the unstable element? Illustrate in a Web-publishable document the manner by which the utopian model was compromised, and fully describe the radical agent.

Phase 2: Contemporary Translation

From a historical perspective, utopian models (although addressing different social/political/economic contexts) share a few common themes that seem to be timeless or universal, and are augmented by more polemical themes that are often reactionary to the context of their invention. To better understand the historical precedents of utopian models, you are asked to choose a utopia from those presented, or identify one independently for study. The study should yield a demonstration of your understanding of the differentiation and relationships between *contemporary utopian agents:*

➤➤ Remove yourself from everyday life. Audit potential Agents for utopian concepts. Focus on technology (communications/media/ubiquitous systems) and study the potentials for appropriation or revisionism in the furtherance of a utopian idea. Create a Web-publishable record of your findings for collective use.

Among the contemporary utopian agents you have identified, define which may be viable candidates for addressing the transposition of the core concepts from your chosen historical utopia into the present day. Elaborate on the possibilities in a discussion.

1 | **CONSTRUCTING SITE** Immerse yourself in everyday life. Define the present day context "site") in relationship to your chosen historical utopian model. Create a Web-publishable presentation of your "constructed site."

Phase 3: Building Utopia

To date, the project has focused more on representation. The student has acted as an interpreter. You are now asked to construct, to be an author. The next several weeks will be spent constructing a habitable (defined by the reconciliation of the core concepts and the mapping of social relations across the space you're working in) utopia that is based upon the re-contextualization of a set of core utopian concepts isolated earlier in the semester. The only requirement is that the student tries to work as closely with the core concepts associated with their earlier studied utopia within the limits of productivity, localizing the same in the context of contemporary social/political/economic conditions. The result should be a Web-publishable and habitable environment that is a fully-reconciled conceptual and aesthetic utopian experience. Several rounds of desk crits and interim presentations culminating in a final presentation of intent and means.

Games + Play in the Summer Desert

KAREN WHITE AND KATIE SALEN

AFTER THE LAST day of the spring semester, most students (and faculty) try to flee Arizona for a cooler temperature and the sight of water. Resisting this trend were a few brave students and visiting faculty who convened in the desert for the first Summer Design Workshop at the University of Arizona. The workshop was set up to accommodate visiting faculty for an exchange of ideas in information on design, technology, and the production of artifacts.

Over the course of three hot weeks students worked with Melissa Niederhelman, designer and educator, of Arizona State University, Bruce Licher, designer and printmaker, Sedona, Arizona, and Katie Salen, designer and educator, of the University of Texas. Each person came in for two days of workshop time. I, the instructor of record, prepared the students for the visits, and worked with them on projects that were sent ahead of time, or reviewed articles, and taught the necessary software skills to produce the work. In hindsight, it was one of my most rewarding teaching experiences.

The workshop offered a wonderful opportunity for students to interface with designers, artists, and educators outside of the normal curriculum offered by our design program. The focus of each workshop was determined by the visiting lecturer; each worked with ideas that he or she was most passionate about sharing with the students. The content thread that wove together the diverse offerings of each participating visitor was the theme "technology and design." Each lecturer was asked to focus the workshop around a specific part of his or her personal research, and tie it in to the use of technology. Each week the specific media changed, but the focus was always on design process and working in teams. Included in each component of the workshop was an opportunity to design.

Broadly speaking, the summer workshop gave students the opportunity to explore collaboration, movement, and interactivity by experimenting with new ideas and processes. Students produced three projects for the class. The first project examined the intersection of new and old technologies through the production of letterpress plates from digital technologies and printing the images on the Vandercook press. The project, given by Bruce Licher, also offered a historical overview of pop music and its influences. The second project, given by Melissa Niederhelman, was a survey and analysis of design trends in Web site design. Students created pre-

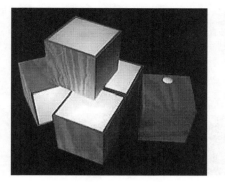

sentations from their observations and made thesis statements about the trends. The last project, given by Katie Salen, was on design, interactivity, and play. For this article, Katie and I will be discussing her component of the workshop, Design + Play.

Zoom In

Workshops have always afforded an interesting opportunity to explore a small idea intensely over the space of a few short days. Released from the often unwieldy demands of longer course projects, students tend to revel in the freedom such workshops allow, both in terms of ideas they are asked to consider, and in methods they are urged to implement. Time and again, I have been pleasantly surprised by the quality of results achieved in a span of less than thirty-six hours. Perhaps it is true that the limits of invention have a correspondingly inverse relationship to the time allowed.

Zoom Out

That being said, workshops must be considered within the larger context of the course structures out of which they grow. Rarely, if ever, do I develop a workshop without ties to material I have been developing in my other courses, and the Design + Play workshop I ran with Karen White's students at the University of Arizona in May 2000 was no exception. For several years I have been teaching a course at the University of Texas called Design and the Social Environment. This course uses the study of socially embedded design systems (like the lottery or board games) as a lens for understanding basic principles of interactive design. In the class, students are asked to consider the ways in which design creates situations of meaningful interactivity for users, from the territorial conflict of musical chairs, to the economically driven scratching of lottery tickets. Students explore issues related to the design of interactive systems through projects focusing on information design, procedural prototyping and appearance modeling, text/image juxtaposition, and translation of user experiences. In addition, the course introduces a study of the creative quality of the play principle in culture as a way to teach design process. But more on this later.

First, a bit of explanation on the structure of this article. For reasons noted above, the Design + Play workshop requires presentation within the context of a larger whole, namely, the course Design and the Social Environment. As such, excerpts from two course assignments have been included here as a means of enhancing an understanding of the work produced in Tucson. Inclusion of this additional material may serve to clarify an approach to the teaching of interactive design through the study of more general design systems.

Games + Play: Enter the Magic Circle

One distinguishing feature of games, and game play more generally, lies in the relationship between an unambiguous, fixed, and closed system of rules that stylize user behavior, and the open and free system of play (interactivity) that emerges once the game begins. Games are governed by rules that suspend ordinary laws, as well as ordinary expectations about how users might behave within a given situation. The pushing and shoving that erupts as players vie for limited seating during a game of musical chairs is seen as perfectly acceptable within the illusory social space of the game; similarly, players attempting to "bluff" their opponent during a game of poker transform a moral directive (thou shall not lie) into a strategic imperative. This ability of games to create a "magic circle," within which player interaction is instantaneously codified and made meaningful, forms the basis for the study of essential interactivity developed by the students in Tucson.

We began the workshop with a general question: In what ways can the phenomena of the magic circle be explored within the context of interactive design? Because meaningful interactivity (like meaningful play) emerges from the design of an experience, rather than from the design of an "interface," we needed to focus on the ways in which a player's experience is shaped by the design of the game, from its "look and feel," to the interactivity proscribed by the relationship between fixed rules and emergent play (see Gamezeit assignment). In order to do this, we first needed to become players ourselves. And so we played.

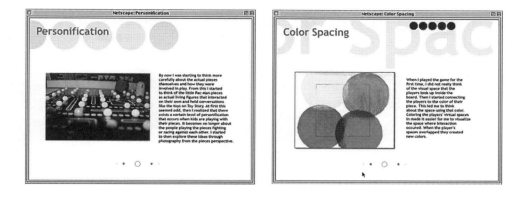

Play

Groups of two to five students were assigned games (selected by me prior to the workshop), ranging from the card game Uno to the digital first-person shooter Quake, and asked to play. Initially, the students were instructed to act as players only, immersing themselves in the pleasure of game play, forgetting for a moment the more academic questions at hand. Once the threshold of the magic circle had been crossed, this was, of course, not a problem. The students engaged in vigorous debate over the rules, laughed, yelled, virtually killed and maimed each other, and were seamlessly transported into highly divergent and interactive spaces. After thirty minutes or so, play was stopped and the students were asked to describe their experience, as a way to reinforce concepts introduced initially. A second, more specific, question emerged from this discussion: What is the essential interactivity of a game and how can it be visualized? Students were then asked to return to game play, this time with the singular goal of identifying their game's mode of essential interactivity. As play resumed, students began to define forms of interaction based on systems of sequential matching (Uno), hunting and gathering (Quake), self-defense (Sissyfight 2000), and linguistic collaboration (My Name is Alice).

Phase II: Rapid Prototyping

While the students had been able to draw some general conclusions about the systems of interactivity governing their games, there was still a need to visualize these systems in order to make their observations actionable within a design context (see lottery assignment). Phase II of the workshop involved a series of quick, one minute, rapid prototyping studies that challenged the students to develop visualizations of their game's essential interactivity. The studies moved from familiar forms of representation (word lists and visual diagrams) to the use of simple materials and actions (a single sheet of paper; a rubber band connected to any other object in the room). Inevitably, while the word lists and visual diagrams were the easiest to complete, rarely did they carry the precision of the latter prototypes, which involved the visualization of concepts without the aid of words or images. For example, the crumpled piece of paper produced as a

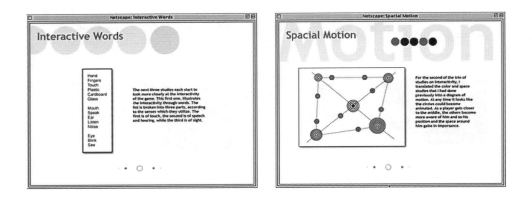

means to visualize the violent interaction of Quake was far more compelling than a diagram of directional arrows. Students were able to immediately recognize that while not all of their studies could single-handedly express the concept they hoped to describe, there was value in the sequence as a whole. As a group, the studies provided a specialized design vocabulary (both formal and conceptual) that would assist them in the next phase of the assignment: the design of a visual interface or animation that communicated the essential interactivity of their game.

Phase III: Interface Design

In addition to an investigation of games and play as objects of study for interactive designers, a parallel aim of the workshop was to introduce the students to forms of technology (Macromind Director, Flash, HTML) that could be used to develop interactive experiences. It is important to note that students were given information about the software on a need-to-know basis—as they created storyboards and schematics for their concepts, students were directed toward certain software features that would support their ideas. Karen gave a short overview of behaviors in Director and Flash—just enough of an introduction to familiarize the students with what was possible—and off they went. The students were encouraged to "play" with the software in the same way they played games: by recognizing the relationship between the rules of the system (i.e., constraints of the software) and the emergent play (or design process) these constraints encouraged. After some initial frustration, the students quickly began to implement their interface concepts, and three short hours later they had completed the assignment. Amazing!

Play as Process

As I mentioned earlier, this workshop assignment, as well as much of the other work included here, uses the study of play as a means to support iteration and creativity within the design process. Four defining qualities of play—that it is free, separate, uncertain, and governed by rules—find effective application within the design process. While students often struggle to under-

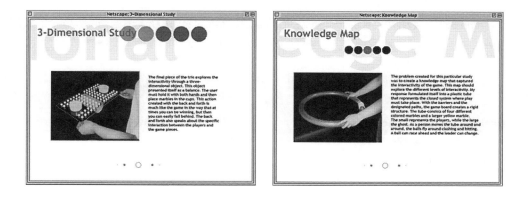

stand the term "process," they almost always understand what is meant by "play." In addition, because students are often learning new software at the same time they are developing their concepts, there is an opportunity to strengthen both experiences through designed play, which encourages students to go back and forth between open exploration and focused research.

Afterword

Once the workshop was complete I was curious to hear Karen's observations. "Overall," she said, "Students found that working in groups during this workshop was really important in terms of brainstorming and production. The groups worked through learning the software and breaking down tasks in order to complete the assignment on time. All work was done in class, and with the intense workshop atmosphere, students used their time for the project. The short nature of the workshop was a bonus in terms of intensity and focus, but more time could have been used to fully understand the software and how it could be used to further the 'magic circle.' It was interesting to see that at first students really were drawn to the more sophisticated games, such as Quake, and were disappointed that their group had been assigned a card game, i.e., Uno. However, once the groups began their work, they lost interest in the other games and stopped believing that the grass was greener on the other side. They recognized the value of their own game to the task at hand."

Suggested Reading

If/Then. Jan Abrams, ed., The Netherlands Design Institute, 1999.

"Lotteryville, USA," Kim Phillips, from *Commodify Your Dissent*, Thomas Frank and Matt Weiland, eds. "The Lottery," Shirley Jackson, [chapter 8 excerpt].

"Rules, Play, and Culture: Towards an Aesthetic of Games," Frank Lantz and Eric Zimmerman, *Merge*, 1999.

"Derivative Sport in Tornado Alley," David Foster Wallace. *A Supposedly Fun Thing I'll Never Do Again*. Little, Brown and Co., 1997.

The Ambiguity of Play. Brian Sutton-Smith. (Cambridge, MA: Harvard University Press, 1997).

Man, Play, Games. Roger Caillois, translated from the French by Meyer Barash. (New York: Free Press of Glencoe, 1961).

The Study of Games. Elliott M. Avedon (and) Brian Sutton-Smith. (New York: J. Wiley 1971).

Design Methods Used in Workshop

Descriptions of these methods are taken from the research Web at *www.id.iit.edu/ideas/methods.html.*

- conceptual prototyping: realization of a design concept in some prototypical form; usually used primarily to demonstrate concept.
- iterative prototyping: producing numerous trial or prototype artifacts for the purposes of testing and evaluation with the goal of successive rounds of refinement.
- rapid prototyping: use of prototype production techniques and materials that allow for the rapid and responsive adjustment of certain attributes of prototypes in response to testing feedback.
- interaction analysis: detailed decomposition and representation of all interactions between people and products, or between people and people, that are involved in the use of a product, service, or system.
- play: free-form invention, experimentation, imagination, and creation.
- sketching: active, visual exploration of concepts, usually done on an individual level.
- storyboarding: visually planning or describing a time-based narrative with a series of key frames.
- semantic analysis: analysis of meaning [both denoted and connoted] of an artifact.
- syntactic analysis: analysis of formal properties of an artifact.
- pragmatic analysis: analysis of the contextual factors influencing the use and understanding of an artifact.

Assignment Excerpt: The Lottery

1 | OBJECTIVES

❶ to explore the issues surrounding the design of an interactive interface: procedural prototyping and appearance modeling, text/image juxtaposition, color, time, and sequence, user interaction

❷ to understand the lottery as a narrative system within multiple contexts (visual, economic, social, etc.)

❸ to place the lottery within the framework of game and play

❹ to investigate the principles of comparative analysis in the design of charts and graphs

2 | PART 1: INTERACTIVE SCHEMATIC

Graphical elegance is often found in simplicity of design and complexity of data. —Edward Tufte

As an introduction to issues of information design, interface design, and comparative analysis, translate an existing lottery ticket into an interactive diagram. The objective of this diagram is to reveal the multiple systems that co-exist within the design of a single ticket. These include systems of interactivity, representation, play, history, economics, etc.

3 | PART 2: INTERACTIVE TICKET Part 2 investigates the design of an interactive lottery "ticket" using principles of information and interface design defined in part 1 of this project. The content of this "ticket" is the lottery itself; specifically, an aspect of the system that you have found personally compelling. Macromind Director will be used as a platform for presentation.

4 | CONSTRAINTS

➤ the ticket must utilize some aspect of interactivity

➤ the ticket can include any or all forms of appropriate media: sound, video, type, image, color

➤ the ticket must include a comparative analysis component such as a chart or diagram

4 | EVALUATION

➤ a significant evaluative component will be based on user testing

➤ a peer review component will be included in the final assessment

➤ criteria for design evaluation will be determined as a class

Course Excerpt: Gamezeit, Fall 1999: Play, Analysis, Iteration

1 | OBJECTIVES

❶ Assessment and analysis methods: What are the ways in which a designer can study an artifact?

❷ Exploration, iteration, and experimentation: How can "play" be used as a method of critical making?

2 | PART I Develop a series of visual studies based on a game of your choosing. These visual studies should represent a critical review of a design artifact, including studies of form, meaning, and context.

❶ Choose a game that is (a) non-digital and (b) has a set of physical components (chess: yes; marco polo: no)

❷ Using "play" as a primary working method, develop a set of studies along three vectors of analysis: (a) rules (visual language: what formal structures define the game?), (b) play (interactivity: what kinds of interactivity arise from game play?), and (c) culture (value: who, what, why?)

❸ Studies (a) may be 2-D, 3-D, 4-D, (b) should explore a range of materials, and (c) should provide an understanding of your game as a self-contained design system.

3 | PART II: KNOWLEDGE MAPS Objectives include: (1) Translation of one form of knowledge (play) to another (mapping), (2) Exploration of forms of visual mapping, and (3) Expression of a dynamic design system through a visualization of interactivity.

➤ part a: Design a "knowledge map" that communicates the forms, methods, and value of the interactivity of your game.

➤ part b: Extend and apply this understanding the to the design of an object of your choice.

Game Design

FRANK LANTZ AND ERIC ZIMMERMAN

Interactive Telecommunications Program, New York University

Overview

Games represent some of the most ancient forms of designed interactivity. And computer and video games are certainly among the most complex and sophisticated artifacts of digital culture today. Yet, game design as a design discipline remains largely unexplored. How do games work? What are the unique qualities of games? What makes game interaction meaningful? How does the cultural status of games affect the design of games? And what can games teach us about interactive design?

This course will introduce students to these questions in a workshop format, focusing on the creation of non-digital games. Readings and discussions in the class will present formal, social, and cultural frameworks for understanding game play and game design. Using these discussions as a starting point, students will plan and create games, both individually and collaboratively. Rather than a course on software, the focus of the course is critical thinking. The goal of the class is for students to develop a sophisticated understanding of how games function. Key skills that will be taught include critical analysis of game design, the ability to rapidly prototype an idea, dynamic systems thinking, and an understanding of games as pop culture. And we'll be playing a lot of games.

Conceptual Model

The course utilizes a conceptual model that considers games as three different kinds of dynamic systems: Games as Rules, Games as Play, and Games as Culture. These are also the three units of the course. This Rules/Play/Culture model will be discussed throughout the semester, but to summarize:

- Games as Rules: games as formal systems of mathematical rules
- Games as Play: games as the social and psychological experience of play
- Games as Culture: games as cultural phenomena

Design Methodology

The focus of this course is the creation of a number of playable games. And the methodology for completing these design assignments is an iterative, prototype-and-testing process. This means that you will be creating playable prototype versions of the games as soon as possible after the project is assigned, and you will make most of your design decisions based on actual play testing. It is very challenging to bring your initial ideas "out of the clouds" and create an actual, playable prototype. For this reason, we have structured each of the design assignments so that one week after the assignment is given, a one-page summary of the project is due; the following week, an initial prototype is due; and one to two weeks after that, the final version is due.

For the game design assignments, we will not be grading you on the finished quality of the cards, game pieces, and other materials you create. Instead, the focus of our grading will be on the game design: the underlying game logic, the designed interactivity that the players enact in the game, and the overall play experience. You should not, for example, spend the few days before a project is due designing beautiful materials. Instead, you should use this time to continue play testing: testing and refining the game design itself.

One of the primary contexts for the work we do in this class is digital game design. However, you will not be creating digital games as part of this course. The games you create in this class will be implemented using non-digital materials. There are several reasons for this. First of all, we want you to create many games over the course of the semester, applying the lessons learned along the way to each new design. Doing even the simplest digital game projects would be too time-intensive to allow for multiple projects. In addition, digital development would involve a great deal of coding, de-bugging, and asset creation—tasks that are not central to the game design itself, which is the main focus of this class. Finally, whether it's digital or not, a game is an interactive system. Creating non-digital games is a valuable exercise in thinking about the fundamental principles of interactivity outside the immediate context of computer technology.

Grading

The class will involve three short paper/presentations, two in-class game creation projects, two longer-term game-making assignments, one digital game proposal, and one final project. Every assignment that students complete in the course will be graded and given a written evaluation. Each assignment is worth a certain amount of points:

Attendance/Participation (including in-class projects)	20
3 Short Papers/Presentations (5 each)	15
1 Digital Game Design	10
2 Longer-Term Game Projects (15 each)	30
Final Project: prototype	5
final version	20
	100

Final letter grades are given on the following scale:

98–100	A+
93–97	A
90–91	A–
88–89	B+
82–87	B
80–81	B–
etc.	

UNIT ONE: Games as Rules

1 | WEEK 1 Discussion Topics: Introductory remarks. Overview of the goals and methods of the course. Formal/structural analysis of games.

➼ Paper 1 assigned: Formal Game Critique

➼ Paper/Presentation 1: Formal Game Critique (2 weeks). Students will write a short paper (two to three pages) reviewing a non-digital game that they haven't played before. The paper should focus on the formal structure of the game and general game design. Students should not just summarize and describe the game, but give a critical analysis by evaluating the success or failure of some aspect of the experience. Students will also give a short (five minutes) presentation of their papers to the class.

➼ Game Project 1 Assigned: Traditional Format Game

➼ Game Project 1: Traditional Format Game (2 weeks). In groups of two, students will create a game within a traditional object-based format such as a board, card, or dice game.

2 | WEEK 2 Discussion Topics: The Structure of Games. Chance, rules, conflict, goals, and strategies. Instructors will bring in games for in-class play, analysis, and discussion.

➼ Proposal for Game Project 1 due

3 | WEEK 3 Presentation of Paper 1 and class discussion

➼ Prototype for Game Project 1 due

➼ Work in-class on Project 1

UNIT TWO: Games as Play

1 | WEEK 4 Discussion Topic: Social Analysis of Games

➼ Game Project 1 due—class play and discussion

➼ Paper 2 assigned: Social Game Critique

➼ Paper/Presentation 2: Social Game Critique (2 weeks). Students will write a short (two to three pages) critique of any game (digital or non-digital), focusing on the way it organizes social interaction. As with the first paper, the emphasis should be on critical analysis rather than on description. Students will also give a short (five minutes) presentation to the class.

- Game Project 2 assigned: Social Game
- Game Project 2: Social Game (3 weeks). Groups of three to four students will design and build a non-digital game with a focus on social interaction. These games should be designed to create interesting social behavior and contexts.

2 | WEEK 5 Proposal for Game Project 2 due

3 | WEEK 6 Presentation of Paper 2 and class discussion
- Prototype for Game Project 2 due
- Work in-class on Project 2

4 | WEEK 7 Discussion Topics: Computer and video games. Instructors will bring in historical and contemporary examples of digital games for class to play and discuss.
- Game Project 2 due
- Game Project 3 assigned: Digital Game Proposal
- Game Project 3: Digital Game Proposal (2 weeks). In groups of two, students will describe a five-page digital game design that incorporates game design insights from the previous assignments. Students will give a ten-minute presentation of their game. A format for the document will be handed out when the project is assigned.

5 | WEEK 8 Game Project 2: Class play and discussion
- Work in-class on Project 3

UNIT THREE: Games as Culture

1 | WEEK 9 Discussion Topic: Cultural Analysis of Games
- Game Project 3 due—class presentations
- Paper 3 assigned: Cultural Game Critique
- Paper/Presentation 3: Cultural Game Critique (2 weeks). Students will write a short (two to three pages) critique of any game (digital or non-digital). The analysis should focus on the cultural implications and context of the game. Past student work has ranged from a personal account of high-school football to a socioeconomic analysis of Brazilian soccer culture to an investigation of the subcultures surrounding church bingo and professional Scrabble. Students will also give a short (five minutes) presentation to the class.
- Final Project assigned
- Final Project (4–5 weeks). Individually or in groups, students will create a finished, playable game of any kind that builds on the previous assignments and readings. A playable prototype is due two weeks after the final project is assigned.

2 | WEEK 10 Discussion Topic: Interactive Narratives, both digital and non-digital
- Final Project proposals due
- Final Project workshop

3 | WEEK 11 Presentation of Paper 3 and class discussion
- ➤ Final Project prototype due
- ➤ Final Project workshop

4 | WEEK 12 Final Project workshop

5 | WEEKS 13 AND 14 Final Project Presentations and discussion.

Additional In-Class Projects

Throughout the semester, in-class projects will be assigned and completed within a single class. Work on these projects counts toward the Attendance and Participation portion of your grade.

Readings

Readings will be assigned each week for the first eleven weeks of the semester, and will be handed out as photocopies the week before the reading is to be discussed. Students are expected to carefully complete each reading and come to class prepared to critically discuss the reading.

Readings in the class will consist of selections from the following books:

The Study of Games, E. Avedon and B. Sutton-Smith
Homo Ludens, Johan Huizinga
Man, Play and Games, Roger Caillois
Grasshopper: Life, Play, and Games, Bernard Suits
Prisoners' Dilemma, William Poundstone
Inside Electronic Game Design, Arnie Katz and Laurie Yates
From Barbie to Mortal Kombat: Games and Gender, J. Castell & H. Jenkins, eds.
The Ambiguity of Play, Brian Sutton-Smith

as well as the following essays:

"Checkmate: Rules, Play, and Culture," Frank Lantz & Eric Zimmerman
"Don't be a Vidiot," Greg Costikyan
"The Video Game as Emergent Media Form," McKenzie Wark

This list of readings is a general guideline for the semester's reading assignments. Depending on student interest, we may adjust the reading assignments as a semester progresses.

Motion Graphics at California Institute of the Arts

MICHAEL WORTHINGTON
Beginning Motion Graphics

MATT MULDER
Beginning Motion Graphics

GEOFF KAPLAN
Advanced Motion Graphics

Program Overview

The Graphic Design program at CalArts consists of both undergraduate and graduate studies. The undergraduate levels have core studio classes that cover all disciplines of graphic design (print, Web, motion, etc.), and motion projects appear in all four years of the BFA program. Outside of the core studio class there are a number of more specialized electives. For the first two years, the BFA students have compulsory electives; in the third and fourth years, the students may choose electives that reflect their particular interests, e.g., motion graphics. The motion graphics classes are split into beginning and advanced classes, both of which are critique-based studio classes—they offer very little technical information. Instead, they concentrate on the concepts behind the work and the visual forms that those ideas may take in order to successfully play themselves out. Technical expertise is offered in separate classes that specialize in using software such as After Effects and Flash. The beginning class tends to be slightly more pragmatic, while the advanced class offers more opportunity for deconstructing how motion works and building one's own idiosyncratic methodologies for making motion graphics.

Graduate students have a separate core seminar class, but also can choose specialized electives such as the motion classes.

The following three syllabi are from the instructors that have taught motion graphics at CalArts over the last year (2000).

Beginning Motion Graphics. *Instructor: Michael Worthington*

MOTION PHILOSOPHY: Since sophisticated new digital tools became affordable and available to graphic designers, the field of motion graphics has burgeoned. Rather than creating After Effects slaves to produce generic motion design for service-industry studios, I am interested in fostering students to become auteurs in the field of motion graphics, to develop their own ideas and structures, and design the surface of the motion. That is not to say that motion designers should become video artists or filmmakers; whether they exist in the commercial realm is up to the individual. I think, however, that it is important for designers to concentrate on making work that remains essentially "graphic" in its manufacture and mode of storytelling: motion pieces that extend and examine graphic language as communication in motion format, that examine new graphic narratives, rather than traditional filmic ones. Though influential and important dialogues can be gleaned from looking at art, animation, and film history and theory, graphic designers have the opportunity to develop and extend visual communication within the field of motion graphics, and to attain the level of critique and intellectual dialogue that exists around printed graphic design.

COURSE OVERVIEW: This class examines the elements of contemporary motion graphics for broadcast, Web animation, and film titles. Students complete projects that isolate and explore certain of these elements. The projects are used as a basis for group critique and discussion. Although the area of focus is dictated by the projects, the projects are intended to have enough creative flexibility to allow each student to create radically different outcomes. When these basic projects are completed, the students are given an extended period to produce a piece of their own choosing, in consultation with the faculty member, for any motion platform they choose.

1 | PROJECT 1: HISTORICAL REVIEW View compilation tape of movie titles, broadcast graphics, design-studio reels, avant-garde animation, video directors' reels, etc. This all too brief exposure to the history of motion is essential an historical platform to depart from (throughout the semester students continue to bring to class interesting pieces of motion graphics that they find).

DISCUSS: which pieces are successful and why, in terms of concepts, timing, impact, use of sound, editing/pacing, narrative structure, image-making, typography, etc.

2 | PROJECT 2: ABSTRACT ANIMATION, TIMING, AND MUSICAL SYNCHRONIZATION View and discuss the collected works of Oscar Fischinger.

BRIEF: Use Macromedia Flash or Director to create a twenty-second animation using geometric shapes in black and white only. Your animation should be synchronized to an audio track. The audio track can be anything you like, but the way your elements move should reflect the audio. Think about scale and depth, hierarchy, narrative, structure, perspective, camera angle, the relationship and interactions between forms, how objects move or have life, and above all, spend some time considering your audio track before you start.

Use Flash/Director purely as an animation tool, work with a 640 × 480 pixel screen, draw shapes in Illustrator or straight in Director. Make your piece twenty seconds long and 24 fps.

- *Presentation 1.* Make a fluid visual sketch of your audio piece. It does *not* have to be a conventional storyboard, but rather a more expressive form of visual notation. Map out the highs and lows, the places where events should happen. You may find it helpful to have many layers of sketches or an underlying 24-fps rigid grid. Use this sketch to plan the actions and events of your animation; it should correlate to the 24 fps in your animation piece. Digitize your audio and make a rough version of your animation.
- *Presentation 2.* Present a final version of your animation, rendered as a quicktime movie, 640 x 480, 24 fps.

➡ *Discuss:* Connections between sound and motion, value of timing and how the feeling/emotion created by music can be transferred/correlated to abstract shapes.

3 | PROJECT 3: OVEREFFECTS Brief: To abstract conventional recognizable footage by overusing Adobe After Effects.

➡ *Presentation 1.* Shoot digital video to document a place of your choosing. Edit the footage down to twenty seconds, use straight cuts, and do not alter sound.
➡ *Presentation 2.* Take your edited footage and "overprocess" it in After Effects. Use multiple effects and filters to remove the imagery from its initial recognizability, and take it toward an abstract realm.
➡ *Discuss:* The limitations of using given filters/effects, the value of combining several effects, and the concept of exploring the far end of the program's capabilities by deliberately overusing effects.

4 | PROJECT 4: GET OFF THE COMPUTER! Brief: Select one of the following words: engulf, absence, mythology, adorable, anxiety, waiting, catastrophe, compassion, dedication, faults, embarrassment, identification, unknowable, jealousy, monstrous, silence, signs, truth.

➡ *Presentation 1.* Using the word as a starting point, make or collect a text that you feel explains or discusses that theme. The text can be written/structured any way you like. Make the text "physical," i.e., not computer-screen based, through transparency, slide, printouts, video projector, conventional animation techniques, etc. Evaluate footage.
➡ *Presentation 2.* Select a soundtrack and edit your footage using straight cuts only. No cross-fades, no After Effects effects. The final piece should be approximately thirty seconds long.
➡ *Discuss:* Advantages and inadequacies of designing through the lens; the ability to create worlds that are not possible to create by using the computer; the "cinematization" of the real world.

5 | PROJECT 5: SELF-INITIATED PROJECT Design and make a piece of motion graphics of your own choosing; content, platform, and length to be decided by you. The project will be broken down into the following loose stages: (1) presentation of written ideas/concepts, (2) presentation of storyboards, (3) presentation of developed key frames, (4) presentation of motion tests, (5) presentation of rough edit, and (6) presentation of final piece.

Beginning Motion Graphics. *Instructor: Matt Mulder*

MOTION PHILOSOPHY: Today's designers are required to do more than simply get a reaction in some instantaneous momentary fashion. We need to engage. We need to entertain. We need to be able to tell stories. In my work and in my teaching I am constantly struggling to balance the rational need to build, manage, and organize my thoughts, methodologies, and tools with the more intuitive desire to orchestrate, experiment, and perform. Dealing with motion graphics means dealing not only with graphic elements, but also with image and sound elements over time. Without at least an understanding of established practices such as storyboarding, key-framing, shot lists, editing, cinematography, etc., we lack the basis from which rebellion would be a positive constructive experience, and our work will very easily end up being trite, redundant, and ultimately boring. In order to press forward, I think we need to train ourselves and our students to commit to ideas fully. Students should be able to tell us exactly what they mean and not rely on applications to mediate it for them.

COURSE OVERVIEW: The purpose of this class is to teach strategies and techniques of graphic storytelling. This class is broad-based. The tools used to realize a project will be up to the student, unless otherwise specified. For example, some of you may chose to use After Effects while others might choose to use Flash. The main emphasis of this class is to introduce students to methods and concepts of designing narrative graphic design. Most class time will be devoted to critiques, quick exercises, discussions, and demonstrations. Various reading and writing exercises will be given throughout the semester. You are required to start a motion journal. This is basically a sketchbook or library of motion tests, found motion, found sound, sound experiments, story ideas, poetry, and anything else you find relevant to your interests. Collect anything and everything you find interesting—commercials, videos, experimental films, photographs, answering-machine tapes, anything that sparks interest.

1 | PROJECT 1: IN-CAMERA STORY Key-framing and storyboarding are essential elements to organizing and telling a story. This project will force you to deal with shot selection and framing. In a single roll (24 exposures) of film using a 35mm camera you are to tell a story about your favorite outdoor location in southern California. It could be about something that happened to you there, complete fiction, a feeling, a documentary. Your story should unfold in sequence across the roll of film—shot 1 on the roll is the beginning of your story and shot 24 is the end of your story. It may take you a few attempts to get it right. I encourage you to take at least three or four rolls of film and pick the best sequence.

You will not have the freedom to rely on happy accidents or layering in the compositing stages to bail you out of a bad story. You should think about what you want to say and execute your in-camera story according to a methodical plan of action.

After you have finished shooting the roll, get 3 × 5s made and attach them together, end to end, in a horizontal strip with tape. Fold your story strip in accordion fashion and bring to class next week for discussion. In addition, write a short synopsis of your story. No cheating please. You will be turning in your story strip and the negatives of the roll you used.

This project requires you to do a little pre-planning before you start. Where will you go? What are the shots you need to tell your story? What is going to be happening over twenty-four frames? Are there characters in your story?

2 | PROJECT 2: THE ANIMATION SMACKDOWN Using your in-camera story from the first project, pick a word that describes your story, the action, the place, etc. You are to animate your word in a manner that reinforces its meaning or message.

Think about irony, surprise, climax, drama, and pace. Be resourceful! Do not rely solely on computer-generated type or Photoshop/After Effects filters. These filters and plug-ins can be useful, but more often than not create trite, derivative, and boring work. Show me evidence of "the hand" in your work. Use analog methods. Use light, collage, silkscreen, acetate, letterpress—whatever you can come up with to make a mark.

For our next class bring a sequence (five or six) of Photoshop frames that demonstrate the action you plan to animate, and an idea or sample of sound(s) you plan to use. We will have individual critiques on what you're up to.

The finished piece should be 480 × 360 pixels, be in a format compatible with QuickTime (.mov, swf) and include music and/or sound fx. There is no specific time or frame count. I would, however, recommend that you work in the five-to-ten second range. Longer pieces will significantly increase the amount of hours required to edit and tweak your animation.

3 | PROJECT 3: THE EINSTEIN TAPES Read *Einstein's Dreams* by Alan Lightman.

Einstein's Dreams introduces you to how flexible the architecture of storytelling can be. One does not have to obey the seemingly linear path of time and space. In fact, by playing with it, you can create intrigue in otherwise benign material.

Choose one of the stories from the book to use as the basis for a sound piece. Interpret how your particular story deals with the architecture of time and space and reflect that in the structure of your piece. Use any and all means to manufacture, record, or pirate music and sounds.

The finished piece should be at least one minute in length. It is to be in digital form, ready to be recorded on a group CD.

4 | PROJECT 4: TWO DOLLARS You are given $2.00. Write a story about what you did with it. Your story does not necessarily have to directly refer to the money (i.e., if you went to the racetrack and bet it, your story might be about something that happened while you were there or about horseracing in general). Be creative about what you do with it—burn it, fold it into a pterodactyl, whatever!

After writing about your experience, create a motion piece using image, typography, and sound. All three elements must be present in the piece. It should last thirty seconds to one minute. Build your piece at 640 × 480 and output to tape.

For next week: Bring in a synopsis of what you did with your newfound wealth and be prepared to tell us what you want to do for this project.

Advanced Motion Graphics. *Instructor: Geoff Kaplan*

MOTION PHILOSOPHY: Can we say that the major proportion of our graphic-design history/knowledge comes out of the Machine Age? If so, then as we move squarely into the digital/information age our methods of representation must change. In order to develop new strategies demanded by the digital age, I ask the class to investigate the medium of the screen, to generate motion marks in an attempt to define the issues we, as graphic designers, are faced with in this post-machine age.

COURSE OVERVIEW: Why "motion graphics"? What happens to our understanding of graphic mark-making when the element of time is introduced? Advanced motion graphics examines this question through a series of assignments and critiques in order to develop individual strategies that each student will need to skillfully deal with time-based marks.

1 | **PROJECT 1: DYNAMIC TYPOGRAPHY (MORPHOLOGY)** *Assignment: Watch the movies Akira and Tetsuo, the Iron Man*

You are an archaeologist/anthropologist with the ability to travel through time and space. You have traveled ahead in time to an uncharted planet. The population is extinct. You have come across the remnants (three or four objects) of the population's "alphabet." It is your job as an archaeologist/anthropologist to "decode" the objects you have found.

- *Presentation 1.* Write an anthropological history about the "letters" you have found. The paper should include an outline of the physical properties of the planet, and how these properties dictated the form of the alphabetic objects discovered. The one rule I am imposing is that the objects must be three-dimensional.

  To begin: start by determining the nature of the planet's gravity and how the gravitational forces affect the object. You might also address whether or not the object is "man-made" and/or organic.

  The paper must be at least 250 words in length. It must be in narrative form, no list making.

- *Presentation 2.* Transpose the written story into images, and tell the narrative with the images.

  How to create the images: (1) Make the objects out of stuff that's around (e.g., *Tetsuo*): garbage, food, whatever . . . recontextualize stuff. It must be 3-D. (2) Take the artifact and videotape it. Capture the material and render as "filmstrip for Photoshop" in After Effects. This creates a strip-like document, one image after the other. In this case: thirty (or fifteen) images per second. If you want to mask an object, you have to do it in every single image. (3) In Photoshop: manipulate the strip, image by image. (4) Open the strip(s) as a movie in After Effects.

  The final form should be a thirty- to forty-five-second piece of motion that tells the story of how the alphabet worked, how it communicated.

2 | **PROJECT 2: DUCK-RABBIT-DUCK-RABBIT** (a drawing that is a duck and a rabbit, but you can never see the two figures at once)

ASSIGNMENT: *Read* Wittgenstein: *Philosophical Investigations* IIXI*;* Various Selected Articles on Gestalt Theory

Discuss aspect blindness and Gestalt "flip-flops" as exemplified by the infamous image of the "duck-rabbit." Discuss how it is possible to produce, within the volume of time and the screen, a suspended or continual "duck-rabbit," the Wittgensteinian push-pull effect.

The assignment itself is to produce a thirty-second PSA, commercial, or TV promo that extrudes a perceptual gestalt flip-flop through time, and comments in some way on Wittgenstein's text. In living up to this challenge (there are *no* other parameters), it falls to each design student to investigate and play with the various means to accomplish their objective. Examples include: figure-ground relationships, scale relationships, color shifts, hiding-revealing, three-dimensional to two-dimensional juxtapositions, etc.

Write a series of questions that you have asked yourselves concerning the nature of screen-based volume (the fourth dimension) during the course of this assignment.

A Field Guide

DAVID REINFURT
Interactive Telecommunications Program, New York University

Precedent

Roger Tory Peterson's *A Field Guide to the Birds*,[1] first published in 1934, changed everything for the nascent sport of birding. Before the guide, birding was practiced largely by hunters and academics. The identification of species was conducted on a bird in the hand, the result of hunting, or a specimen delivered to a laboratory. Ornithological training was required to accurately identify a bird and to place it in the phylogenetic taxonomy. *A Field Guide to the Birds* proposed a simple, but revolutionary thesis: A bird can be identified quickly and accurately in the field based on its unique visual qualities.

Throughout his life, Roger Tory Peterson drew pictures of birds. He began in seventh grade when a teacher suggested he join a Junior Audubon Club. He became quickly engrossed in drawing and watching birds. By the time he finished high school, Peterson claimed to know the existing *Reed's Pocket Guide to Birds* by heart. This fat, checkbook-sized volume included, on each spread, a portrait and a descriptive text of each of the common species. Peterson's field sketches of birds led him to pursue a career in art. He studied at the Art Students League (1927–1928) and the National Academy of Design (1929–1931) in New York City. Living in New York, he met many of the leading ornithologists, including Ludlow Griscom. Griscom had developed the idea of field marks, which can be used to distinguish one bird from another at a distance. Peterson was exposed to a larger group of people who shared his fascination with birds. He left New York convinced that a guide arranged visually rather than biologically would find an audience.

Peterson's Field Guide was a synthesis of several existing ideas, and he credited his visual training with enabling him to develop the concept. *A Field Guide to the Birds* organized the birds not through ornithology, but rather by visual similarities of form and structure. The Chimney Swift was placed with the Sparrows, because they looked the same. The Philadelphia Vireo and Ruby-Crowned Kinglet were compared with the confusing Fall Warblers. This was radical.

Further, the drawings of the birds were not handsome portraits like the paintings in *Reed's Pocket Guide to Birds*, but were purposely diagrammatic. On a plate that included six to ten birds, arrows point to the unique visual characteristics that could be used to accurately identify that bird from all of the others in the guide. The Wood Pewee is distinguished by its conspicuous wing bars and yellow bill, and the Western Kingbird by its yellow belly and black tail. This system of visual notation was called the Peterson Identification System.

Finding a publisher for the new guide was difficult. Peterson's manuscript, including illustrations and his meticulously terse text, was rejected at four New York publishing houses. Houghton Mifflin agreed to publish the book, but considered it such a gamble that they could not pay royalties on the first one thousand of the two thousand copies to be printed. Peterson accepted immediately. The first printing of two thousand copies of the field guide sold out in a matter of days. *A Field Guide to the Birds* is currently in its fourth edition, and has inspired numerous imitators.

By arranging birds according to their visual differences and rendering these differences clearly, the field guide opened up birding to a broad audience. Birds could now be identified in the field rather than in the hand. Peterson replaced the rifle with field binoculars and, in doing so, he turned "looking" into a viable sport.

The Importance of Field Studies

Friday, September 3, 1999, page B1, *New York Times* Metro Section: "A Field Guide to New York City Busses."[2] The half-page graphic stopped me as I flipped through the paper. Presented in a derivative of the Peterson Identification System were seven species of New York City busses. There was a diagrammatic drawing of each kind, a map showing their range, a terse description, and a name. I was compelled to study this guide. I wasn't driven by an innate fascination with busses, but, instead, because I see these specimens daily moving through their city habitat. Before, I had only the crude word "bus" to describe what I saw plodding down the street. After studying the field guide, I had a new language. In the following days and weeks, my world expanded slightly and I could see what was invisible to me before. It was no longer a bus that stopped to pick me up or rolled up 10th Avenue, it was an RTS-04, an Over The Road, or maybe an Orion 5, distinguished by its flat front and boxy shape. Since encountering this Field Guide, I have become a bus-watcher of sorts, able to identify all seven types easily, and only recently experiencing the thrill of spotting the Nova L.F.S, only one of which is known to travel New York City streets. This connection between design, language, and my daily experience in the city was powerful.

In Elements of Visual Language, the class that I teach at the New York University Interactive Telecommunications Program, I emphasize that design yields meaning when it makes connections to existing sets of conditions and other bodies of knowledge. This is something that I learned in graduate school, specifically in a set of assignments given by Paul Elliman at Yale University. He stressed the explicit connection to another body of knowledge by giving a thematic topic to his classes, whether it was the clouds, the night sky or public transport.

My class at NYU is filled with students from varied backgrounds. They are beginning the two-year graduate program and the course is required. For many, it is the first formal class that they have had in graphic design. In order to get them started on making visual work right away,

I attempt to connect all of the assignments directly to their everyday experience. This is meant to suggest that design is not something done only in a secluded studio, or arrived at by revelation, but is a mundane and direct process of making a series of decisions. The students leave the class and pursue a broad range of electronic projects through their two years of study. One assignment that they complete in my class is to design a field guide.

I try to engage the city with assignments. The field guide assignment requires students to spend a majority of their time in the field (city) looking at small differences in a group of similar objects, and to render these differences clearly. Their Field Guides must communicate concisely and must be useful in the field. The assignment turns in on itself at the end, as I ask that students exchange field guides with one another and spend the next week in the field attempting to use the guide. They document their sightings with photographs.

The city is a system that isn't predictable. Bell Atlantic is switching all of their payphones to Verizon, graffiti have been "erased," downtown C trains have been replaced by E trains for service to World Trade Center, making all local stops. By engaging the processes of the city, I want to make explicit that accident, coincident, and external factors are a crucial part of design.

The field guide offers an internal set of criteria for judging its success. It works if it allows small differences to be clearly read in the field. The existing form of the field guide provides a useful set of formal and structural conventions for the students to respond to. Each design decision can be weighed against the criteria: Is it easier to read the visual differences in my set of things? Students must consider how to represent their objects, by drawing, photography, in isolation, or in context. Finally, the field guide assignment asks students to spend a considerable amount of time looking at similarities and differences. The assignment stresses formal connections within a set of things, which is a part of what graphic design can do well.

Many have pursued a serial working method which suggests the process of a field guide. Wilson Alwyn "Snowflake" Bentley compulsively recorded and cataloged snowflakes.[3] In 1884, at age nineteen, he began making photomicrographs through an inexpensive telescope, and continued throughout his life. In total, he recorded 5,381 individual snowflakes, no two the same. A farmer by trade, he cataloged other visual phenomena, including daily weather, using a consistent notation system: the sizes of raindrops (developing a system still in use), 649 auras that he searched for in the evening, and even the smiles of actress Mary Pickford. Bentley's original subject was his most successful. His photographs of snowflakes reveal a visual structure not immediately visible, and they made permanent a transient experience (the falling snow). He wasn't taken seriously by the scientific community until late in his life. Perhaps his method, rooted in looking at visual similarities and differences, was a challenge to a formal scientific education.

Artist Ed Ruscha has often worked in series, making books of typologies with small collections of photographs.[4] In 1963, he made his first, *Twenty-Six Gasoline Stations*. It was a collection of filling stations that he had often seen while driving from his birthplace in Oklahoma City to his residence in Los Angeles. Other books followed, including *Various Small Fires*, *Some Los Angeles Apartments*, *Thirty-Four Parking Lots*, and *Nine Swimming Pools*. In these works, the photographs reveal the wide variety of visual forms that exist inside one category. William Eggleston's *Guide*, his seminal book of color photographs of Mississippi and Tennessee, uses a similar approach.[5] German photographers Bernd and Hilla Becher provided some of the best known typologies. They made exhaustive catalogs of common structures, grouped together to reveal visual similarities and differences. *Cooling Towers Wood-Steel* is a collection of nine photographs made between 1959 and 1977.[6] The straight photographs are presented as a collection, rendering the differences visible.

In the film *Smoke*, by Paul Auster and Wayne Wang, Auggie Wren owns a tobacco store in Brooklyn that is the locus of the story.[7] Auggie has a collection of photographs spanning fifteen years that he has made at the same time each day from the same location just outside of the storefront. He has arranged the photographs chronologically in endless albums. The motivation for this project is never revealed, but Auggie seems to be following the systematic method of a field guide.

The Assignment

This is the assignment as given to "Elements of Visual Language" class at New York University Interactive Telecommunications Program:

Design a field guide.

1. Find a set of seven to fifteen similar things readily available in the New York City habitat
2. Record them. (Photographs can be made in context [field photography] or in a controlled setting [studio photography]. Drawings can be used. Other methods are possible. This depends on what you wish to communicate.)
3. Make a "a pictorial key using obvious similarities and differences of form and structure." (Your field guide can be any finished size, but must fold down to a size that someone [me] could take with them and use in the field [city]. It may be produced in any way that you want: photocopy, color photocopy, computer printout.)

Here are some field guide notes:

- A field guide is about the small differences between similar things
- A field guide is based on the visual differences
- One thing that design can do well is to render these visual differences clearly
- A collection should be homogeneous so that small differences can be read
- A field guide is based on direct, in the field, observation
- You should use things readily found in New York City environment

Responses and Findings

Responses to the assignment vary along consistent lines. I try to make it clear that the clever choice of a subject for the field guide is not important. The subject should be readily available in the city. The subjects should be as similar as possible, so that small differences can be clearly rendered. The most important part of the activity is the close looking and deciding how to communicate these differences. Often, two students will choose the same subject.

One successful response was *A Field Guide to Waste Receptacles* in Manhattan. This guide is approximately 4" × 6" and accordion-folded. It is largely white with a series of photographs of public trashcans, each silhouetted, one per panel. The descriptions and names are given on the reverse. Clearly presented, the sequence of trashcans immediately makes legible the differences in the eight kinds. These differences are largely in the outline shape of the trashcans.

Another response was *A Field Guide to Manhole Covers*. A popular topic, but this time it was done differently. The student chose to concentrate on one city block, 22nd Street between Park Avenue South and Fifth Avenue. Square-format photographs of the manhole covers are presented in a grid. The visual differences can be clearly read. Additionally, the texture and astounding variety of manholes found on that single block makes a nice connection to the infinite visual variety available in the city.

A third response, *A Field Guide to Street Vending Carts*, was produced by a student who was coincidentally pursuing a degree in Oceanography. The topic had been attempted previously with limited success. In this guide, the street-vendor carts are organized by the number of umbrellas, and a colored generic silhouette opens each section. Following the opening are specific photographs of the street vending cart specimens as seen in the field. The move from generic to specific makes the differences in vending-cart types clear.

The inevitable dividend of the assignment is the other body of knowledge. In the process of making design and satisfying the criteria, students learn about payphones, trashcans, city birds, manhole covers, curb finishes, busses, police uniforms, and paving patterns. This is useful.

N O T E S

1. Roger Tory Peterson, *A Field Guide to the Birds* (Boston: Houghton Mifflin Company, 1934).

2. David W. Dunlap and Al Granberg, "A Field Guide to New York City Busses" in *New York Times* Metro Section, B1 (New York: The New York Times, September 3, 1999).

3. Joe Laniado, "Cold Comfort" in *Frieze* issue 53 (London: Durian Publications Ltd., 2000).

4. Neal Benezara and Kerry Brougher, *Ed Ruscha* (Zurich: Scalo, 2000).

5. William Eggleston, *William Eggleston's Guide* (New York: Museum of Modern Art, 1976).

6. Peter C. Bunnell, *Photography at Princeton* (Princeton: The Art Museum, Princeton University, 1998).

7. Paul Auster and Wayne Wang, *Smoke and Blue in the Face: Two Films* (New York: Miramax Books, 1995).

Designing Experience for a Functional Object

MASAMICHI UDAGAWA

Interactive Telecommunications Program, New York University

Class Description

What does "designing experience" mean? It is an act of choreographing a series of events in the minds of others. How is it different, for example, from making a movie? In the case of linear narrative media, such as music, film, or book, an experience is pre-determined by the maker and "spoon-fed" to the audience (at least at the mechanical level of perception). However, in the case of a functional object, such as a product, a prescribed event does not reveal itself until the user interacts with it. Therefore, the design must solicit the user for a desired action, which triggers the product's functionality/experience. Here, the user's experience is an inseparable element of the functional system.

The class will explore the nature of designing experience in three successive projects. First, various ways of describing experience will be discussed. Secondly, the class will re-design an existing experience of a functional object, such as an ATM or vending machine. Thirdly, the class will design a new experience as a vehicle of integrating the user and novel functionality. The students will be encouraged to explore a new vocabulary of interactivity, to expand the lexicon of interactive experience, and to examine the societal role of designing experience.

In short, designing experience is like installing a minefield, a trap anticipating how people behave in a certain context, as opposed to fireworks, an entertainment.

Prerequisite

Introduction to Computational Media. Though it is not a mandatory requirement, any degree of knowledge of Physical Computing, Motion Graphics, Graphic Design, and Industrial Design is a good addition.

Evaluation Criteria

Grading will be based on deliverables and general class participation. Rigorous investigation is a requirement. Class attendance is mandatory.

Schedule Flexibility

Due to the instructor's professional activity, there may be an occasional rescheduling of a class meeting time. The instructor will use his best efforts to avoid such situations, but when unavoidable, he would appreciate participants' cooperation.

Syllabus

1 | **PROJECT 1: DESCRIBING EXPERIENCE** An interactive journal or simulation of memorable experience (description/simulation of experience through interactive media).

The first step toward designing experience is to establish methods of reading and describing experience.

Existing description methodology for time-based artifacts, such as music score, storyboard or task flow chart, may provide an interesting reference. Computer-based tools provide us with totally new ways of visualization that may be suitable to describe complex experiences. We will start the project with exploring alternative ways of documenting and visualizing existing "ordinary" experiences. Here, various aspects of the event need to be captured and converged into a single piece. Time line may be used as a basic structure, though, as in music, our impression of time does not correspond to mechanical clock movement.

There are two ways to address this assignment though they are not purely exclusive.

The first approach is to describe the experience as a story. The second approach is to simulate/recreate the experience.

- ➻ **WEEK 1** *Activity:* introduction of the class • introduction of project 1 • discussion regarding various description methods of experience • discussion regarding characteristic differences among various media • discussion regarding the reading materials • assignment 1a (documentation of experience with traditional media such as text, photograph, sketch, video, object, etc.) given • discussion about assignment 1a (focusing on time/space relationship characteristic for each medium) • assignment 1b (documentation of experience with digital media such as Director) given. *Deliverables:* name card (3" × 5" card with (1) e-mail address, (2) individual background information, and (3) a mug shot)
- ➻ **WEEK 2** *Activity:* individual presentation of MATERIALS (photos, objects, stories, sounds, etc.) and PLAN • discussion. *Deliverables:* assignment 1a
- ➻ **WEEK 3: SEPTEMBER 26** *Activity:* review assignment 1b (individual presentation) • discussion regarding the difference between assignment 1a and 1b • introduction of project 2 • group formation (four groups). *Deliverables:* assignment 1b presentation • formation of four groups for project 2

2 | **PROJECT 2: REDESIGNING EXPERIENCE** The second step explores methods of breaking conventions without losing practicality of use. We will pick an existing automated vending machine in public space, analyze it, form a point of view (design concept), and then redesign the experience.

- ➤ **WEEK 4** *Activity:* group presentation: RESEARCH REPORT of the current practice (photos, videos, drawings, stories, etc.) and PROJECT PROPOSAL (please review appendix 1 for more detail) • discussion regarding project 2 framework (from the reading materials) • discussion regarding the interface in public spaces (ADA, multi-lingual . . .) • review NYCT MetroCard Vending Machine (presentation of the instructor's portfolio). *Deliverables:* RESEARCH REPORT and PROJECT PROPOSAL (composed in Web pages or director slide-show)
- ➤ **WEEK 5** *Activity:* group presentation: THREE USER SCENARIOS and THREE STORY-BOARDS. *Deliverables:* THREE USER SCENARIOS (representing different users) and THREE STORYBOARDS
- ➤ **WEEK 6** *Activity:* group presentation: refined THREE USER SCENARIOS, THREE STORY-BOARDS, and hardware/software design SKETCHES and MOCK-UPS (foam or cardboard or 3-D computer model). *Deliverables:* refined scenarios, storyboards and hardware/software SKETCHES and MOCK-UPS
- ➤ **WEEK 7** *Activity:* group presentation: STEP-BY-STEP INTERACTION STORYBOARDS (Director demo or slide show) illustrating three user scenarios, revised hardware/software concept mock-ups (foam or cardboard models or 3-D computer model). *Deliverables:* STEP-BY-STEP INTERACTION STORY BOARDS (Director demo)
- ➤ **WEEK 8** *Activity:* project 2 final presentation • introduction of project 3. *Deliverables:* final hardware/software mock-ups and presentation package for the instructor.

3 | PROJECT 3: NARRATIVE SPACE – AN INTERACTIVE INSTALLATION* Narrative space is a product with the simple function of telling a story. Naturally, a space is an interactive medium that requires the viewer/user's participation. As the viewer/user navigates through the space, the story unfolds. Each group will select an existing museum in New York City and choose a subject that relates to the specific museum. Then, design and construct an interactive installation that communicates the selected subject through digital interaction. The installation should be conceived as a portion of a fictitious exhibition that the selected museum might be interested in realizing. The installation should be designed to be a potentially semi-permanent exhibition. The experience created by the installation needs to be repeatable.

4 | PROJECT 3: HOME – AN AUGMENTED LIVING* HomE is an electronically enhanced living style. Each group will come up with a product/service concept and its user experience prototype. Unlike Project 2, here students are encouraged to explore various sentimental values of the product/service.

- ➤ **WEEK 9** *Activity:* group formation, project discussion and the instructor's presentation. *Deliverables:* documentation of Project 2
- ➤ **WEEK 10** *Activity;* group presentation: RESEARCH REPORT of the current practice (photos, videos, drawings, stories, etc.), PROJECT PROPOSAL. *Deliverables:* RESEARCH REPORT, PROJECT PROPOSAL
- ➤ **WEEK 11** *Activity:* group presentation: THREE USER SCENARIOS and THREE STORY-BOARDS. *Deliverables:* THREE USER SCENARIOS and THREE STORY BOARDS

➤ **WEEK 13** *Activity:* desk crit

➤ **WEEK 14** *Activity:* final presentation

Appendix 1 (Project 2): What Should Be in a Project Proposal?

During the first session of Project 2, each group will present their project concept together with a written document, namely, the project proposal.

A project proposal should contain: objective, design criteria, solution, and user scenario (deliverable in second week of project 2).

Objective section should state the basic reason-of-existence of the proposed project. The section should contain: (1) main goal of the project (i.e., to ease the traffic congestion of NYC, to reduce the cost of distributing your product, etc.), (2) context analysis and problem statement (i.e., what's wrong with current practice, etc.), and (3) target user groups (i.e., who's going to use it). Please note that to satisfy different needs, there will always be more than one type of user—subway cars can be used by rider, driver, conductor, maintenance crew, authority, city, etc. Later in the scenario development, you will explore motivations and activities of various users in a narrative format.

Design criteria section provides guidelines for potential solutions. It may contain such phrases as ". . . in order to achieve . . . (goal) . . . the solution must do . . . and cost . . . , easy-to-understand, visually pleasing, meet ADA, etc. . . ." Design criteria can be seen as a hit list that states a series of must-have characteristics to make this project successful.

Solution section is the beginning of the actual design proposal. If design criteria contains "vandal proof," solution section may say ". . . the housing needs to be constructed out of 3mm thick stainless steel, etc. . . ." It is a possible way to meet the design criteria; thus, to achieve the goal. You may be able to imagine more than one solution (this is always the case). Then, you may state "opportunities and challenges" to encourage informed trade-offs (i.e., . . . by using this new technology XXX, we can . . . , however, the technology XXX costs U.S. $5 billion, and will take ten years to develop. On the other hand, the existing technology ZZZ is available for $500.00 and it does 80 percent of technology XXX . . .).

User scenario describes how the proposed solution can be used and satisfies the goal in narrative form. It is a detailed description of the solution in the context of actual use. By using various fictitious characters (defined in the target user section), rationale of the project will be examined. Like a character in a novel, though he or she is a fictitious existence, the user in a scenario must act according to a set of reasonable motivations. If the character in your scenario has to behave oddly, your concept contains some irrational or unnatural elements.

In summary, the most important point about a project proposal is to make a rational (and convincing) argument about "why someone needs your new invention." Creating a logical structure is crucial to making someone understand your point. So, let's focus on creating a logical structure! At this stage, you do not need to spend time perfecting "Good Writing." A series of bullet points are perfectly okay. Clarity is more important than the volume of the text. This is a fictional project; therefore, the strength of your rationale (story) is the only foundation you can build your stuff upon.

In an actual project proposal, in business, there are usually a lot more elements, such as various schedules, budgets, estimated return-on-investment, risk analysis, competition and market analysis, distribution plan, user demographics, technology analysis, etc. However, in this project, we will focus on creating a front-end user experience and exercising rational thinking in design. That is to say, how to design a good argument.

 **Biographies**

SEAN ADAMS is a partner at AdamsMorioka, Inc. in Beverly Hills. He currently teaches typography and design theory at California Institute of the Arts.

ERIK ADIGARD, along with Patricia McShane, is the founder of the design and illustration studio, M.A.D. His work crosses all media and ranges from experimental design to corporate communications. Additional information about activities, exhibits, and publications can be found at M.A.D.'s Web site *www.madxs.com*.

BOB AUFULDISH is a partner in Aufuldish & Warinner and an affiliate associate professor at the California College of Arts and Crafts, where he teaches graphic design, typography, and new media, and is design director of Sputnik CCAC, a student-staffed design office producing work for the College. His first interactive project was produced on a Mac IIcx. Bob has a BFA and MFA in graphic design from Kent State University, Ohio.

AARON BETSKY joined the San Francisco Museum of Modern Art as curator of architecture and design in February 1995. In 1997, he mounted "Icons: Magnets of Meaning," a large exhibition of mass-produced objects. He assembles five to six exhibitions a year on subjects in design, and, through the Architecture and Design Forum of the Museum, has helped organize several dozen lectures, public symposia, and competitions. In 1995, he co-founded the San Francisco Prize, an annual competition that has elicited designs for the Philip Burton Federal Plaza (1996), Union Square (1997), and Harvey Milk Plaza (2000). Mr. Betsky has published nine books on architecture, most recently *Architecture Must Burn* (Thames & Hudson, 2000).

J. D. BIERSDORFER, who has written extensively about technology for the *New York Times*, majored in theatre at Indiana University and came to computers late in life. If she can learn this stuff, anybody can.

ANDREW BLAUVELT leads a hybrid life in Raleigh, North Carolina, where he is director of graduate studies in graphic design at North Carolina State University.

RED BURNS is a founding member of the Board of the New York New Media Association, and also serves as a board member on The New York Times Digital Advisory Board, The Charles H. Revson Foundation, Media Lab Europe, The Visual Media Task Force, The Convergent Media Group, Earthnoise, Bluefly.com, ProBono.net and Skoodles. In the past year she was named to *Silicon Alley's* 100 and *Crain's New York Business* listed her as one of the 100 top leaders of New York's economy, as well as one of the top 100 most influential women in business. *Interactive Week* picked her as one of the "Top 25 Influential People on the Net," and she was named one of *Newsweek's* "50 for the Future," and *New York Magazine's* "New York Cyber Sixty."

ANNE BUSH teaches graphic design and graphic design history at the University of Hawaii at Manoa. Her design work has been recognized by the AIGA, the ACD, *EYE* magazine, and *I.D.* magazine. Her writing has appeared in *Visible Language, Design Issues*, the *ACD Journal, Emigre, Zed*, and *TipoGrafica*. She has been a visiting artist at the American Academy in Rome, and is currently a fellow at the Camargo Foundation in France where she is writing a book on the discourses of travel and travel guidebooks.

DENISE CARUSO is a scholar at Interval Research in Palo Alto, a laboratory run by the computer industry pioneer David Liddle. She was a visiting lecturer at Stanford University in the Human-Computer Interaction program in the university's Computer Science department. In 1994, Caruso launched Technology & Media Group. She was also the founding editor of *Digital Media,* the seminal newsletter in the emerging new media industry. For five years she was anchor columnist for the *San Francisco Examiner's* Sunday technology section. Her essays and analysis have been published in a wide variety of publications, including the *Wall Street Journal, Columbia Journalism Review, WIRED, I.D. Magazine,* the *Utne Reader,* and the *New York Times.*

KYLE COOPER is the designer of over 100 titles for film and television. In 1996, Kyle Cooper and his founding partners, Chip Houghton and Peter Frankfurt, bought the Los Angeles operations from parent company RG/A, forming the design and production company, Imaginary Forces (IF). Since then, Cooper and his design team at IF have extended their work from film titles to trailers, broadcast graphics, commercials, and print, creating graphics for HBO, show openings such as *Ally McBeal,* and directing commercials for Gatorade, Reebok and Janus. With its first feature film, *Blade,* IF is moving further into content development for film, television, and print publication. He is currently directing his first feature film, *New Port South,* for Touchstone Pictures.

HILLMAN CURTIS, principal of hillmancurtis.com, inc., a design firm in New York City, represents the cutting edge of motion graphic design on the Web today. His expert and innovative use of motion graphic design has garnered him the Communication Arts Award of Excellence, the One Show gold, New Media Invision Bronze, the South by Southwest Conference "best use of design" and "best of show," *How* magazine Top 10 Web site, features in major design magazines and books, as well as a growing reputation around the world. Hillman has appeared as keynote speaker at design conferences in Japan, Paris, New York, San Francisco, Chicago, and Atlanta. His company's current client roster includes Intel, Iomega, 3com, Hewlett Packard, Ogilvy One, DSW, SonicNet, Macromedia, Capitol Records, Lycos, WebTV, Sun, and others. His book, *Designing Flash Motion Graphics* (MacMillian USA) is a best seller.

MEREDITH DAVIS is professor and department chair of graphic design At North Carolina State University where she teaches courses in Master of graphic design and PhD in design programs. She has chaired efforts of the American Institute of Graphic Arts to redefine standards for college-level graphic design programs in the United States and is a member of the AIGA Advance for Design group which seeks to define models for practice and education in experience design.

HUGH DUBBERLY is a design planner and teacher. At Apple Computer in the mid eighties and early nineties, Hugh managed cross-functional design teams and went on to manage creative services and corporate identity for the entire company. While at Apple, he served at Art Center College of Design in Pasadena as the first and founding chairman of the computer graphics department. He later moved to Netscape and became vice president of design. Recently, he has started a new company, Dubberly Design Office, which focuses on planning Web applications.

GEOFFRY FRIED is chair of the design department at the Art Institute of Boston at Lesley University. He has been a designer and educator for the past seventeen years and has taught at Boston University, Northeastern University, and Rhode Island School of Design.

DIANE GROMALA is an associate professor in the School of Literature, Communication, and Culture, and a member of GVU (Graphics Visualization and Usability Center) at Georgia Tech. Gromala's work in innovative interface design and emerging technologies has been exhibited and performed worldwide. She is on the editorial board of *Postmodern Culture*, a reviewer for international computer science organizations, and chair of the Art and Design Gallery at SIGGRAPH 2000.

STEVEN HOSKINS is assistant professor in the Department of Communication Arts + Design at Virginia Commonwealth University and is coeditor *of Loop: AIGA Journal of Interaction Design Education*. After practicing print design and illustration in the 1980s and 1990s, he received an MFA in graphic design from Rhode Island School of Design. He has specialized in interactive media design professionally and academically for the last six years.

MARIE KACMAREK is the vice president of design/creative director for Circle.com, where she oversees the creative direction of all projects originating in the San Francisco office. Prior to joining Circle.com, she was a creative director for Yosho, Inc., where she orchestrated a new identity for the company, and founded Floating Code, an interactive design and animation studio. Marie's other work experiences include art direction of commercial animations for United Airlines, McDonald's and Ameritech. She publishes and art directs "Urban Sounds," *www.urbansounds.com,* combining the Web and electronic music. Awards that she has received include: ITVA Gold Philo Award, American Graphic Design Award, and the Gold Aurora Award.

GEOFF KAPLAN is the founder of General Working Group. Previously, he worked for Imaginary Forces in Los Angeles. He produces motion graphics for television, movies, and Web-based media.

DAVID KARAM is half of the San Francisco–based Post Tool, founded with partner Gigi Biederman in 1993. Post Tool's multimedia work has been featured in numerous recent books and most major design publications, including *Eye*, *I.D.*, *Graphis*, and *AIGA Journal*, as well as in *Rolling Stone* and Japan's *Popeye*. Their work is in the collection of the San Francisco Museum of Modern Art and the Cooper-Hewitt National Design Museum, and both Karam and Biederman have lectured internationally on the subject of design and technology. In addition to its other awards, Post Tool was a Chrysler Award nominee for Innovation in Design in 1995 and 1997. David also served as the director of the Design and Media department, and as the assistant chair of graphic design at the California College of Arts and Crafts.

ISAAC KERLOW plays a key role to the Walt Disney Company in efforts related to digital art production in a variety of wide-ranging new media. Prior to this post, Isaac led Disney Interactive's group of digital artists and animators responsible for developing and producing CD-ROM, online and platform games. Before joining Disney in 1995, Isaac spent a decade at Pratt Institute in New York where he was a tenured professor and the founding chairman of the Department of Computer Graphics and Interactive Media. Isaac served on the NY/AIGA Board of Directors, 1989–1991, and was a juror for the Art Directors' Club 78th Annual Awards and the Webby 2000 Awards.

FRANK LANTZ is one of the founding members of the New York new media design studio R/GA Interactive, where he served as creative director for seven years. He left R/GA in 2000 to join the instant-delivery e-commerce company Kozmo.com as vice president of design. He teaches classes in game design and interactive narrative at the Interactive Telecommunications Program at New York University.

JONATHAN LIPKIN is assistant professor of multimedia design at Ramapo College, photographer, and the author of many journal articles and a book on digital photography for Harry N. Abrams.

CAROLYN MCCARRON is a communications strategist for Waters Design in New York City, where her responsibilities include graphic design, strategic design planning, content development, and writing. She previously worked as a senior designer for Houghton Mifflin Company in Boston. She has a B.F.A. in graphic design from Rhode Island School of Design, and an M.A. in advertising and communications design from Syracuse University. She has written articles for *Communication Arts, Adobe Magazine,* and the *AIGA Journal.*

KATHERINE MCCOY is senior lecturer at Illinois Institute of Technology's Institute of Design, and was co-chair of design at Cranbrook Academy of Art for twenty-four years. As a partner of High Ground

Tools and Strategies for Design, she organizes continuing educational programs for designers. Her design practice includes graphic design and design marketing for an international range of cultural, educational, and corporate clients. She is an elected member of the Alliance Graphique Internationale, a fellow of the Industrial Designers Society of America, and has served as president of the American Center for Design and the IDSA.

MATTHEW MULDER lives in Los Angeles. He is a founding partner of wideopenspaces, a multidisciplinary design studio investigating, authoring, and designing for narrative media.

KATHERINE NELSON is a design writer and senior editor at *PRINT* magazine. Her writing has appeared in *Sony Style* and *Harper's Bazaar* among other publications. She is currently at work on the launch issue of *eDesign,* a new digital-design magazine to be published this fall by RC Publications, Inc.

MELISSA NIEDERHELMAN is a designer, writer, and currently assistant professor of graphic design in the School of Design at Arizona State University where she teaches interactivity, design research and planning, as well as interdisciplinary courses involving design and business students. Her research interests include issues of design education, the Internet and design as a cultural influence, and interdisciplinary opportunities in visual communication design.

NANCY NOWACEK is an independent designer living and working in Brooklyn, New York.

RAYMOND PIROUZ *(raymond@r35.com)* is a designer and author of several books, and as a number of articles published online and in traditional media. In his spare time, he is CEO of R35, Inc. *(www.r35.com)* and founder/president of R35 edu *(www.r35.com/edu).*

DAVID REINFURT runs O R G, a graphic design practice in New York City, and teaches in the Interactive Telecommunications Program at New York University. See also *http://www.o-r-g.com.*

KATIE SALEN is an assistant professor of design at the University of Texas at Austin. Her research focuses on utilizing a broad design practice to investigate ideas about the dynamic relationship between cultural identities and their expression through visual language. In addition to serving as editor and designer of *Zed* she is currently writing a book for MIT Press, Game + Design, with Eric Zimmerman, which uses games as a model of study for interactive design. She is also working as a designer and animator for Flat Black Films, and is a founding member of Condu1t, (a digital film and gaming engine).

LOUISE SANDHAUS is codirector of the graphic design program at CalArts and a partner in the multi-disciplinary design firm, Durfee Regn Sandhaus, which develops material and electronic "information spaces." She is a participant in "Re-Thinking Exhibitions," a series of six speakers who explore the possibilities of alternative exhibition strategies, and is coeditor and codesign director for the *American Center for Design Journal,* "New Media. New Narratives?" Ms. Sandhaus has an

M.F.A. in Graphic Design from CalArts and is a Post-Graduate Laureate from the Jan van Eyck Akademie, Maastricht, The Netherlands.

MICHAEL SCHMIDT is an associate professor teaching undergraduate and graduate graphic design courses at the University of Memphis. He also works in the areas of curatorial research, print design, design writing, and independent digital filmmaking. Michael's current live action/graphic film project is titled "Normal to Oily," and is due for release in the fall of 2001.

RACHEL SCHREIBER is an artist and writer living in Baltimore, Maryland. Her videos, digital works, and writings have been exhibited, published and screened internationally. Currently, she is the coordinator of the Master of Arts in digital arts program at the Maryland Institute, College of Art. Schreiber received a B.F.A. in graphic design from the Rhode Island School of Design, and her M.F.A. in Photography and Critical Writing from the California Institute of the Arts. In 1995–96 she participated in the Whitney Independent Study Program in New York.

J. J. SEDELMAIER is president of J. J. Sedelmaier Productions, Inc., White Plains, NY. The award-winning studio has brought to life many of the seminal broadcast-animation projects of recent years, ranging from the launch season of MTV's *Beavis and Butthead* to an ongoing series of edgy shorts for NBC's *Saturday Night Live* and hundreds of animated commercials. Sedelmaier and his studio have received numerous creative awards, including the Animated Film Society/ASIFA Hollywood's Annie Award for Best Animated Commercial, gold medals from the New York Festivals, Art Directors Club, Broadcast Designers Association Awards, IBA Awards, and a top award from the Annecy animation festival in France. Clients include all the major television networks, Volkswagen, Converse, Nike, Burger King, 7UP, and Hawaiian Punch.

LORETTA STAPLES is a Managing Director with Scient, an international e-business strategy consulting firm. Before joining Scient, she taught graphic and interface design at the University of Michigan School of Art and Design.

DUGALD STERMER is an illustrator, author, and teacher living in San Francisco.

GUNNAR SWANSON is a Ventura, California–based graphic designer who can be found at *www.gunnarswanson.com.* He was the director of the multimedia program at California Lutheran University, the head of the graphic design program at the University of Minnesota Duluth, and has taught graphic design at the University of California, Davis and at Otis College of Art and Design in Los Angeles.

CHARLES H. TRAUB is chair and creator of the M.F.A. Photography and Related Media department at the School of Visual Arts, a photographer, and the author of seven books.

MASAMICHI UDAGAWA, a principal of Antenna Design New York Inc., graduated from Chiba University in Japan, then joined the Yamaha Product Design Laboratory in 1987. There, he designed electronic musical instruments, including the award winning YS200 synthesizer. After receiving his M.F.A. from Cranbrook Academy of Art in 1991, he worked at Emilio Ambasz Design Group in New York. From 1992 to 1995, Masamichi was a senior designer at Apple Computer Industrial Design Group in Cupertino, where he designed a number of products such as the PowerBook 5300/3400 series. He also worked closely with Apple's research laboratory, Advanced Technology Group, on research projects addressing novel user experiences. From 1995 to 1997, he ran a New York satellite studio of Ideo Product Development. He has also been involved in design education since 1993. Currently, he is an associate professor, teaching user-centered design process at New York University's Interactive Telecommunications Program.

TUCKER VIEMEISTER was Executive Vice President, Research and Development, of Razorfish, giving physical form to ideas, needs, desires, and brands across all kinds of information platforms, including virtual products. Prior to this he was frogdesign's New York studio head—the global design group founded by Hartmut Esslinger. He co-founded Smart Design, a New York–based industrial design consultancy which was responsible for a lot of fun, functional, and profitable stuff, like OXO Good Grips.

DAVID VOGLER is the chief creative officer of Mutation Labs, a new media studio that creates multi-user content, digital toys, and wireless entertainment. Vogler is a consultant to MTV Networks and a frequent guest lecturer at the School of Visual Arts and Carnegie Mellon University's Human Computer Interaction Institute. David can be reached at *david@davidvogler.com*.

LISA WALTUCH is a creative director, focusing on user experience design at Icon Nicholson, a Web development company in New York City. Currently, she is working with Walmart.com and Walmart stores to integrate their online and offline experiences through technology. Prior to this project, she established the overall creative direction for the Metropolitan Museum of Art Web site. In addition to her work with Icon Nicholson, she is an adjunct faculty member at New York University teaching interactive design in the graduate Interactive Telecommunications Program (ITP). Before joining Icon Nicholson, Lisa worked with various interactive media including Web sites, interactive television, CD-ROMs and laser disks. Lisa has a B.A. in graphic design and art history from Stanford University and an M.F.A. in graphic design from the Rhode Island School of Design.

BRUCE WANDS is the chair of the M.F.A. Computer Art department and director of computer education at the School of Visual Arts in New York. He is a digital artist and composer/musician. He was chosen by *Time Out New York* as "One of the 99 People to Watch in 1999," and has lectured and exhibited his creative work internationally. His computer art, photography, music, and writing explore the invention of new forms of narrative and the relationship between visual art and music. His Web site: *www.brucewands.com* and e-mail: *bruce@sva.edu*. He is currently writing a book entitled *Digital Creativity* for John Wiley & Sons publishers. He has a B.A. with honors from Lafayette College and an M.S. from Syracuse University.

LYNDA WEINMAN is the director and owner of the Ojai Digital Arts Center, a state-of-the-art teaching facility devoted solely to the World Wide Web and author of numerous books on Web design, including *Coloring Web Graphics, Deconstructing Web Graphics,* and *Lynda Weiman's Web Graphics Resource Library.* Her Web site, *www.lynda.com,* offers information, demos, and practical demos from her books.

KAREN WHITE is a designer, educator, writer, and artist. She is an assistant professor of visual communications at the University of Arizona School of Art. Her current research examines the relationship between design, culture, and technology. Her work has been seen in *Adobe Magazine, FATE Journal, Zed,* and *Visual Resources Journal.* Additionally, her artwork has been shown in numerous national and international galleries and juried exhibitions. She has won awards from the College Design Association and Adobe. She received her M.F.A. from Virginia Commonwealth University. She can be contacted at *kmwhite@u.arizona.edu.*

MICHAEL WORTHINGTON is the codirector of the Graphic Design program at CalArts, and also runs Worthington Design, a small design studio in Los Angeles. His recent work includes design-writing and editorial projects, as well as graphic design and typography for print and screen.

DAVID YOUNG is cofounder and partner of Triplecode, a Los Angeles–based interactive media design studio. He has been on the faculty at Art Center College of Design and involved with their new media curriculum development. He holds an M.S. in Visual Studies from the MIT Media Lab's Visible Language Workshop, and a B.A. in Computer Science from University of California Santa Cruz.

NATALIE ZEE is the interactive design director of Rich Media and is the cofounder of the Internet Research and Development Group at marchFIRST in San Francisco. She is an author, designer, teacher, and regular speaker at conferences around the country on the subject of Web design.

ERIC ZIMMERMAN is a game designer, artist, and academic. He is the founder and CEO of gameLab, a New York City–based game development company. His non-computer projects include the interactive paper book, *Life in the Garden* (created with Nancy Nowacek), and installations in galleries and museums. Eric has taught at MIT's Comparative Media Studies program, NYU's Interactive Telecommunications program, and the M.F.A. Digital Design program at Parsons School of Design.

MARINA ZURKOW is a director and art director who works in film, animation and print. Her most recent project is the award-winning animated series, "Braingirl" *(www.thebraingirl.com).*

Index

Books from Allworth Press

The Education of a Graphic Designer
edited by Steven Heller (paperback, 6¾ × 9 ⅞, 288 pages, $18.95)

The Education of an Illustrator
edited by Steven Heller (paperback, 6¾ × 9 ⅞, 288 pages, $19.95)

Starting Your Career as a Freelance Illustrator or Graphic Designer
by Michael Fleishman (paperback, 6 × 9, 256 pages, $19.95)

Careers By Design: A Business Guide for Graphic Designers, Third Edition
by Roz Goldfarb (paperback, 6 × 9, 256 pages, $19.95)

Mastering 3D Animation
by Peter Ratner (paperback, 8 × 9⅞, 344 pages, includes CD-ROM, $35.00)

Business and Legal Forms for Graphic Designers, Revised Edition
by Tad Crawford and Eva Doman Bruck (paperback, 8½ × 11, 240 pages, includes CD-ROM, $24.95)

AIGA Professional Practices in Graphic Design
The American Institute of Graphic Arts, edited by Tad Crawford
(paperback, 6¾ × 10, 320 pages, $24.95)

Graphic Design History
Edited by Steven Heller and Georgette Balance (paperback, 6¾ × 9 ⅞, 352 pages, $21.95)

Graphic Design Timeline: A Century of Design Milestones
by Steven Heller and Elanor Petit (paperback, 6¾ × 9 ⅞, 288 pages, $19.95)

Graphic Design and Reading: Exploration of an Uneasy Relationship
edited by Gunnar Swanson (paperback, 6¾ × 9 ⅞, 240 pages, $19.95)

Looking Closer 3: Classic Writings on Graphic Design
edited by Michael Bierut, Jessica Helfand, Steven Heller, and Rick Poynor
(paperback, 6¾ × 9 ⅞, 304 pages, $18.95)

Looking Closer 2: Critical Writings on Graphic Design
edited by Michael Bierut, William Drenttel, Steven Heller, and DK Holland
(paperback, 6¾ × 9 ⅞, 288 pages, $18.95)

Looking Closer: Critical Writings on Graphic Design
edited by Michael Bierut, William Drenttel, Steven Heller, and DK Holland
(paperback, 6¾ × 10, 256 pages, $18.95)

Please write to request our free catalog. To order by credit card, call 1-800-491-2808 or send a check or money order to Allworth Press, 10 East 23rd Street, Suite 510, New York, NY 10010. Include $5 for shipping and handling for the first book ordered and $1 for each additional book. Ten dollars plus $1 for each additional book if ordering from Canada. New York State residents must add sales tax.

To see our complete catalog on the World Wide Web, or to order online, you can find us at *www.allworth.com.*